GUIDE TO MANUSCRIPT COLLECTIONS

Western History Collections, University of Oklahoma

Compiled and Edited by
Donald L. DeWitt

HERITAGE BOOKS
2014

HERITAGE BOOKS
AN IMPRINT OF HERITAGE BOOKS, INC.

Books, CDs, and more—Worldwide

For our listing of thousands of titles see our website
at
www.HeritageBooks.com

Published 2014 by
HERITAGE BOOKS, INC.
Publishing Division
5810 Ruatan Street
Berwyn Heights, Md. 20740

Copyright © 1994 Donald L. DeWitt

Other Heritage Books by the author:
*CD: Guide to Manuscript Collections,
Western History Collections, University of Oklahoma*

All rights reserved. No part of this book may be reproduced or transmitted in any form or by any means, electronic or mechanical, including photocopying, recording or by any information storage and retrieval system without written permission from the author, except for the inclusion of brief quotations in a review.

International Standard Book Numbers
Paperbound: 978-0-7884-0117-6
Clothbound: 978-0-7884-9032-3

TABLE OF CONTENTS

Introduction — v

Manuscript collections — 1

Index — 257

INTRODUCTION

The Western History Collections is a special collection within the University of Oklahoma library system. The beginning of the Western History Collections dates to 1927, when history professor Edward Everett Dale started the Frank Phillips Collection. In 1948, the University of Oklahoma library created a separate Division of Manuscripts headed by university archivist Gaston Litton. Both Dale and Litton pursued aggressive acquisition policies, and their combined success established the University of Oklahoma as a significant manuscript repository. The University Libraries administration merged the Frank Phillips Collection and the Division of Manuscripts in 1967, and designated the combined holdings as the Western History Collections.[1] In addition to the manuscript collections described in this guide, the Western History Collections also holds 60,000 books, 250,000 photographs, 3,500 maps, and 1,500 sound recordings. These combined holdings reflect the development of the American west and American Indian cultures, with a specific emphasis on the history of Oklahoma and the southwest.

Two previous guides to the manuscript holdings of the Western History Collections have been published. Gaston Litton prepared a mimeographed guide to the Division of Manuscript holdings in 1952.[2] The Litton guide included over 250 manuscript collections, but it was not widely distributed. Eight years later, the University of Oklahoma press published Arrell Gibson's *A Guide to Regional Manuscript Collections...* .[3] Gibson's guide had 694 entries and represented the combined manuscript holdings of the Phillips Collection and the Division of Manuscripts. While both guides remain useful, they describe less than one-half of the manuscript collections now available at the Western History Collections. This guide remedies that situation by describing all manuscripts holdings accessioned through 1993.

---

[1] For a thorough review of the administrative history of the Frank Phillips Collection, the Division of Manuscripts and the Western History Collections, see H. Glenn Jordan, "Western History Collections at the University of Oklahoma," *Chronicles of Oklahoma* 54 (Fall 1976): 370-380.

[2] Gaston Litton, "Oklahoma: A Guide to Holdings of Regional Manuscripts. Preliminary Draft. September 1, 1952." Mimeographed guide, Western History Collections, University of Oklahoma, Norman, Oklahoma.

[3] A. M. Gibson, *A Guide to Regional Manuscript Holdings in the Division of Manuscripts, University of Oklahoma Library* (Norman: University of Oklahoma Press, 1960).

THE HOLDINGS

The curators of the Western History Collections have presented the University of Oklahoma with an admirable and valuable research collection. The 11,000 linear feet of manuscript holdings date from the sixteenth century and cover a wide range of subject matter. The holdings are multi-disciplinary in content, and anthropologists, sociologists, economists, linguists, genealogists, and geographers as well as historians find them useful. There are, however, areas of exceptional strength that should be noted. Records and papers relating to the Indians of Oklahoma and the southwest are a case in point.

The Western History Collections has over 270 manuscript collections relating to Indians. Foremost among them is the Cherokee Nation Papers, a collection of 85 linear feet that encompasses the development of the Cherokee Nation in Indian Territory, from approximately 1830 to 1907. Researchers using this collection will encounter a wealth of material on schools, censuses, per-capita payments, law enforcement, intruders, land issues, and governmental affairs within the Cherokee Nation. This collection also incorporates the personal correspondence of Stand and Sarah C. Watie, James Madison Bell, and the Ridge and Boudinot families.

Choctaw Nation history is well represented by the Peter Pitchlynn and Green McCurtain collections. Pitchlynn was an attorney and Choctaw Nation delegate to Washington, D.C. His papers reflect life in the Choctaw Nation for the period preceeding the Civil War. Besides his personal correspondence and diaries, the Pitchlynn papers include correspondence relating to the Choctaw Nation's participation in the Civil War, claims of the Choctaw Indians against the federal government, and the removal of Choctaw Indians to Indian Territory. Covering a later period, the Green McCurtain papers offer a unique perspective on the reluctance of the Choctaw Nation to embrace Oklahoma statehood, and the subsequent movement to form a separate Indian state from Indian Territory. The collection contains McCurtain's correspondence as principle chief of the Choctaw Nation and many of his messages to the general council of the Choctaw Nation.

Other collections such as the Kaw Indian Agency Collection, and the Southern Plains Indian Agencies Collection document the history of Indians in western Oklahoma, and their relations with the federal government. The records of Cruce, Cruce, and Bleakmore, Roscoe Cate, and Melvin Cornish, all attorneys specializing in Indian claims, are untapped resources for those interested in the procedures for establishing Indian heritage and citizenship. Family collections provide yet another perspective on Indian life, and the Samuel Robertson and Jerry Whistler Snow collections both contain insightful correspondence on life in Indian Territory during the 19th, and early 20th centuries.

While there are more Indian-related collections in the Western History Collections than any other subject area, business collections are the most voluminous. Railroad records, for example, are plentiful. The Chicago, Rock Island, and Pacific Railroad Collection, the Oklahoma Transportation Company Collection, and the Guy B. Treat Collection are sources offering over 500 linear feet of records on railroads for the period 1853-1984. The Chicago, Rock Island, and Pacific Collection includes minutes of the board of directors, extensive documentation on mergers, litigation files, records on its real estate holdings, and voluminous graphic records relating to rolling stock, depots, bridges, and maintenance of its track throughout the company's operating area. The Oklahoma

Transportation Company Collection and the Guy B. Treat Collection focus on the development and operation of smaller, central Oklahoma railroads such as the Oklahoma City Railway, the Metropolitan Railway, the El Reno Interurban Railroad, and the Norman Interurban Railroad. These two collections include minutes of board of directors meetings and records relating to operations, finances, and labor unions representing railroad employees.

The Western History Collections also has in excess of 400 linear feet of records from thirty-one Oklahoma banks for the period 1891-1951. They include ledgers recording the daily financial transactions of the banks, minutes of the board of directors, and correspondence reflecting the operation of the banks and their relations with other financial institutions within the state and region.

Added to this body of commercial records are those of numerous retail businesses. Typical are the records from the Redwine Trading Company's business activities in the southeastern Oklahoma town of Spiro, and the Zweigel Merchandise Company in Atoka, Oklahoma. The Redwine Trading Company Collection offers twenty-one linear feet of financial and operating records of the company's general store, cotton gins, and funeral home. The Zweigel Collection includes over fifty feet of correspondence and financial records from Abraham Zewigel's general merchandise store, and includes records relating to his interests in oil, gas, and mining leases on Choctaw Indian lands. Another outstanding business collection is that of the Chickasha Milling Company. Operating in the town of Chickasha, Oklahoma, its 452 linear feet of records provide an excellent source for the study of grain marketing in the southwest for the period 1899-1952.

Oklahoma's mining interests are represented in the Kali-Inla Coal Company Collection of 219 linear feet that span the years of 1893-1944. Besides documenting the course of the mining industry in Indian Territory and Oklahoma, this collection contains a wealth of information about labor relations. Of specific interest is a subgroup of records within the Kali-Inla Coal Company Collection relating to the Bache-Denman Coal Company's preparation and development of the landmark case *The United Mine Workers of America, et al. vs the Coronado Mining Company et al.* Forty-two linear feet of records and papers from the Oklahoma Federation of Labor are an additional source for the history of organized labor in Oklahoma.

The papers of seven Oklahoma governors provide opportunities for research on Oklahoma politics. Collections of governors' papers at the Western History Collections include those of territorial governors Thompson B. Ferguson and Abraham J. Seay. They are accompanied by those of state governors Raymond D. Gary, Charles N. Haskell, Henry S. Johnston, Johnston Murray, Leon C. Phillips, James B.A. Robertson, and John C. Walton. The Western History Collections also is the repository for the Republican Party of Oklahoma, and holds over 125 linear feet of records relating to the party's activities in the state and its relations with the national party. Socialism in Oklahoma can be studied by reviewing the papers and publications in the Thomas W. Woodrow collection. Records relating to Oklahoma agricultural politics are found in the collections of Homer Duffy and John Andrew Simpson, both active in national and state farm organizations.

Diaries and manuscript accounts of frontier and pioneer life received special attention during the preparation of this guide. As a result, the collection summaries and index note a significant number of these primary sources. The Civil War, travel in western states, and Oklahoma land runs provided opportunities for many personal reminiscences. Women, particularly, found the keeping of a diary and the writing of family historical accounts an outlet for relating the hardships of settling a new area. Flora Ramsey, for example, described her experiences in the land run of 1889, and her family's subsequent settlement in the Stillwater, Oklahoma, area. Cassandra Sawyer Lockwood recounted her journey to the Cherokee Nation in the 1830s, and left a valuable description of life at Dwight Mission. Later in the 19th century, Emma DeKnight recorded her experiences as a teacher at the Chilocco Indian School and the Oto Indian School at Red Rock Agency in Indian Territory. Less dramatic, perhaps, but still significant, is the diary of Caro Emerson who wrote of her student life at Bethany College in Topeka, Kansas, in the 1890s.

Other collections of materials relating to women are also present in the Western History Collections. The Lois Lenski Collection, for example, contains nine linear feet of her manuscripts of stories for children, the original art work she used to illustrate her stories, her speeches, and her personal correspondence. Complementing the Lenski Collection is that of Alberta Wilson Constant, an author of short stories and historical fiction. The Constant Collection also includes manuscripts of her work and correspondence with her publishers, agents, and reading public. Non-fiction work by women authors is represented by the collections of Elizabeth Mahala Kirk Boyer and Elsbeth Estelle Freudenthal. Boyer, who wrote under the name of Betty Kirk, is known for her work on Mexico and U.S. foreign policy, and Freudenthal, for her writings on the history of aviation, and aviation in Latin America. Both collections contain manuscripts, correspondence, and extensive research materials pertinent to the authors' writings.

An area of collection strength generally not found in manuscript repositories is that relating to the history of medicine in Oklahoma and Indian Territory. The Western History Collections, however, holds over 130 collections of physicians papers. These collections contain information on illnesses and diseases in the region, birth and death records, accounts of treatment and records of prescriptions, and personal reminiscences of medical practice in Oklahoma and Indian territories. Physicians' collections, along with those relating to dentistry, pharmacy, medical societies, and hospitals provide a unique source for the development of the medical profession in Oklahoma.

HOW TO USE THE GUIDE

All collections in this guide are arranged alphabetically by collection title. Each entry has up to seven information fields that are included to help researchers analyze collections. Figure 1 illustrates a typical entry and identifies each of the fields. An index follows the section describing the collection entries. The index is keyed to an entry number assigned to each collection. Entry numbers appearing in the index in bold-face type refer to a collection by the same name. The others indicate that the referenced entry contains some information by or about that specific person, place, subject, or event. To find all collections that relate to a specific subject, place, event, or person, one first turns to index, finds the desired subject listing and notes the entry numbers following it. Researchers can then turn to the specific entry(s) cited and read the summary to see if the collection merits further examination.

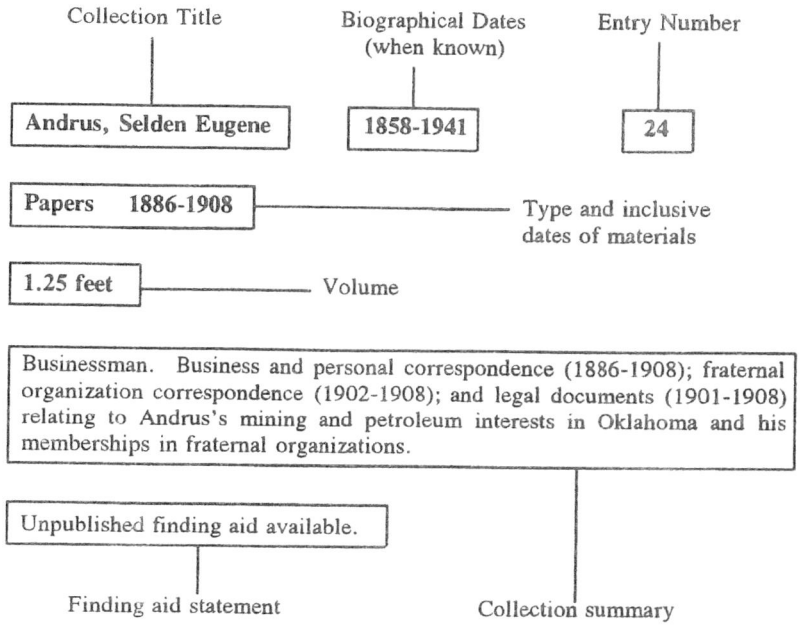

Figure 1. Information fields for collection entries.

ACKNOWLEDGMENTS

Compilation of this guide began in 1987, and since that time a number of people have contributed to the final product. Bradford Koplowitz, the assistant curator for the Western History Collections, provided valuable advice on the format, edited many of the entries and supervised the processing of many previously undescribed collections. Western History Collections graduate assistants Kayla Barrett, Bill Dobbins, Bradley Gernand, Carol Mathias, Ray Miles, Mary Rausch, and Kristina Southwell, also played a major role in the preparation of this guide. They analyzed the content of collections, wrote entries for new collections, revised entries from previous guides, recommended appropriate subject headings, and answered numerous questions about specific materials in collections. Shirley Clark provided invaluable assistance with word processing applications and final preparation of the manuscript. The generous assistance of all of these people speeded the completion of the guide. The work of all former curators of the Western History Collections and their assistants needs to be acknowledged. Their success in acquiring many of the collections in this guide accounts for much of the richness evident in the Western History Collections today.

Donald L. DeWitt
Curator

MANUSCRIPT COLLECTIONS

Abrams, Abner W. 1
Papers 1881-1916
.10 foot

Businessman. Correspondence (1893-1916) concerning lead and zinc mining in Oklahoma, the automotive business in Baxter Springs, Kansas, and real estate holdings, along with a program (1881) of a funeral service for Lucy Grey.

Adams, Joseph Quincy 2
Papers 1654-1911
.10 foot

University professor. An Elizabethan commonplace book (1654) with typescript; inventories (1870-1918) of the rare book collections of Adams Stevenson and Henry Stevenson; personal correspondence (1882-1911) of E. J. Doggett, of Bristol, England, regarding rare book collecting; and an inventory (n.d) of rare books at the William Bennett Bizzell Memorial Library, University of Oklahoma.

Adams, Ramon Frederick (1889-1976) 3
Papers 1942-1958
1.33 feet

Writer. Manuscripts of three of Adams's books, "A Genius in Chaps," "Cowboy Lingo," and "Come an' Get It," along with his correspondence (1942-1958) with other writers, collectors of western lore, fans, and publishers.

Aderhold, Thomas 4
Records 1921-1949
.33 foot

Superintendent. Minutes (1921-1935); statistical reports (1934-1949); and correspondence (1931-1942) of the El Reno Sanitarium, a general proprietary hospital, the first in Oklahoma to train and graduate a class from its school for nurses.

Albert Pike Hospital Collection 5
Records 1917-1948
12 feet

Hospital for women and crippled children. Admittance records and ledgers (1917-1948) of the Albert Pike Hospital, McAlester General Hospital and All Saints Hospital, all in McAlester, Oklahoma. Also included in the collection is a certificate of incorporation (1928) granted by the state of Oklahoma to the Albert Pike Hospital.

Alexander, Ira Olyen (b. 1906) 6
Papers 1950-1952
.10 foot

Collector. Genealogical material (1950-1952) concerning the Alexander, Sellers, Chisum, and Bourland families; notes (ca. 1952) on the early histories of Paris, Texas, and Bennington, Oklahoma; and printed material (1950-1951) on organized labor in Oklahoma.

Allen, Neva 7
Ledgers 1911-1912
2 items

Hosteler. Two registers (1911-1912) from the Hotel Dewey in Dewey, Oklahoma.

Allen, Susie Keefer 8
Papers 1911-1940
8 items

Collector. An obituary (ca. 1925) of Lewis Keefer; a discharge certificate (1911); pension certificates (1914-1926) for Keefer and his widow, Ann; a statement (ca. 1940) by former state senator Walter Bruce Allen concerning conditions at the Granite (Oklahoma) Penitentiary; and copies of two letters (1940) from Allen concerning the death of former state senator Ralph Busey.

Alley, Charles 9
Diary 1861-1865
1 item

Soldier. A typescript of a diary (1861-1863, 1865), kept by Lt. Charles Alley, Company "C," Fifth Iowa Cavalry with an appendix containing the regiment's organization and strength.

Alley, John 10
Papers 1890-1940
2.50 feet

University professor. A letter (1912) to Alley from Victor M. Locke, Jr., principal chief of the Choctaws, listing present and former principal chiefs of the Five Civilized Tribes, and discussing the status of the Choctaw government; a four-page manuscript (n.d.) entitled "For the First Time: The True Story of the Last Oklahoma Indian Uprising as Told by the Man Who Put It Down" as related to Alley by Col. Roy V. Hoffman of the Oklahoma National Guard; Hoffman's official reports (1909) concerning the Crazy Snake Rebellion, along with Governor Charles N. Haskell's orders (1909); correspondence (1926-1942) concerning Kingfisher College; documents (n.d.) about the Dalton family; and miscellaneous research notes and professional correspondence (1920-1942) accumulated by Alley as a professor of government.

Allman, George 11
Papers 1917-1952
.33 foot

Oil field worker. Personal correspondence (1945-1950); war ration books, bills and receipts (1944-1948); Catholic church programs (1951); road maps and travel guides; farmers handbooks (1947-1951); and telephone directories (1928-1950) from Oklahoma and Texas towns.

Alpha Epsilon Delta Collection 12
Records 1932-1951
1.33 feet

Professional organization for pre-medical students. Correspondence (1938) of the officers of the University of Oklahoma Kappa Chapter of Alpha Epsilon Delta; biographical data forms (1936-1946) for each member of the organization; petitions (1947-1948) from local collegiate chapters nationwide requesting admittance to the national organization; publications (1932-1951), including *The Scalpel*, published by the national organization; and brochures (1946), with form letters enclosed, explaining the Graduate Record Examination, a scholastic aptitude test for graduate students.

American Association of University Women Collection 13
Records 1923-1949
9 feet

Professional organization. Minutes (1920-1949) and correspondence (1934-1946), along with other records (1923-1949) including membership lists, reports, newspaper articles, bulletins, yearbooks, histories, by-laws, and related materials from the state of Oklahoma chapter and the University of Oklahoma chapter of the American Association of University Women.

American Indian File Collection 14
Printed materials 1939-1975
.75 foot

Subject file. Publications (1939-1975) of the Bureau of Indian Affairs and other state and federal government agencies, along with reprints of articles regarding the American Indian. Included in the collection is a report (1970) entitled, "President Nixon's Indian Legislative Program."

American Indian Institute Collection 15
Records 1956-1974
8 feet

Indian advocacy organization. Minutes (1958-1960) of annual conferences; correspondence (1956-1974); and newsletters and other publications (1956-1974), all concerning Indian education, civil rights, tribal council proceedings, and Indian youth programs.

American Legion Post 303 Collection 16
Records 1944-1950
5.50 feet

Veterans organization. Awards, bulletins, and committee reports (1946-1950); correspondence (1946-1950); financial records (1946-1950); minutes of meetings (1944-1950); membership applications (1946-1949); and scrapbooks (n.d.) of the University of Oklahoma American Legion post.

Unpublished finding aid available.

American Red Cross of Beckham County Collection 17
Records 1916-1921
2 feet

Local Red Cross chapter. Correspondence (1916-1921); minutes (1917-1921); financial records (1917-1921); and a history of the Beckham County (Oklahoma) chapter formed during World War I.

Unpublished finding aid available.

American Red Cross of Cleveland County Collection 18
Records 1917-1919
1 item

Local Red Cross chapter. A scrapbook history of the Cleveland County (Oklahoma) chapter formed during World War I.

Ames, Charles Bismark (1870-1935) 19
Printed material 1902-1920
.66 foot

Judge. Promotional literature and a speech (1902-1903) by Ames on Oklahoma statehood; pamphlets (1915-1918) regarding American involvement in World War I; reports (1914) of earnings and expenses of the Oklahoma City *Times* Company; and correspondence (1907-1919) regarding Oklahoma and Oklahoma City politics.

Ames, H. B. (b. 1873) 20
Records 1901-1934
3 feet

Physician. Office records (1901-1934), including ledgers, bills, patient case histories, correspondence, and insurance papers documenting Ames's practice of medicine in Alva, Oklahoma.

Unpublished finding aid available.

Amos, French Stanton Evans 21
Papers 1928-1937
.10 foot

University professor. Grade books (1929-1937) from Amos's courses in government and an unpublished manuscript (1928) by Amos entitled "The Yazoo Land Frauds."

Anderson, R. M. 22
Papers 1893
1 item

Physician. Lecture notes (1893) taken by Anderson while a medical student.

Anderson, R. R. (1851-ca. 1930) 23
Papers 1887-1923
2 items

Physician. A daybook (1918-1923) and a medical notebook (ca. 1887) of diseases and treatments.

Andrus, Selden Eugene (1858-1941) 24
Papers 1886-1908
1.25 feet

Businessman. Business and personal correspondence (1886-1908); fraternal organization correspondence (1902-1908); and legal documents (1901-1908) relating to Andrus's mining and petroleum interests in Oklahoma and his memberships in fraternal organizations.

Unpublished finding aid available.

Anthony, Travis Dan (1914-1993)   25
Papers 1926-1989
.75 foot

Teacher. Correspondence (1926, 1974-1989); newspaper articles (1982-1989); manuscripts (n.d.); and publications (1935-1987) either by or about Travis D. Anthony, and relating to Anthony's family, his life in rural Oklahoma, and his student experiences at the University of Oklahoma in the 1930s.

Anti-Horse Thief Association Collection   26
Records 1892-1902
.25 foot

Vigilante group. Constitutions (1892-1895); rosters (n.d.); minutes (1895-1902); and proceedings (1895-1901) of Chapter 35 of the Anti-Horse Thief Association located in Fairview, Oklahoma Territory.

Arnold, Ben   27
Scrapbook 1938-1950
1 item

Lawyer and judge. A scrapbook of news clippings (1938-1950) documenting Arnold's career as an attorney and judge.

Arthur, Patti Joy   28
Scrapbook 1915-1917
1 item

Collector. A scrapbook (1915-1917) kept by Patti Arthur, who graduated from the University of Oklahoma in 1917, about her college experiences.

Asahl, John   29
Ledger 1903-1904
1 item

Merchant. An account book (1903-1904) from Asahl's hardware store in Ramona, Indian Territory.

Ashbrook, William   30
Records 1853-1855
3 items

Collector. Deeds (1853-1855) to land in Missouri.

Ashley, Charles   31
Manuscript ca. 1951
1 item

City clerk. A list of mayors of Claremore, Oklahoma, from 1900 to 1949, including the index numbers to city record books where their records can be found.

Atoka State Bank Collection 32
Records 1905-1935
25 feet

Bank. Records (1905-1935), including tellers daily balance books, discount rate books, draft registers, daily statement books, tellers cash journals, reconciliation registers and a photocopy of the bank's articles of incorporation.

Austin, William Claude (1880-1946) 33
Papers 1920-1943
71.33 feet

Lawyer. Case and client files (1920-1943) from Austin's law firm in Altus, Oklahoma, in which Robert B. Harbison and David Ross Rutherford were associate members.

Ayer, Hugh M. 34
Printed materials 1952-1953
4 items

Historian. Reprints (1952-1953) from the *Indiana Magazine of History*, and a paper read at a historical society convention, all written by Ayer, concerning the medical career of Joseph Rodes Buchanan.

Babcock, James M. (b. 1926) 35
Papers 1900-1953
.10 foot

Archivist. Correspondence (1951-1953) concerning the University of Oklahoma's Western History Collections and the nomination of Luther H. Evans for the post of Librarian of Congress, along with history-related printed materials (1900-1953).

Bacon, Charles W. 36
Records 1891-1917
11 items

Pharmacist. Certificates and diplomas (1891-1917) awarded to Bacon during his career as a pharmacist in Oklahoma.

Badger, Ina 37
Papers 1898-ca. 1925
5 items

Collector. A yearbook (1898-1899) of the Pioneer Club, a women's club in

Chickasha, Oklahoma; two letters (n.d.); notes (ca. 1925) about early settlers on Bitter Creek near Chickasha; and a notebook (n.d.) of recipes.

Bailey, Hurshel 38
Records 1846-1930
1.66 feet

Collector. Bills, land deeds, leases, and correspondence of the Cocke family (1846-1930) and of the Ben Lafayette and Brothers Company (1900-1910) of Checotah, Indian Territory.

Unpublished finding aid available.

Baker, Jesse Albert (1853-1925) 39
Papers 1853-1928
.10 foot

Judge. An election certificate (1906) and a letter (1907) from William H. Murray regarding Baker's service as a delegate to the Oklahoma Constitutional Convention; letters (1898-1922) from territorial governor Cassius M. Barnes, Oklahoma governor J. B. A. Robertson and state supreme court justice Summers Hardy; a transcript (ca. 1890) of the story of Baker's participation in the run into the Cherokee Strip; and one copy of *The Barking Water* (1928), a magazine published in Wewoka, Oklahoma.

Baldwin, Delmar H. 40
Papers 1820-1950
.33 foot

Collector. One letter (1937) from former U. S. marshal Chris Madsen; a proclamation by Oklahoma Territory governor Cassius M. Barnes welcoming Theodore Roosevelt; a reprint (n.d.) of a publication entitled *Opening of Kiowa, Comanche, Apache and Wichita Indian Lands in the Territory of Oklahoma*; a program of the Roosevelt Rough Rider Reunion of 1900 in Oklahoma City, Oklahoma Territory; a typescript (n.d.) entitled "Oklahoma Criminals with a History, 1889-1933;" a copy of a magazine (1899) entitled *Buffalo Bill's Wild West and Congress of Rough Riders of the World*; and a textbook (n.d) entitled *The American Spelling Book* by Noah Webster.

Balyeat, Frank Allen (1886-1971) 41
Printed materials 1774-1960
.33 foot

Educator. Typescripts and notes (1926-1957) regarding Baptist missionaries to the Indians; a history (1960) of schools in Kiowa County, Oklahoma; publications (1953-1957) of the Bureau of Indian Affairs concerning American Indians and Indian education; a booklet (n.d.) on Sequoyah and the Cherokee syllabary; notes and correspondence (1926) concerning Joseph Samuel Murrow and Bacone College; a leaflet (1958) describing El Meta Bond College; and correspondence (1960) concerning Oklahoma post offices.

Bandy, Mary 42
Records 1890-1931
1.25 feet

Collector. Land title abstracts of property (1890-1931) located in Kingfisher County, Oklahoma.

Bank of Udall Collection 43
Records 1891-1896
1 item

Bank. A daybook (1891-1896) of individual accounts from the Bank of Udall, Oklahoma.

Barbour, John (1872-1950) and Robert Barbour (1871-1953) 44
Records 1889-1952
40.66 feet

Pharmacists. Ledgers and account books (1889-1952); business correspondence (1900-1916); a drug registration record book (1900-1945); and athletic literature (1911-1918) from the Barbour Drug Store, which John and Robert Barbour opened in Norman, Oklahoma Territory, in 1889.

Barker, N. L. 45
Ledger 1945
1 item

Physician. A daybook (1945) listing appointments from Barker's medical practice in Paris, Texas.

Barnes, Arch 46
Papers 1877-1900
.10 foot

Collector. Correspondence (1877-1900) concerning Barnes's family matters and property taxes.

Barnes, D. Elijah (b. ca. 1850) 47
Papers 1876-1879
2 items

Physician. A diploma (1876) awarded to Barnes by the University of Louisville granting him a degree in medicine and a certificate (1879) licensing Barnes to practice medicine in Texas.

Barnes, Sudie McAlester (1873-1953)   48
Papers 1875-1920
.33 foot

Housewife. A diary (1880s) kept by Barnes while at Baird College in Clinton, Missouri; a published letter (n.d.) from J. J. McAlester, founder of McAlester, Oklahoma, and a prominent figure in territorial politics, to the Dawes Commission and the Choctaw Commissioners; and correspondence (1900-1929) relating to Barnes and her family's business and personal affairs.

Barrett, Hershel   49
Manuscript 1850-1890
1 item

Pioneer. A short, typewritten manuscript (n.d.) entitled "Frontier Experiences of Hershel Barrett" recounting Barrett's participation in the Oklahoma land run of 1889 and subsequent life in Earlsboro, Oklahoma Territory.

Bass, Altha Leah Bierbower   50
Papers 1847-ca. 1960
.33 foot

Historian. Essays (1847-1850) written by Sarah Worcester, a daughter of missionaries to the Cherokees, while a student at Mount Holyoke Female Seminary; unpublished manuscripts (ca. 1950-1960) by Altha Bass, entitled "The Inheritance of Alice Robertson," "I Raise This Glass to Jennie," "Harriet Bunce Wright, a Charleston Lady Among the Choctaws," "A Summer Thanksgiving--the Seneca Green Corn Festival," and "Standing Bear of the Ponca Nation," along with correspondence and research notes (ca. 1957) regarding William L. Bear, and his role in the founding of Osborne, Kansas.

Bass, Henry Benjamin (1897-1975)   51
Papers 1861-1966
12 feet

Historian and collector. Materials (1962-1965) from Bass's participation with the Oklahoma Civil War Centennial Commission, including general correspondence and correspondence regarding Abraham Lincoln; and subject files regarding Civil War historical sites, events, personalities and programs received from other state commissions. Also included in the collection are Bass's travel diaries (1943-1966); correspondence (1933-1936) to and from patriotic societies; correspondence (1935-1940) from J. Edgar Hoover regarding conferences on crime; speeches (1935-1940) by Hoover; and reports (1933-1936) from conferences regarding crime.

Bates, S. R. 52
Records 1930-1943
1 foot

Physician. Patient account ledgers (1930-1943) and other financial records from Bates's medical practice in Wagoner, Oklahoma.

Battenburg Press Collection 53
Printed materials ca. 1950-1955
.10 foot

Commercial press. Books (1951-1954), pamphlets, calling cards, Christmas cards, announcements and other items printed by the Battenburg Press in Norman, Oklahoma.

Battey, Thomas C. 54
Papers 1824-1897
.33 foot

Teacher. Battey's diaries (1872-1884) and correspondence with family members (1873-1874) regarding his experience as a teacher of Indians, along with a book (1876) by Battey entitled *Life and Adventures of a Quaker Among the Indians* and containing substantial manuscript revision.

Baum, F. J. 55
Printed materials 1899-1925
.25 foot

Physician. An account book (1899-1901) from his medical practice and a manuscript and printed copy (1925) of an article by Baum entitled "The Modern Management of Acute Gonorrhoea."

Baumgartner, Frederick M. and A. Marguerite Baumgartner 56
Papers 1930-1987
4 feet

Ornithologists. Correspondence (1930-1978), research notes (1930-1978) and preliminary manuscripts (1979-1987) regarding the habits and species of birds indigenous to Oklahoma and accumulated by the Baumgartners while writing their book entitled *Oklahoma Bird Life*.

Unpublished finding aid available.

Beam, J. P. 57
Records 1929-1941
2 items

Physician. Two ledgers (1929-1941) relating to Beam's medical practice.

Bell, Earl L. 58
Papers 1869-1966
.33 foot

Collector. Receipts (1869-1909) for business transactions between Thomas J. Stephenson and merchants of Vicksburg, Mississippi; contracts (1881) with the Northern Pacific Railroad Company for the sale of land in Washington and Idaho territories; and letters (1876-1930) to the railroad from homesteaders regarding their purchases of land from the railroad.

Bell, Jack 59
Papers 1937-1970
2.66 feet

Journalist. Manuscripts and galley proofs (1960-1962) of books by Bell including *The Johnson Treatment*, *Mr. Conservative: Barry Goldwater*, and *The Splendid Misery*; and typescripts of interviews (1960-1965) with Hubert H. Humphrey, Lyndon B. Johnson, John F. Kennedy, and Robert F. Kennedy. Bell's correspondence (1945-1970) with political figures, including Dwight D. Eisenhower, Everett Dirkson, Barry Goldwater, J. Edgar Hoover, Hubert H. Humphrey, Lyndon B. Johnson, Edward M. Kennedy, Richard M. Nixon, William Proxmire, Douglas MacArthur, Nelson A. Rockefeller, Harry S. Truman and Adlai E. Stevenson is in the collection, along with newspaper articles (1937-1970) written by Bell on various topics.

Unpublished finding aid available.

Bell, Robert E. 60
Papers 1936-1977
.25 foot

Anthropologist. Correspondence (1949); notes (n.d.); and publications (1948-1951) concerning a field trip headed by Bell in 1949 to the Harlan Site, near Fort Gibson, Cherokee County, Oklahoma. Included in the collection are notes (1950) by Kenneth Orr concerning the Spiro Site in LeFlore County, Oklahoma and minutes (1939-1942), along with related records (1936-1943) of the Oklahoma State Archaeological Society.

Belt, Robert V. 61
Papers 1885-1898
.33 foot

Government employee and attorney. Five letter books (1885-1898) containing correspondence from Belt, an assistant commissioner of Indian affairs, to government officials regarding the administration of federal Indian policy and legal matters of his private law practice.

Belvin, G. N.   62
Papers 1874-1929
.33 foot

Collector. A collection of documents (1874-1929), written mostly in English, but with many in the Choctaw and Creek Indian languages. The papers include correspondence, postcards, bankbooks, mortgages, wills, speeches, allotment certificates, homestead patents, deeds, licenses, and printed materials. The documents in English indicate that much of the collection concerns the Four Mothers Society.

Benson, Mildred June Tompkins (1915-1981)   63
Papers 1952-1981
28 feet

Mayor. Agendas and minutes (1954-1981) of the Norman, Oklahoma, city council and of several city government boards, including those governing environmental and noise pollution and the quality of water; publications, including newsletters and brochures, published by the League of Women Voters of the United States; and one manuscript, jointly authored by Benson and Cortez A. M. Ewing, regarding presidential nominating politics in 1952. Benson was active in Norman politics and her papers reflect the governance of the municipality for the period 1954-1981.

Unpublished finding aid available.

Benson, Robert R.   64
Papers 1890-1962
2.33 feet

Historian. Manuscripts and typescripts (n.d.) by Benson regarding Lee Vining Creek, California; the boundaries of New Mexico, Colorado, and No Man's Land and the panhandle of Oklahoma; the Pecos River; the tri-state corner of Oklahoma, New Mexico and Colorado; Charles Goodnight's trail; and several other locales in the American west, along with a history (n.d.) of the American Garden Service.

Benton, Joseph Horace (1898-1975)   65
Papers 1815-1970
1.66 feet

Professor. Correspondence (1815-1893) from Benton's family; correspondence (1892-1896) from Giuseppe Verdi and Francesco Tamagno; memorabilia (1913-1970) concerning Lynn Riggs; scores (1911-1926) of Hadyn's "The Seasons" and Mendelssohn's "Elijah"; four Japanese music books, one autographed by Puccini; programs (1899-1968) from various musical productions; scrapbooks (1900-1967) of reviews and programs; clippings (1924-1939); and posters (1924-1934) advertising the performances of Benton, a University of Oklahoma professor of voice who sang professionally under the name of Joseph Bentonelli.

Unpublished finding aid available.

Berry, Josie Craig 66
Letter 1937
1 item

Collector. A letter (1937) written to Josie Craig Berry from Ralph Ellison, Pulitzer Prize winning author of "Invisible Man."

Berry, Roger M. 67
Printed materials 1909-1939
3 items

Collector. An annual report of the city of Norman, Oklahoma, (1938-1939); a news clipping regarding early University of Oklahoma faculty member Vernon Louis Parrington; and a scrapbook of photos, programs, calendars, and brochures (1909-1914) depicting student life at the University of Oklahoma.

Berry, Virgil (1866-1954) 68
Papers 1895-1953
.50 foot

Physician. Clippings (1951-1953) of Berry's column in the *Okmulgee Daily Times*; copies of the American Medical Association delegates handbook and program (1908); and a typescript memoir entitled "Experiences of a Pioneer Doctor in Indian Territory" in which Berry describes his medical practice in Chouteau, Indian Territory, 1890; his experiences as the first physician in Wagoner, Indian Territory, 1891-1898; as a physician to the Seminole tribe, 1898-1901; and as a physician in Wetumka, Oklahoma, 1901-1909, and Okmulgee, Oklahoma, 1909-1947.

Berry, William Aylor (b. 1915) 69
Papers 1941-1950
1 foot

Lawyer. Campaign material (1950) from Berry's race for the Democratic nomination to the fifth Oklahoma congressional district, including press releases, radio spots, speeches, and three scrapbooks of newspaper clippings, along with a scrapbook (1941-1946) containing material about Berry's experiences as a prisoner of war of the Japanese in the Philippine Islands.

Berthrong, Donald J. 70
Papers 1750-1879
13 feet

History professor. Photocopies of correspondence (1786-1918) of government officials regarding Great Plains Indian tribes and their relations and treaties with the United States; treaties (1803-1875) between these tribes and the United States; maps (1750-1876) of treaty areas; and manuscripts (1965) regarding the Indians of the Great Plains.

Unpublished finding aid available.

Betts, D. C. 71
Records 1916-1941
1.33 feet

Merchant. Business correspondence (1927-1940); ledgers recording cash sales (1918-1928); business accounts (1916-1941); and expenses (1917-1934) from the D. C. Betts Supply Company, suppliers of mining equipment, in Quapaw, Oklahoma.

Unpublished finding aid available.

Betzinez, Jason (b. 1860) 72
Manuscript 1942
1 item

Farmer. A 145-page manuscript (1942) entitled "My People -- A Story of the Apaches."

Bevan, Wilbur Harrison 73
Papers 1907-1942
1 item

Collector. A journal (1914-1918) containing quotations, poetry, lecture notes, and notes for self-improvement collected during Bevan's service in World War I, along with lists of personal property (1936-1938), school memorabilia (1907-1911), and correspondence (1942).

Bienfang, Ralph David (b. 1905) 74
Papers 1900-1945
2 feet

Pharmacist and university professor. Bound sketchbooks (1933-1952) of animals and plants; manuscripts (1956-1957), notebooks (1932-1948), and workbooks (1939-1941) written by Bienfang and relating to pharmacognosy; correspondence (1942) and printed material (1944-1945) relating to U. S. Army pharmacy; and Bienfang's collection of postage stamps and seals (ca. 1930-1960).

Unpublished finding aid available.

Biggers, Jesse and Helen Biggers 75
Printed materials 1892-1940
1.10 feet

Collectors. Travel brochures (ca. 1920-1940); postcards, greeting cards, and calendars (1892-1908); books (ca. 1920-1930), including cookbooks and do-it-yourself guides, along with other miscellaneous printed material (ca. 1900), including University of Oklahoma directories, programs, and similar university-related items.

Unpublished finding aid available.

Billings, James F. 76
Papers 1878-1897
.10 foot

School superintendent. Correspondence (1878-1897) from James F. Billings, city magistrate and superintendent of schools in Clay Center, Kansas, to his family concerning business affairs, illnesses, social events, and daily life in several Kansas towns.

Bizzell, William Bennett (1876-1944) 77
Papers 1910-1945
11.25 feet

University president. Personal and business correspondence (1910-1945), including correspondence from Bizzell's tenure as president of Texas A&M College, his association with Drury College in Springfield, Missouri, and letters of condolence to his family upon his death; official correspondence (1925-1941) from Bizzell's tenure as president of the University of Oklahoma; University of Oklahoma sociology department lecture notes and class materials (1941-1943); correspondence, circulars, and reports (1941-1944) from Bizzell's tenure as a director of the Federal Home Loan Bank of Topeka, Kansas; reprints (n.d.); manuscripts of articles and speeches (n.d.) by Bizzell; correspondence (1940-1944) concerning Bizzell's publications; a genealogy of the Bizzell family; and class notes (ca. 1920) taken by Bizzell while attending Baylor and Columbia universities.

Blachly, Lucile Spire and Charles Dallas Blachly (1883-1959) 78
Papers 1924-1955
6 feet

Physicians. Correspondence (1924-1955) regarding personal affairs and selected national affairs such as health care, socialized medicine, the threat of nuclear weapons, and the U. S. government's response to those issues. The correspondence also refers to the Oklahoma County Consumers Council, a depression-era federal agency established by the National Emergency Council. Other series include manuscripts (ca. 1915-1935) by the Blachlys on various aspects of national health, and a short autobiography of Lucile Blachly; certificates and diplomas (1928-1950) awarded the Blachlys for the practice of medicine; minutes (1934-1936) of the meetings of the Oklahoma County Consumers Council, and of its committees; and publications (ca. 1932-1936) of the Oklahoma County Consumers Council regarding the results of surveys by that agency investigating the prices of food and the availability and quality of housing and health care in the Oklahoma City, Oklahoma, area. Correspondents include Eleanor Roosevelt and Pitirim Sarokin.

Black, Albert Hamilton (1936-)   79
Manuscript 1492-1985
1 item

Tribal historian. A typewritten manuscript (ca. 1985) by Black entitled "Ceremony of the Earth People," and regarding the history and religious ceremonies of the Cheyenne and Arapaho Indians from the time of first contact with Europeans to the 1980s. The author details the procedures and appropriate time of each ceremony.

Blakemore, Jesse Lee (1862-1953)   80
Records 1913-1931
2.66 feet

Physician. Account books (1913-1929) and daybooks (1916-1931) from Blakemore's medical practice in Muskogee, Oklahoma.

Blanchard, James Lyon   81
Letter 1852
1 item

A copy of a letter (1852) by Blanchard describing his journey to the California gold-mining camp of Placerville and events in the camp.

Blanding, Donald Benson (1894-1957)   82
Papers 1938-1946
.10 foot

Poet and author. Correspondence (1940-1946) of Don and Dorothy Blanding regarding his books and poetry, and their travels and friends; postcards (1940-1946) from the Blandings sent from various points in their travels; newspaper clippings (n.d.) regarding Blanding and his books; and poetry (n.d.) by Blanding.

Blanton, Jr., (Mrs.) James T.   83
Papers 1827-1941
3 items

Collector. A biographical sketch (1939) of Smith Paul who was raised by the Chickasaw Indians and for whom Pauls Valley, Oklahoma, is named, along with two lists (ca. 1941) of inscriptions taken from tombstones in the old Indian cemeteries at Pauls Valley, and Whitebead, a historic village in the Chickasaw Nation and now in Garvin County, Oklahoma.

Blew, W. Bryan 84
Records 1949-1950
1 foot

Collector. Records (1949-1950), including correspondence and scrapbooks of Oklahoma Lions clubs during Blew's term as a district governor.

Boatman, Andrew Nimrod "Jack" (b. 1887) 85
Papers 1922-1951
.10 foot

Attorney. Correspondence (1922-1951) regarding the University of Oklahoma Alumni Association, of which Boatman was president in 1924 and 1925, and Oklahoma politics.

Bodine, John James 86
Papers 1956-1957
.10 foot

Ethnologist. Three letters (1956-1957) describing Bodine's travels in Mexico and Guatemala. He was employed as a manager of a large ranch in Guatemala and one letter (n.d.) describes the ranch and its native employees.

Boggs, Herbert Otho 87
Papers 1830-1889
8 items

Collector. Photocopies of Choctaw Indian documents including an occupation permit (1889); a sales brochure (n.d.) from the Sacred Heart Abbey in Sacred Heart, Oklahoma; a letter (1845) from George Harkins describing the condition among the Choctaws since their removal from Mississippi to Indian Territory; and a letter (1874) from Peter Pitchlynn to his nephew W. B. Pitchlynn regarding Choctaw politics.

Boirun, G. D. 88
Papers 1897-1921
3 items

Farmer. A ledger (1897-1901) of prices and kinds of liquor sold in a saloon in Burnett, Indian Territory; a ledger (1917-1921) in which Boirun chronicled the weather and day-by-day activities on his farm near Burnett, including a record of farm sales and purchases (1897-1902); and a letter (1908) from Mrs. Boirun's sister describing the problems of farming in the Van Alstyne, Texas, area.

Bollinger, Clyde John 89
Papers 1915-1978
8 feet

Geography professor. Papers (1915-1978), including correspondence between Bollinger and other geographers; research notes with calculations for Bollinger's solar atlas; and reprints of eight articles by Bollinger.

Bond, George M. (1847-1922) 90
Printed materials 1916-1951
5 items

Judge. An obituary (1922) of Bond, the first county judge of Jefferson County, Oklahoma; a list (n.d.) of Bond's brothers and sisters and their birth dates; a certificate of election (1916) to the Oklahoma legislature; and two broadsides (1951) advertising the sale of a Hereford bull.

Bone, Kathleen 91
Papers 1903-1906
7 items

Collector. Allotment certificates (1903-1906) for land in the Chickasaw Nation, Indian Territory.

Boomer Literature Collection 92
Printed materials 1859-1905
1 foot

Subject collection. Flyers, leaflets, and handbills (1859-1905) advertising land in Oklahoma, both settled and unsettled, along with booklets, leaflets and handbills (1859-1905) advertising the new cities, counties, and regions of the territory. The collection also contains a proclamation (1893) by territorial Governor William Renfrow, and a commencement ceremony program (1882) from Indian University in Muskogee.

Boone, Charles A. 93
Records 1925-1966
3 feet

Pharmacist. Financial ledgers (1925-1966) recording daily purchases and sales of a drug store in Sentinel, Oklahoma.

Booth, G. R. 94
Records 1905-1915
.25 foot

Physician. Four daybooks (1906-1910) and one account ledger (1911-1915) from Booth's medical practice near Hughes, Oklahoma.

Bosworth, Caroline M. 95
Printed materials 1942-1945
7 items

Collector. Seven World War II ration books (1942-1945) issued by the Oklahoma City, Oklahoma, ration board.

Boudinot, Frank J. 96
Printed materials 1893-1910
.25 foot

Politician. Typescripts of newspaper editorials and articles (1893-1910) regarding the activities of Boudinot, an attorney and political leader in the Cherokee Nation and the Keetoowah Society.

Boudinot, W. P. (d. 1898) 97
Printed materials 1870-1899
.25 foot

Editor. Typescripts of articles (1870-1899), by or about W. P. Boudinot, from various Cherokee Indian newspapers and relating to the Indian policy of the federal government, the Cherokee Orphan Asylum, land transfers, and railroads in Indian Territory.

Bowen, Myrtle Evans (1898-1975) 98
Papers 1898-1975
.10 foot

Pioneer. Biographical and genealogical material (1898-1975) written by Bowen describing frontier and pioneer life in Oklahoma and Indian territories.

Boyd, David Ross (1853-1936) 99
Papers 1899-1957
.75 foot

University president. Correspondence (1899-1943) between Boyd, his family, and others, including Edward E. Dale, William B. Bizzell, and George B. Parker, regarding the establishment of the University of Oklahoma, its formative years, and the tenure of Boyd as its first president; speeches (n.d.) delivered by Boyd regarding the university and its early faculty and personalities; newspaper clippings (n.d.) regarding Boyd and the university; contracts (1892) signed by Boyd and the university's Board of Regents hiring him as president; certificates (1903-1924) of appreciation and recognition awarded Boyd by institutions and organizations; obituaries and memorials (1936-1937) of Boyd; genealogies of the Boyd and Ross families; event programs (1900-1909) recording university fine arts, athletic, baccalaureate and commencement activities, as well as those of the Norman, Oklahoma, chapters of the Y.M.C.A. and Y.W.C.A.; songs, music, and yells (ca. 1905) of the University of Oklahoma; and posters (1902-1907) advertising University of Oklahoma football games and fine arts events. Also included in this collection is a manuscript by Mary Alice Boyd, daughter of David Ross Boyd, describing the Boyds' life in Arkansas City, Kansas, their move to Oklahoma Territory, and their impressions of, and experiences in early Norman, Oklahoma, and at the University of Oklahoma, with accounts of tornadoes, lawless Indians, racial tension, and personalities.

Boydston, Samuel M. (b. 1884) 100
Papers 1908-1927
.25 foot

Union activist. Financial secretary's ledger (1908-1911) for United Mine Workers Local #1864 (Wilburton, Oklahoma); correspondence (1916-1922) concerning Boydston's activities as an Oklahoma United Mine Workers board member from Sub-District #1, U.M.W. #21, including member complaints submitted for arbitration.

Boyer, Dave H. (b. 1874) 101
Papers 1913-1946
.25 foot

Politician. Correspondence (1913-1946) regarding Boyer's term in the Oklahoma state senate, a political appointment for his son Wilfred (1931), and his own appointment as senate auditor (1933).

Braden, John 102
Printed materials 1938-1948
.10 foot

Philatelist. Thirty-one envelopes bearing cancelled stamps, mostly commemorating the first day of issue of the 1948 stamp honoring Will Rogers, along with one noting National Air Mail Week in 1938. Many of the envelopes commemorating Rogers have scenes of Claremore, Oklahoma, Rogers's home town.

Bragg, Arthur Norris (b. 1898) 103
Papers 1934-1968
10.33 feet

Zoologist. Correspondence (1946-1967) with colleagues and associates regarding Bragg's research and publications; reprints of articles (1934-1968) in his subject field, along with galley proofs and book manuscripts (n.d.) by Bragg regarding amphibians and the zoology of Oklahoma.

Brandt, Joseph August (b. 1901)   104
Papers   1915-1980
4 feet

University president. Correspondence (1940-1980) with professors, academic deans and administrators of the University of Oklahoma, the University of Oklahoma Press, and others; speeches (1948-1950) by Brandt; and articles (1940-1948) written or collected by Brandt.

Unpublished finding aid available.

Branen, Joseph L.   105
Records   1941-1949
1 foot

Collector. Chapter reports (1948-1949) and correspondence (1948-1949) from Branen's term as district governor of Oklahoma Lions clubs, along with programs (1941) for the fiftieth anniversary of the Marshall (Oklahoma) Christian Church.

Branson, Carl Colton (1906-1975)   106
Papers   1900-1975
8 feet

Geologist. Correspondence (1900-1975) regarding the geology of Oklahoma, and the affairs of the Oklahoma Geological Survey, of which Branson was a long-time director.

Brazell, James C. (1868-1948)   107
Papers   1911-1948
.10 foot

Oilman and aviator. A scrapbook (1932-1948) of photographs, clippings, and memorabilia relating to Brazell's interest in flying, along with a copy of an account (1911) of the Civil War experiences of Brazell's father, J. H. Brazell.

Breeding, (Mrs.) W. K.   108
Printed materials   1932
4 items

Song writer. Musical scores and lyrics of two songs (1932) by Breeding entitled "My Dearest" and "Life I Love Best."

Brennan, John   109
Letter   1867
1 item

Soldier. A letter (1867) by Brennan concerning his service in the Confederate Army during the Civil War.

Bressie, R. M. (b. 1848)   110
Papers 1885-1975
.10 foot

Rancher. Genealogical papers (1885-1975) of the Bressie family, including correspondence (1885-1975), news clippings (1950-1960), and reminiscences (1963) concerning the local history of Bressie, Oklahoma, and Ford, Oklahoma.

Brillhart, Norman W.   111
Printed materials 1960-1974
.33 foot

Collector. Newspaper clippings on forts, battles, monuments, and trails (1960-1974), with an emphasis on George Armstrong Custer. Three items describe the 1965 dedication of the restored Fort Washita, Oklahoma.

Briscoe, Isaac   112
Letters 1849-1850
2 items

Pioneer. Two letters (1849-1850) from Isaac Briscoe to his wife, Nancy, describing his situation in the California gold fields near Sacramento.

Broaddus, Bower (1888-1949)   113
Papers 1930-1949
6.66 feet

Judge. Findings of fact, conclusions of law, and case files (1940-1949) from Broaddus's tenure as a judge for the eastern, northern, and western districts of the Tenth Federal District Court; case files (1933-1940) from Broaddus's law practice in Muskogee, Oklahoma; business and personal correspondence (1930-1949); and speeches (n.d.) of Broaddus and others.

Bronson, Edgar S. (1858-1924)   114
Scrapbook 1917-1927
1 item

Editor. A scrapbook (ca. 1927) of newspaper clippings by and about Bronson who was editor of the *El Reno American* and secretary of the Oklahoma State Press Association.

Brooks, Stratton Duluth (1870-1949)   115
Papers 1918-1919
.33 foot

University president. A scrapbook (1918-1919) containing letters and photographs sent to Brooks from Oklahomans who were fighting in World War I. The letters describe military life, fighting, and the writers' reactions to the war.

Broome, Bertram C.   116
Papers 1890-1937
.66 foot

Author. Manuscripts (n.d.) of fictional stories by Broome set in the American southwest in the late 1800s, and entitled "Pagan of the Mesa," "Navajo Gold," "Injun Toll," and "Trail Dust." The collection also includes correspondence (1927-1934) and watercolor and ink drawings by Broome.

Brown, Benjamin H.   117
Papers 1914-1920
3 items

Physician. A reprint of an article (1914) published by the Muskogee County (Oklahoma) Medical Society and entitled "Report of the Committee on Tuberculosis and Tuberculosis Anti-Sera;" a typescript of a speech (1919) by Brown to the Oklahoma State Medical Association entitled "Diagnosis of the Pathological Heart;" and a typescript (ca. 1920) entitled "An Analysis of the Hospital Situation in Muskogee."

Brown, Hugh   118
Printed materials 1821-1865
2 items

Collector. Two typescript copies of a journal (1821-1865) recounting John Brown's study of law in Lexington, Kentucky, 1821-1822, and his activities and expenses as a planter, lawyer, and insurance agent in Camden, Arkansas, 1852-1865.

Brown, John F. (1843-1919)   119
Printed materials 1870-1907
.25 foot

Indian chief. Typescripts of news articles (1870-1907) relating to mining and grazing leases, Dawes Commission proceedings, tribal government, and politics of the Seminole Nation, along with editorials concerning John F. Brown, a businessman and principal chief of the Seminoles from 1877-1902.

Brown, Phillip (ca. 1867-1951)   120
Papers 1898-1933
6.66 feet

Merchant. Correspondence (1898-1933); cotton record books (1904-1928); journals (1917-1933); ledgers (1904, 1921-1922); and daybooks (1923-1925) relating to the Brown Brothers Mercantile Store in Eufaula, Oklahoma, which bought cotton and invested in real estate.

Unpublished finding aid available.

Brown, W. H. 121
Manuscript 1933-1969
1 item

Judge. A typescript (ca. 1969) by Brown chronicling the invention of the parking meter in Oklahoma City, Oklahoma, and Brown's role in its development.

Bryan, Frank 122
Papers 1928-1958
.33 foot

Geologist. Correspondence (1928-1932) concerning arrowheads, and contemporary affairs with Gilbert Floyd of England and others, along with two manuscripts (ca. 1958) entitled "The Llano Estacado" and "Lewisville: Its Place in the Pleistocene Picture."

Bryan, J. R. 123
Papers 1896-1917
12 items

Physician. Notebooks (1906-1907) containing descriptions of diseases, cures, treatments and remedies, and diplomas and certificates (1896-1917) awarded Bryan by medical schools and the Selective Service office of Caddo County, Oklahoma.

Bryan, John A. 124
Records 1882-1909, 1944
.25 foot

Collector. Two ledgers (1882-1909) from the post office at Nelson, Indian Territory, listing materials received and delivered, and a roster of members (1944) in the Oklahoma State Medical Association.

Bryant, William J. 125
Printed materials 1875-1878
2 items

Indian chief. Two typescripts of news articles (1875-1878) from Choctaw Nation newspapers. One concerns the nomination of Bryant for principal chief, the other deals with Bryant's approval of a Choctaw Nation law.

Buchanan, F. R.   126
Records 1915-1941
.66 foot

Physician. Daybooks (1921-1922) and ledgers (1915-1941) from Buchanan's medical practice in Canton, Oklahoma. The collection also includes an inventory (1941) of office equipment and medical instruments.

Buchanan, James Shannon   127
Papers 1850-1937
2 feet

Professor and university president. Correspondence (1902) related to Buchanan's attempts to have power and water companies established in Norman, Oklahoma; lecture notes (n.d.) for history classes; draft copies (n.d.) of his book *The History of Oklahoma*; Katherine Buchanan's lecture notes (n.d.) as a teacher at University High School, Norman, Oklahoma; papers (1912) relating to the history of the University of Oklahoma; personal correspondence and legal papers (1893-1927) of the Buchanan family; printed propositions, journals, and committee reports (1906-1907) to the Oklahoma Constitutional Convention; guides (n.d.) for the study and teaching of English; and Delta Kappa Gamma bulletins (1936-1937).

Unpublished finding aid available.

Buffett, Richard H.   128
Papers 1918-1927
12 items

Collector. Correspondence (1918) with Havemeyers-Seamans Oil Company and Seamans Oil Company, both of Oklahoma City, Oklahoma, concerning Alvah H. Buffett's stock purchases. Also included in the collection are five stock certificates (1921-1927) from the Continental Asphalt and Petroleum Company and the Healdton Petroleum Company.

Burchardt, August Gustave (1906-1988)   129
Records 1952-1955
.66 foot

Collector. Correspondence, publications, bulletins and membership lists, all dated 1952-1955, from international and Oklahoma Lions Club organizations, of which Burchardt was a district governor.

Burchardt, George M.   130
Directory 1926
1 item

Collector. A city telephone directory (1926) for Frederick, Oklahoma.

Burchardt, William **131**
Papers 1960-1965
3.33 feet

Author. Correspondence (1960-1965) to and from Burchardt concerning the Western Writers of America. The collection also contains numerous manuscripts (n.d.) of short stories and articles by Burchardt dealing with the American west.

Unpublished finding aid available.

Burdine, C. A. **132**
Papers 1903-1909
.10 foot

Government employee. Letters (1903-1909) from Burdine to his wife describing life in Indian Territory, especially in the town of Tishomingo, and his work as a member of the Dawes Commission.

Bureau of Government Research Collection **133**
Papers 1889-1962
6 feet

University research bureau. Proceedings and debates of the Oklahoma Constitutional Convention (1906-1907); reports of studies made by the Oklahoma State Planning Board (1936-1938), the Oklahoma Tax Commission (1935-1936), the Oklahoma State Legislative Council (1947-1952), the University of Oklahoma College of Business Administration (1950), and the Bureau of Government Research (1951-1961); typescripts (1910-1931) of newspaper articles relating to the Socialist Party of Oklahoma; and a chart (1962) showing the organization of Oklahoma state government.

Unpublished finding aid available.

Burney, B. C. **134**
Printed materials 1878-1891
6 items

Indian chief. Typescripts of editorials (1878-1891) on Burney's governorship of the Chickasaw Nation from 1878-1880, and of his messages to the Chickasaw Nation legislature which originally appeared in the *Star Vindicator*, the *Cherokee Advocate*, and the *Purcell Register*.

Burns, David A. **135**
Papers 1920-1968
5 items

Collector. Photocopies of articles (1920-1960) concerning Governor Ernest W.

Marland and Lew Wentz; a photocopy of a speech (1932) by Marland regarding money trusts; and a college history class paper (1968) by Burns entitled "Characterizations of E. W. Marland."

Burns, Samuel Lee (b. 1876) 136
Papers 1899-1905
3 items

Physician. Certificates (1899-1905) issued to Burns authorizing him to practice medicine and surgery in the Creek Nation and in the southern district of Indian Territory.

Burton, Patricia 137
Printed materials 1960-1969
.33 foot

Collector. Newspaper articles (1960-1969) and related materials on the history and development of the Shetland pony breed.

Busby, Orel (ca. 1890-1965) 138
Papers 1918-1959
3 feet

Judge. Correspondence (1942), speeches (1942), and clippings (1942) concerning Busby's unsuccessful candidacy for the Democratic nomination for U. S. senator from Oklahoma; correspondence (1918) concerning Busby's successful candidacy for a judgeship in Pontotoc County, Oklahoma; correspondence (1924-1927) from Busby's term as a regent of the University of Oklahoma; and correspondence (1935-1937) concerning his unsuccessful bid for the nomination to a federal judgeship in Oklahoma.

Bush, Charles C., II 139
Papers 1749-1965
5 feet

Professor. Instructional materials (1749-1965) for college history courses; student papers (1963); manuscripts (n.d.) and published materials (1941-1960) regarding historical events; and correspondence (1950-1965) to and from Bush regarding historical events and research, along with an original letter (1829) regarding Tecumseh and the Battle of the Thames in 1813, written by a soldier who participated.

Unpublished finding aid available.

Bushyhead, Dennis Wolf (1826-1898) 140
Papers 1879-1922
.50 foot

Indian chief. Correspondence (1879-1897); annual messages (1879-1882); speeches (1879-1887); an autobiography (1880); proclamations (1879-1885); and other papers (1879-1922) relating to political matters in which Bushyhead was involved as principal chief of the Cherokee Nation from 1879-1887, and a representative to the Dawes Commission, and to the controversies growing out of the Cherokee Strip Livestock Association's operations.

Butcher, Nahum Ellsworth (b. 1872)　　　　　　　　　　　　　　　　141
Papers 1957
1 item

School superintendent. A transcript of an interview (1957) conducted by Frank A. Balyeat with Butcher, the first freshman enrolled at the University of Oklahoma (1893), recounting his experiences at the university and, later, as superintendent of West Norman (Oklahoma) schools.

Butcher, W. H.　　　　　　　　　　　　　　　　　　　　　　　　　142
Printed materials 1890-1930
.10 foot

Collector. Political pamphlets (1893-1916); a speech (1896) by William Jennings Bryan; and booklets (1890-1930) concerning social and labor organizations, such as the Masons, the American Federation of Labor, and the Knights of Labor.

Byrd, William L. (b. 1844)　　　　　　　　　　　　　　　　　　　143
Printed materials 1888-1906
.25 foot

Indian chief. Typescripts of Byrd's messages (1889-1892) to the Chickasaw Nation legislature along with editorials (1888-1891), interviews (1891), and articles (1891-1906) concerning Byrd as governor of the Chickasaw Nation from 1888-1894 and, later, Chickasaw delegate to Washington, D.C.

Cable Temperance Union Collection　　　　　　　　　　　　　　　144
Records 1884-1886
1 item

Civic organization. A notebook containing the constitution, by-laws, and proceedings of the Cable Temperance Union of Cable, Illinois. The book also contains inspirational songs and readings.

Caddo County Medical Association Collection　　　　　　　　　　　145
Papers 1904-1941
2 items

Professional organization. Ledgers (1904-1941) containing minutes of the Caddo

County (Oklahoma) Medical Society, from its inception through its evolution into the Caddo County Medical Association.

Calloway, John R.   146
Papers 1920-1945
.10 foot

Physician. Note cards (1920-1930) recording patient accounts from Calloway's medical practice in Pauls Valley, Oklahoma, and abstracts of lectures (1940-1945) on surgical diagnosis and pediatrics published by the Oklahoma State Medical Association.

Camp Supply Collection   147
Letterbook 1869-1878
1 item

Military post. A letterbook (1869-1878) containing copies of letters sent; lists of names of captured Cheyenne and Arapaho Indians; data relating to their provisioning and outfitting; and reports on hostile bands kept by the commissary supply officer at Camp Supply, Indian Territory, which was established in 1868 as a base for operations against the plains Indian tribes.

Camp, Earl F. (b. 1892)   148
Records 1922-1940
5 items

Physician. Ledgers (1922-1940) recording Camp's patient treatment and billing records for both his medical practice and the hospital he operated in Buffalo, Oklahoma.

Campbell, Anson   149
Papers 1965-1967
2 items

Collector. A letter (1967) regarding the Campbell family history and a typescript (ca. 1965) regarding the Bullock family of Lindsay, Oklahoma, and the family's contribution to the development of early Lindsay.

Campbell, Charles Duncan (b. 1877)   150
Papers 1901-1921
.10 foot

Oil man and postmaster. Correspondence (1905-1907) from Wilbur E. Campbell concerning his oil company and the Prairie Oil Company, his purchase of a Tulsa, Oklahoma, sub-division, and the introduction of a land purchasing bill into the 1907 Oklahoma legislature. Also included in the collection is a letter (1907) from T. S.

Boyers concerning Boyers's family history, and letters (1901) from W. T. Flynn concerning Campbell's appointment as postmaster of Apache, Oklahoma Territory.

Campbell, J. F. (1876-1934)   151
Records   1906-1934
5 feet

Physician. Ledgers (1906-1934) and daybooks (1921-1934) in which Campbell's fees and services from his Mangum, Oklahoma, medical practice were recorded.

Campbell, John Sidney, Sr.   (1875-1961)   152
Records   1899-1934
8 feet

Businessman. Account ledgers of the Campbell Hardware Store (1909-1934) and the Campbell Funeral Home (1899-1918), both of Fairland, Indian Territory, and Oklahoma. The funeral home ledgers record the names of the deceased persons for whom undertaking services were provided and include some biographical and cause-of-death information.

Campbell, Robert Boyers   153
Papers   1907-1948
.10 foot

Collector. A letter (1907) from W. E. Campbell to his son, R. B. Campbell, describing the successes of his [W. E. Campbell's] oil company; news clippings regarding oil in Oklahoma; and a reprint (1948) of an article regarding the elder Campbell.

Campbell, S. W.   (b. ca. 1850)   154
Manuscript   1926
1 item

Collector. A manuscript (1926) recounting a journey made in 1857 by Campbell's family over the Oregon Trail to Colorado to prospect for silver.

Campbell, Walter Stanley   (1877-1957)   155
Papers   1800-1964
77 feet

Professor. Personal correspondence (1897-1957); correspondence with Campbell's relatives (1822-1896); correspondence with publishers and literary agents (1920-1958); literary manuscripts (ca. 1914-1957); diaries, notebooks, and journals (1901-1926); and business papers (ca. 1925-1959) regarding Campbell's writings on the west, Indians, and Oklahoma, with emphasis on transportation, fortifications, cowboys, wars and battles, criminals and outlaws, and Indian chiefs, along with original Indian art by Carl Sweezy.

Unpublished finding aid available.

Canton, Frank M. (d. 1927) 156
Papers 1886-1927
3 feet

Lawman. Canton's correspondence (1893-1927) while a U.S. deputy marshal and Oklahoma adjutant general; reminiscences (n.d.) of his experiences in Texas, Oklahoma, Wyoming, and Alaska; newspaper clippings (n.d.) about his experiences; and related artifacts (1896-1915). The collection also contains both biographical and autobiographical material on Canton.

Unpublished finding aid available.

Capshaw, Madison T. J. (1856-1920) 157
Papers 1884-1920
4 items

Physician. Handwritten accounts (1890-1920) of Capshaw's experiences as a physician in Norman, Oklahoma Territory, and during the World War I influenza epidemic; and of the childhood of his son, Walter Capshaw. The collection also contains a diploma (1884) issued to Madison T. J. Capshaw by the Memphis Medical College in Tennessee granting him the M.D. degree.

Carlisle Barracks Collection 158
Papers n.d.
2 items

Collector. Hand-printed, bound manuscripts (n.d.) in the Ethiopian/Amharic language, brought to the United States from Africa during World War II and which are believed to be a regional religious text.

Carlock, Arlie Ernest (1873-1936) 159
Papers 1896-1936
3 items

Physician. A news clipping (1896) announcing Carlock's commencement from the Missouri Medical College in St. Louis, Missouri; a letter (1897) from a former classmate regarding the alumni of the class of 1896 and the destruction of the college by fire; and a biographical sketch (1936) of Carlock, detailing his long career as a physician in Indian Territory and Oklahoma, with an account of the establishment of a hospital at Hartshorne, Oklahoma, and the reasons for its failure.

Carmen First National Bank Collection 160
Records 1903-1934
4 feet

Bank. Ledgers (1903-1934); tellers cash books (1905-1908); and discount and collection registers (1905-1917) from the First National Bank of Carmen, Oklahoma.

Carpenter, Everett 161
Papers 1911-1977
.10 foot

Petroleum geologist. Correspondence (1950-1977) between Dan H. Carpenter and Everett Carpenter's associates regarding Everett's fiftieth anniversary as a petroleum geologist. Some letters concern the history of petroleum geology. Other materials in the collection include Everett Carpenter's geology thesis (1911) and petroleum-related publications.

Carpenter, Paul Simon (1895-1949) 162
Papers 1910-1956
2.66 feet

Professor of music. Correspondence (1910-1956) to and from Carpenter regarding his university studies at the Conservatoire National in Paris, his appointment to the faculty of the University of Oklahoma in 1914, his 1946 appointment as Dean of Fine Arts at the University of Oklahoma, the designation of a university building as Carpenter Hall, and his book *Music, An Art and a Business* which was unfinished at the time of his death; financial records (1940-1949) of Carpenter, including cancelled checks, bills, and receipts; note cards (n.d.) containing a bibliography of music books; scrapbooks (n.d.) containing musical scores with accompanying research notes; and publications (1870-1954) including musical scores, performance programs, and journals. Also included in the collection is a two-page genealogical listing (ca. 1949) tracing the Carpenter family history from 1675 to 1949.

Unpublished finding aid available.

Carriker, Robert C. (1940-   ) 163
Manuscript 1970
1 item

Historian. A manuscript (1970) of Carriker's book *Fort Supply, Indian Territory: Frontier Outpost on the Plains* which was published by the University of Oklahoma Press.

Carseloway, James Manford 164
Papers 1859-1937
3 items

Historian. A manuscript (1883) containing instructions to the Cherokee National Council's Washington, D.C., delegation as approved by D. W. Bushyhead, principal chief; a typescript concerning a flowing oil well brought in during 1859 in the Cherokee Nation; and correspondence (1937) describing the history of Grand River Dam in Oklahoma.

Carson, Frank L. 165
Papers 1902-1918
.10 foot

Physician. Lecture notes used at Tulane University (1902) and the Mayo Clinic (1906); correspondence (1917-1918) concerning Carson's service in World War I; and a professional paper by Carson about the treatment of tetanus.

Carter, Frank C. (1862-1954) 166
Papers 1930-1956
1 foot

Politician. Correspondence (1938-1956) regarding farm mortgages, Carter's campaigns and election as state auditor in 1938 and as Oklahoma secretary of state in 1942, his retirement from political office in 1946, and his death in 1954; a scrapbook (1930-1948) of clippings and correspondence about Carter's political career; and a certificate (n.d.) from the Oklahoma Sheriffs and Peace Officers Association honoring him for a lifetime of service to Oklahoma law enforcement.

Carter, M. L. (d. 1923) 167
Records 1911-1924
.10 foot

Physician. An account book (1911-1913) in which Carter recorded house calls he made in Choctaw County, Oklahoma, the services rendered to each patient, and the fees charged, along with an account ledger (1923-1924) in which Carter recorded the same information for in-office treatment.

Casey, Alvin Harold 168
Records 1933-1955
.25 foot

Collector. Correspondence (1944); committee assignments (1954-1955); financial statements (1933-1946); and annual reports (1946-1954) of the Guthrie, Oklahoma, Lions Club.

Cass, Lewis 169
Papers 1825-1839
.10 foot

Army officer and statesman. Copies of letters (1825-1839) from Gen. Matthew

Arbuckle, Montfort Stokes, and Jean Pierre Chouteau written at military posts in Indian Territory to Secretary of War Lewis Cass concerning the attempt to gather the plains Indian tribes at Camp Mason on the Canadian River for a peace conference, along with other detailed observations on Indian affairs.

Cate, Roscoe Simmons (1876-1954)   170
Papers 1819-1970
5.33 feet

Indian attorney. Diaries (1939-1949) kept by Cate; manuscripts (1876-1924) in the Creek language; copies of correspondence (1838-1937) in English, signed by officials connected with Indian affairs, including Maj. Gen. Thomas S. Jessup, Opothleyaholo, and Albert Pike; and a compilation of names and locations of Creek towns in Alabama and Oklahoma, along with briefs, trusts, and correspondence, all relating to the court case (1937-1938) concerning the estate of Jackson Barnett, one of Oklahoma's wealthiest Indians.

Unpublished finding aid available.

Cates, P. M.   171
Ledger 1927-1937
1 item

Merchant. An account ledger (1927-1937) showing the wages, wholesale purchases, and bank balances of Cates's dry-goods business in Maysville, Oklahoma.

Cattle Brands Collection   172
Poster n.d.
1 item

Subject collection. A poster (n.d.) entitled "Chart of Texas Cattle Brands Used Throughout the State with Attached Booklet Identifying Each Brand."

Caudron, Theophile (1880-1970)   173
Papers 1912-1970
1 foot

Priest. Clippings (1912-1970) concerning Monsignor Caudron's mediation in the labor disputes at Henryetta, Oklahoma, his long career as pastor of St. Michael's Catholic Church in Henryetta, Oklahoma, his work as superintendent of the church school, his retirement in 1965, his return to his native Belgium, the subsequent closing of the school, and Caudron's death in 1970; correspondence (1965) to and from Caudron concerning the closing of the upper six grades at St. Michael's Catholic School in Henryetta, Oklahoma; and telegrams from prominent political figures, including a letter from President Franklin D. Roosevelt.

Cayuga Nation Papers 174
Papers 1985-1953
.10 foot

Indian tribe. Correspondence (1895-1953) concerning claims by the Cayuga Indians against the state of New York, the United States, and the St. Lawrence Power Company.

Center For Studies in Higher Education Collection 175
Records 1970-1986
10 feet

Research center. Records (1970-1986), including correspondence, reports, and subject files from the Oklahoma Center for Studies in Higher Education regarding the center's operation and mission as well as its participation in a number of special projects, including a training program (1972-1979) for education administrators from Saudi Arabia. Also in the collection are records relating to higher education colloquiums sponsored by the center, the University of Oklahoma Budget Council, the Athletics Council, the University of Oklahoma seal, accreditation programs, and program audits.

Unpublished finding aid available.

Certificates and Diplomas Collection 176
Printed materials 1849-1960
4 feet

Series collection. Certificates, diplomas, and awards (1849-1960) issued by governmental entities, private and public institutions, and organizations to individuals as awards, academic degrees, appointments to office, acknowledgments of service, and expressions of appreciation.

Unpublished finding aid available.

Chaat, Robert P. 177
Records 1900-1908, 1939-1948
.10 foot

Clergyman. A minute book (1900-1908) kept by the secretary of the Apache Indian Mission at Fort Sill, Oklahoma; manuscripts (n.d.) concerning the history of the Dutch Reformed church schools, the Comanche Mission, the Warm Springs Apaches, and Indian conversion to Christianity, along with booklets, pamphlets, and newsletters (1939-1948) regarding the history and constitution of the Dutch Reformed Church, and the evils of narcotics.

Chandler National Bank Collection　　　　　　　　　　　　　　　　　　　178
Records 1894-1910
8 feet

Bank. Ledgers (1898-1909); note ledgers (1907-1910); journals (1894-1908); remittance registers (1894-1900); and discount registers (1895-1898) recording daily business transactions of the Chandler National Bank of Chandler, Oklahoma Territory.

Chaney, Warren P. (b. 1878)　　　　　　　　　　　　　　　　　　　　　　　179
Papers 1864-1935
.10 foot

Government employee. Correspondence (1904-1908); recollections (1955); allotment records (1908); Civil War papers (1864); and published materials (1932-1954) relating to Indian Territory events of the early twentieth century and reflecting Chaney's experiences while traveling through the Choctaw and Chickasaw nations as clerk-in-charge of the Choctaw-Chickasaw allotment division of the Dawes Commission.

Chapman, Berlin Basil (1900-　)　　　　　　　　　　　　　　　　　　　　180
Papers 1889-1955
1 foot

Historian. Photocopies of correspondence, reports, and news articles (1889-1955) by Chapman regarding the history of Oklahoma Territory, including Lincoln County, the towns of Chandler, Mountain View, and Stillwater, and the Boomers led by David L. Payne. The collection also contains material relating to Oklahoma State University and the loyalty oaths required of the state's college and university faculties during the early 1950s. Also included is a proclamation (1923) by Governor J. C. Walton declaring martial law in Okmulgee County, Oklahoma.

Chapman, T. Shelby　　　　　　　　　　　　　　　　　　　　　　　　　　181
Records 1895-1911
1 foot

Physician. A typewritten account of the first meeting of the Indian Territory Medical Association in 1899; certificates (ca. 1900); copies of magazines (ca. 1910-1930); three letters (1904) of condolence on the death of Chapman's son; and seven account books (1895-1911) from his medical practice in McAlester, Oklahoma.

Checote, Samuel (1819-1884)　　　　　　　　　　　　　　　　　　　　　182
Printed materials 1867-1886
.25 foot

Indian chief. Typescripts of messages (1875-1883) of Checote, first principal chief of the Creek Nation under the Muskogee Constitution of 1867, to the House of

Kings and Warriors; newspaper editorials (1872-1883) on Checote and George W. Grayson from the *Vindicator* and the *Cherokee Advocate*, along with a biographical sketch (1926) of Checote.

Chelsea (Indian Territory) Town Records Collection   **183**
Records 1893-1899
.33 foot

Municipality. Minutes of the Chelsea, Indian Territory, city council (1893-1896); city assessments for 1899; summons for witnesses (1896-1897); and a warrant (1899) for disturbing the peace.

Cherokee Bibliography Project Collection   **184**
Papers ca. 1984
15 feet

Research project. Notes and bibliographic materials (ca. 1984) used in the compilation of an unpublished bibliography regarding the Cherokee Indians and Cherokee Nation.

Cherokee Bilingual Education Project Collection   **185**
Printed materials 1972-1976
1 foot

Educational project. Publications (1972-1976) of the Cherokee Bilingual Education Project of Tahlequah, Oklahoma, including teachers guides and students primers in both Cherokee syllabary and Roman script. The collection includes sample materials from a similar project from Mississippi produced for Cherokee Indians in that state.

Cherokee Nation Papers   **186**
Papers 1801-1982
83 feet

Indian tribe. Official correspondence, letter books, reports, chiefs messages, speeches of delegates, proceedings, laws, court decisions, acts, leases, election returns, registers of removal claims, and clippings relating to the affairs of the Cherokee Nation. Specifically included are groups of records and papers relating to the *Cherokee Advocate* (1869-1906); the Cherokee boundary survey (1871-1873); the Cherokee census (1868-1901); the Cherokee Outlet (1871-1896); citizenship (1856-1904); the Creek War or the William Cobb murder case (1880-1885); the Dawes Commission (1894-1907); delegations, agents, and attorneys (1816-1910); the Eastern (North Carolina) Cherokee (1871-1906); education (1856-1906); elections (1856-1901); the insane asylum (1874-1907); intruders (1868-1902); legislative affairs (1837-1905); licenses, permits, and fees (1856-1902); United States-Cherokee disputes (1874-1899); executive documents (1801-1909); financial records (1868-1909); national officers (1856-1902); the national prison and high

38

sheriff (1870-1900); Old Settlers Band (1875-1902); pardons and commutations (1876-1897); per-capita payments (1875-1902); railroads (1866-1900); rewards and extraditions (1877-1888); smallpox (1882-1900); suspensions (1877-1896); town lots (1858-1911); the Vann murder case (1879-1881); Cherokee Nation printed documents (1800-1982); Stand and Sarah C. Watie papers (1832-1881); Ridge and Boudinot family papers (1835-1890); James Madison Bell papers (1836-1908); general correspondence (1836-1908); Cherokee Treaty Fund claims (1837-1850); Civil War records (1861-1866); and general documents (1824-1893).

Unpublished finding aid available.

Chi Delta Phi Collection 187
Records ca. 1934-1948
.33 foot

Literary society. Two scrapbooks (1934-1948) containing correspondence and reports (1936-1948), membership records (1934-1948), by-laws (1939) and event programs of the University of Oklahoma Alpha Sigma chapter of Chi Delta Phi, a national collegiate literary society.

Chi Upsilon Collection 188
Records 1919-1955
.50 foot

Professional geology society for women. Correspondence (1921-1941); minutes of meetings (1920-1921); constitutions and by-laws (1920-1955); newspaper articles (n.d.); and manuscripts (1919-1937) regarding the establishment, history, members, and operation of the Alpha chapter (University of Oklahoma) of Chi Upsilon.

Chicago, Rock Island and Pacific Railroad Collection 189
Records 1853-1984
487 feet

Railroad company. Corporate records arranged in the five functional sub-groups of executive files; legal files; engineering records; property accounting; and real estate and industrial development records. Record series of the executive sub-group include minutes (1905-1915, 1947-1975); annual reports (1884-1908, 1915-1932, 1941, 1948-1975); subject files (1900-1984); Executive Committee minutes (1953-1955, 1971-1974); monthly letters to the Board of Directors (1921-1972); correspondence (1913-1976); corporate files of associated railroads (1910-1975); liquidation files (1968-1984); and stock ledgers (1853-1864, 1906-1933). In the legal sub-group are subject files (ca. 1925-1979); correspondence (1969-1976); contracts (1900-1910, 1930, 1950-1960); merger files-Union Pacific (1963-1975); merger files-other railroads (1920-1980); litigation files (1930-1980); legislation files-state level (1908-1920); and liquidation files (1975-1984). The engineering sub-group consists of projects files (1890-1975); graphics, including maps, tables, station blueprints, track layouts, bridges, engines and cars, total-system diagrams, and statistical charts (ca. 1890-1980); structural notes (1916-1917); and capital expenditures (1940-1941, 1947, 1966-1968). In the property accounting sub-group are grand summaries (1942-1972); valuations (1915-1981); money control files (1903-1904, 1935-1942); original cost data files (1934-1941); general balance sheet statements (1959-1964); and revenues and expenditures files (1902-1903, 1928-1944). The real estate and industrial development sub-group includes real estate sales files (1937-1974); abstracts of title (1859-1902, 1911-1931); industrial area files (1956-1977); lease records (1902-1925); quit claim deeds and tax records (1890-1907); land contracts (1941-1943); and station master files (1979).

Unpublished finding aid available.

Chickasaw Nation Collection   190
Papers   1871-1933
.25 foot

Indian tribe. Typescripts of laws (1871-1881) and newspaper articles (1874-1933) relating to the lands, institutions, and the affairs of the Chickasaw Nation, Indian Territory.

Chickasha Milling Company Collection   191
Records   1899-1952
452 feet

Grain milling company. Correspondence (1914-1952); financial records (1899-1952); and associated agricultural and economic historical materials, all pertaining to the operation of the Chickasha Milling Company of Chickasha, Oklahoma. Also included in the collection is a typewritten history (1899-1952) of the company.

Unpublished finding aid available.

Childs, (Mrs.) William Oscar   (1868-1957)   192
Papers   1926-1956
.66 foot

Philanthropist. Correspondence (1926-1955) concerning the Childs's move to Oklahoma in the 1920s and William O. Childs's subsequent involvement in the Oklahoma oil industry, his membership in the Scottish Rite of Freemasonry, his death in 1936, and Mrs. Childs's memorial gifts of chime carillons to the Scottish Rite Temple, Guthrie, Oklahoma, and to the University of Oklahoma in 1955, including the acceptance speech (1956) at the University of Oklahoma's dedication of the chimes, and an original purchase agreement (1955) for one of the three chimes Mrs. Childs donated.

Choate, Mary Treadwell (b. 1884)   193
Papers   ca. 1750-1927
.25 foot

Collector. The collection contains five books, including an eighteenth-century Bible; receipts and promissory notes (1809-1889); tax receipts (1871-1929); and a recipe for medicine (1839), all from the family of May Treadwell Choate, who settled first in Texas in the 1850s, and then came to Oklahoma in 1905.

Choctaw Nation Papers 194
Records and printed materials 1868-1936
17 feet

Indian tribe. Acts, laws, bills, and resolutions (1896-1910) of the Choctaw Nation; typescripts of newspaper articles (1868-1936), mainly about political matters such as elections, allotment, and the Dawes Commission, along with four ledgers (1902-1911) which were the journals of record and contain the minutes of the Choctaw Nation Council.

Unpublished finding aid available.

Choska Trading Company Collection 195
Records 1902-1907
2 items

Trading company. Ledgers (1902-1907) recording the daily commerce of the Choska Trading Company, a general merchandise store which operated in the Creek Nation villages of Choska, and Porter, Indian Territory.

Chouteau, Myra Yvonne (ca. 1929-   ) 196
Printed materials 1932-1950
.33 foot

Ballerina. Articles (1932-1950) concerning Chouteau's direct ancestor and first white settler in Oklahoma, Jean Pierre Chouteau, his brother, Auguste Chouteau, founder of St. Louis, Missouri, her dance career from childhood appearances at such events as Pioneer Day parades to membership in the Ballet Russe de Monte Carlo, and her acquaintance with Oklahoma political figures such as Governor Ernest W. Marland.

Christopher, Ernest Randell (1897-1967) 197
Records ca. 1940-1959
82 feet

Postmaster. Records (ca. 1940-1959) of the U.S. post office in Bartlesville, Oklahoma, of which Christopher was postmaster, including employee records and correspondence with the U.S. Post Office Department in Washington, D.C., regarding service in Bartlesville, Oklahoma, along with publications and correspondence (ca. 1950-1959) of the American Legion organization and its posts in Oklahoma. Included among the American Legion materials is information regarding its National American Commission, of which Christopher was a member, and "Man of the Year" awards, which he received.

Chupco, John (d. 1881)   198
Typescript 1874
1 item

Indian chief. A typescript of a news article (1874) from the *Cherokee Advocate* entitled "A Protest by John Chupco, P. P. Pitchlynn, et al," in which Chupco, Pitchlynn, and a number of Indian leaders protest efforts by white men to stop the formation of a ruling general council of Indians for Indian Territory, as provided by the Treaty of 1866, and efforts to extend a federal territorial government over Indian Territory.

Ciereszko, Leon   199
Printed materials and artifacts 1915-1917
.33 foot

Collector. Camp Fire Girl instruction manuals for leather and pine needle crafts, a Camp Fire Girl ceremonial dress, and beaded choke necklace. Also included is a booklet from the Camp Fire Outfitting Company describing the ceremonial dress.

Cities Service Oil and Gas Corporation Collection   200
Records 1896-1982
40 feet

Petroleum-related corporation. Administrative reports (1913-1980) and publications (1923-1982) regarding the history and operations (1896-1982), both domestic and international, of the Cities Service Oil Company, later the Cities Service Oil and Gas Corporation, as well as of other energy industry companies. Also included are biographical sketches of corporate officers such as Arthur W. Ambrose, Singer B. Irelan, J. Edgar Heston, Robert L. Kidd, and Henry Doherty.

Unpublished finding aid available.

Civil Rights Commission Collection   201
Records 1957-1961
.50 foot

Federal commission. Minutes (1960) of the Oklahoma Advisory Committee, along with correspondence (1958-1961) and publications (1957-1961) of the U.S. Commission on Civil Rights and the Oklahoma Advisory Committee, all relating to civil rights in Oklahoma.

Clarita Farmers State Bank Collection   202
Records 1913-1944
3 feet

Bank. Ledgers and cash account books (1922-1944) recording the daily business of the bank and also containing the by-laws, articles of incorporation, and minutes (1913) of stockholders meetings of the "96" Ballard Oil and Gas Company of Inola, Oklahoma.

Clark, Ben 203
Papers 1863-1907
.10 feet

Interpreter and scout. Military orders and personal correspondence (1863-1907), most notably from Gen. Nelson A. Miles, received by Clark while serving as an interpreter and scout for the U. S. Army at Fort Reno, Indian Territory.

Clark, Carter Blue 204
Printed materials 1922-1974
.33 feet

Historian. Photocopies of articles (1923-1927) from Ku Klux Klan journals such as *Kourier Magazine* and *Imperial Night-Hawk*, including many with articles about the Klan in Oklahoma; newspaper articles (1922-1924) on the Klan in Oklahoma; papers (1923-1924) relating to Oklahoma Governor John C. Walton and the Klan; Klan pamphlets and handbooks (1920s) and interview transcripts (1972-1974) with Ira M. Finley, Albert S. Giles, and Leon Hirsch regarding the Klan in Oklahoma.

Clark, Joseph J. 205
Papers 1908-1935
.10 foot

Physician. Correspondence (1933) to Clark from friends; receipts (1935) for goods purchased by Clark; a notebook (n.d.) of medical notes recorded by Clark; a daily journal (1934); and one ledger (1934-1935) in which Clark recorded patient accounts.

Clarke, (Mrs.) Hulbert S. 206
Printed materials 1924-1959
.50 foot

Professional golfer. A scrapbook (1926-1930) containing photographs, news clippings, and correspondence regarding Georgia Lee Clarke's career as a professional golfer.

Clarke, John R. 207
Papers 1926-1932
.10 foot

Politician. Correspondence (1926) to Clarke from Henry S. Johnston, and others concerning political issues and Clarke's campaign for the 1926 gubernatorial election in Oklahoma; pamphlets (1926) from Clarke's campaign, and Henry S. Johnston's platform for the same race; and an article (1926) from the *Muskogee Daily Phoenix* giving the election results by county. The collection also includes a letter (1932) to Clarke from Franklin D. Roosevelt concerning Clarke's platform.

Clarkson, Addie W. (1869-1950) 208
Papers 1908-1926
.10 foot

Physician. Account ledgers (1908) from Clarkson's medical practice at the Wheelock Academy in Millington, Oklahoma, and at Valliant, Oklahoma. The collection also includes A. M. Clarkson's class notes (1926) from the University of Oklahoma.

Classen, Anton H. (1861-1922) 209
Papers 1900
4 items

Realtor. Correspondence (1900) between Classen and Governor Theodore Roosevelt of New York, regarding Roosevelt's attendance at the Rough Rider's reunion of 1900 in Oklahoma City, Oklahoma Territory.

Cleckler, Frank Stuart (1922-1978) 210
Papers 1922-1978
8 feet

Philanthropist. Correspondence (1923-1974); financial records (1922-1978); travel logs and manuscripts (1964-1978) of trips to Australia, Oceania, the Near East, and the Far East; and posters (ca. 1940) by British Railways advertising the policy at its Preston, England, station of forbidding local boys of "engine spotting" from the platform. Also included in this collection are publications (1941-1963), including a dedication program of a U.S. naval air station in the Philippines, and travel booklets advertising Hong Kong, the Federation of South Africa, and one published by the U.S. embassy in Teheran, Iran, regarding the pleasures of travel there.

Clements, Frank B. (1896-1955) 211
Papers 1933-1953
2.66 feet

Collector. Correspondence (1933-1953) of Clements regarding Lions International activities in Tulsa, Oklahoma, and the state of Oklahoma, and publications, including *The Roar*, newsletter of the Tulsa Lions Club, and the *Official Proceedings* (1936-1947) of the Lions International conventions.

Cleo State Bank Collection 212
Ledgers 1900-1933
12 feet

Bank. General ledgers (1902-1932); reconciliation books (1916-1925); trial balances (1901-1903); bills receivable registers (1900-1914); collection registers (1900-1913); draft registers (1900-1915); remittance registers (1900-1908); cash sales books (1907-1914); tellers cash books (1900-1933); and cash books (1914-1920), all documenting the accounting functions of the Cleo State Bank in Cleo Springs, Oklahoma.

Unpublished finding aid available.

Cleveland County (Oklahoma) Children's Clinic Collection 213
Records 1927-1956
.10 foot

Medical facility. Correspondence (1949-1956); board meeting minutes (1937-1945); a clinic history (n.d.); and financial records (1938-1953) relating to the operation of this children's clinic.

Clifton, Robert T. 214
Manuscripts 1970
2 items

Author. Two manuscript copies (1970) of Clifton's book, *Barbs, Prongs, Points, Prickers and Stickers: A Complete and Illustrated Catalogue of Antique Barbed Wire*, published by the University of Oklahoma Press.

Cline, (Mrs.) B. F. 215
Records ca. 1920-1940
.33 foot

Merchant. An account ledger (1920-1940) from Cline's Department Store in Medford, Oklahoma.

Co-operative Publishing Company Collection 216
Records ca. 1900
3 items

Publishing company. Unpublished manuscripts (ca. 1900) entitled "Early History of the Co-operative Publishing Company," concerning the beginning of the company, its executives, and early gains and losses; "History of the State Capitol" describing the State Capitol Printing Company printing plant from founding to incorporation and including names of early executives; and "An Historical and Economical Brief of Guthrie and Logan County, Oklahoma," which includes sketches of the area's industry and scenic beauty, along with a description of the 89er Celebration, an annual event recognizing pioneers of the 1889 land run into Oklahoma Territory.

Coachman, Ward 217
Printed materials 1877-1878
3 items

Indian chief. Typescripts of messages (1877) and an editorial (1878) concerning an attempt to unite Creek political factions, and to promote the Creek constitution of 1867.

Cobb, Isabel (1858-1947) 218
Papers 1893-1913, 1959
2 items

Physician. A record book (1893-1913) listing Cobb's patients and house calls, and a brief biography of Cobb written by her nephew.

Coffey, John L. (b. 1898) 219
Record 1725
1 item

Collector. A document (1725) of proceedings before a royal notary concerning the death of a member of the Fourche family and his new world estate. The document is in French with no translation.

Coins, Tokens, and Money Collection 220
Artifacts 1816-1924
.10 foot

Numismatic collection. Trade tokens (1892-1920) issued by retail stores in Oklahoma and Indian territories, and Oklahoma, along with currency issued by the Bank of Augusta, Georgia (1816), the Confederate States of America (1863-1864), the states of Arkansas (1863) and North Carolina (1862), and by the Church of Jesus Christ of Latter Day Saints in Salt Lake City, Utah (1896).

Colbert, Winchester (1810-1880) 221
Printed materials 1866-1908
2 items

Politician. A typescript of a letter (1866) from Colbert to Stand Watie, along with a brief biography (1908) of Colbert.

Colcord, Charles Francis (1859-1934) 222
Papers 1885-1935
15.33 feet

Civic leader and businessman. Correspondence (1901-1935) relating to Colcord's oil and other business activities; general correspondence (1909-1930) to Colcord; and correspondence (1909-1930) from Colcord, his wife, Harriet Scoresby Colcord, his sons, Ray and Sidney Colcord, and his brother, Will C. Colcord; genealogical material (n.d.) concerning the Colcord family; scrapbooks and newspaper clippings (1910-1934) relating to Colcord, including some concerning the 1934 Charles F. Urschel kidnapping case, for which Colcord offered a reward; miscellaneous printed material (1920-1934) collected by Colcord; and a manuscript of his autobiography published in 1970.

Unpublished finding aid available.

Coldiron, Daisy Lemon (1876-1946)   223
Papers 1918-1950
1 foot

Poet. Correspondence (1918-1941) with her publishers, the Oklahoma Tuberculosis Association, and with local political candidates about women's suffrage; a ledger (1924-1937) listing poem titles, publishers, and payments; and scrapbooks (1920-1941) containing published and unpublished poems, essays, and greeting card manuscripts, copies of Coldiron's column "Letters From Aunt Sallie," and articles from literary and political sources on issues such as suffrage, prohibition, censorship, and eugenics. Also included in the collection is a typed manuscript of "Ballads of the Plains" which was published posthumously in 1950.

Cole, Coleman   224
Printed materials 1875-1879
.33 foot

Indian chief. Typescripts of correspondence (1875-1879) relating to Choctaw participation in the proposed Indian Union growing out of the Okmulgee Council; published speeches (1877-1878); Choctaw Tribal Council proceedings (1873-1878); accounts of Choctaw court cases (1877); and other papers (1875-1879) pertaining to the problem of intruders, tribal citizenship, and royalties from Choctaw coal lands, all during the period of Cole's tenure as principal chief, 1874-1878.

Cole, Redmond S. (1881-1959)   225
Papers 1894-1956
38 feet

Judge. Correspondence (1894-1947) regarding the personal affairs of Cole, politics and government at both the state and local levels, and legal cases before the Oklahoma court system; legal briefs (1909-1925) of Oklahoma cases; publications (1908-1956) regarding politics and government at the local, state, and national levels; and speeches (n.d.) delivered by Cole before civic, fraternal, and other groups.

Coleman, Emma Alberta White (1863-1949)   226
Printed materials 1889-1927
2 feet

Photographer. Business and personal correspondence (1890-1910), along with advertisements and mail-order catalogs (1889-1927) for photography, art, needlework, garden supplies, household products, patent medicines, and women's clothing and dress patterns. The bulk of the material dates from 1903 to 1914.

Unpublished finding aid available.

Collins Coal Company Collection 227
Records 1938-1949
2 feet

Coal company. Employee records, including wage reports (1938-1942), payrolls (1940-1947), record of orders and employees pay (1939-1948), and a time book (1942-1947); shipment records (1943-1947); correspondence (1941-1949); financial reports (1940-1947); expenses and sales accounts (1937-1946); and Bituminous Coal Producers Board reports (1939-1942), all from the Collins Coal Company in Krebs, Oklahoma.

Unpublished finding aid available.

Collins Hardware Store Collection 228
Records 1902-1920
1.50 feet

Hardware store. Ledgers (1902-1920) from this retail business in Hydro, Oklahoma, along with catalogs (1902-1920) of jewelry, saddlery, stoves, and other hardware store merchandise.

Collins, Arza Bailey and John D. Arnold 229
Papers 1907-1936
.75 foot

Government employee. Diaries (1912-1933) kept by Collins recording his travel and activities as a U.S. farmer for the Sac and Fox Indian Agency; correspondence (1924-1929) relating to lease disputes; weekly reports (1922-1925) to the Shawnee Indian agent, and other records (1907-1936) relating to the Sac and Fox and Iowa Indians in Oklahoma.

Collums, (Mrs.) Garner G. 230
Printed materials 1947-1950
.33 foot

Collector. Invitations (1947-1950); newspaper clippings (1948-1950); newsletters (1949-1950); and directories (1947-1948) from Norman, Oklahoma, clubs and organizations such as the University of Oklahoma Faculty Club, the University Women's Club, the Y.W.C.A., the Girl Scouts, and the Red Cross.

Colonial Dames Collection 231
Papers 1852-1894
1.33 feet

Collector. Correspondence (1859-1862) regarding the Choctaw Indians and Spencer Academy; correspondence (1864-1871) concerning the Omaha Indian mission in Nebraska; correspondence (1861-1864) dealing with the Civil War, and correspondence (1852-1894) from Charles S. Rogers to Mrs. Orlando S. Lee, mostly regarding student life, family illnesses, and duties as a minister.

Unpublished finding aid available.

Combest, George Marion (1866-1926) 232
Papers 1899-1927
.10 foot

Physician. A diary (1899) detailing Combest's participation in the Spanish-American War; certificates (1896-1906) of honorable discharge from military service, registration as a physician in Indian Territory, and pension eligibility from previous military service, along with articles (1918-1926) concerning Combest's enlistment into the medical reserve force in 1918, his obituary in 1926, and medals earned during his military career. The collection also includes Combest's unpublished biography (n.d.) entitled "Life and Works of George Marion Combest: Oklahoma Pioneer Medical Doctor" by Christine Combest Millsap.

Commerce First State Bank Collection 233
Records 1911-1950
17 feet

Bank. General ledgers (1918-1921); collection registers (1919-1926); discount registers (1915-1936); tellers cash books (1917-1929); journals (1915-1920); voucher registers (1913-1916); distribution of expense ledgers (1917-1938); and overdraft registers (1944-1950) from the First State Bank of Commerce, Oklahoma, along with records (1915-1935) of the city of Commerce; a treasurer's register (1917-1919) from Ottawa County, Oklahoma; and business records (1911-1930) from a lumber company and a drugstore, apparently in Miami, Oklahoma.

Unpublished finding aid available.

Commercial National Bank Collection 234
Ledger 1935-1936
1 item

Bank. An account ledger (1935-1936) from the Commercial National Bank of Muskogee, Oklahoma.

Confederate States of America Indian Affairs Collection 235
Papers 1861-1864
.25 foot

Subject collection. Provisions returns (1861); memoranda (1861-1862); and correspondence (1862), all regarding the provision of rations by the Confederate States of America to the Five Civilized Tribes, and to the Osage, Comanche, and Caddo Indians.

Conkling, Richard A. (1885-1952) 236
Papers 1914-1953
.10 foot

Petroleum geologist. Correspondence (1921-1922) to Conkling from his colleagues concerning personnel changes at Roxana Petroleum Corporation, Ardmore, Oklahoma, including Conkling's resignation as head geologist in 1922 and his subsequent employment; an employment contract (1914) between Conkling and the Bataafsche Petroleum Maatshappij, an allied corporation of Roxana Petroleum based in the Netherlands; and certificates (1929-1946), issued to Conkling by the University of Oklahoma. Also included is a reprint of a biographical article (1952) written by Albert S. Clinkscales shortly after Conkling's death.

Conlan, Madeline Czarina Colbert 237
Papers 1756-1932
.33 foot

Historian. Typewritten manuscripts (1920-1938), including research notes, speeches and reports on the history and culture of Oklahoma's Indian tribes and their leaders, with an emphasis on the Choctaws.

Conn, J. L. 238
Papers 1895
2 items

Collector. Copies of two letters (1895) from Amos Ewing to William McKinley concerning an upcoming Oklahoma territorial convention, the Free Home bill, and delegates to the St. Louis convention at which McKinley would be nominated for the presidency of the United States.

Connelley, William Elsey (1855-ca. 1929) 239
Papers 1854-1925
2.33 feet

Author. Correspondence (ca. 1923) regarding the Benders of Kansas, and the genealogy of families in Big Sandy Valley, Kentucky; notebooks (ca. 1854-1913) concerning the Civil War, William Quantrill, Indians, linguistics, border wars, Kansas history prior to the 20th century, and the genealogy of families of Big Sandy

Valley, Kentucky; clippings (ca. 1855-1900) concerning Indian mythology, legends, and relations with whites, the Civil War within Kansas and adjoining states, as well as other Kansas history; manuscripts (ca. 1902) concerning politics, Indian mythology, folklore, linguistics, and relations with whites, John Brown, William Quantrill, and Kansas history; and pamphlets (1857-1925) concerning politics within and between Indian and white groups, Indian mythology, folklore, linguistics, "Wild Bill" Hickok, and John Brown. The collection also includes diaries (1858-1911) of Connelley, and of George Ela who writes of Kansas farm life, local Indian groups and their linguistics, and his Civil War experiences at Pine Bluff, Arkansas.

Unpublished finding aid available.

Connors State Agricultural College Collection 240
Typescript 1951
1 item

State college. A transcript of the proceedings (1951) of the opening ceremony for the Jacob Johnson Library at Connors State Agricultural College in Warner, Oklahoma.

Constant, Alberta Anne Wilson 241
Papers 1930-1983
9 feet

Author. Correspondence (1930-1983) of Edwin and Alberta Constant with friends, admirers, publishing companies, and agents regarding family affairs of the Constants, the authorship, publication, and distribution of her works, and public appearances by Alberta Constant; publicity items (n.d.) generated by Constant's writings; subject and reference files (n.d.) of Constant regarding topics of interest or on which she wrote; manuscripts (n.d.) of the fiction and non-fiction works by Constant; and publications (1945-1953), including newsletters, magazines, and journals, containing articles or stories by Constant.

Unpublished finding aid available.

Cook, Benjamin R. 242
Records 1872-1948
1 foot

Collector. Three account books (1872-1874) and a fire insurance policy (1889), along with statements and receipts (1879-1880) from the Hester Mercantile Store, Boggy Depot, Indian Territory, owned by George B. Hester. The collection also contains printed election returns (1930-1948) from Atoka County, Oklahoma.

Cook, F. L. (d. 1950) 243
Manuscript n.d.
1 item

Physician. A manuscript (n.d.) by Cook describing the symptoms, progression, and treatment of syphilis.

Cooksey, Harold S.   244
Papers 1954-1970
9 feet

State employee. Oklahoma Wildlife Conservation Commission minutes (1961-1969); monthly reports (1958-1969); financial reports (1963-1969); budgets (1962-1970); federal aid budgets (1966-1970); correspondence (1961-1970); fisheries reports (1962-1968); deer and game reports (1958-1969); legislation (1962-1968); wildlife and conservation publications, and government documents relating to the Little River Reservoir (Lake Thunderbird), all accumulated by Cooksey while he was a member of the above commission.

Unpublished finding aid available.

Cooper, Ann Mayer   245
Manuscript 1949
1 item

Pioneer. A typewritten manuscript (1949) written by Cooper concerning the history of Lincoln County, Oklahoma, and including information on early county officials and the land runs into the Sac & Fox, Iowa, and Kickapoo Indian reserves.

Copeland, Fayette, Jr.   246
Papers 1915-1971
5.50 feet

Professor. Correspondence (1841-1968); research notes (1835-1914); reference materials (1910-1961), including book reviews; publications (1886-1971); and manuscripts (1892-1953) by Fayette and Edith Copeland regarding the University of Oklahoma and its School of Journalism, the history of journalism in general, and the lives of social reformer Kate Barnard and George Wilkins Kendall. The collection also includes copies of Kendall's correspondence, financial records, and personal journals.

Unpublished finding aid available.

Coppadge, Ethel (1882-1965)   247
Printed materials 1883-1965
.33 foot

Collector. A membership roster (1942), convention proceedings (1906-1929), and other materials (1883-1965) relating to Oklahoma's Woman's Relief Corps and, specifically to the Stillwater, Oklahoma, chapter.

Cornell, Kearns Bryon (b. ca. 1890) 248
Printed materials ca. 1950
3 items

Politician. An article (1950) concerning the announcement of Cornell's candidacy for the U.S. congress, and explaining his platform which included advocacy of a return of prohibition; a pamphlet (ca. 1950) in comic book format entitled "Here's What A Republican Congress Did For You;" and a letter (1950) to James Babcock giving a brief personal history of Cornell.

Cornish, Melven (b. ca. 1870) 249
Papers 1876-1940
20 feet

Attorney. Case files (1903-1904) and letterbooks (1900-1905) relating to Choctaw and Chickasaw Indians citizenship claims; dockets (1903-1904) for the central and southern divisions of the U. S. District Court; an account book (1899); and a record book (1876) entitled *Proceedings of the Court of Claims, Choctaw Nation*, along with clippings (1896-1907) and published court documents (1900-1940) relating to Chickasaw and Choctaw Indian cases represented by the law firm of Mansfield, McMurray, and Cornish in U.S. courts.

Court, Nathan Altschiller (1881-1968) 250
Printed materials 1896-1950
.33 feet

Mathematician. A biography (n.d.) of Court, and a bibliography (n.d.) of his writings and publications; school inspection reports and certificates (1896-1905) from Poland; and articles (1923-1950) by Court regarding the fields of mathematics and geometry.

Covey, Arthur (1877-ca. 1960) 251
Printed materials 1877-1960
3 feet

Artist. Publications (1925-1960) describing Covey's art, sketches, and lithographs.

Covington, J. A. 252
Diaries 1863-1900
.10 feet

Government employee. Photocopies of diaries (1863-1900) kept by Covington and describing his work at the Cheyenne-Arapaho Indian Agency and his travels to Alaska during the Klondike gold rush.

Crawford, L. E. 253
Papers 1885-ca. 1949
.10 foot

Author. Manuscripts (n.d.) of articles dealing with cattle branding, and cowboy life and work, and lists of cattle brands used in western Oklahoma, the Texas panhandle, and western Kansas.

Creek Nation Collection 254
Papers 1849-1943
.33 foot

Indian tribe. Court decisions, treasury warrants, and related legal documents (1868-1900); correspondence (1873-1898); and typescripts of newspaper articles (1849-1943); all relating to land, institutions, and the affairs of the Creek Nation, Indian Territory. Correspondents include Samuel Checote, Ward Coachman, Joseph M. Perryman, and Isparecher.

Cress, Sherry Marie 255
Papers 1861-1956
.10 foot

Collector. The diary (1861-1865) of Charles Knott, recording his experiences as a soldier in the Eleventh Indiana Volunteer Infantry during the Civil War and detailing his participation in the battles of Shiloh, Fort Donelson, and Corinth. Also included are letters (1885-1956) about the diary.

Crittendon, William Dial 256
Legal document 1690
1 item

Collector. A vellum document (1690), in French, regarding the sale of an orchard near Orleans, France.

Cross, George Lynn (1905-) 257
Manuscript 1926
1 item

University president. A copy of Cross's M.A. thesis (1926) entitled "The Ontogeny of the Vascular Elements in Zea Mays."

Crouch, Aziel Henry (b. ca. 1866) 258
Papers 1904-1916
3 items

Physician. Certificates (1904-1916) authorizing Crouch to practice medicine in

Oklahoma, and appointing him a medical examiner for the Aetna Life Insurance Company and a camp physician for the Modern Woodmen of America.

Cruce, Cruce, and Bleakmore Collection 259
Papers 1899-1935
25 feet

Law firm. Legal documents and correspondence from the law firms Cruce, Cruce, and Cruce (1899-1901); Cruce, Cruce, and Bleakmore (1901-1912); and Potter and Cruce (1912-1928) reflecting the firm's practice representing Chickasaw Indian citizenship and allotment claims, banking interests, and oil and gas companies. Also in the collection are correspondence and speeches from Lee Cruce's gubernatorial campaign of 1907 and his senatorial campaign of 1930.

Crumbo, Woody (b. 1912) 260
Art prints n.d.
2 feet

Artist. Prints (n.d.) of works by Potawatomi Indian artist, Woody Crumbo.

Cuddeback, Frank J. (b. ca. 1904) 261
Manuscript 1926-1940
1 item

Mining engineer. A typescript (n.d.) describing the lead and zinc mining operations, 1926-1940, in the tri-state district of Oklahoma, Kansas, and Missouri.

Curry, Arthur R. 262
Notebook 1921-1923
1 item

Librarian. A notebook (1921-1923) labeled "To My Successor," in which Curry lists his activities, functions, and duties as the reference librarian for the University of Oklahoma library.

Cushing Refining and Gasoline Company Collection 263
Records 1927-1945
2 feet

Refining and gasoline company. Correspondence (1927-1945) to and from other petroleum companies regarding orders and shipments of petroleum products, and from federal agencies concerning the rationing and price regulation of gasoline during World War II; pamphlets (1941-1943) from federal agencies concerning gasoline rationing and price controls during World War II; and additional business records (ca. 1935-1945) concerning Cushing's production. Also included in this collection is a blueprint (n.d.) of an underground oil tank.

Custer County Medical Society Collection 264
Ledger 1904-1909
1 item

Professional organization. A ledger (1904-1909) containing the minutes, roll of membership, and financial accounts of the Custer County (Oklahoma) Medical Society.

Custer County State Bank Collection 265
Records 1900-1938
27 feet

Bank. Balance ledgers (1900-1920); collection registers (1911); daily statement books (1900-1938); deposit ledgers (1906-1920); discount registers (1901-1933); distribution ledgers (1911-1912); general ledgers (1926-1935); transfer ledgers (1906-1936); tellers cash books (1900-1932); and related records, all detailing the daily financial transactions of the Custer County State Bank of Arapaho, Oklahoma, and Oklahoma Territory.

Unpublished finding aid available.

Cutler, Violona 266
Printed materials 1929-1953
.10 foot

Collector. Publications (1929-1953) and manuscripts (1950) regarding social work among the aged, young, and physically handicapped in Oklahoma.

Cutlip, C. Guy (1881-1938) 267
Papers 1867-1967
5 feet

Judge. Records (1930-1931) of the Oklahoma Bar Association's board of governors; speeches (1927-1936) by Cutlip; manuscripts (n.d.) regarding the history of Seminole County, Oklahoma, Wewoka, Oklahoma, and the Seminole Indian Nation; Seminole Indian land allotment certificates (1901-1902); Cutlip's travel diaries and personal diaries (1920-1936); records (1905-1910) of the Wewoka Masonic Lodge; and a financial ledger (1867-1872) of the Wewoka Trading Company.

Unpublished finding aid available.

Dahlberg, Sophie Little Bear 268
Papers 1861-1979
.25 foot

Collector. Photocopies of birth and death certificates and related genealogical materials of members of the Little Bear family including Bacon Rind, Haynes Little Bear, Dora Pah Se To Pah, Jack Portillo, Sophie Little Bear Dahlberg, Edward L. Chouteau, and Rosalie Capitaine Chouteau. Also in the collection are tombstone inscriptions from the Kiowa Indian cemetery near Duncan, Oklahoma, and the Dyeo Mission cemetery near Lawton, Oklahoma, along with a checklist of Osage Indian songs in the Library of Congress and published information about Osage Indian traditions.

Dale, Edward Everett (1879-1972) 269
Papers 1865-1948
80 feet

Historian. Correspondence (1902-1972), student papers (n.d.), theses and dissertations (1932-1933), and personal research materials (1832-1967) regarding the history of Oklahoma, Oklahoma Territory, and Indian Territory, the Indians of North America, and the American southwest; teaching materials used by Dale at Harvard (1913-1920) and the University of Oklahoma (1921-1952); administrative and other files (1936-1941) of the Works Progress Administration's Indian-Pioneer History Project for Oklahoma; U.S. government documents (1897-1957); and presidential papers of University of Oklahoma presidents James Shannon Buchanan (1911-1929) and Stratton D. Brooks (1915-1922).

Unpublished finding aid available.

Danforth, Thatcher O. 270
Letter 1863
1 item

Soldier. A letter from Union soldier Thatcher Danforth to his mother written from somewhere near Vicksburg, Mississippi. He comments on the excitement caused by a naval battle on the Mississippi River and adds that he expects to be moved south of Vicksburg soon.

Dangerfield, Royden James (1902-1969) 271
Papers 1914-1948
3 feet

Professor. Reprints (1914-1940) and manuscripts (ca. 1930-1948) of both published and unpublished works by Dangerfield, including a history of Oklahoma political campaign platforms from 1890 to 1914; *The Hidden Weapon: The Story of Economic Warfare*, and other works dealing with international relations, Oklahoma state and local government, and national and foreign affairs; and research notes (ca. 1930-1948) concerning the Oklahoma land run of 1889, Oklahoma politics, international law, and international relations, including research material relating to the allied blockade of Germany during World War II.

Unpublished finding aid available.

Daniel, Harley A. 272
Papers 1936-1956
2 feet

Collector. Correspondence (1936-1954) regarding the Lions Club organization in Oklahoma; a poster (1953) advertising Daniel's campaign for governor of his district Lions Club; publications (1952-1954) of the Lions Club; and club reports (1954) from towns and cities throughout Oklahoma, listing membership and activities.

Daniels, Opherita Eugenia 273
Papers 1920-1979
.10 foot

Teacher. An autobiographical manuscript (ca. 1979) by Daniels, the first Afro-American to enter the University of Oklahoma's School of Social Work, along with news articles (1920-1979) regarding her attendance at the University of Oklahoma.

Danner, Clyde 274
Papers 1894-1945
.10 foot

Collector. Teaching contracts (1894-1926) for P. M. Danner's employment in Arkansas, and Beckham and Caddo counties, Oklahoma. Also included are a land patent (1906), a warranty deed (1915) to land in Caddo County, and newspaper clippings (1940s) from World War II.

Darnell, E. E. 275
Records 1911-1953
.50 foot

Physician. Journals and ledgers (1911-1953) from Darnell's medical practice in Colony, Oklahoma, along with a copy of a report (1923) of the Oklahoma Commissioners of Charities and Corrections.

Daugherty, Charles L. 276
Papers 1907-1913
.66 feet

State official. Correspondence, circulars, pamphlets, and labor regulations (1907-1913) to and from Charles L. Daugherty while serving as Oklahoma's first commissioner of labor, and concerning issues such as labor legislation, organized labor, open and closed shops, child labor, the Democratic Party, local elections, and political appointments.

Daughters of the American Revolution Collection 277
Records 1914-1957
.50 foot

Women's club. Minutes (1914-1944) and publications (1919-1957) of the Daughters of the American Revolution, Black Beaver chapter, Norman, Oklahoma.

Davis, Robert Murray 278
Papers n.d.
.50 foot

English professor. Critiques (n.d.) of literary works, especially those by Evelyn Waugh; and research materials (n.d.) regarding Waugh's works, as well as those by Donald Barthelme, Charles Molesworth, and Matthew Bruccoli.

Davison, Oscar William (b. 1905) 279
Printed materials 1940-1949
.66 foot

Collector. Publications (1940-1949), including reports, circulars, press releases, newsletters, and clippings relating to legislative programs sponsored by the Oklahoma Education Association.

Dawson, Herron Victor (b. ca. 1905) 280
Papers ca. 1950-1981
.33 foot

Composer. Manuscript songs (n.d.) written and published by Dawson.

Dawson, Winnie M. 281
Papers 1911-1967
4.33 feet

Teacher. Manuscripts (1952-1967) regarding the history of Wanette, Oklahoma, and its schools, along with Protestant religious song books (1911-1913).

Unpublished finding aid available.

Day, John Lewis 282
Printed materials 1910-1941
.10 foot

Physician. A daybook (1910-1911); a pamphlet (1913) on preparation for childbirth; reprints of two articles (1932, 1941) by Day; and a copy of *Harlow's Weekly* (1935) which contains a story about Day.

Dean, Samuel C.   283
Papers 1896-1906
.10 foot

Physician. A ledger (1902-1906); a memorial to Charles D. Frick (1902); and an indexed ledger of class notes taken by Dean while a student at Barnes Medical College, St. Louis, Missouri, 1896-1900.

DeBarr, Edwin S. (1859-1950)   284
Papers 1870-1950
1.33 feet

University professor and chemist. Correspondence and reports (1897-1950) regarding essays, autopsies, chemical analyses, and consultations conducted by DeBarr; services rendered by DeBarr as expert witness in legal cases; the DeBarr family and personal affairs; members of the University of Oklahoma faculty and Board of Regents; and the construction and laboratory fittings of the University of Oklahoma's chemistry building, including a report (1870-1872) on the survey of the Indian Meridian boundary through Indian Territory.

Unpublished finding aid available.

Debo, Angie Elbertha (1890-1988)   285
Papers 1953-1976
.66 feet

Historian. A galley proof and original typescript for the book *Geronimo* (University of Oklahoma Press, 1976); correspondence (1967-1972) written by Debo on behalf of Alaskan Indians to regain their tribal lands; and newspaper clippings (1953-1954) of Debo's column in the *Daily Oklahoman*.

Decker, Charles Elijah (1868-1958)   286
Papers 1861-1957
5.33 feet

Professor. General correspondence (1911-1957); papers (1923-1950) regarding the University of Oklahoma chapter of the geology fraternity, Sigma Gamma Epsilon; correspondence (1925-1942), membership lists, and expense records (1934-1935) from the Oklahoma Academy of Science; manuscripts, reprints, and research correspondence (1932-1934) from Decker's research on the geology of Oklahoma and on grapholites; correspondence (1925-1946) and notebooks (n.d.) concerning the Methodist Episcopal Church in Norman, Oklahoma; correspondence and printed material (1931-1952) concerning the University of Oklahoma; and correspondence and printed material (1913-1955) from geological associations and other universities.

Unpublished finding aid available.

DeKnight, Emma H. 287
Diary 1886-1892
1 item

Teacher. A diary (1886-1892) kept by DeKnight and relating her experience as a teacher at the Chilocco Indian School and the Oto school at the Red Rock Indian Agency. The diary emphasizes the time DeKnight spent among the Otos and includes a list (1887) of her Oto students.

Delaware Indian Agency Collection 288
Records 1867-1874
2 items

Indian tribal agency. A manuscript allotment list (1867) prepared by the federal government when the Delaware Indians moved from their reservation in Kansas to settle along the Caney River, Indian Territory, along with a printed Delaware allotment list published in 1874.

Delta Tau Delta Collection 289
Ledger 1922-1958
1 item

Collegiate social fraternity. A ledger (1922-1958) containing rosters of initiates of the University of Oklahoma Delta Alpha chapter of Delta Tau Delta fraternity.

Dennis, Frank Landt, Sr. (b. 1907) 290
Papers 1928-1988
.75 foot

Journalist and attorney. Correspondence (1933-1988); certificates (1933-1941); ribbons and patches (1929-1947); cartoons (n.d.); publications (1928-1988); newspaper clippings (1928-1939); and a scrapbook (1928-1935) chronicling the life of Frank Dennis as a student at the University of Oklahoma and as an editor. Also included in the collection are teletype printouts (1962) from an unidentified wire service detailing news of the United States' first manned orbital space flight by John Glenn in the space capsule *Friendship*.

Denver, James William (1817-1892) 291
Papers 1849-1891
.50 foot

Lawyer and U.S. Army general. Correspondence (1855-1888) from the Denver family, from politicians concerning national politics and political appointments, and from Denver's legal practice, including cases involving damage claims for cotton illegally seized by the U.S. government during the Civil War; a manuscript account (n.d.) of Denver's activities as a Union brigadier general, 1861-1863; a pamphlet (1884) endorsing Denver as a Democratic nominee for the presidency; typescripts of a journal (1850) kept by Denver during an overland journey from Fort Leavenworth, Kansas Territory, to California; pamphlets (1865-1891) of speeches by Denver and others; bills for legislation in which Denver had an interest; and a genealogical chart (n.d.) of the Francis Xavier Rombach family.

DeRosier, Arthur H.   292
Papers 1780-1903
.10 foot

Collector. Photocopies of correspondence (1780-1842) between William and Diana Dunbar regarding the American Revolution, New Orleans, Louisiana, and the Napoleonic wars in Europe, along with correspondence (1901-1903) between the U.S. Department of the Interior and its surveyor, Charles L. Wood, regarding townsite locations and surveys in Indian Territory.

DeStwolinski, Louis C.   293
Papers 1844-1958
.10 foot

Amateur radio operator. Postcards (1933-1958) from amateur radio operators in numerous states and foreign countries confirming radio contacts with DeStowlinski, along with a certificate (1844) of land purchase issued to Nathan Bass by the United States for land in Mineral Point, Wisconsin.

Detrick, C. H.   294
Papers 1880-1897
6 items

Interpreter. A Comanche-English dictionary (ca. 1895), with a Comanche alphabet and diacritical markings, compiled by Detrick while serving as an interpreter for the Red Store Trading Post at Fort Sill, Indian Territory. Also included in the collection are typescripts (n.d.) on the Comanche language, customs and conventions, the Lord's Prayer in Comanche, a translated Comanche reminiscence with language notes and explanations, and a typewritten memoir (ca. 1890) by Detrick about his work at the Red Store Trading Post.

DeVilliers, Myrtle   295
Papers 1891-1904
.10 foot

Collector. Quapaw tribal records (1891-1904) relating to governmental affairs, tribal schools, labor contracts, and farm leases, along with legal documents (1900) pertaining to the settlement of the estate of George Bingham, an early settler among the Quapaw Indians.

Dewlen, Al 296
Papers 1961
.66 foot

Author. A manuscript (1961) of Dewlen's award-winning book, *Twilight of Honor*, with accompanying research notes.

Diamond Jubilee Commission Collection 297
Records 1982
1 foot

Official state commission. Records (1982) of the commission, including correspondence, proclamations, resolutions, and reports, along with calendars of commission-sponsored activities celebrating Oklahoma's seventy-fifth anniversary of statehood.

Dill, C. A. 298
Typescript 1868-1869
1 item

Collector. A typescript of the journal (1868-1869) of Lt. P. V. Hardman, an officer on Gen. George Armstrong Custer's staff, Seventh U.S. Cavalry, detailing the Battle of the Washita from the Osage scouts' reconnaissance to the departure of the Cheyenne prisoners for Fort Supply, Indian Territory.

Dinkler, Frank A. 299
Ledger 1893-1902
1 item

Pharmacist. An accounts receivable ledger (1893-1902) from the Jewel Drug Store in Hennessey, Oklahoma Territory. The book includes lists of the pharmaceuticals used and the prices paid for them.

Disney, Richard Lester (b. 1887) 300
Papers 1940-1951
3 feet

Judge. Majority and dissenting opinions (1940-1951) by Disney of cases heard while serving on the U.S. Board of Tax Appeals from 1936 to 1951.

Ditzler, Walter Linginfelter (1892-ca. 1978) 301
Printed materials 1952-1967
2 items

Attorney. Poems (1952-1967) by Ditzler about his children and grandchildren, including some family data.

Division of Manuscripts Collection 302
Papers 1682-1969
4 feet

Subject collection. Letters, reports, publications, and manuscripts reflecting the history of Oklahoma and of its American Indian tribes and nations, including correspondence (1813-1839) from U.S. government officials concerning policy toward the Indians, especially in regard to the Indian removal, and correspondence (1862) from Confederate Army officer Albert Pike in regard to Confederate States of America policy toward the Indians. Also included in this collection is a group of French colonial documents (1682-1794), along with diaries and journals (1770-1877) of travelers on the American frontier. The collection contains material on a variety of topics and researchers are urged to consult the inventory to determine the full scope of the collection's contents.

Unpublished finding aid available.

Division of Manuscripts Map Collection 303
Printed materials 1630-1986
3,918 items

Map collection. Maps and atlases (1630-1986), both domestic and foreign, of North America, Oklahoma, Oklahoma and Indian territories, and the world. Included are maps of colonial French North America, of the locations of Indian tribes and reservations in the United States throughout its history, and of the early territorial west and southwest. Specific collections of Oklahoma interest include the Sanborn Fire Insurance Company maps for the cities and towns of Oklahoma, and the Fred L. Wenner Collection of maps relating to the Cherokee Strip and the Territory of Oklahoma.

Unpublished finding aid available.

Dixon, A. 304
Records 1908-1944
1.25 feet

Physician. Patient account records from Dixon's medical practice in the Kingfisher County towns of Lacey, Oklahoma (1908-1909), Kiel, now Loyal, Oklahoma (1915-1917), and Hennessey, Oklahoma (1920-1944), along with Dixon's records of births attended throughout the county and of drugs he prescribed (1917-1918).

Donnelley, Herndon Ford (b. 1900) 305
Printed materials 1982
3 items

Collector. Correspondence and brochures (1982) regarding the establishment of the Individual Opportunity Achievement Ranch at Perkins, Oklahoma, along with a research paper (n.d.) about the Donnelley family, by Diana Inskip, entitled "The Study of a Pioneering Seamstress."

Doody, Maurice   306
Printed materials 1953-1954
3 items

Cobbler. A booklet (1954) by Doody entitled *Modern Shoe and Foot Helps* about tanning, the working of leather, and the making and repairing of shoes, along with two manuscripts (1953-1954) by Doody on the trend of education in the United States.

Doran, Lowry A. (1886-1966)   307
Typescripts 1892-1942
.50 foot

Collector. A typescript of the diary (1892-1893) kept by Abraham J. Seay, governor of Oklahoma Territory; typescripts of newspaper articles (1943) concerning foreign affairs and U.S. foreign policy; and two typescript copies of "How War Came" by Forrest Davis and Ernest K. Lindley, published in the *Ladies Home Journal* (1942) and concerning America's entrance into World War II.

Dorrance, Lemuel (1876-1921)   308
Papers 1896-1921
5 items

Pharmacist. A diploma (1896) from the University of Oklahoma School of Pharmacy, one of the first two diplomas granted by the university; two certificates (1896-1897) from the Oklahoma Board of Pharmacy and the Oklahoma Pharmaceutical Association; a log of correspondence (1920-1921) kept by Dorrance in Nicaragua; and a copy of *Southern Pharmaceutical Journal* (1955) with an 1896 photograph of Dorrance.

Dowd, Jerome H. (b. 1864)   309
Papers 1891-1943
1.66 feet

Sociologist. Personal correspondence (1930-1954) and manuscripts of books and articles written by Dowd while a sociology professor at the University of Oklahoma from 1907-1947. The manuscripts include two copies of Dowd's "The Negro in American Life" (1926); three unpublished manuscripts entitled "Seeing the World by Tramping and Ford Car," (1939), "The New World as Viewed by the Prophets and Interpreted by Jerome Dowd," (1943), and "Social Aspects of Art" (n.d.); and two article-length manuscripts dealing with Oklahoma prison reform and juvenile delinquency.

Drake, Noah Fields (1864-1945) 310
Papers 1894-1948
.10 foot

Geologist. Geological reports (1916-1935) from oil and gas companies in Oklahoma; reprints of articles (1897-1945); and two field notebooks and a class notebook (1894-1895) belonging to Fields, a professor of geology and mining at the University of Arkansas.

DuBois Family Collection 311
Manuscript ca. 1849
1 item

Family collection. A brief history (ca. 1849) of the DuBois family recounting the arrival of Louis DuBois in America in 1661, the purchase of land from Indians, the captivity of Catherine DuBois by Indians, and family participation in the American Revolution.

Duffy, Homer 312
Records 1943-1968
2 feet

Collector. Correspondence, tax records, audits, and financial statements (1943-1968) of the Oklahoma Farmers Union, and of its subsidiary organizations, the Oklahoma Farmers Union Supply Association (1950-1957), and the Union Mutual Insurance Company (1947-1968); financial statements (1954-1955) of the Oklahoma Farmers Union Service Corporation and the Oklahoma Farmers Union Cooperative (1956-1960); financial reports (1961-1964) of the Mid-Continent Farmers Cooperative; and correspondence and financial reports (1949-1955) of the National Farmers Union.

Unpublished finding aid available.

Dugan, Eva Ellsworth 313
Papers 1898-1952
.33 foot

Music instructor. Personal correspondence (1917-1924); a poem (ca. 1924) regarding the South Canadian River; performance programs (1928) of the Oklahoma City Symphony Orchestra and of the University of Oklahoma Children's Sooner Orchestra (1917-1918); and news clippings (1941-1945) regarding World War II.

Duke Indian Oral History Collection 314
Papers 1890-1968
20 feet

Oral history collection. Typescripts of interviews (1967-1972) conducted with hundreds of Indians in Oklahoma, regarding the histories and cultures of their respective nations and tribes. Related are accounts of Indian ceremonies, customs, social conditions, philosophies, and standards of living. Members of every tribe resident in Oklahoma were interviewed. The collection includes the original tapes on which the interviews were recorded as well as microfiche copies of the typescripts.

Published finding aid available.

Duke, James Monroe   315
Records 1902-1926
5 items

Collector. Land deeds (1903-1908) issued by the Choctaw and Chickasaw nations; Choctaw Indian land allotment certificates (1903-1904); stock ownership certificates (1918-1923) issued by Oklahoma associations and companies; and a letter (1926) by Oklahoma congressman William W. Hastings in reply to charges made by his political opponent.

Dukes, Gilbert W. (b. 1849)   316
Printed materials 1877-1905
.25 foot

Indian chief. Typescripts of correspondence (1900-1901) written during Dukes's tenure as principal chief of the Choctaw Nation and relating to leases, stock raising, and Choctaw Indian schools, together with speeches (1900-1902); biographical information (1901); and political writings (1900-1905) reflecting the problems involved in the transition from tribal government to territorial, and, ultimately, state jurisdiction.

Duncum, Floy   317
Papers 1941
3 items

Collector. Memoirs (n.d.) of James Louis Avant, relating his experiences as bailiff of the U.S. District Court for Western Arkansas at Fort Smith, Arkansas, and as disciplinarian of the Kiowa Indian schools at Anadarko, Oklahoma Territory, along with anecdotes of a hunting trip in the Kiamichi Mountains (Oklahoma), plus two obituaries (1941) of Avant.

Durant, William A. (1866-1952)   318
Printed materials 1926, 1937
2 items

Indian chief. Two typescripts of newspaper articles (1926, 1937) about Durant including an account of the operation of the Oklahoma land department.

Duvall, Preston Van Buren 319
Manuscript 1938
1 item

Pioneer. A typed manuscript (1938) concerning the life of Preston Duvall and his experiences in the 1893 land run into the Cherokee Strip.

Dwight Mission Collection 320
Papers 1957
1 item

Subject collection. A biographical letter (1957) by Charles C. Torrey in which the history of Dwight Mission is noted.

Eagle-Picher Mining and Smelting Company 321
Records 1939-1974
4 feet

Mining company. Correspondence (1967-1974) related to geophysical consultants; equipment records and inventories (1939-1970) for the central mill; general ledgers (1940-1945, 1949-1951); a check ledger (1939-1945); and survey and drill records, all relating to the company's Oklahoma operations.

Unpublished finding aid available.

Edwards, Archibald Cason (b. ca. 1910) 322
Papers 1875-1987
104 feet

Investment broker. Correspondence (ca. 1875-1950) of the Robert James Edwards and J. S. Handy families; business correspondence (ca. 1890-1945) from Edwards's investment-securities firm, R. J. Edwards, Inc., including University of Oklahoma dormitory and Memorial Union building bonds (1946-1948); and concert and theatre programs (1928-1987) from musical and theatre productions throughout the United States and, particularly, in Oklahoma City, and at the University of Oklahoma.

Edwards, Thomas Allison (1874-1955) 323
Manuscript 1949
1 item

Attorney. A twenty-page manuscript entitled "Early Days in the C & A" which was published in the *Chronicles of Oklahoma* (Summer, 1949) and in which Edwards recounts his experiences as a teacher and lawyer after coming to Washita County, Oklahoma Territory, in 1898.

El Reno Citizens National Bank Collection 324
Records 1891-1930
15 feet

Bank. Financial records (1891-1930) including ledgers, journals, remittance registers, draft registers, loans and discount registers, collections registers, and daily balance books reflecting the daily commerce of the bank and that of its predecessor, the El Reno Bank, of El Reno, Oklahoma.

Elder, Frederick Stanton (b. 1868) 325
Papers 1889-1904
.10 foot

University professor. Correspondence (1900-1902) and speeches (1902-1904) relating to Elder's involvement in the controversy over selling Oklahoma school lands.

Elk City Community Hospital Collection 326
Printed materials 1931-1953
5 items

Co-op health facility. Brochures (1931-1953) describing services provided by the Elk City, Oklahoma, hospital and the costs of each service.

Elk City Farmers National Bank Collection 327
Records 1920-1930
10 feet

Bank. Financial records (1920-1930) including correspondence, ledgers, journals, certificates of deposit registers, discount registers, and tellers cash books in which the daily business of the bank was recorded. The collection includes records of an institutional predecessor, the German State Bank, also in Elk City, Oklahoma.

Elk City First National Bank Collection 328
Printed materials 1901-1951
2 items

Bank. Booklets printed by the bank to mark its fiftieth anniversary (1951) and tracing the history of the bank and of Elk City, Oklahoma.

Elkins, Harrison H. 329
Papers 1952
2 items

Merchant. Poems (1952) by Elkins including one entitled "Sooners and Settlers."

Elliott, J. Ross 330
Papers 1975
4 items

Genealogist. A letter (1975) from Elliott commenting on the Boyd family, along with a manuscript (n.d.) and newspaper clippings (1975) tracing the genealogy of the David Ross Boyd family, including its coat of arms.

Ellison, (Mrs.) C. D. 331
Papers 1834-1956
4 items

Collector. A pamphlet (n.d.) entitled "Darlington, the Indian's Friend," which chronicles the life of the Cheyenne-Arapaho Indian agent and Quaker missionary, Brinton Darlington; a speech (1945) by Edgar S. Vaught giving a brief history of Oklahoma; and a diary (1891-1893) kept by Caro Emerson while a student at Bethany College, Topeka, Kansas.

English, Frank Miller (1861-1931) 332
Papers 1901-1974
4 feet

Businessman and civic leader. Correspondence (1901-1914) relating to English's banking career and civic activities in Lawton, Oklahoma, along with personal financial records (1901-1924), including receipts and cancelled checks.

Unpublished finding aid available.

English, William M. 333
Papers 1935-1950
1 foot

Businessman. Correspondence and reports (1935-1939) relating to English's land sales and rentals in the Shattuck, Oklahoma, area, along with personal correspondence (1935-1950) with his family, friends, and civic organizations.

Unpublished finding aid available.

Epton, Hicks Byers (1906-1972) 334
Records 1860-1880
.10 foot

Collector. Discharge certificates (1860-1880) issued to Seminole freedmen, including David Bowlegs, by the U. S. Army, for service rendered during and after the Civil War.

Erdmann, E. M. 335
Papers 1884-1891
2 items

Collector. An autograph book (n.d.) written in German and a class grade record book (1884-1891) by a German student.

Erwin, A. M. 336
Records ca. 1921-1942
.50 foot

Physician. Ledgers (1921-1928) and birth records (1925-1942) from Erwin's medical practice in Nowata County, Oklahoma.

Eta Kappa Nu Collection 337
Records 1942-1957
.25 foot

Professional society. Records of the University of Oklahoma Beta X chapter of Eta Kappa Nu, a national electrical engineering honorary fraternity, including the chapter's petition (1943) for admittance to the national body, and its correspondence (1943-1957).

Evans, Arthur W. (b. 1908) 338
Papers 1816-1968
.66 foot

Collector. Correspondence (1906-1968); certificates (1891-1918); and news clippings (1928-1939) regarding University of Oklahoma president Arthur Grant Evans, federal funding for schools in Indian Territory, the issue of separate statehood for Oklahoma and Indian territories, and Evans's participation in the United States' propaganda effort in World War I; a typescript regarding the history (1816-1831) of the Presbyterian church and missions in the eastern Cherokee Nation; a diary (1887) of A. G. Evans; and original records (1830-1857) of the New Echota Church in the Cherokee Nation as recorded by Samuel A. Worcester, church clerk.

Evans, Charles 339
Correspondence 1862-1893
.10 foot

Collector. Correspondence (1862-1863) between Lt. Lyle Garrett of the Twenty-third Iowa Infantry, and his wife, Mary Garrett. His letters describe camp life, attitudes toward officers, and troop movements in Missouri, Arkansas, Texas, Louisiana, Mississippi, and Alabama. Garrett also describes the general conduct of the war, soldiers' views about action in other theaters of the war, attitudes concerning the South, slavery, and the destruction caused by the war. The collection also contains three letters (1866-1893) regarding the Garrett family in general.

Evans, Oren F. 340
Papers. 1940-1950
.33 foot

Geology professor. Manuscripts (1940-1950) of geological articles and fiction stories written by Evans.

Ewing, Cortez Arthur Milton (1896-1962) 341
Papers 1910-1951
20.33 feet

University professor. Manuscripts (1933-1961) of Ewing's papers on political theory and of his book *Essentials of American Government*; research materials (ca. 1930-1960), including information on impeachment and primary elections; lecture notes (ca. 1920-1930) and other teaching materials (ca. 1930-1960); correspondence (ca. 1930-1960); and speeches (ca. 1920-1950), all relating to American government.

Unpublished finding aid available.

Ezell, John Samuel (1917-) 342
Papers 1955-1984
.33 foot

Historian. A transcript of an oral history interview (1984) conducted by Herbert R. Hengst with John S. Ezell, recounting Ezell's tenure as dean of the University of Oklahoma College of Arts and Sciences; research and seminar papers (1955-1980) written by Ezell's students and colleagues, including three by Jack Ericson Eblen concerning the growth of the Afro-American slave population in nineteenth-century America and Cuba, and one by Gary L. Cunningham concerning gambling in frontier Kansas.

Fairland, Oklahoma, Municipal Records Collection 343
Records 1909-1945
4 feet

Municipality. Correspondence (1933-1936) relating to the finances of the city of Fairland, Oklahoma; copies of city ordinances (1935); a financial record book (1912-1926); two ledgers (1921-1924); a receipt book (1933); books of treasurer's warrants (1930-1936); and a daybook (ca. 1920) containing records of water bonds, electric bonds, and sinking funds.

Unpublished finding aid available.

Farley, Alan W. 344
Papers 1833-1966
2.50 feet

Collector. A typewritten manuscript (n.d.) in which Homer W. Wheeler describes his life as a U.S. Army scout; numerous broadsides, newspapers, and handbills (1840-1966) regarding the settlement of Kansas, along with a wide variety of other documents (1833-1965) collected by Farley and relating to the Civil War, settlement of Kansas, Indian battles on the Great Plains with an emphasis on Kansas, and on the history of the west in general.

Unpublished finding aid available.

Farmers State Bank Collection 345
Ledger 1913-1918
1 item

Bank. A general ledger (1913-1918) from the Farmers State Bank of Park Hill, Oklahoma.

Farmers Union Cooperative Gin Company Collection 346
Records 1927-1948
.10 foot

Agricultural cooperative organization. By-laws (1927) of the company, minutes (1927-1936) of the meetings of its members and directors, and a company financial statement (1948).

Feaver, John Clayton (1911-) 347
Papers 1968-1975
1.66 feet

Philosophy professor. Resource files (1974-1975) compiled by Feaver while chairing the Commission on Curriculum for the University of Oklahoma College of Arts and Sciences, including correspondence and memoranda from outside consultants; information on curriculum programs at other universities; correspondence, memoranda and reports from subcommittees; curriculum proposals; committee minutes; and copies of the final report. Also files (1968-1970) compiled by Feaver while chairing the University Constitution Drafting Committee, including correspondence; memoranda; drafts; faculty comments on drafts; bibliographies, notes, and clippings.

Ferguson, Milton James (1879-1954) 348
Grade book 1906
1 item

Librarian. A grade book for a course in bibliography taught by Ferguson at the University of Oklahoma in 1906.

Ferguson, Thompson Benton (1857-1921) 349
Papers 1901-1911
2.66 feet

Governor. Letterbooks of correspondence sent (1902-1911) and letters received (1901-1911) by Ferguson during his term as governor of Oklahoma Territory, along with a scrapbook containing newspaper clippings about Ferguson.

Unpublished finding aid available.

Ferguson, Walter Scott (1886-1936) 350
Papers 1863-1960
17.33 feet

Banker. Business and personal correspondence (1883-1951), the majority concerning Walter Ferguson's tenure as vice-president of the Exchange National Bank in Tulsa, Oklahoma; a book-length manuscript (n.d.) on the Choctaw Indians; brand books (1906-1918) of Walter Ferguson; correspondence (1902-1906) to Thompson B. Ferguson, governor of Oklahoma Territory; typescripts of annual reports (1904-1905) of Thompson B. Ferguson as governor of Oklahoma Territory to the secretary of the interior; and correspondence (1928-1942) to Lucia Loomis Ferguson concerning her syndicated newspaper column "One Woman's Opinion," along with manuscripts (ca. 1930-1962) and clippings (ca. 1928-1942) of her column.

Unpublished finding aid available.

Feuquay, Courtland Matson (1890-1949) 351
Papers 1885-1948
7 feet

Attorney and state senator. General correspondence (1915-1940) of Feuquay; his personal correspondence (1923-1925) as a state senator; Works Progress Administration work relief lists (1934-1935); case records (1917-1948) of railroad litigation in which Feuquay served as counsel; Selective Service directives (1941-1946); American Legion-related papers (1919-1924), including "40 et 8" materials; a diary (1885) of Feuquay's grandfather, W. B. Holland; and an account book (1905-1908) of Feuquay's father, J. W. Feuquay.

Unpublished finding aid available.

Field, J. Walker 352
Speech 1904
1 item

Assistant attorney general. A speech entitled "The Essentials of a Great Republic" written by Field in 1904 while a member of The Forum, a University of Oklahoma student literary and debating society.

Fillman, Irvin 353
Papers 1951
7 items

Treasure hunter. Correspondence (1951) from Fillman to Oklahoma governor Johnston Murray, describing excavations around Comanche, Oklahoma; from Murray to Fillman, forwarding Fillman's letter to Morris L. Wardell, a professor at the University of Oklahoma; and from Wardell to Fillman, and Wardell to Murray, acknowledging receipt of Fillman's original letter.

Findlay, James Franklin 354
Papers 1934-1938
.10 foot

Collector. Records (1934-1938) chronicling the origin, organization, and function of the Independent Men's Association of the University of Oklahoma, including typescripts (n.d.) regarding the history of the organization and a mailing list (n.d.) of persons to whom its publications were mailed, along with publications (1934-1938), including the local chapter newsletter *The Roundup*, and a program from the first national conference of the Independent Student's Association, held at the University of Oklahoma.

Fink, John Berlin (1886-1960) 355
Papers 1834-1957
6 feet

Collector. Correspondence (1933-1955); books (1833-1959) about railroads; printed material (1935-1960) also about railroads and including travel brochures and timetables; maps (1834-1883, ca. 1955), relating to early military posts in Oklahoma Territory and surrounding states; and notebooks (1934) kept by Fink.

Unpublished finding aid available.

Finney, Thomas McKean and Frank Florer Finney 356
Papers 1827-1977
8 feet

Indian traders. Papers of Thomas M. Finney, Indian trader at Gray Horse, Osage Agency, Oklahoma Territory, and of Frank F. Finney, historian and employee of the Indian Territory Illuminating Oil Company, including correspondence (1925-1936) relating to T. M. Finney's book *Pioneer Days of the Osage Indians, West of '96*; historical materials (1827-1977) such as correspondence, news clippings, magazine articles, and bibliographic notes of Frank Finney on topics such as the Cherokee Strip, the Osage Indian Agency, Gray Horse Trading Post, the Dalton Gang, Kaw Indian Agency, Buffalo Bill, Pawnee Bill, peyotism, President Herbert Hoover's early days in Pawhuska, Oklahoma, and Maria Tallchief; field notebooks (1915-1949) kept by Frank Finney while an employee of the Indian Territory Illuminating Oil Company; finished and unfinished articles and stories (1891-1969) by Frank Finney, Thomas Finney, and J. E. Finney including research notes, newspaper clippings, and magazine articles; and oil and gas files (1896-1972) of Frank Finney with articles and documents primarily relating to the Indian Territory Illuminating Oil Company and oil and gas leases on Osage Indian lands.

Unpublished finding aid available.

First, Francis Ray, Sr. (b. 1887) 357
Ledger 1911-1915
1 item

Physician. A ledger (1911-1915) of patient accounts in which patient ailments and the remedies prescribed were recorded. The last page tallies the number of abortions, births, deaths, and the causes of death.

Fisher, Daniel G.   358
Papers 1912-1937
.66 foot

Journalist. Correspondence (1912-1937) between Fisher and numerous authors regarding their contribution to literature and thoughts concerning their prominent works. The correspondents include Sherwood Anderson, Winston Churchill, Clarence Darrow, Hamlin Garland, Will James, Helen Keller, Ring Lardner, Charles A. Lindbergh, David Lloyd George, Robert Latham Owen, Burton Rascoe, Agnes Repplier, Sigfried Sassoon, Upton Sinclair, William Allen White, and Owen Wister.

Fisher, Te Ata   359
Papers 1913-1983
6.50 feet

Performer. Correspondence (1934-1983) to and from Fisher, along with printed materials (1935-1976) she used as resource material for her performances as a storyteller and interpreter of Indian folklore and culture. The collection also includes a scrapbook (1936) of a Scandinavian tour, along with some correspondence (1922-1953) and printed material (1913-1936), mostly reprints, relating to Clyde Fisher, a naturalist and Te Ata Fisher's husband.

Fisk, Charles W. (ca. 1860-1939)   360
Papers 1902-1939
.10 foot

Physician. Official transactions (1906) of the joint session of the Oklahoma state and Indian Territory medical associations; official publications (1906-1935) of the Oklahoma State Medical Association; correspondence (1926-1939) regarding Fisk's appointment as consulting surgeon to the Chicago, Rock Island, and Pacific Railroad, and certificates of election (1902-1908) to the position of city councilman in Kingfisher, Oklahoma Territory, and Oklahoma.

Fite, Gilbert C.   361
Papers 1912-1967
6 feet

Historian. Reports, correspondence, and publications (1926-1952) regarding the Mount Rushmore national monument, including correspondence (1925-1940) from its creator, Gutzon Borglum; photocopies of Borglum's diary (1925); papers (1912-1948) regarding former governor of South Dakota, Peter Norbeck; a manuscript by Fite regarding consumer cooperatives; official files (1966-1967) of the search committee appointed to recommend a candidate to become the eighth president of the University of Oklahoma; personal files regarding agricultural farm relief programs and a typescript of George Peek's diary (1932-1933).

Unpublished finding aid available.

Fitzpatrick, H. L.   362
Papers 1955-1961
4 feet

Publisher. Resource files (1955-1961), including correspondence, newspaper clippings, tear sheets, drafts, and illustrations, all used by Fitzpatrick for publishing the *Oklahoma Almanac*.

Fletcher, Margaret Catherine   363
Diary 1879-1914
1 item

Housewife. A bound photocopy of Margaret Catherine Fletcher's diary (1879-1914) which includes information regarding the history, politics, economics, and everyday life of the Flint District, Cherokee Nation; descriptions of early Tahlequah, Indian Territory, and Fort Smith, Arkansas; and detailed genealogical information concerning the Adair, Bixby, Fletcher, Guthrie, and Sanders families, including lineage charts and personal name indexes.

Flitch, Sylvester (1847-1900)   364
Printed materials 1881-1883
2 items

Cattleman. Guides (1881-1883) to cattle brands in the Cherokee Strip, Indian Territory, Kansas, and Texas, published by cattlemen's associations of those areas.

Flora, Snowden Dwight (1879-1957)   365
Papers 1920-1957
3 feet

Meteorologist. Printed materials on adverse weather conditions, especially hail and tornadoes, arranged by state; statistics and charts (ca. 1920-1950); weather maps (1930-1955); newspaper clippings (1935-1955) and correspondence (1928-1957) concerning hail and tornadoes; clippings (1913-1955) by and about Flora; biographical materials, including Flora's awards and papers charting his career with the U.S. Weather Bureau; and a notebook (1899) Flora kept as a geography student.

Unpublished finding aid available.

Folsom, Lee W.   366
Papers 1867-1910
.66 foot

Journalist. Folsom family correspondence (1902-1908); a notebook (1897-1899) indicating the subjects studied by Folsom while a student at Atoka Baptist Seminary and Folsom's personal account books (1905-1910). The collection also includes annual reports (1895-1900) of the U. S. Board of Indian Commissioners; a copy of the acts and resolutions (1897) of the general council of the Choctaw Nation; a hymnal (n.d.) written in Choctaw; two copies of the *Laws of the Choctaw Nation*

(1866-1891) written in English and Choctaw; a Choctaw *New Testament* (1906); a Choctaw *Pentateuch* (1867) and a letter (1885) in Choctaw from Alfred Folsom to Rainie Winthrop.

Folsom Training School Collection 367
Records 1920-1986
1.5 feet

School. Business and legal records (1922-1975) of the Folsom Training School, a Methodist mission school for Indians located in Smithville, Oklahoma; Folsom Reunion Association correspondence and mailing lists (1968, 1985-1986); history of Sealey Chapel Methodist Church with announcements (1966, 1970, 1981-1986) of Folsom reunions; and an article concerning the school.

Unpublished finding aid available.

Foreman, Stephen (1807-1881) 368
Papers 1837-1881
.10 foot

Missionary. Typescripts of Foreman's journals (1862-1868) describing life in the Cherokee Nation during the Civil War, along with letters (1864-1881) written by Foreman regarding the same, and letters (1837-1881) to members of the Foreman family.

Forsyth, George Alexander (1837-1915) 369
Papers 1868-1915
10 items

Army officer. Photostatic copies of Forsyth's formal report (1869) of the Battle of Beecher Island; lists (1868) of casualties; general field orders (1868); and correspondence (1872-1915) concerning veterans of this 1868 battle with the Northern Cheyenne Indians.

Fort Gibson First National Bank Collection 370
Records 1904-1930
18 feet

Bank. Financial records from the Fort Gibson (Oklahoma) First National Bank, including a cash book (1908); cashiers check registers (1919-1938); a circulation register (1917-1935); a collection register (1911-1916); commission books (1922-1930); a daily balance ledger (1904-1906); daily statement ledgers (1907-1941); daybooks (1913-1924); discount registers (1904-1920); general ledgers (1904-1932); journals (1904-1939); letters of credit books (1908-1924); liability ledgers (1922-1937); a minute book (1906-1922); notary records (1911-1916); order books (1906-1921); a payment ledger (1916-1917); reconcilement registers (1909-1937); record of checks cashed ledgers (1924-1926); bonds registers (1918-1919); tellers cash books (1906-1937); and a time certificates of deposit ledger (1911-1929). The collection also includes a town treasurer's monthly report ledger (1923-1926) and the Muskogee County treasurer's record ledger (1908-1909).

Unpublished finding aid available.

Fort Gibson Quartermaster Collection 371
Letterbooks 1879-1890
5 feet

Military post. Correspondence documenting Fort Gibson's significance in carrying out the U. S. government's Indian policy regarding the Indian pacification program following the Civil War. Included in the collection are letters sent (1879-1890), five volumes and one index volume; and registers of letters received (1879-1880 and 1886-1890), two volumes.

Fort Smith, Subiaco, and Eastern Railway Company Collection 372
Records 1908-1916
.25 foot

Railroad company. A ledger (1908-1916) in which the finances of the Fort Smith, Subiaco, and Eastern Railway Company were recorded. The records show profits, losses, and business relations with other area railroads, including the Arkansas Central Railroad.

Foster, Del Oneita 373
Sheet music 1956
1 item

Amateur song writer. A collection of nineteen musical compositions written, arranged, and privately published (1956) by Foster. Several have Oklahoma themes.

Fowler, David (b. 1877) 374
Printed materials 1889-1956
6 items

Labor leader. Printed reports (1951-1956) regarding a welfare and retirement fund for miners; handbills (n.d.) relating to miners organizations; two printed copies of a speech (1952) by the United Mine Workers of America president; and two issues (1957) of the *United Mine Workers Journal*.

Fowler, Richard Gildart (1916-1992) 375
Papers 1924-1980
12 feet

Professor. Correspondence (1924-1980); lecture notes and tests for classes in physics taught by Fowler at the University of Oklahoma; manuscripts (1958-1969) for textbooks authored by Fowler; correspondence with Fowler's publishers; research notes (1943-1979) arranged by research project; and project histories and documentation (1952-1972) for contracted research projects conducted by Fowler, a University of Oklahoma physics professor.

Unpublished finding aid available.

Franklin, William Monroe (b. 1874) 376
Papers 1874-1956
.66 foot

Attorney and state senator. Printed materials (1926-1947) concerning the Oklahoma Farmers Union and Franklin's political campaigns; copies of laws (1905-1945) drafted by Franklin; his speeches (1915-1916); newspaper clippings (1943-1947) containing his editorials; and biographical material (1874-1958).

Frayser, E. B. 377
Ledger 1870-1872
1 item

Physician. A ledger (1870-1872) in which Frayser recorded lecture notes taken while a medical student in St. Louis, Missouri.

Frederickson, Mary Brownlee 378
Papers 1920-1930
.33 foot

Writer. Typescripts and manuscripts (1920-1930) of poetry, and stories regarding the Oklahoma oil fields and oil industry, all by Mary B. Frederickson.

Freedom State Bank Collection 379
Ledger 1920-1933
1 item

Bank. A ledger (1920-1933) containing financial transactions of the Freedom State Bank in Freedom, Oklahoma.

Freeman, Margaret 380
Papers 1895-1872
.10 foot

Homemaker. Correspondence (1859-1872) between Margaret Freeman in Springfield, Illinois, and her children in Texas. The Freeman family owned land near Lancaster, and Starlight, Texas, and was engaged in homesteading and cattle ranching. Many of the letters describe farm and ranch life, cattle drives, and exchanges of family news. These letters also contain information about local politics and racial attitudes.

Freudenthal, Elsbeth Estelle (1902-1953) 381
Papers 1900-1953
8 feet

Economist and author. Correspondence (ca. 1940-1950); research notes (ca. 1900-1950); manuscripts (ca. 1900-1950); printed material (1930-1953); and a bibliography (ca. 1930), all relating to the history of aviation and Latin American aviation, with an emphasis on Alberto Santos-Dumont and Pan American Airways.

Unpublished finding aid available.

Fritts, Mary 382
Printed materials 1969-1972
1 foot

Collector. Copies of radical political magazines and pamphlets (1969-1972), covering such subjects as civil rights, ecology, and the Vietnam War.

Fuller, Agnes 383
Papers 1894-1923
.10 foot

Teacher. Certificates and teaching contracts (1894-1923); a teaching assignment (1907) from the U.S. Indian Service at McAlester, Indian Territory; and the Choctaw spelling book *Chata Holisso* (n.d.), printed by the Richmond Presbyterian Committee of Publication containing the alphabet, symbols, tables, vocabularies, the Ten Commandments and the Lord's Prayer, names of animals, money tables, and moral essays, all in the Choctaw language.

Fulton, J. S. (d. 1950) 384
Papers 1904-1950
14 feet

Physician. Correspondence (1930-1950); medical records (1914-1950); and certificates and citations (1922-1948) relating to Fulton's medical practice in Atoka, Oklahoma, along with minutes (1904-1911) of the Atoka County Medical Society.

Unpublished finding aid available.

Funk, Rose 385
Papers 1886-1945
1 foot

Collector. Personal correspondence (1894-1908); diplomas (1894-1905); and certificates (1910-1925) of the Funk family; books (1886-1899), including a *Majestic Cookbook* (1899) and a telegraphic code book; plus an autograph book (ca. 1900); a scrapbook (n.d.); and composition books (n.d.) belonging to Rose Funk; together with calendars (1898); printed invitations (1892-1902); greeting and postcards (ca. 1900); travel brochures (ca. 1920-1945); a cigar band collection (ca. 1914); and legal papers (1894-1906) from the files of attorney John Funk.

Gaillardia Garden Club Collection 386
Records 1927-1954
3 items

Women's club. Notebooks (1927-1954) containing programs, membership lists and minutes, along with a history of this Norman, Oklahoma, club that sponsored local beautification projects.

Gaither, Edna 387
Printed materials 1860-1956
.33 foot

Collector. Clippings (1860-1956) on Missouri-Kansas-Arkansas-Oklahoma border history concerning subjects such as Indians, border industries, monuments, and landmarks, the Civil War on the border, and on famous persons such as George W. Carver and Belle Starr.

Galen Society Collection 388
Records 1932-1952
.10 foot

Professional organization. Correspondence (1933-1948); the club constitution (1948); membership lists (1932-1948); minutes (1938-1939); account ledgers (1932-1950); and memorabilia of this pharmacy-related organization at the University of Oklahoma.

Gallaher, William M. (1877-1955) 389
Papers 1925-1954
1.66 feet

Physician. Correspondence (1925-1950); manuscripts (n.d.) on medical topics; and account ledgers and daybooks (1925-1950) from Gallaher's general practice in Shawnee, Oklahoma, along with publications (1950-1954) concerning Oklahoma medical laws and the health and pension plans of the Chicago, Rock Island, and Pacific Railroad.

Gamble, Richard Dalzell (b. 1925) 390
Printed materials 1853-1866
.33 foot

History professor. Photocopies of correspondence (1853-1854) from the letterbook of the commanding officer of Fort Union, New Mexico; typescript of the diary (1853-1854) of Caleb Burwell Rowan Kennerly, entitled "Diary of a Journey to California, 1853-1854;" photocopies of articles on the founding of D'Hanis, Texas, and on exploring expeditions through the American southwest; and notecards (n.d.) made by Gamble while conducting historical research on the southwest.

Gardner, Florence Guild Bruce (1900-1955)   391
Papers 1940-1953
1 foot

Author. Book manuscripts by Gardner, including "Woman: Her Power and Glory" and "Lillie of Six-Shooter Junction;" correspondence (1940-1953) regarding Gardner and the release of her books; a poster (1940) advertising the release of "Lillie ...;" newspaper clippings (1940-1953) regarding the release of Gardner's books, and of her death; music scores (1942-1944) regarding the end of World War II, Gen. Douglas MacArthur, and the absence of Christianity in Great Britain; and publications (1940-1948), including Gardner's book *He is Risen: A History of the Wichita Mountains Easter Pageant*, and a copy of *The Official Peace Officer* concerning the death of Anthony Mark Wallock, a minister who was a strong advocate of the pageant. Also included in this collection are two scrapbooks concerning the subjects described above.

Gardner, Jefferson (ca. 1846-1906)   392
Printed materials 1894-1906
.10 foot

Indian chief. Typescripts of newspaper articles (1894-1906), including speeches and letters, by and about Gardner, a principal chief of the Choctaws, and also relating to such issues as slavery, financial affairs, tribal factionalism, and the allotment of land by the Dawes Commission.

Gardner, Oscar   393
Printed materials 1950-1955
5 items

Teacher. Booklets and brochures (1950-1955) describing the Goodland Indian Orphanage and School in Goodland, Oklahoma.

Garretson, Henry David   394
Records 1904-1923
.25 foot

Collector. Abstracts of title (1911-1919) for land in Pittsburg County, Oklahoma; an abstract of title (1904) for the townsite of Quinton, Indian Territory; and government bonds (1915-1923) from the Republic of Germany and the Kingdom of Hungary.

Garrity, Richard M.   395
Printed materials 1986
4.33 feet

Collector. Newsletters of the Model Railroad Interest Group (1960-1985) for which Garrity served as editor, plus his notes and typescripts for the same. Also included are correspondence (1950-1988); published and unpublished articles by Garrity, and others, regarding railroad development around Ripley, Oklahoma, and Eureka

Springs, Arkansas; Oklahoma natural history; Oklahoma local history; and solar energy. The collection also contains numerous sound recordings on cassette tapes.

Garvin, Isaac L. 396
Printed materials 1877-1879
7 items

Indian chief. Typescripts of legislation (1877-1879) enacted by the Choctaw Nation council concerning the courts, schools, timber lands, and coal mining.

Gary, Raymond Dancel (1908-1993) 397
Papers 1955-1958
41.66 feet

Oklahoma governor. Papers (1955-1958) of Oklahoma governor Raymond D. Gary, including commissions and appointments; correspondence concerning bills before the state legislature; radio speeches and press files; correspondence concerning the teachers retirement referendum; alphabetical files of Gary's executive assistant, Clarence Burch; minutes of meetings and correspondence from the commissioners of the land office; files of the budget office, including payroll information; reports and correspondence concerning other individual state boards and committees; appointments and general correspondence of the governor's office; welfare files, including claims and correspondence organized by county; correspondence concerning pardons, paroles and extraditions; and correspondence filed by organization, by personal name, and from out-of-state.

Unpublished finding aid available.

Gassaway, Percy Lee (b. 1885) 398
Certificates 1920-1934
7 items

Judge. Certificates (1920-1934) proclaiming Gassaway's admission to the Masonic Order, his election as a district judge, and his nomination by the Democratic Party of Oklahoma for congress.

Gatchell, Theodore Dodge 399
Papers 1881-1957
.50 foot

Collector. Manuscripts (1900-1901); typescripts (1880-1933); publications (1881-1957); and cartoons (1884-1942), all regarding the principal cotton expositions held throughout the southern United States from 1881 to 1937, including those at Charleston, Atlanta, Nashville, Jamestown, and New Orleans.

Gee, Robert L. (1878-1954) 400
Records 1926-1954
.33 foot

Physician. An account ledger (1929-1933); surgical supply catalogs (1926-1929); and an eyeglass catalog (1931) kept by Gee, an ear, nose, and throat specialist in Hugo, Oklahoma.

Geissler, Arthur H.   401
Scrapbooks 1895-1928
1.50 feet

Diplomat. Scrapbooks containing news clippings, magazine articles, government documents, pamphlets, photographs, handbills, and memorabilia accumulated by Geissler while serving as U.S. ambassador to Guatemala and reflecting events throughout Central America for the period 1922-1928.

Gibson, Arrell Morgan (1921-1987)   402
Papers 1817-1871
.66 foot

Historian. A collection of research materials (1817-1871) gathered for use in writing projects. Most of the material deals with Fort Smith, Arkansas, and the Civil War in Indian Territory.

Gibson, Iva Thomas   403
Papers 1947-1960
.10 foot

Poet. Correspondence (1947-1958) to Gibson commenting on her progress as a lay teacher in the Methodist Church and on her inspirational poetry. Also included in this collection are published materials (1949-1951) from writers organizations to which she belonged, along with magazines containing poems she wrote and announcing the publication of her poetry.

Giessmann, Gary   404
Papers and records 1862-1957
1 foot

Collector. Letters (1862-1863) from Union soldier Robert Stansberry to his family; business records (1904-1929) from the Southwest Merchandise Company; Sanders family correspondence and records (1870-1957); and a diary (1886) by an unknown author recounting a trip from Carrolton, Arkansas, to Indian Territory.

Unpublished finding aid available.

Gildart, W. B.   405
Letter 1899
1 item

Collector. A photocopy of a letter (1899) to W. B. Gildart of Stockbridge, Michigan, from J. B. Gildart of Austin, Texas, in which the latter comments on the

Gildart family extensively, and, especially, on the activities of the Gildarts who served in the Confederate Army.

Gilkey, Jessie Lone Clarkson 406
Papers ca. 1936
2 items

Composer. A music manuscript of "The OU Chant" composed by Gilkey in 1936, along with a letter (n.d.) commenting on the composition.

Gilkey, John E. 407
Records 1903-1907
1 foot

Grocer. Ledgers (1903-1907) containing the names of customers and what they bought and paid for goods from John Gilkey's Norman, Oklahoma, grocery and feed store.

Gillespie, F. E. 408
Manuscript 1951
1 item

Postmaster. A brief history (1951) of Kiowa County, Oklahoma, written by Gillespie.

Gillespie, John D. 409
Manuscript 1963
1 item

Collector. A typescript (1963) of several documents written in Cherokee with a translation by Gillespie, one of which deals with the death of Sequoyah.

Gilliland, J. W. 410
Letter 1893
1 item

Collector. A photostatic copy of a letter (1893) by Newt Locke to his brother, Tom, describing in detail his participation in the land run of 1893 into the Cherokee Strip, with accounts of the settlement of Hennessey, Oklahoma Territory, and Enid, Oklahoma Territory, of the people who settled there, and with a description of their modes of transportation. The letter concludes with Locke's decision to return to the United States due to his disenchantment with Oklahoma Territory.

Gist, Chris 411
Papers 1836-1841
7 items

Collector. Military papers (1836-1841) of Brig. Gen. Greenup White concerning his commissions from the state of Missouri.

Gittinger, Roy (1878-1957) 412
Papers 1864-1957
1.10 feet

Professor. Correspondence (1913-1955) regarding early faculty and student affairs at the University of Oklahoma, including enrollment, credit, and grading; hand-drawn maps (n.d.) of the American west; note cards (n.d.) containing information regarding the history of the University of Oklahoma; and publications (1914-1947) from schools, organizations, and associations in Oklahoma.

Unpublished finding aid available.

Gladney, Essa 413
Diaries 1925
2 items

Librarian. Two diaries kept by Gladney for January, and February, 1925. They briefly chronicle Gladney's daily activities for these two months.

Glasstone, Samuel 414
Papers 1968
2 feet

Professor. Book manuscripts (1968), including a rough draft, final manuscript, and galley proof for Glasstone's *The Book of Mars*, published by the National Aeronautics and Space Administration in 1968.

Glickman, Mendel 415
Papers 1932-1967
.10 foot

Architect. Correspondence (1932-1967) between Glickman and Frank Lloyd Wright concerning their collaboration on construction projects, along with a few unidentified blueprints.

Goddard, Eunice May Stewart (1923-   ) 416
Papers 1942-1978
.10 foot

Collector. Photocopies of U.S. government reports (1945-1959); publications (1945-1978); and notecards (n.d.) by Goddard, all in regard to the U. S. Naval Air Technical Training Center and the U. S. Naval Air Station in Norman, Oklahoma.

Golobie, John 417
Manuscript ca. 1865
1 item

Immigrant. A typescript of the autobiography (ca. 1865) of John Golobie, a nineteenth-century immigrant to America from Yugoslavia, describing, in detail, life in his native country, his coming to America, and his impressions of the culture and people he found there.

Gomes, Pat 418
Papers 1864-1875
.10 foot

Collector. Photocopies of documents (1864-1875) relating to the Worcester Willey family and Dwight Mission, Indian Territory.

Good, Nancye 419
Papers 1920-1922
.10 foot

Collector. Correspondence (1922) regarding the Oklahoma gubernatorial election campaign of 1922, and its coverage by the *Tulsa Tribune*; speaking itineraries (1922) of candidate John C. Walton; programs (1920-1922) of fine arts events at the University of Oklahoma; and one political campaign broadside, "John Writes Tate a Letter - and Tate Answers It," comparing the qualities of candidates John Fields and Jack Walton.

Goodland Indian School Collection 420
Printed materials 1940-1956
5 items

Indian school and orphanage. Newspaper clippings (1956); brochures (1950); pamphlets (1955); and a published history (1940) of the Goodland Indian School, a Presbyterian orphanage founded for Choctaw Indians, but later expanded to serve orphans from other tribes as well.

Goodrich, Harold Beach 421
Papers 1904-1943
.25 foot

Petroleum geologist. Correspondence (1931-1943) of Goodrich regarding his geological interests and research; blueprints and charts (ca. 1930) showing geological data, as well as one entitled "Graphic History of Oklahoma Oil Production, 1930," all compiled by Goodrich; news clippings (ca. 1940) regarding geological developments; data in manuscript form regarding the availability of oil in California; and a bibliography of sources regarding oil in California, compiled by Goodrich.

Gordon, Charles Ulysses 422
Printed material 1950
2 items

Postmaster. Mimeographed copies, signed by the author, of Gordon's poem (1950), *The American Flag*.

Gould, Charles Newton (1868-1949)   423
Papers 1897-1948
11 feet

Geologist. Correspondence (1914-1941) regarding personal matters, Oklahoma place names, and the geology of Oklahoma; manuscripts (1907-1946), both book-length and shorter, and both published and unpublished, regarding the history, place names, and geology of Oklahoma; book reviews (n.d.) of Gould's works; poetry (n.d.) by Gould; speeches (n.d.) delivered by Gould; and newspaper clippings (1900-1946) regarding Gould's life and his writings.

Unpublished finding aid available.

Governor's Interstate Indian Council   424
Minutes 1950
1 item

State organization. Minutes of the third meeting of the council, held on December 7-8, 1950 in Oklahoma City, Oklahoma.

Graham, Gideon Wesley (1867-1950)   425
Printed materials 1928-1949
.10 foot

Wildlife conservationist. Printed cards and one-page leaflets (1928-1949) expressing Graham's views concerning the conservation and protection of wildlife in Oklahoma. Also in this collection is one card advertising Graham's campaign (ca. 1930) to save the Cherokee Indian language.

Grass, Frank and Patty Grass   426
Papers 1876-1957
.33 foot

Collectors. Correspondence (1876-1900) between members of the Helpenstein family, who settled in Oklahoma Territory, in 1889; a scrapbook of newspaper articles (n.d.) concerning the history of Palo Pinto County, Texas; and a ledger (1907) belonging to L. E. Patterson.

Grayson Family Papers   427
Papers 1834-1919
1 foot

Family collection. Correspondence (1834-1919) regarding Creek Indian history, including tribal politics, tribal factionalism, the Green Peach War, sale of Creek lands in Alabama, removal, allotment of land, and related administrative matters. Correspondents include George W. Grayson, Washington Grayson, Pleasant Porter, Return J. Meigs, Samuel Checote, James A. Garfield, and Dennis W. Bushyhead.

Unpublished finding aid available.

Grayson, Ambrose T. 428
Papers 1905
2 items

Physician. A menu (1905) for a luncheon at the Hotel Threadgill, Oklahoma City, Oklahoma Territory, at which the Oklahoma County Medical Society was host to the Tri-State Medical Association; and a personal letter (1905) from Grayson to his family in Alabama.

Griffith, Alfred 429
Records 1842-1931
.66 foot

U.S. Navy physician. Correspondence (1860-1913) to and from Griffith regarding his participation in the Civil War, his later membership in a U.S. Navy expedition to Darien, Panama, and also regarding the New Hope Seminary in the Choctaw Nation; diaries (1864-1870) regarding Griffith's naval travels abroad, his stay in Lisbon, Portugal, and his emigration to Indian Territory; naval medical reports and requisitions (1870-1871); a petition (1894) of the residents of Sans Bois, Choctaw Nation, requesting that Griffith become their physician; certificates (1900-1917) advising him of his election as superintendent of schools for the southern district of Indian Territory, and of his membership in medical associations; a passport (1871) issued to Griffith for travel in France; manuscripts (1864-1865) by Griffith detailing his participation in Gen. William T. Sherman's march to the sea through Georgia and North Carolina during the Civil War; and publications (1888-1931), including Grand Army of the Republic encampment programs, a booklet entitled *Songs of the Darien Expedition*, and college graduation and event invitations.

Griffitts, James Addison (1859-1931) 430
Papers 1906-1940
.25 foot

Minister. Publications (1907-1940), including *The Christian Workers Magazine*, booklets produced by the American Friends (Quakers) regarding an African mission and national service efforts, and one textbook used at the Friends Hillside Mission in Indian Territory and Oklahoma; and minutes (1906-1907) of the ministry and oversight meetings held at the Friends mission at Vera, Indian Territory. The minutes of only two meetings are recorded. The collection also includes a biographical sketch of Griffitts.

Grimes, Mary E. (1891-1950) 431
Papers 1910-1950
8 feet

Teacher. Personal correspondence (1916-1950) and diaries (1919, 1941), along with photographs, scrapbooks, and sheet music reflecting her life and career as a teacher of music at the Walters, Oklahoma, high school, and her community service activities.

Grisso, D. Horton 432
Papers 1851-1865
.33 foot

Collector. Diaries (1851-1865) of John F. Lafferty who enlisted in Company "E" of the Ohio militia and served during the Civil War. Included are hand-drawn maps of Union battlefield maneuvers and artillery batteries, as well as listings of daily rations given each soldier. The diaries are written almost exclusively in Pitman-style shorthand and have not been translated.

Grisso, Walker D. (1905-1965) 433
Papers 1953-1965
10 feet

Oil producer and lawyer. Correspondence (1953-1965) between Grisso, Arthur McAnally, and Col. John Virden on subjects such as the American southwest, the Albert Jennings Fountain murder case, the Maxwell land grant, the University of Oklahoma Board of Regents, western saloons, and the oil industry in Oklahoma.

Unpublished finding aid available.

Guthrie District Medical Association Collection 434
Minutes 1900-1940
1 item

Professional association. Minutes (1900-1940) of the Guthrie (Oklahoma) District Medical Association meetings, including a petition signed by association members requesting that school children be immunized.

Guy, William M. (1845-ca. 1907) 435
Printed materials 1887-1907
.10 foot

Indian chief. Typescripts of newspaper articles (1887-1907), including editorials and messages of Guy as governor of the Chickasaw Nation, on the issues of Chickasaw tribal legislation and the disputed gubernatorial election of 1888.

Guymon First National Bank Collection 436
Records 1906-1928
8 feet

Bank. General ledgers (1906-1918); journals (1907-1910); a discount register (1906-1910); daily balances (1908-1918); draft registers (1906-1907); expense ledgers (1906-1907) and tellers cash books (1906-1928) from the First National Bank of Guymon, Oklahoma.

Haas, Mary R. 437
Printed materials 1941-1954
.10 foot

Anthropologist. Reprints (1941-1954), mostly relating to the Muskogean language, along with a dictionary (1953), compiled by Haas, of the Tunica Indian language.

Hackett, Helen 438
Artifacts 1888-1920
.33 foot

Collector. Ribbons, medals, and buttons (1888-1920) from various political campaigns and conventions, political parties, and fraternal organizations, plus a notary public seal.

Haddix, J. F. 439
Records 1921-1947
.66 foot

Collector. Minutes of stockholders meetings (1921-1928); stock certificates (1921-1947); and a stock certificate register (1923-1933), all from the Farmers Cotton Gin Company of Maysville, Oklahoma.

Hadsell, Sardis Roy (1876-1942) 440
Papers 1900-1942
.50 foot

English professor. Correspondence (1916-1942); freshmen English placement exams and results (1936-1940); and English department circulars and course outlines (1929-1940) from the University of Oklahoma; a report of an audit (1905) of the university's finances; manuscript accounts by Hadsell of the early history of the University of Oklahoma, including "[Vernon L.] Parrington in Oklahoma," (n.d.), "A History of the University of Oklahoma," (1929), and "Twenty-Eight Years After," (1928) which relates Hadsell's experiences with the 1900 expedition of the Oklahoma Geological Survey, plus a typescript of Hadsell's diary from that expedition.

Hague, Lyle L. (b.1895) 441
Papers 1930-1938
3.33 feet

Farmer. Personal and business correspondence (1930-1938); minutes (1930-1938); financial reports (1930-1933); journals (1930-1938); and printed material (1930-1938), relating to the Farmers National Grain Corporation, the Oklahoma Grain Growers Association, the Farm Credit Administration, the U.S. Department of Agriculture, and other farming organizations.

Unpublished finding aid available.

Hainer, Bayard Taylor (1866-1933) 442
Papers 1887-1933
.50 foot

Judge. Correspondence (1906-1927); commissions and appointments (1898-1906) to the Oklahoma Territory supreme court; certifications as an attorney (1897-1909); and clippings (1900-1933) concerning Hainer's career as an Oklahoma Territory supreme court justice and Federal Trade Commission attorney.

Haines, Sarah Deborah (ca. 1891-ca. 1958) 443
Artifacts 1913
4 items

Collector. Four University of Oklahoma Class of 1913 pins belonging to Sarah Deborah Haines.

Hair, Fannie M. Townsend 444
Papers 1901-1911
10 items

Collector. Newspaper clippings (1901); certificates (1901-1911) from the U. S. Land Office, Lawton, Oklahoma; and a manuscript (n.d.) written by Fannie M. Townsend Hair concerning the naming and route of the Chisholm Trail in Oklahoma, with comments by Edwin C. McReynolds.

Hall, David 445
Papers 1970-1974
1.33 feet

Governor. Papers (1970-1974), including appointments, radio speeches, correspondence, and press files of Oklahoma governor David Hall concerning state prisons, federal disaster relief, agriculture, and politics.

Hall, Horace Mark (1854-1945) 446
Manuscript ca. 1958
1 item

Physician. A transcript of letters (1871-1873) written by Horace Mark Hall while he was working as a ranch hand in Texas. The letters are edited, with an introduction and detailed footnotes, by Joseph S. Hall.

Hallinen, Joseph E. 447
Papers 1903-1973
.10 foot

Naturalist. Correspondence (1903-1973) concerning Hallinen's employment; a transcript of an interview (1973) with John A. Hallinen Jr., regarding Joseph E. Hallinen's life; legal documents (1903) regarding Andrew Hallinen's estate; and a catalog (1933) of Joseph E. Hallinen's library.

Halsell, Harold Hallet (b. 1892) 448
Papers 1930-1943
4 items

Merchant. Two typewritten manuscripts (1930 and 1943) by Harold H. Halsell, concerning the life of his father, Oscar D. Halsell, and early Oklahoma City, Oklahoma, along with two letters (1932) concerning the Williamson, Halsell, Frasier Grocer Company.

Hamilton, (Mrs.) C. P. 449
Ledgers 1917-1925
2 items

Merchant. Two account books (1917, 1924-1925) from the Hamilton Hardware Store in Hollis, Oklahoma.

Hamilton, Charles W. 450
Papers 1909-1962
2.66 feet

Petroleum geologist. Correspondence with the Mexican Gulf Oil Company (1912-1922); Hamilton's family correspondence (1909-1926), including some (1914) concerning the Mexican Revolution; general business correspondence (1911-1923), including some with E. L. DeGolyer; Hamilton's geology class notes (1914-1915); Hamilton's diary (1912-1914); printed material and reports (1913-1959) concerning oil production in Oklahoma, the Middle East, and Central and South America; and a draft of a book-length work by Hamilton entitled "Americans in the Middle East."

Unpublished finding aid available.

Hamon, Earl (b. 1911) 451
Papers 1914
1 item

Collector. An architect's specifications (1914) for the construction of Newkirk High School, Newkirk, Oklahoma.

Hancock, William Box (1860-ca. 1934) 452
Memoirs 1812-1925
1 item

Cowboy. A typewritten autobiography (ca. 1925) of Hancock's life as a cowboy, primarily at the Woodard and Oge ranch near San Antonio, Texas. It also describes five of his trips up the Western Trail driving cattle, and the towns of San Antonio, Rockport, Fort Griffin, and Alpine, Texas, Camp Supply, and Fort Reno, Indian Territory, and Dodge City, Kansas, along with accounts of his work on ranches in Dakota Territory.

Harbison, Robert B. 453
Papers 1938-1942
1.66 feet

Lawyer. Correspondence (1938-1942) pertaining to Harbison's term as a senator representing district five, encompassing Jackson and Tillman counties, in the Oklahoma state legislature.

Unpublished finding aid available.

Hardin, Joe 454
Manuscript 1952
1 item

Photographer. A poem (1952) written by Hardin commemorating the Sons of the United Confederate Veterans.

Hargett, Jay L. 455
Papers 1792-1935
.66 foot

Collector. Typescripts of correspondence (1816-1870), mostly regarding missionary work among the Choctaw and Cherokee Indians; diaries (1914) recounting travel in the eastern United States and in the Galena, Kansas, area; a students notebook (n.d.) containing class notes, poetry, and miscellaneous notes; an account book (1860s-1890s) recording purchases and daily expenses; and personal correspondence (1894-1902) between Edwin Ludlow writing from Mexico as superintendent of the Mexican Coal and Coke Company and his wife who was residing in Hartshorne, Indian Territory. Correspondents writing about missionary activities include Cyrus Byington, Israel Folsom, David Folsom, Nathaniel Folsom, Peter Pitchlynn, Stand Watie, and Cyrus Kingsbury.

Hargrett, Lester (1902-1962) 456
Papers 1951
.50 foot

Writer and bibliographer. The manuscript, galley sheets, and page prints (1951) of *Oklahoma Imprints*; photocopies of manuscripts (1836, 1881) relating to the extension of the western boundary of Arkansas and the granting of rights-of-way to the Chicago, Texas, and Mexican Central Railway Company and to the St. Louis and San Francisco Railway Company.

Harjo, Lochar (d. 1879) 457
Printed materials 1875-1879
5 items

Indian chief. Typescripts of newspaper articles (1875-1879) of Harjo's inaugural speech as principal chief of the Creeks, on governmental affairs during his administration, and, subsequently, on his impeachment.

Harlow, James Gindling (b. 1912) 458
Printed material 1969-1976
1 foot

Educator. Promotional pamphlets (1968-1971) produced by the National Aeronautics and Space Administration concerning the Apollo Space missions; pamphlets (1966) and photocopies of articles (1969-1975) concerning economics and management, along with calendars (1970-1976), desk diaries (1973-1976), and appointment calendars (1972-1975) belonging to Harlow and his wife.

Harlow, Victor E. (1876-1959) 459
Papers 1859-1950
1 foot

Publisher. Research materials (1859-1950), including notes and rough drafts of Harlow's book *Jesus the Man* and other religious monographs, along with a manuscript copy of Charles F. Colcord's memoirs.

Harper, Robert Henry (1869-ca. 1933) 460
Manuscript 1933
1 item

Physician. A six-page statement (1933) by Robert H. Harper, explaining why he requested that no religious services be held for him after his death.

Harrall, Stewart (1906-1964) 461
Printed materials 1947-1951
.10 foot

Publicity officer. Printed material, including reports and lists of participants from the Sixth Annual National Conference on Higher Education (1951); a clippings file (1947-1948) from the *Tulsa World* and the *Tulsa Tribune* concerning the University of Oklahoma; and publicity material (1950-1951) from Johnston Murray's 1950 gubernatorial campaign.

Harris, C. Johnston (1856-ca. 1922) 462
Printed materials 1892-1922
.66 foot

Indian chief. Typescripts of newspaper articles (1892-1922) on Cherokee Nation governmental issues such as allotment, the Dawes Commission, land transfers, and tribal politics during Harris's tenure as chief of the Cherokees and his service in the Cherokee senate.

Harris, Cyrus H. (1817-1888) 463
Printed materials 1872-1905
.10 foot

Indian chief. Typescripts of newspaper articles (1872-1905) on Chickasaw Nation governmental issues such as tribal factionalism, elections, schools, and the allotment of land during Harris's tenure as governor of the Chickasaw Nation.

Harris, Giles Edward (1878-1938) 464
Printed materials 1902-1938
.10 foot

Physician. A laboratory notebook (1902-1903); weekly public health reports for the United States (1909); a copy of the second biennial report (1910-1912) of the Oklahoma State Public Health Department; Harris's obituary; and a letter (1917) from Oklahoma governor Robert L. Williams regarding selective service registration.

Harris, James A. (1870-1947) 465
Papers 1853-1947
2 feet

Businessman. Correspondence (1900-1943) concerning Harris's activities with the Oklahoma Republican Party, of which he was state chairman from 1909-1924; legal correspondence, papers, deeds, and mortgages (1900-1947) from Harris's real estate business in Wagoner, Oklahoma; clippings (1914-1918); accounts and receipts (1853) from Harvey Harris, James Harris's father; and a genealogy (1924) of the Harris family.

Harris, Robert M. (1851-1927) 466
Printed materials 1896-1927
.33 foot

Governor. Typescripts of newspaper articles (1896-1927) regarding Harris's term as governor of the Chickasaw Nation from 1896-1898 and Chickasaw legislation, along with biographical information on Harris.

Harrison, Jacob 467
Printed materials 1905
3 items

Indian chief. Typescripts of newspaper articles (1905) regarding Harrison's impeachment and removal from office as chief of the Seminoles and, John Brown, his replacement.

Harrison, Walter M. (1888-1961) 468
Papers 1915-1961
10 feet

Journalist. Personal correspondence (1930-1961); military papers (1918-1959); political campaign materials (1949-1959); biographical materials (1915-1961); business correspondence (1931-1961); Pulitzer Prize Board materials (1938-1942); Will Rogers Memorial Commission papers (1938-1961); National Cowboy Hall of Fame files (1955); and Civil War Centennial Commission materials (1953-1961), all reflecting Harrison's personal affairs and his association with the above organizations while an editor for the *Daily Oklahoman* and the owner of *The North*

Star, along with papers (1949-1959) regarding his service as a city councilman for Oklahoma City, Oklahoma.

Unpublished finding aid available.

Harrison, William H. (1876-1929) 469
Printed materials 1901-1937
5 items

Indian chief. Typescripts of speeches and correspondence (1901-1937) by Harrison, a principal chief of the Choctaws, on the subject of the allotment of Choctaw lands.

Harrod, Neva Belle 470
Papers 1901-1957
2 feet

Teacher. Correspondence (1917-1918) with U.S. soldiers during World War I; and newspaper clippings (1901-1957) concerning President McKinley's assassination, World War I, Charles Lindbergh, World War II, and other major news stories of the twentieth century.

Unpublished finding aid available.

Hart, (Mrs.) Hugh 471
Manuscript 1887-1939
1 item

Writer. A history (ca. 1939) of the Presbyterian church in Pauls Valley, Oklahoma, written by Hart.

Haskell and LeFlore Counties Medical Society Collection 472
Records 1936-1951
.33 foot

Professional organization. Correspondence (1945-1952); minutes (1941-1952) of meetings; financial records (1939-1947); and miscellaneous printed materials (1936-1952) from the Haskell and LeFlore Counties (Oklahoma) Medical Society.

Haskell, Charles Nathaniel (1860-1933) 473
Papers 1863-1929
.50 foot

Governor. Correspondence (1863-1929) concerning Haskell's political career; speeches (1907-1952) made by Haskell; newspaper clippings (1908-1938); and notes (n.d.) concerning his involvement with the Oklahoma Constitutional Convention in 1906.

Hatfield, Edna Greer Porter 474
Papers 1831-1958
1 foot

Collector. Transcripts of interviews (ca. 1930-1958) with pioneers who took part in the 1893 land run into the Cherokee Strip. The interviews contain descriptions of the land run, hardships encountered, sod houses and dugouts, agriculture, religion, schools, and other socio-economic aspects of life in the Cherokee Strip. Township maps showing the location of original settlers in the Cherokee Strip accompany the interviews. The collection also includes historical, religious, social, and anecdotal information about the Indian tribes that lived in the eastern portion of the Cherokee Strip such as the Tonkawa, Kansa (Kaw), and Ponca Indians. Correspondence (1871-1875) and field notebooks (1869-1871) written by Orville Smith and T. H. Barrett during a survey of the Sisseton and Wahpeton Indian reservations in Dakota Territory make up the final part of the Hatfield Collection.

Hathaway, A. H. 475
Records 1892-1954
3 feet

Physician. Ledgers and journals (1892-1954) in which patient accounts were recorded, along with Hathaway's observations on daily weather conditions, particularly those regarding the dust storms of the 1930s.

Hayes, James H. 476
Records 1903-1929
.10 foot

Physician. Ledgers (1903-1929) in which Hayes recorded patient accounts and fees charged. The collection also includes a booklet (1923) of poetry by Oklahoma poet Ina Gainer.

Haynes, Micajah P. (1851-1939) 477
Printed materials 1857-1897
6 items

Physician. A receipt (1857) for the sale of a slave, along with Haynes's enrollment forms (1897) establishing his eligibility for Cherokee citizenship.

Healy, Frank Dale, Jr. (b. 1897) 478
Manuscripts ca. 1920-1950
2 items

Rancher. Two manuscripts, one (1950) by Frank Dale Healy, Jr., concerning Healy family history and life in the Oklahoma panhandle area during territorial days, including a description of related photographs; and one (ca. 1920) written by George Henry Healy, concerning ranching on Padre Island, Texas.

Heffner, Edna Swenson 479
Papers 1947-1980
5 feet

Educator. Correspondence (1947-1980) and newsletters concerning missionary work and Bible translation, mainly in Peru and Nigeria, along with commencement programs from the University of Oklahoma (1947), and Central Grammar School (1953).

Unpublished finding aid available.

Heffner, Roy E. (1895-1949) 480
Papers 1874-1947
18 feet

University professor and photographer. Personal correspondence (1904-1940) of Heffner and his wife, much of it from missionaries; printed material (ca. 1920-1940) relating to missionary activities and to the University of Oklahoma; scrapbooks containing newspaper clippings and personal items; and posters publicizing church events.

Unpublished finding aid available.

Heflin, Cleo Eugene (1911-1986) 481
Papers 1950-1981
1.75 feet

Author. Correspondence (1950-1981); research notes (n.d.); journal articles (1915-1979); and one unpublished manuscript (n.d.), all regarding the Caddo Indians.

Hefner, Robert Alexander (b. 1874) 482
Papers 1874-1947
.10 foot

Mayor. A biography (1874-1956) of Hefner, mayor of Oklahoma City, Oklahoma; a genealogy of the Hefner family; mayoral speeches (1947) to the city council of Oklahoma City; a first issue (1956) of the magazine *Independent Oil*; and a news magazine (1947) of the First National Bank Building in Oklahoma City.

Henderson, Arnold G. 483
Papers 1965-1970
11 feet

Professor. Source materials (1965-1970), including correspondence, research notes, interview forms, survey forms, and reports accumulated in compiling housing surveys and environmental studies of various Indian tribes, with an emphasis on the Cheyenne and Arapaho.

Unpublished finding aid available.

Hendricks, James R. (b. 1817) 484
Papers 1859-1902
1 foot

Judge. General and family correspondence (1865-1902); notebooks and journals (1862-1887); speeches (1866-1888); and legal documents (1859-1894) dealing with the Cherokee National Party, the Cherokee Nation Blind Asylum, pensions, and Cherokee Indian medicines.

Hendrickson, Gwen (b. 1897) 485
Manuscript 1950
1 item

Homemaker. Gwen Hendrickson's reminiscences (1950) about her father, Samuel Harvey Hendrickson, who settled on the Cheyenne and Arapaho lands in 1892.

Hennessey High School Collection 486
Papers 1880-1980
.10 foot

Public school. Term papers and reports (1980) regarding the history of Hennessey, Oklahoma, and surrounding communities, written by students in Hennessey High School's writing class, with an emphasis upon the Czechoslovakian immigrants who settled the area.

Hennings, A. E. 487
Records 1929-1950
.33 foot

Physician. A ledger (1929-1950) in which Hennings recorded patient accounts and services rendered, and a news clipping (1950) regarding a gift of land by Hennings to the Oklahoma Medical Research Foundation.

Hensley, Claude 488
Papers 1860-1940
.10 foot

Journalist. Typescripts of correspondence (1879) and memoirs (1860-1874) concerning Quanah Parker; the first telephone in Indian Territory; life at Fort Sill, and Fort Reno, Oklahoma Territory; and the hunting of buffalo; along with an account (1940) by E. H. Linzee describing the development of Oklahoma Territory.

Herbert, Harold Harvey (1888-1980) 489
Papers 1918-1959
49 feet

Professor. Departmental and personal files (1918-1959) compiled by Herbert as director of the University of Oklahoma School of Journalism, concerning faculty, students, the College of Liberal Arts and Sciences, and general University of

Oklahoma business, along with materials relating to committees and associations with which Herbert and the School of Journalism were connected.

Herring, Alvin J. (d. 1954) 490
Records 1922-1925
5 items

Collector. An account book (1923-1924) and notebooks (1922-1925) containing lists of photograph negatives from the Deal Studio in Chelsea, Oklahoma.

Hertzog, Anna Laura Brisky (1873-1963) 491
Papers 1904-1948
2 items

Educator and civic leader. A combination account book, scrapbook, and family diary (1904-1948) which includes descriptions of the mining boom in the Wichita Mountains and early school board meetings in Comanche County, Oklahoma, along with a manuscript (n.d.) entitled "Pioneer Days in Comanche Co."

Hewes, Leslie (b. 1906) 492
Papers 1901-1912
.33 foot

Geography professor. Township maps (ca. 1937) of the Cherokee Nation of Oklahoma on which Hewes plotted the following data: what groups (categorized by degree of Indian blood, intermarried citizens, or freedmen) settled which allotments, along with the classification of these allotments and the appraised value per acre of each. Hewes used the information included on these maps to write his dissertation, "The Geography of the Cherokee Country of Oklahoma" at the University of California in 1940.

Hewitt, Robert C. 493
Papers 1923-1953
.50 foot

Army officer. Personal correspondence (1942-1944) to family members regarding Hewitt's military service and war-related experiences as a bombardier in the U.S. Army Air Force; additional correspondence (1944-1953) to the Hewitt family from E. C. McCallum of Stanolind Oil and Gas Company; telegrams (1943-1944); medals (1944); personal records (1923-1946); and news clippings (1943-1946), all relating to Robert C. Hewitt up to the time of his death in 1944.

Heydrick, L. C. 494
Papers 1901-1953
.33 foot

Oil prospector. Correspondence (1901, 1931-1939, 1944, 1953) relating to Jesse A. Heydrick's discovery of oil in Red Fork, Oklahoma; a manuscript (1931) of unpublished chapters for John W. Flenner's *History of Early Oil Developments in*

Oklahoma; legal papers (1901); newspaper clippings; and a bound report (1953) by Heydrick entitled "Red Fork Discovery, June 1901."

Hicks, Jimmie 495
Manuscript 1990
1 item

Educator. An unpublished manuscript (1990) by Jimmie Hicks entitled "A Critique of the PBS Television Program, 'Indians, Outlaws and Angie Debo,' The American Experience, #103." In this eighteen-page paper, Hicks introduces the principals, offers a point-by-point criticism of the program, discusses Debo's book, *And Still the Waters Run*, the controversy over its publication, Joseph Brandt's effort to have it published, and defends Edward E. Dale's role in the controversy.

Hilbert-Price, Shirley 496
Papers 1963-1987
4.50 feet

Political activist. Legislative bills and resolutions (1975-1985); correspondence (1972-1986); publications (1972-1987); and memorabilia (n.d.), including banners, bumper stickers, pins, buttons, and sound recordings, all regarding the status of women's rights in Oklahoma and the United States, and the campaign for the Equal Rights Amendment.

Unpublished finding aid available.

Hill, Francis M. 497
Printed materials 1950-1951
2 items

Collector. Booklets (1950-1951) advertising the sale of Hereford cattle at the Honey Creek Ranch near Grove, Oklahoma. The booklets describe the stockbreeding techniques employed at Honey Creek Ranch, one of the first ranches in Oklahoma to adopt scientific breeding techniques.

Hill, George Washington (1834-1925) 498
Records 1858-1907
.10 foot

Merchant. Land titles and deeds (1858-1879) from Georgia and the Cherokee Nation, Indian Territory; an admission ticket to the 1900 Democratic Party national convention, and minutes (1900) of the Vinita, Indian Territory, Democratic Club; an election poll list and tally sheet (1907) from Vinita, Indian Territory, and one court document (1886) of the Cooweescoowee District Court, Cherokee Nation.

Hill, Weldon 499
Papers 1957-1968
3.33 feet

Author. Book and short story manuscripts (1957-1968) regarding fictional themes, authored by Hill, using both his pen name, Weldon Hill, and his real name, William R. Scott. Titles include *Onionhead* (1957), *One of the Casualties* (1964), *The Long Summer of George Adams* (1961), *Rafe* (1966), and *A Man Could Get Killed That Way* (1967).

Unpublished finding aid available.

Hine, L. T. 500
Papers 1903-1935
.10 foot

Real estate agent. Correspondence (1925-1935), including legal and financial documents from Hine's real estate business in Purcell, Oklahoma; oil leases (1925); and correspondence and papers (1909-1926) relating to the Fraternal Order of Eagles of which Hine was a member.

Hines, M. D. 501
Papers 1858-1942
.10 foot

Businessman. Financial agreements and correspondence (1858-1942) relating to family affairs and Hines's farm, cattle ranch, and nursery near Maysville, Arkansas. One letter (1868) describes preparations for a cattle drive from Boggy Depot, Indian Territory, to Maysville, Arkansas.

Hinkel, John W. 502
Papers 1894-1908
3 items

Collector. Correspondence (1894-1897) to and from Freeman E. Miller, a professor at Oklahoma Agricultural and Mechanical College, regarding Miller's publications; pamphlets (1896-1908); and printed advertisements from publishers.

Hinkhouse, Steven 503
Ledger 1889-1897
1 item

Collector. A Chicago, Rock Island, and Pacific Railroad Company station log from Durant, Iowa, for the period 1889-1897.

Hinsdale, Harriet 504
Papers 1895-1966
.10 foot

Collector and author. Manuscripts (ca. 1948) by Helen Hinsdale; copies of magazine articles (1895-1966), including some from an 1895 issue of *McClure's Magazine*; and newspaper clippings (1894-1966), all concerning Robert Louis Stevenson.

Hipes, Jessie James
Records 1908-1947
.66 foot 505

Physician. Records (1908-1947) from Hipes's medical practice, including prescriptions for glasses, patient case histories, and financial records, along with certificates (1911-1947) and diplomas (1908-1910) issued to Hipes by government health agencies and universities.

Hisel, (Mrs.) O. R.
Papers 1950-1951
3 items 506

Historian. Bound typescripts of three unpublished works by Hisel entitled "Oklahoma Federation of Music Clubs" (1950); "Missionary Federation of Muskogee, Oklahoma" (1950); and "Presbyterian Pioneers and Personalities, 1825-1951" (1951).

Historic Oklahoma Collection
Printed material 1900-1987
19.33 feet 507

Vertical file. Newspaper clippings and brochures containing information on selected subjects, events, and places significant to Oklahoma's history. The index to this guide includes each subject, event, or place, identified at the folder level in this collection.

Historic Oklahoma Collection-Biographies
Printed material 1900-1987
4.66 feet 508

Vertical file. Newspaper clippings and tear sheets containing biographical information on prominent and historically significant Oklahomans. The index to this guide includes the people documented in this collection.

Holbrook, Ralph Winfrey (ca. 1870-ca. 1952)
Records 1899-1944
.50 foot 509

Physician. Ledgers and notebooks (1899-1944); matriculation records (1896-1899); and birth memoranda for the years 1925-1941. These records document Holbrook's medical training and his medical practice in Payne County, Oklahoma, from 1896 to 1944.

Holbrook, Richard Burkey
Papers 1900-1915
1 foot 510

Editor. Correspondence (1900-1915) between Holbrook, his wife, Mabel Jackson

Holbrook, and others regarding his editorship of the *Pawnee Dispatch*, family matters, and social life in Pawnee, Oklahoma.

Holdenville Schubert Music Club Collection 511
Scrapbook 1907-1957
1 item

Social club. A scrapbook (1907-1957) containing newspaper clippings and memorabilia documenting the history of Holdenville, Oklahoma's, Schubert Music Club.

Hollem, Anna Iverson 512
Papers 1892-1935
.10 foot

Collector. Correspondence, teaching certificates and examination scores, letters of recommendation, and tax receipts belonging to Charles L. Hollem, Anna Hollem's husband. All materials are from the years 1892-1901, except for souvenirs from Hollem's lumberyard and letters describing Hollem's funeral in 1935. The papers reflect Hollem's activities as a school teacher in Oklahoma Territory, and as owner of the first lumberyard in Lawton, Oklahoma.

Holmberg, Gustaf Fredrik (d. 1936) 513
Papers 1921-1936
.10 foot

Professor. Correspondence (1921-1935); manuscripts (n.d.); speeches (n.d.); and newspaper clippings (n.d.) relating to Holmberg's career as dean of the University of Oklahoma School of Fine Arts, 1907-1936.

Holt, Smith Lewis and James Doepel Holt 514
Papers 1829-1870
5 items

Collectors. An account book (n.d.) of W. M. Lewis; a ciphering book (1829) belonging to Samuel D. Jackson; a deposition and petition (1870) of Elizabeth and Angeline Carter; and a warrant (1870) issued by George W. Campbell.

Holtzendorff, Crichton Brooks (1886-1958) 515
Papers 1919-1922
.10 foot

Attorney. Financial records (1919-1922); notes (1920-1922); correspondence (1921-1922); legal documents (1920); and a newspaper clipping (1922), all relating to a legal dispute over utility rates between the city of Claremore, Oklahoma, and the Oklahoma Natural Gas Company.

Hoops, Mary Griffith (1842-1898) 516
Manuscript 1864-1866
1 item

Pioneer. A photocopy of a typewritten memoir (1887) by Mary Griffith Hoops, published in the *Marion Record* in 1925, describing the 1864-1866 settlement of her family in Marion, Kansas. It includes information on the early history of the area, life on the frontier, a meeting with Kit Carson, and a trading post on the Santa Fe Trail.

Hopeton State Bank Collection 517
Records 1903-1910
2 items

Bank. Two general ledgers (1903-1910) of the State Bank of Hopeton, Oklahoma.

Horton, Guy K. (b. 1912) 518
Manuscript ca. 1979
1 item

Attorney and state legislator. An unpublished, typewritten memoir (ca. 1979) of Horton's life in southwestern Oklahoma as an attorney and state legislator. The memoir contains references to his family, his boyhood, his college years, and especially, to Oklahoma politics and his career as a state legislator.

Hoskinson, William Earl (b. 1887) 519
Papers 1873-1973
2 feet

Collector. Correspondence (1914-1973); financial and tax records (1901); clippings (n.d.); and family memorabilia (ca. 1905-1950) of William E. Hoskinson. The collection also includes a family history (1970) entitled "Thomas Bowman Hoskinson: Of Ohio, Texas, and California," and hymnals (1873-1907).

Unpublished finding aid available.

Hoss, Henry Sessler (ca. 1882-1921) 520
Papers 1898-1931
.10 foot

Physician. An account book (1917); notes (1904) from a course of lectures on obstetrics; two letters (1898, n.d.); and obituaries of Hoss, who practiced medicine in Muskogee, Oklahoma, from 1906 to 1921. The collection includes a memoranda calendar (1931) from A. R. Gregory.

Hosterman, Jacob (1831-1903) 521
Ledger 1859-1862
1 item

Shoemaker. An account book (1859-1862) kept by Hosterman, who practiced his shoemaking trade in and around Mechanicsville, Iowa, during the years 1859-1862. A recipe for ink is included at the back of the book.

Hotchkiss and Cronkhite Loan and Investment Company Collection   522
Ledger 1905-1914
1 item

Financial institution. A daybook (1905-1914) of the Hotchkiss and Cronkhite Loan and Investment Company of Watonga, Oklahoma.

Hotema, Solomon E.   523
Manuscript 1907
1 item

Indian chief and minister. A typescript of an article (1907) concerning Hotema, a Choctaw chief and Presbyterian minister, and his release from prison.

Houghton, Fred Ernest (1854-1943)   524
Records 1901-1943
.25 foot

Merchant. A daily account book (1919-1920); a trade token advertising Houghton's stores; and photocopies of other financial records (1901-1943) belonging to Houghton, who owned general merchandise stores in the towns of Guthrie, Coyle, Cashion, Meridian, and Goodnight, Oklahoma.

House, Roy Temple (b. 1878)   525
Papers 1939-1951
.33 foot

Professor. Manuscripts (n.d.) of short stories by Roy Temple House, Emil Lucka (in German), José de la Cuadra, and others; correspondence (1939-1951) concerning House's work with the University of Oklahoma and *Books Abroad*, much of it from Ada P. McCormick.

Houston, Temple (1860-1905)   526
Speech 1898
1 item

Attorney. A typescript of a speech (1898) by Temple Houston at the laying of the cornerstone of Northwestern State Teachers College, Alva, Oklahoma.

Howard, Walter Alonzo (1883-1970)   527
Papers 1919-1928
1 foot

Physician. Correspondence (1924-1927) from Howard's tenure as secretary-treasurer of the Rogers County (Oklahoma) Medical Society; military examination records (1920-1927) created while Howard was a designated medical examiner for the U.S. Veterans Bureau; and personal correspondence (1918-1927) from Howard's activities with the American Legion and the American Red Cross, along with reprints of articles on medical subjects.

Howe, A. N. 528
Manuscript 1883-1938
1 item

Cowboy. Transcript (n.d.) of a personal reminiscence by Howe regarding his experience in the west including visits to Dodge City, Kansas, Beaver County, Oklahoma, and No Man's Land (the Oklahoma panhandle). Also included are words to a song entitled "The Little Old Sod Shanty on My Claim."

Howell, O. E. (b. 1877) 529
Papers 1907-1946
4 items

Physician. A copy of a speech (1946) by Howell in which he recounts his experiences as a country physician in Oktaha, Oklahoma (1904-1929). Also included are copies of the *Saturday Evening Post* (1907), the *Illustrated London News* (1915), and a copy of a flyer advertising the movie *Ashes of Vengeance*, starring Norma Talmage.

Hudson, Waddie (b. ca. 1865) 530
Papers 1847-1951
.33 foot

Collector. Papers (1847-1951) of the Hudson family, including letters (1855, 1860) from Jefferson Davis and L.Q.C. Lamar to Thomas J. Hudson; Hudson's commission (1861) as a major in the Confederate Army; and a letter to Hudson from M. H. Thomson concerning the prices of household goods. Also included in this collection are eight notebooks of official notary records (1905-1907) of William F. Rasmus of Tahlequah, Indian Territory; a ledger (1870) from Rasmus's general store in Flint, Indian Territory; two funeral registers (1903-1909) from John W. Stapler and Son; and a scrapbook (n.d.) prepared by Waddie Hudson for his grandson, Gordon Hudson Council.

Huff, Thomas J. (b. 1884) 531
Printed materials 1907-1949
.10 foot

Collector. Programs (1907-1949) from musical recitals, concerts, and plays in central Oklahoma, along with valentines and political flyers (n.d.).

Huffman, John 532
Records 1864-1871
6 items

Collector. An account book (1864-1871) of Jacob C. Huffman's personal expenditures, and five advertising cards.

Huggard, Christopher James (1954-   ) 533
Thesis 1828-1910
2 items

Historian. Huggard's thesis (1987) entitled "The Role of the Family in Settling the Cherokee Outlet," with chapters regarding the land run of 1893, settlement and housing patterns, and interaction with neighbors. Also in this collection is an unpublished paper by Huggard entitled "Culture Mixing, Everyday Life Among the Choctaw in the Mid-Nineteenth Century."

Hughes, Jim 534
Papers 1948-1957
.33 foot

Labor official. Scrapbooks (1948-1957) of newspaper clippings concerning investigations of labor problems, legislation, and strikes; copies of the *United Mine Workers Journal* (1957); a typescript of a speech (1957) Hughes presented to the Oklahoma State Federation of Labor; a labor convention program (1957); and a contract for the publication of "A Labor History of Oklahoma."

Hughes, John Elmer (1878-1947) 535
Printed material 1906-1951
1 item

Physician. A published memoir (1951) in which Hughes describes his medical practice in Shawnee, Oklahoma, beginning in 1906, and his travels in Alaska, Europe, South America, Africa, and Indochina.

Hume, Carlton Ross (1878-1960) 536
Papers 1838-1948
10.50 feet

Attorney. Personal and business correspondence (1893-1948) relating to Hume's family, his attendance at the University of Oklahoma, his contact with the university as an alumnus, and his law practice as an attorney for the Caddo Indians. Also included are numerous legal documents (1838-1948) relating to Indian claims and the Indians of Oklahoma, the Shirley Trading Post, the Anadarko, Oklahoma, area and the University of Oklahoma.

Unpublished finding aid available.

Hundley, John (b. 1872) 537
Records 1900-1942
7 feet

Businessman. Account books (1913-1937); daily statement ledgers (1914-1918);

correspondence (1913-1919); tax receipts (1912-1917); stock inventories (1923-1942); and financial records (1920-1937) from Hundley's general store, plus assorted business papers (1900-1936), all relating to Hundley's enterprises in and around Calvin, Oklahoma.

Unpublished finding aid available.

Hunt, Blanche Seale 538
Papers 1936-1951
.33 foot

Author. A scrapbook containing a complete set of Hunt's *Little Brown Koko* children's stories (1936-1951) clipped from magazines.

Hunt, J. O. 539
Records 1853-1903
7 items

Physician. An account book (1898-1903); a notebook (1876) of medicinal recipes and accounts; and matriculation and lecture tickets (1853) from the Medical College of Georgia, all belonging to Hunt or relating to Hunt's medical practice in Wallis, Indian Territory.

Hunter, H. A. 540
Ledger 1912
1 item

Collector. A ledger entitled "List of real estate owned by J. E. Campbell and E. B. Lawson jointly. November 25th, 1912."

Hunter, Thomas W. 541
Printed materials 1902-1903
3 items

Indian leader. Typescripts of newspaper articles (1902-1903) concerning Hunter's appointment of E. P. Pitchlynn as a light horseman and his authority to do so.

Huntley, A. A. (d. 1933) 542
Papers 1897-ca. 1900
2 items

Physician. A manuscript of a paper (1900) read by Huntley before the Beckham County (Oklahoma) Medical Society, and a reprint of an article (1897) written by Huntley and Delano Ames.

Hurley, Patrick Jay (1883-1956) 543
Papers 1900-1956
188 feet

U.S. ambassador. Correspondence, reports, and articles (1900-1956) regarding Hurley's positions as national attorney for the Choctaw Nation, including enrollments, land questions, and the Mississippi Choctaw Indians; assistant U.S. secretary of war and U.S. secretary of war; a special presidential representative to the Soviet Union, Great Britain, Afghanistan, and the Middle East; U.S. ambassador to China during World War II, including correspondence regarding American and Allied efforts in the Far Eastern Theatre: Correspondents include Winston Churchill, Franklin D. Roosevelt, Louis Mountbatten, Mao Tse-Tung, Chiang Kai-Shek, Herbert Hoover, Douglas MacArthur, Henry A. Wallace, Joseph Stilwell, Helen Keller, and Cordell Hull, as well as officials of the diplomatic corps such as Averell Harriman and Harry Hopkins.

Unpublished finding aid available.

Hurst, Irvin 544
Manuscript 1957
1 item

Writer. An annotated manuscript (1957) for Hurst's book *The 46th Star*, a history of Oklahoma's Constitutional Convention.

Hutto, Robert W. (b. 1885) 545
Papers 1929-1946
.66 foot

Banker. Business correspondence (1929-1946) and printed materials (1944-1946) relating to the Norman, Oklahoma, Chamber of Commerce, and to the Oklahoma Bankers Association, plus bound copies (1944-1946) of *The Oklahoma Banker*.

Hyde, Clayton H. (1868-1950) 546
Papers 1881-1946
13.66 feet

Farmer. Personal correspondence (1881-1946) of Clayton H. Hyde, including copies of speeches and public statements; correspondence (1909-1939) with local, state, and national farm, business, and political organizations, together with informational circulars on their activities.

Unpublished finding aid available.

Hydro First National Bank Collection 547
Records 1903-1951
25 feet

Bank. Financial records (1903-1951), including correspondence, ledgers, draft registers, daily statements, distribution of expenses, and insurance records of the Bank of Hydro, the Hydro First National Bank, and the Farmers National Bank, all of Hydro, Oklahoma.

Impson, Hiram 548
Letter 1940
1 item

Collector. A letter (1940) written by Paul McKennon, recounting his experiences in the Seminole Nation (1894-1896) with an explanation of how criminals were punished under Seminole law.

Independent Order of Odd Fellows Collection 549
Printed materials 1904-1911
7 items

Fraternal organization. Publications of Independent Order of Odd Fellows lodges in Indian and Oklahoma territories (1904-1907), and in the state of Oklahoma (1907-1911).

Indian-Pioneer Papers Collection 550
Papers 1861-1936
22 feet

Oral history collection. Typescripts of interviews conducted during the 1930s by government workers with thousands of Oklahomans regarding the settlement of Oklahoma and Indian territories, as well as the condition and conduct of life there. Consisting of approximately 80,000 entries, the index to this collection may be accessed via personal name, place name, or subject.

Unpublished finding aid available.

Indian Territory Medical Association Collection 551
Records 1881-1904
.33 foot

Professional organization. Minute books (1881-1904) recording the proceedings of the Indian Territory Medical Association and a college term paper (1956) regarding the history, origin, and governance of the Indian Territory Medical Association.

Indian War Veterans Collection 552
Papers 1937-1956
.50 foot

Veterans organization. Correspondence (1930-1954), including personal data sheets on veterans of Indian wars and letters requesting assistance in obtaining pensions; diary extracts (1866-1893) describing experiences in various Indian wars, especially from 1860-1900, against the Apaches, Arapahos, Cheyennes, Comanches, Dakotas, Kiowas, and Paiutes; a manuscript (n.d.) written by Gen. T. H. Slavens, entitled "San Carlos, Arizona in the Eighties; The Land of the Apache," describing Indian activity in the San Carlos area, 1849-1894; and publications which include issues of *Winners of the West* (1937-1944), *The Veteran Corps Bulletin* (1952, 1954), *The*

William McKinley Camp Bulletin (1954), *War Path* (1955-1956), and the *Proceedings* of the twenty-fifth annual convention of Indian wars veterans.

Internal Provinces of New Spain Collection   553
Papers 1704-1789
1 foot

Spanish colonial governmental unit. Copies of documents (1704-1789) from the Spanish archives of New Mexico relating to Indian relations, military defense, trade, and general colonial conditions in New Mexico, with notes from Ralph Emerson Twitchell's guide *The Spanish Archives of New Mexico*.

Unpublished finding aid available.

Isparhecher (1828-1902)   554
Printed material 1884-1908
.25 foot

Indian chief. Typescripts of letters (1891-1898); speeches (1884-1898); editorials (1896-1906); and biographical accounts (1903-1908), all relating to Isparhecher while a principal chief of the Creek Nation on subjects such as tribal factionalism, finance, land titles, and related government affairs.

Jackson, Jacob Battiest (b. 1845)   555
Printed material 1896
1 item

Indian chief. A typescript of a newspaper article (1896) regarding Jackson's election as a principal chief of the Choctaw Nation.

Jackson, Robert Edward Jr. (b. 1891)   556
Papers 1906-1907
3 items

Collector. An autograph book (1906) kept by Jackson while a page at the 1906 Oklahoma Constitutional Convention, containing the names of each delegate attending; a printed copy (1907) of the new constitution, along with county boundaries and election ordinances; and one parliamentary procedures manual (1906) used by Jackson during the convention and entitled *Rules, Roster and Standing Committees of the Constitutional Convention*.

Jacobson, Oscar Brousse (1882-1966)   557
Papers 1916-1945
1 foot

Professor. Newspaper editorial cartoons (1918-1930) regarding World War I and the post-war period; civilian defense correspondence (1917-1920) and publications (1942-1945), including plans, papers, and blueprints detailing civilian defense of the University of Oklahoma in the event of enemy attack; biographies (n.d.); and

Jacobson's unpublished manuscript (ca. 1954) regarding Oklahoma artists and the status of art in Oklahoma through 1930.

Jameson, John (b. 1897) 558
Records 1891-1911
1 item

Rancher. A ledger (1891-1911) containing financial transactions of the Jameson ranch in Indian Territory, along with personal and family information. Included is a home remedy for "weak lung," using as ingredients glycerine, whiskey, and white rock candy.

Jamieson, W. C. 559
Papers 1915-1937
.10 foot

Farmer. Bulletins (1918-1921) released by the National Board of Farm Organizations; a letter detailing an automobile journey through Oklahoma in 1930; a letter regarding presidential candidate Alfred M. Landon; and correspondence (1919-1920) regarding the creation of a dairy farmers league for the Oklahoma City, Oklahoma, market.

Jarboe, (Mrs.) W. C. 560
Manuscript 1890-1913
1 item

Pioneer. In 1913 Jarboe wrote this account of her family's move from Texas into Indian Territory, and their subsequent move to Greer County, Oklahoma. The manuscript contains anecdotes about their experiences with Choctaw and Kiowa Indians, as well as a general description of hardships faced by pioneers.

Jayne, Mary Prosser 561
Papers 1896-1924
.33 foot

Missionary. Correspondence (1915) and pamphlets (1924) of missionary, Robert Hamilton, stationed in Shawnee, Oklahoma, regarding his work there; and manuscript notes (n.d.) by Jayne, regarding missionary work at the Cheyenne and Arapaho Indian Baptist Mission, and the class of 1896 of the Baptist Missionary Training School.

Jazhe, Benedict 562
Printed materials 1680-1963
.10 foot

Collector. Maps (1680-1963); government documents (1917-1960); a bibliography (n.d.) of sources; and a checklist of names (n.d), all relating to the Fort Sill Apache Indians.

Joblin, Walter Ridgway (1873-1950) 563
Records 1902-1943
6.33 feet

Physician. Records of Joblin's medical practice in Porter, Indian Territory, and Oklahoma, including ledgers listing patients and fees charged (1902-1943); narcotics purchased and administered (1933-1939); and personal and household expenses (1933-1942).

Unpublished finding aid available.

John, Walter N. 564
Records 1894-1949
.10 foot

Physician. Ledgers (1923-1938) in which John recorded patient visits and services rendered; a diploma (1894) issued to John, along with a biography and news clippings (1894-1949) regarding his life and career.

Johnson, B. F. 565
Records 1898-1954
2 items

Physician. Ledgers (1898-1954) listing patient visits and charges from Johnson's practice as a physician and pharmacist in Fairview, Oklahoma.

Johnson, Bob 566
Papers 1849-1873, 1908
.10 foot

Collector. A short, typewritten copy of a travel diary (1908) describing a trip through Kansas and Oklahoma, along with copies of three letters (1849-1873). One letter is from Beni Wingate writing from Ft. Gibson, Indian Territory, in 1850 about family matters; the second is from George Mower, writing from the Platte River in Nebraska Territory in 1849 and commenting on what he has seen since leaving St. Joseph, Missouri; and the third (1873) is a brief letter of introduction for a salesman operating out of Denison, Texas.

Johnson, Edgar Allen (1880-ca. 1955) 567
Records 1919-1950
13 feet

Physician. Case histories (1934-1950); fee books (1919-1950); and obstetric records (1934-1950) from Johnson's practice as a specialist in obstetrics and radiology in Hugo, Oklahoma.

Johnson, Edith Cherry (b. 1879) 568
Papers 1919-1951
2 feet

Journalist. Correspondence (1922-1945) from Johnson's readers concerning their personal problems and their opinions about her editorials and columns in the *Daily Oklahoman*; typescripts (1934-1948) of articles by Johnson; clippings (1919-1951) of her columns and of articles about her; letters (1921) endorsing Oklahoma senator John Golobie for the post of U.S. minister to Yugoslavia; and papers (1949-1950) from Johnson's tenure as secretary of Oklahoma Goodwill Industries, Inc.

Johnson, Edward Bryant (1865-1935) 569
Papers 1882-1929
7 feet

Banker and rancher. Correspondence (1882-1929); legal and financial records (1896-1928); diaries (1928-1929); and related biographical items concerning the banking, ranching, oil interests, and life of Edward Johnson, a Chickasaw Indian businessman and banker in Norman, Oklahoma.

Johnson, Henry Lee 570
Printed material 1945
1 item

Physician. A copy of *A Standard Practice Manual for Use in State Hospitals for Mental Disorders*, a manual (1945) written by Johnson while serving as the assistant superintendent for the Western Oklahoma Hospital, a psychiatric hospital at Fort Supply, Oklahoma.

Johnson, Martha Sherwood Finch 571
Papers 1954
3 items

Poet. Copies of three letters (1954) from Johnson to Mrs. Copeland, possibly Edith Copeland.

Johnson, William E. 572
Papers 1912-1917
.10 foot

Government employee. A letter (1914) describing Johnson's trip to Russia, along with newspaper clippings (1912-1917) of stories about Johnson and his work to prevent the sale of alcoholic beverages to Indians. Among the clippings is a two-page article (1917) written by Johnson and entitled "Ten Years of Prohibition in Oklahoma."

Johnston, Douglas H. (1858-ca. 1940) 573
Printed materials 1896-1936
1 foot

Indian chief. Typescripts of newspaper articles and editorials (1896-1936) regarding Johnston as governor of the Chickasaw Nation and issues such as tribal government, land, mineral resources, finances, claims, education, and the ownership of slaves.

Johnston, Henry Simpson (1870-1965) 574
Papers 1891-1960
51 feet

Governor. Correspondence (1900-1960) relating to Henry Simpson Johnston's political and legal careers, and to his affiliation with various fraternal organizations; legal papers (1909-1934) documenting court cases with which Johnston was involved; speeches and other papers (1914-1930) relating to his political campaigns; and printed material and newspaper clippings (1920-1960) collected by Johnston.

Unpublished finding aid available.

Johnston, Paul Imbrie (b. 1886) 575
Records 1927-1972
3 feet

Business executive. Corporate records (1934-1972), including articles of incorporation and minutes of the Oklahoma Public Services Corporation, the Oklahoma-Kansas Natural Gas Company, and the Continental Investment Corporation; operating manuals (1927-1930) of the Eason Oil Company, the Mid-Continent Petroleum Corporation, the Independent Oil and Gas Company, and the Transcontinental Oil Company; and a notebook (1957) labelled "Proxy Contest," including lists of stock sales and stock holders for the Atlantic Oil Corporation.

Jones, Dovie 576
Papers 1870-1892
2 items

Collector. A ledger (1870) with entries in the Choctaw language belonging to Wilson N. Jones, a principal chief of the Choctaws, and containing information regarding a general store he operated in Cade, Indian Territory. Also included is a copy of a speech (1892) by Jones to the Choctaw general council.

Jones, John Paul 577
Ledger 1923-1924
1 item

Physician. A ledger (1923-1924) in which Jones recorded services rendered and fees charged.

Jones, Lydia Caroline Baggett (1843-1934) 578
Papers ca. 1900-1988
5 items

Pioneer. Photocopies of Jones's account of pioneer life in early Montague County, Texas, from 1854 to approximately 1867, describing early settlers and raids by Comanche Indians; census returns from 1860 and 1870 for the Jones and Baggett families, taken from *Early Records of Montague County, Texas* (1982); an obituary

(1934) of Jones; a roll of the Nacogdoches (Texas) Mounted Volunteers; and notes (1988) on the genealogy of the Jones and Baggett families.

Jones, Stephen   579
Papers 1964-1977
8 feet

Lawyer. Correspondence (1971-1973) of the American Civil Liberties Union and the Oklahoma Civil Liberties Union; court records (1971-1973); testimony (1972-1973); transcripts, prisoners petitions, and prison records (1971-1977); and publications (1964-1976) of the American and Oklahoma civil liberties unions, all relating to Jones's service as general counsel to the Oklahoma chapter of the American Civil Liberties Union and his successful representation of Bobby Battle in the landmark case *Battle vs. Park Anderson*.

Unpublished finding aid available.

Jones, Wilson N. (ca. 1831-1901)   580
Printed materials 1890-1935
.10 foot

Indian chief. Typescripts of newspaper articles (1890-1935), including speeches, editorials, and official documents which focus on Choctaw tribal politics, land allotment, and mineral rights on Choctaw Indian lands.

Jordan Drug Store Collection   581
Records 1921-1928
.50 foot

Pharmacy. Prescriptions filled at this Oklahoma City, Oklahoma, pharmacy for the period 1921-1928.

Jordan, Glenn   582
Printed materials 1860-1977
.50 foot

Historian. Research materials (1860-1977) gathered by Jordan while preparing his dissertation on Joseph S. Murrow and Bacone College, including photocopies of Murrow's diary (1867-1869).

Jordan, John D.   583
Papers 1839-1903
.10 foot

Collector. A letter (1842) to Stand Watie from John R. Ridge regarding the Ross faction and the death of James Foreman, and a biography (n.d.) of Stand Watie, compiled by the Daughters of the Confederacy.

Jordan, Omar L.   584
Records 1940-1948
.66 foot

Collector. Correspondence (1941-1948) regarding Oklahoma Lions Club business, and publications (1940-1941) issued by the Lions Club, including a history of Oklahoma club district 3-A.

Journeycake, Charles (1817-1894)   585
Printed materials 1936-1964
.10 foot

Indian chief. A typescript of a biography (n.d.) of Charles Journeycake, and newspaper clippings (1936-1964) regarding the Journeycake home, and his career.

Judy, Thomas J. (1861-1936)   586
Manuscript 1884-1936
1 item

Rancher. A typewritten, twenty-seven page memoir (ca. 1936) of Judy's life as a pioneer rancher in No Man's Land (the Oklahoma panhandle area). The memoir recounts the hardships of ranching in what is now Beaver County, Oklahoma, and the lawlessness of that area.

Jumper, John (1823-1896)   587
Printed materials 1874-1928
.10 foot

Indian chief. Typescripts of newspaper articles (1874-1929) by and about Jumper, and regarding the Peace Council of 1874, and the status of Christian missions in the Seminole Nation.

Kagey, Joseph Newton (1890-1959)   588
Papers 1850-1959
.10 foot

Educator. Newspaper clippings (1946-1959) and a history (1954) of the Seneca Indian School; a pamphlet (1950) and booklet (ca. 1951) regarding the history of the Goodland Indian Mission; and an obituary (1959) of Kagey.

Kali-Inla Coal Company Collection   589
Records 1903-1944
219 feet

Coal mining company. Correspondence, financial reports, leases, legal reports and general reports, all dated 1903-1944, regarding the operation and management of the Kali-Inla Coal Company of Hartshorne, Indian Territory, and Oklahoma, and that of its subsidiary coal companies and related firms. Special correspondence files include those regarding labor union activity, mining accidents, company housing, relations with railroads, and insurance. Also included in this collection are equipment catalogs (ca. 1910-1944) containing advertisements and information regarding miner and mining supplies. In addition to reflecting the mining industry in Oklahoma, the collection also contains information on mining operations in Colorado, West Virginia, and Arkansas.

Unpublished finding aid available.

Kaufman, Kenneth Carlyle (1887-1945) 590
Papers 1908-1942
.10 foot

Editor. Manuscripts (1929-1940) of poetry, short stories, and plays; printed material (1930-1942), including literary publications; a bibliography (n.d.) of Oklahoma writers; and certificates and diplomas (1908-1926) received by Kaufman.

Kaw Indian Agency Collection 591
Records 1887-1939
15.33 feet

Indian agency. Farming and grazing leases (1903-1937); oil and gas leases (1913-1932); allotment records (1902-1936); financial and property records (1887-1927); employee records (1903-1918); correspondence (1901-1939); and general subject files (1895-1932) of the agency for the Kansa (Kaw) Indians.

Unpublished finding aid available.

Kay County State Bank Collection 592
Records 1898-1901
4 feet

Bank. Four deposit ledgers (1898-1901) from the Kay County (Oklahoma) State Bank.

Keith, Harold (1903-   ) 593
Papers 1930-1970
1.50 feet

Writer. Corrected manuscripts (n.d.) for *Boy's Life of Will Rogers* and *Rifles for Watie* both written by Keith; programs (1930-1970) of University of Oklahoma athletic events; and letters (1942-1946) from University of Oklahoma students and alumni, mostly athletes, serving in the U.S. armed forces during World War II, to Keith and members of the University of Oklahoma athletic department.

Keller-Clarke Seed Store Collection 594
Records 1908-1953
4 feet

Retail business. Ledgers (1927-1929); receipts, invoices, and bank books (1920-

1921); legal papers (1920); correspondence (1930-1943); and blueprints (1920), all concerning the Keller-Clarke Seed Store in Shawnee, Oklahoma, together with reports (n.d.) of Oklahoma agricultural colleges; typescripts (n.d.) of radio advertisements; and minutes (1908) of the Shawnee (Oklahoma) Fanciers Association.

Unpublished finding aid available.

Kennedy, John C. (1910-1993)   595
Papers 1906-1990
4 feet

Insurance executive. Correspondence (1957-1990); speeches (1959-1983); Democratic political campaign literature and memorabilia (1960-1980); scrapbooks (1938-1955); and newspaper clippings (1906-1993) relating to Kennedy's businesses and investments, his support of the Democratic Party in Oklahoma and nationally, his appointment as an alternate delegate to the U.S. mission to the United Nations, his service as a commissioner of the Oklahoma State Highway Department, and his travels in the U.S. and worldwide.

Unpublished finding aid available.

Kennedy, John Fitzgerald (1917-1963)   596
Printed materials 1963
.33 foot

Subject collection. Newspapers and news magazines (1963) published in the United States and the Federal Republic of Germany, regarding Kennedy's visit to West Germany, and West Berlin, in June, 1963, and his assassination in November, 1963. All items in this collection bear cover stories regarding, or are special editions devoted to, President Kennedy, and his death.

Kennedy, Kay Don   597
Records 1903
3 items

Collector. Three $500 bonds (1903) issued to fund the Oklahoma Territorial University, the Agricultural and Mechanical College, and the Normal School.

Kennedy, L. P.   598
Letter 1887
1 item

Clergyman. A letter (1887) from Judge Isaac C. Parker advising Kennedy as to the legality in Texas of marriages performed in Indian Territory.

Kerley, J. W.   599
Ledger 1903-1922
1 item

Physician. An account and prescription ledger (1903-1922) from Kerley's medical practice in Cordell, Oklahoma.

Kerr-McGee Corporation Collection 600
Printed material 1928-1978
.66 foot

Energy corporation. Photocopies and printed material (1928-1978) issued by the public relations department of the Kerr-McGee Corporation, including biographical information on Robert S. Kerr and Dean A. McGee; reports (1976-1977) to the Securities and Exchange Commission; reference material (n.d.) used for the report on drilling operations in the corporation's annual reports (1960-1966); chronologies of corporate history and general statistics (1962-1977); an index (1977) to the minutes of the board of trustees meetings; and clippings and press releases (1975-1977), including information on Karen Silkwood.

Kibbey, W. Beckford 601
Manuscript 1929
1 item

Rancher. A typewritten, ten-page, daily account (1929) of Kibbey's activities to defend his hacienda in northern Sonora, Mexico, against revolutionary forces and the counter demands of Mexican federal troops during a short-lived revolt in 1929.

Kibler, Nell 602
Papers 1828-1888
5 items

Collector. An oath of allegiance (1862) to the United States; a history (1863) of the Confederate Army's Dublin Provost Guard; a letter (1828) from an ancestor of Kibler regarding the hardships of life in Michigan Territory; and schoolbooks (1885-1888).

Kiebler, W. G. 603
Records 1920-1927
.10 foot

Physician. Five journals (1920-1927) recording patients' names and fees charged, from Kiebler's medical practice in Enid, Oklahoma, and a 1927 edition of *The Skeleton*, a yearbook from the training school for nurses in Enid, Oklahoma.

Kinder, George 604
Printed materials 1904-1950
2 items

Collector. A booklet (1904-1905) entitled *Souvenir*, listing the teacher and pupils of Mount Pleasant School in Blaine County, Oklahoma Territory; and one entrance ticket (1950) to the 1950 Sugar Bowl football game in New Orleans, Louisiana, at which the University of Oklahoma football team won its first national championship.

King, (Mrs.) A. J. 605
Papers 1856-1876
.10 foot

Collector. Typescripts of letters (1856-1865) by Abraham J. Seay, second governor of Oklahoma Territory, regarding the role of the American Party in Missouri, and Seay's experience and views regarding the Civil War; and a typed manuscript (1856-1876) regarding the history of Seay's parents and family.

King, Charles Francis Xavier (d. ca. 1981) 606
Papers 1960-1975
2 feet

Professor. Unpublished manuscripts (1951-1975) on western history themes including the Battle of the Washita in 1868, the establishment of Fort Gibson, Indian Territory, and its cemetery, and the westward migration of the Cherokees; and lecture notes (n.d.) used by King to teach American, European, and Russian history.

King, Donald 607
Papers 1897-1914
.25 foot

Collector. Issues of the *Colony Mercantile Company Store News* (1912-1914), an in-house newsletter of a retail store run by the King family and serving the Cheyenne-Arapaho reservation, plus an issue of the *Colony Courier* (1910); and three commencement and wedding invitations (1897-1910).

Kingfisher College Collection 608
Records 1894-1964
1 foot

College. Administrative records (1894-1964), including a report (1917) of the president; administrative correspondence (1921-1928); constitutions of the college (1895-1964); papers of the college's board of trustees; alumni ballots (1927) regarding the future of the college; and a certificate of amended incorporation. Also included are publications such as *The Halcyon*, a yearbook (1914), *The Kingfisher*, a newsletter (1903-1909), and the *Kingfisher College Bulletin* (1903-1921).

Kingsbury, Cyrus (1786-1870) 609
Records 1819-1869
1.50 feet

Missionary. Photocopies of the correspondence (1818-1869) and reports (1820-1859) of Cyrus Kingsbury, Presbyterian missionary among the Choctaw Indians, regarding the Choctaw removal to the Indian Territory, the Civil War, and slavery.

Unpublished finding aid available.

Kiowa County Historical Society Collection 610
Manuscripts 1911-1945
7 items

Historical society. Anonymous manuscripts (1911-1945) regarding crime and criminals, and specifically concerning Frank Nash, a bank robber and murderer from Hobart, Oklahoma.

Kirk, Betty (1904-1984) 611
Papers ca. 1940-1970
10 feet

Journalist. Manuscripts of articles; correspondence; research notes; and reprints (all ca. 1940-1970) used by Elizabeth Mahala Kirk Boyer, who wrote under the pen name, Betty Kirk, in researching her articles and books concerning U.S. politics, Mexico, and international relations.

Kirkpatrick, Albert J. 612
Papers ca. 1932-1968
.50 foot

Pianist. Musical score (n.d.) entitled "Grand River Suite," written for string orchestra by S. A. McReynolds, along with original compositions (1932-1968) and travel sketches and short stories (ca. 1963-1968) by Kirkpatrick. Also included are sound recordings (ca. 1990) of Kirkpatrick playing his compositions.

Klapps Drug Store Collection 613
Records 1901-1913
.10 foot

Pharmacy. Two books (n.d.) containing formulae for home remedies, and a poison and narcotics register (1901-1913) from Klapps Drugstore in Tecumseh, Oklahoma.

Kliewer, Heinrich 614
Papers 1892-1898
.10 foot

Government employee. Work reports (1892-1898) filed by Kliewer, a farmer employed by the Cheyenne-Arapaho Indian Agency, Darlington, Oklahoma Territory, to assist Indians in their agricultural activities. The reports include number of days worked, the number of Indians assisted, acres plowed, rods of fencing built or repaired, acres planted, houses improved or repaired, and the general condition of the Indians' stock and crops.

Knights Templar of Oklahoma Collection 615
Printed materials 1920-1934
.10 foot

Fraternal order. Official proceedings (1920-1934) of conclaves held by the Knights Templar of Oklahoma.

Kobel, Raleigh (1877-1951) 616
Printed material 1915-1952
.10 foot

Merchant. Clippings (1915-1951) concerning John F. Wheeler and his descendants, the history of Sallisaw, Oklahoma, and the Cherokee Nation.

Korn, Anna Lee Brosius (b. ca. 1870) 617
Papers 1927-1955
.10 foot

Club woman. A typescript of a lecture (n.d.) entitled "Progress and Development of Missouri Since 1860 from Gleanings Here and There," for presentation to the Missouri division of the United Daughters of the Confederacy; a yearbook (1927) published by the National Society, United States Daughters of 1812 of Oklahoma; and programs and clippings (1930-1955) concerning Korn and her club activities.

Kraettli, Emil Rudolph (1890-1979) 618
Papers 1900-1959
.33 foot

University administrator. Reports (1900-1928) of the University of Oklahoma Board of Regents; financial papers (1906-1915); faculty lists (1908-1913) of the university; and a letter (1933) from Oklahoma governor William H. Murray to Brig. Gen. Charles F. Barrett ordering guards posted at the University of Oklahoma football stadium.

Krugers, Albert 619
Records 1838-1903
4 items

Investor. Three deeds (1838, 1857) for land in Vermont, and one deed (1903) for land in Oklahoma City, Oklahoma Territory.

Kruis, Roland (b. 1923) 620
Poster 1931
1 item

Collector. A poster (1931) announcing a benefit performance by Will Rogers at the University of Oklahoma.

Ku Klux Klan Women Collection 621
Records 1923-1928
.66 foot

Social club. Official correspondence (1926-1928); membership lists (1924-1928);

minutes (1924-1928); booklets (1923-1928); songsheets (n.d.); flyers (n.d.); and memorabilia (1923-1928) from this Alfalfa County, Oklahoma, women's group.

Kuyrkendall, Louis C. (d. 1956)   622
Records 1853-1955
12 feet

Physician. General correspondence (1906-1955); examination reports (1924-1944) of injured Missouri, Kansas, and Texas Railroad Company employees; examination reports (1943-1950) prepared for the Oklahoma Department of Public Welfare; correspondence (1929-1950) regarding workers compensation cases; examination reports (1940-1949) for the Civil Aeronautics Administration; and daybooks and account ledgers (1920-1948) from Kuyrkendall's medical practice in McAlester, Oklahoma. Also included in the collection are reprints of articles authored by Kuyrkendall and a prescription book (1853) belonging to Kuyrkendall's grandfather.

Ladies Aid Society Collection   623
Records 1884-1913
.25 foot

Social organization. A ledger (1884-1913) showing expenditures, dues, and account balances of the Ladies Aid Society of Bismarck, North Dakota.

Lahman, Marion Sherwood (1872-1954)   624
Papers 1936-1950
.33 foot

Botanist. A manuscript (1950), with drawings, entitled "Some Cacti of Our Southwest" by Lahman; papers (1936) from the meetings of the Cactus and Succulent Society of Oklahoma City, Oklahoma; and paintings (1950) by Lahman of western wild flowers.

Lain, Everett S. (b. 1873)   625
Papers 1893-1952
.33 foot

Physician. A biography (1923) of Lain; a typescript of a speech (n.d.) by Lain to the Oklahoma State Medical Association; news clippings regarding medicine in Oklahoma; a patient accounts ledger (1900); and financial journals (1933, 1938) from Lain's medical practice. Also included in this collection is a publication of the Epworth Methodist Church of Oklahoma City, Oklahoma, entitled *The Epworth Spotlight*, and several articles which Lain wrote on herpes research, x-ray technology in Oklahoma, and skin diseases among Oklahoma Indians.

Lamb, Ellis   626
Records 1910-1915
.33 foot

Physician. Records (1910-1915), including ledgers, personal correspondence, and billing receipts from Lamb's medical practice in Clinton, Oklahoma.

Langsford, William (b. 1869) 627
Records 1899-1939
2.33 feet

Physician. Records (1899-1939), including daybooks, patient hospital records, prescriptions, and certificates and licenses, all relating to Langsford's medical practice in Oklahoma City, Oklahoma.

Lansden, J. B. (1877-1953) 628
Records 1913-1939
.66 foot

Physician. Six ledgers (1913-1939) recording patients and fees from Lansden's medical practice in Granite, Oklahoma.

Las Dos Americas Collection 629
Records 1940-1951
.10 foot

Social club. Minutes (1940-1951) and correspondence (1940-1951), in Spanish, of Las Dos Americas, the University of Oklahoma Spanish club.

Latty, James Monroe (1861-1937) 630
Papers 1898
3 items

Farmer. A letter (1898), with typescript copies, by James M. Latty of Muskogee, Indian Territory, to his brother in Idaho, describing his intention to move west so that his children would receive a better education.

Lawton, Sherman Paxton (1908-1971) 631
Papers 1927-1968
2 feet

Professor. Television scripts and publicity (1951-1959) for "The Open Window;" radio scripts (1953) for "Labor's Side of the News" and "Wake Up to Yesterday;" correspondence (1945-1961); manuscripts (ca. 1935-1960) of articles and short stories; curriculum material (1934-1960); and printed material (1927-1968) accumulated by Lawton, while a professor of communication at the University of Oklahoma.

Unpublished finding aid available.

Layton, Helen Elizabeth Blackert 632
Papers 1840-1916
.33 feet

Collector. A manuscript of *Pilgrims of the Plains* by Kate Smith Aplington, published in 1913; correspondence (1912-1914) concerning the publication of the book; a manuscript of "Life and Writings of Samuel A. Deming by his Brother" (1849); and newspaper clippings (1840-1916), all belonging to Helen Layton, niece of Kate Aplington.

Ledbetter, Eugene P. 633
Papers 1892-1952
2.33 feet

Attorney. Case files (1892-1952) of Ledbetter, an Oklahoma City, Oklahoma, attorney, concerning oil, gas, and railroad leases and stock; the payment of Oklahoma supreme court justices salaries (1933-1935); and the payment of a reward offered for the arrest of George "Machine Gun" Kelly (1934).

Unpublished finding aid available.

Ledbetter, Walter A. (b. 1863) 634
Papers 1914
3 items

Attorney. A copy of the contract, bond, and specifications (1914) for the Oklahoma state capitol building in Oklahoma City, Oklahoma.

Lee, Ottie 635
Papers ca. 1936-1947
.10 foot

Collector. Newspaper clippings (1936-1947) relating to R. C. "Crockett" Lee; a typescript (n.d.) of an article on Lee by J. J. McAlester, grandson of Col. J. J. McAlester; a list (n.d.) of officials of the Missouri, Kansas, and Texas Railroad; and correspondence (1939-1946) to and from Lee concerning Oklahoma and national politics.

LeFlore, Carrie 636
Papers 1886-1892
.10 foot

Housewife. Personal correspondence (1886-1892) with friends and family and reflecting her life as the wife of Basil LeFlore, a principal chief of the Choctaw Indians, along with expressions of condolence on the death of her husband.

Lenski, Lois (1893-1974) 637
Papers 1907-1972
9 feet

Author and illustrator. Manuscripts (1918-1971) of works by Lenski; original art work (1917-1939); and typescripts of speeches and articles (1932-1970) by Lenski; business and personal correspondence (1912-1972); biographical materials (1930-

1970) on Lenski, including a scrapbook compiled by Letha Barde; and information (1956-1972) concerning other Lois Lenski collections.

Unpublished finding aid available.

Leslie, Samuel B. (b. 1874) 638
Records 1906-1952
.10 foot

Physician. Correspondence (1906-1952) relating to Leslie's service with the Oklahoma State Board of Medical Examiners, the Oklahoma State Medical Association, and the American Medical Association, and examination questions (1939-1945) used by the State Board of Medical Examiners to certify Oklahoma physicians.

Letterhead Collection 639
Printed materials 1865-1919
.25 foot

Subject collection. Samples of official letterheads and envelopes printed for the territorial and state governments of Oklahoma, Indian Territory, cities and towns, businesses, and organizations, all selected as representative of the stationery style of their period.

Lewallen, Wesley P. (1862-1943) 640
Records 1904-1932
1 foot

Physician. Patient account ledgers (1904-1932) and a daybook (1926-1930) from Lewallen's medical practice in Canadian, Oklahoma.

Lewis, Powell K. (1879-1955) 641
Records 1901-1954
1 foot

Physician. Daybooks (1936-1952); ledgers (1924, 1937-1942); receipt books (1946-1954); personal financial and legal records (1921-1938); a pamphlet of medical formulae (1912); and a *Guide to First Year Laboratory Work* (1901), all from Lewis's medical practice in Sapulpa, Oklahoma.

Lewis, Walter E. 642
Papers 1920-1991
.10 foot

Amateur ornithologist. Two manuscripts (ca. 1920) about birds in northwest Oklahoma (panhandle area), eight letters between Walter E. Lewis and Margaret Nice (1922-1932); four letters between John Tomer and Wayne S. Lewis (1990-1991); and a pamphlet (n.d.) about Walter Lewis as a candidate for the office of Oklahoma state representative.

Liberty National Bank Collection 643
Records 1911-1930
24 feet

Bank. Financial records (1911-1930) including correspondence, general ledgers, a computation register, a distribution of expenses ledger, tellers cash books, and an insurance policy register from the Stockyards National Bank and Guaranty Bank, which were absorbed by the Liberty National Bank of Oklahoma City, Oklahoma.

Ligon, Mary Louise 644
Papers 1906-1925
7 items

Collector. A manuscript (n.d.) describing a saloon fight; a typescript (n.d.) entitled "Fundamental Principles of Plant Breeding," by Isaac Renfro; newspaper clippings (1925); and a permit (1906) issued to Elkins, Webster, and Bayleas to sell insurance in Indian Territory.

Lilley, (Mrs.) John B. 645
Diary 1842-1857
1 item

Missionary. A typescript of a diary (1842-1857) kept by the wife of John B. Lilley, a Presbyterian missionary to the Seminole Nation. The diary describes the Lilleys' arrival among the Seminoles, the hardships of living in Indian Territory, problems with slaves, friction between the Creeks and the Seminoles, Wild Cat's (Coocoochee) departure for Mexico, and tensions prior to the Civil War.

Lillie, Foress B. (1885-1926) 646
Papers 1872-1949
5 feet

Pharmacist. General correspondence (1887-1923); diaries (1886-1920); printed materials (ca. 1895-1934), including postcards, greeting cards, and magazines; scrapbooks (n.d.) regarding the history of Guthrie, Oklahoma; correspondence (1887-1889) relating to the passage of pharmacy laws in Oklahoma; a minute book (1889-1921) of the Oklahoma Territorial Board of Pharmacy; the constitution of the Oklahoma Pharmaceutical Association (1907); a report (1907) to the governor of Oklahoma on pharmacy in the state; and ledgers and correspondence (1887-1901) from Lillie's Drug Store, Guthrie, Oklahoma.

Unpublished finding aid available.

Lillie, Gordon William (1860-1942) 647
Papers 1911-1943
8.5 feet

Rancher and businessman. Mostly correspondence (1911-1943), but also including legal and financial papers, newspapers, and printed materials regarding Lillie and his ranching and business enterprises. The collection includes an autobiographical sketch and references to several Indian chiefs.

Unpublished finding aid available.

Lincoln County Medical Society Collection 648
Records 1904-1944
.10 foot

Professional organization. Society minute books (1904-1944) and correspondence (1928-1938) regarding the county medical Poor Fund and Cancer Committee, as well as society-sponsored proposals for improving medical care in Lincoln County, Oklahoma.

Lindsey, Newton Harvey (1870-1934) 649
Papers 1951
2 items

Physician. A biographical sketch (1951) of Lindsey's life and his contribution to Pauls Valley, Oklahoma, along with an article (1951) by Kathleen Lindsey on being a physician's wife.

Lindsey, Ray H. 650
Papers 1863-1864
.10 foot

Collector. Letters (1863-1864) written by Thomas G. Lindsey to his wife Laura during the Civil War, while serving with the Twenty-sixth Alabama Infantry Regiment in Virginia and Georgia.

Lininger, Herbert K. (d. 1953) 651
Papers 1621-1907
.10 foot

Collector. Deeds (1901-1907) issued in Oklahoma and Indian territories, and servant indentures (1621-1849) signed and issued in Great Britain.

Lions Club Collection 652
Records 1954-1955
.33 foot

Civic club. Membership and activity reports (1954-1955) and correspondence (1954-1955) with the local chapters of the Lions Clubs in district 3L which included southwestern Oklahoma.

Lions International Collection 653
Printed materials 1954-1955
.10 foot

Civic club. Copies of the *Lions Club Official Directory* (1954-1955).

Little, Jesse Samuel   654
Papers 1900-1930
.10 foot

Physician. Ledgers (1904); daybooks (1904-1908, 1930); and lecture notes, matriculation tickets, and lecture schedules (1900-1902) from Fort Worth University, all belonging to Little who practiced medicine in Minco, Oklahoma.

Litton, Gaston   655
Papers 1849-1987
9 feet

Archivist. Manuscripts and unpublished materials (1837-1940) relating to Douglas H. Johnston, governor of the Chickasaw Nation, the history of the Chickasaw and Choctaw Indian nations, and the enrollment of the Eastern Band of Cherokee Indians; lecture notes, class assignments and other materials (1950-1953) relating to courses Litton taught at the University of Oklahoma; radio scripts (1948-1949) from a program entitled "Great Men and Books" broadcast over WNAD, Norman, Oklahoma; and books, articles, and presentations (1955-1975) authored by Litton and relating to archival administration and librarianship in Latin America.

Unpublished finding aid available.

Livezey, William Edmund (b. 1903)   656
Papers 1932-1951
.66 foot

Professor. Letters (1932-1940) recommending senior students for admission to the University of Oklahoma President's Class; corrected manuscripts (n.d.) for *Mahan on Sea Power*, University of Oklahoma Press, 1947, and *The Philippines and the United States*, University of Oklahoma Press, 1951, the latter co-authored with Garel A. Grunder. The collection also includes correspondence and minutes (1939-1950) of the Oklahoma Memorial Union Board of Governors.

Locke, Victor M., Jr.   657
Papers 1900-1927
.10 foot

Indian chief. Typescript of newspaper articles (1900-1927) regarding the allotment of land in the Choctaw Nation and Locke's role in the Choctaw tribal government.

Logan County Road Record Collection   658
Records 1896-1905
.25 foot

County government. A ledger (1896-1905) containing applications for the construction of new roads in Logan County, Oklahoma Territory. Each application bears the applicant's justification for the road, along with a map plotting its exact course in relation to section, range, and township lines.

Logan, Leonard M. (1891-1974) 659
Papers 1925-1961
2.50 feet

University professor. Correspondence (1950-1958) with the U.S. Department of the Interior, congressmen, and the U.S. Bureau of Indian Affairs; reports (1956-1963); newspaper clippings (1925-1961) concerning Indian affairs; and manuscripts (1948) by Logan entitled "The Care of Chronic and Convalescent Patients in Oklahoma," and "Norman and Cleveland County, A Resource Inventory."

Unpublished finding aid available.

Long, Charles Alexander (b. 1881) 660
Manuscript 1905-1971
1 item

Minister. Memoirs (1971) of Charles Alexander Long, who graduated from the University of Oklahoma in 1905, and served as a Methodist missionary to Brazil, 1911-1952.

Longstreet, James 661
Letter 1837
1 item

Army officer. A letter (1837) from Maj. James Longstreet in San Antonio, Texas, to Maj. Gen. George Gibson in which Longstreet requests $10,000 to purchase supplies for an upcoming campaign against the Indians.

Lottinville, Savoie (1906-) 662
Papers 1953-1977
1.33 feet

Editor. Edited manuscripts of "Travels in North America, 1822-1824" by Paul Wilhelm, Duke of Württemburg, and "Life of George Bent" by George E. Hyde; articles (1964-1977) by Lottinville on George Milburn, the University of Oklahoma seal, and the Rhodes Legal History Collection; a letter (1966) from E. N. Roberts to R. L. Disney, relating the meeting in 1883 of John Roberts with a woman claiming to be Sacajawea; and a notarized statement (1953) of Frank M. Wyncoop concerning the Sand Creek Massacre.

Lovelace, Bryan W. 663
Papers 1850-1858
.10 foot

Collector. An original journal (1850) kept by Joseph R. Smith of New York, in which he recorded his experiences while on a surveying expedition through Indian

Territory. Entries detail the expedition's encounters with hostile Comanches, friendly Osages, severe weather, and hordes of insects. Also included in this collection are photocopies of a legislative document (1858) and a published article (1850), both regarding Creek Nation boundaries.

Loy-McDonald Clinic Collection 664
Records 1938-1948
1 foot

Medical facility. Laboratory test results (1938-1939); receipt books (1945-1948); and an equipment catalog (1939) from the Loy-McDonald Clinic in Pawhuska, Oklahoma.

Lucka, Emil (1877-1941) 665
Papers ca. 1939
.10 foot

Author. Typescripts of unpublished essays (ca. 1939) by Lucka, an Austrian author who sent them to literary colleagues in Oklahoma for safekeeping after he fell into disfavor with the German occupation forces in Austria.

Luster, Dewey William "Snorter" 666
Papers 1925-1980
1.33 feet

Coach. Correspondence (1941-1980); notebooks of football plays (1929-1945); and speech notes, reminiscences, and clippings (1925-1980) of Luster, the University of Oklahoma head football coach from 1941-1945.

Unpublished finding aid available.

Lyles, Harold L. 667
Printed materials 1912-1913
2 items

Collector. A pamphlet (1913) of speeches by representative Claude Weaver of Oklahoma in the House of Representatives, and a pamphlet (ca. 1912) containing excerpts of Weaver's speeches, including his closing speech in defense of William T. Peoples, charged with the murder of Eugene McLaughlin, at Peoples's trial in 1902.

Mackey, (Mrs.) Clifton Marion 668
Papers 1912-1977
1 foot

Housewife. Correspondence (1912-1977) between Alice Hurley Mackey and her brother, Patrick Hurley, and including Hurley's correspondence with Herbert Hoover, Henry Luce, Franklin D. Roosevelt and Madame Chiang Kai-shek, regarding Hurley's duties as the national attorney of the Choctaw Nation, a colonel in the American Expeditionary Forces, secretary of war during the Hoover administration, and as an ambassador during World War II. Also in this collection is a diploma (1912) issued to Alice Hurley by the Sisters of Saint Joseph Carondelet in Missouri.

Unpublished finding aid available.

Madsen, Christian C. (b. 1850) 669
Papers 1886-1967
6 items

Soldier. Enlistment papers (1872-1886) and two letters (1926-1937) of Christian Madsen, who served with the Fifth Cavalry, U.S. Army. The collection also contains a letter (1967) to Jack D. Haley from John A. Minion, who claims that Madsen was with the Seventh Cavalry at the time of the Custer Massacre.

Maguire, Grace Adeline King (1880-1951) 670
Printed materials 1885-1935
2 feet

University professor and librarian. Newspaper clippings (1885-1935) concerning Abraham Lincoln, and of Maguire's weekly article "Lights and Shadows;" books (1891-1927) and printed materials (1891-1906) relating to the Roman Catholic Church; a scrapbook (n.d.) of Maguire's; and documents (1902-1914) from the U.S. Land Office at Lawton, Oklahoma, along with correspondence (1917) concerning the James D. Maguire Store in Norman, Oklahoma.

Unpublished finding aid available.

Malone, E. L. 671
Papers 1904-1905
.10 foot

Oil field worker. Letters (1904-1905) from E. L. Malone to his wife and son, describing oil field life and Oklahoma Territory boom towns.

Manos, Grace C. 672
Letter 1953
1 item

Business manager. A copy of a letter (1953) from Fred G. Cowles, part owner of the *McAlester News-Capital*, to Walter C. Johnson, briefly describing the history and ownership of the *McAlester News-Capital*.

Marable, Mary Hays (1889-1959) 673
Papers 1935-1954
6 feet

Librarian. Research notes (n.d.) and biographical information used in Marable's book *Handbook of Oklahoma Writers* (1959), along with bibliographic materials (n.d) and newspaper clippings (1935-1954) of book reviews written by Marable and others.

March, (Mrs.) Abe   674
Printed materials 1951-1952
.33 foot

Collector. Material from Lawton, Oklahoma's fiftieth anniversary celebration, including a script (1951) for a pageant entitled "Neath August Sun"; a copy of "Lawton's Golden Anniversary, 1901-1951" (ca. 1951); copies of the *Lawton Constitution* (August, 1951); programs (1951-1952); and the yearbook (1952) of the Lawton Pioneer Club, Inc.

Marquart, Vida   675
Papers 1892-1895
4 items

Collector. Invitations (1892-1895) to attend the exercises of Knights Templar at Guthrie, Oklahoma Territory, and Oklahoma City, and the 1895 graduation exercises of the University of Oklahoma.

Marland, Ernest Whitworth (1871-1941)   676
Papers 1937-1938
3 items

Governor. A letter (1938) supporting Marland's campaign for election to the U.S. senate; a promotional card (1938) from his campaign; and a printed speech (1937) by Governor Marland to the Oklahoma legislature.

Marriott, Alice (1910-   )   677
Papers 1930-1968
21 feet

Anthropologist. Correspondence (1926-1961); manuscripts (n.d.) of Marriott's books and articles; research notes (n.d.); and printed materials (1930-1968) accumulated by Marriott in the course of her research for her numerous books and articles relating to Indians. Included in the collection are book-length manuscripts entitled "Maria, the Potter of San Ildefonso," "The Ten Grandmothers," "Indian Annie," and the "Valley Below."

Unpublished finding aid available.

Marriott, Sydney C.   678
Papers 1917-1941
.10 foot

Accountant. Programs (1927-1941) from conventions and meetings of the National Aid Life Association; one issue each of *The Highway Magazine* (1917) and *The*

N.A.L.A. News (1927); and a handwritten musical composition (n.d.) entitled *Oklahoma, I'm Coming Back to You.*

Marriott-Rachlin Collection 679
Papers 1963-1975
3 feet

Anthropologists. Correspondence (1963-1975); research materials (1963-1975); and manuscripts (n.d.) of Alice Marriott and Carol Rachlin accumulated during their collaboration on several essays and articles relating to Indian society, mythology, and peyotism.

Unpublished finding aid available.

Marrs, Frederica S. Dewey 680
Papers 1861-1912
.33 foot

Collector. Commissions, orders, and property reports (1881-1906) regarding Frederick Stanley Dewey's service as a contract surgeon, and as an assistant surgeon with the U.S. Army in the Philippines; correspondence (1898-1912) regarding a lawsuit over a land claim in Oklahoma Territory; matriculation cards and notices of examination results (1877-1879) from St. Louis (Missouri) Medical College; and a journal (1884), all belonging to Frederick S. Dewey. Also included are commissions, orders, property reports, and discharge papers (1861-1867) regarding George H. Dewey and his service as assistant surgeon with the Eleventh, and 109th Illinois Volunteer Infantry regiments.

Marrs, James Wyatt (ca. 1896-ca. 1963) 681
Papers ca. 1922-1963
31 feet

Professor. Manuscripts, galley proofs, reviews, and letters (ca. 1940-1960) accumulated by Marrs for his book *The Man on Your Back*; research material on social parasitism (1930-1963); and sociology class materials (1922-1963), including lecture notes and student term papers from classes taught by Marrs, a University of Oklahoma sociology professor, 1922-1963.

Martin, Cy (1919-1980) 682
Papers 1966-1975
2.33 feet

Author. Manuscripts (1968) of "Your Horoscope," children's stories, and books (1973-1975), all written by Martin; magazines (1966-1975), some containing stories by Martin; and biographical information on Cy Martin who wrote under the pen name of William Stillman Keezer.

Unpublished finding aid available.

Martin, Richard L. (b. 1847) 683
Papers 1860-1907
5 items

Rancher and postmaster. Two letter-size tablets containing rough drafts (1860-1907) of Martin's correspondence and a brief account of his experiences in Indian Territory during the Civil War. Some correspondence (1882-1907) concerns land allotment and Indian opposition to Oklahoma statehood.

Martin, Thomas Pugh, Jr. 684
Papers 1873-1952
1 foot

Banker. Programs of Oklahoma City businessmen's clubs, including the Oklahoma Club (1925-1931) and the Men's Dinner Club (1913-1914); a program of an Oklahoma City banquet honoring Gen. John J. Pershing (1920); currency issued by the Confederate States of America (1864) and the federal and state governments of Mexico (1915-1916); programs of the inaugurals of Oklahoma governors Lee Cruce (1911) and John C. Walton (1923); a manuscript (1933) by Martin regarding early telephone service in Marlow, Oklahoma; and showbills (1912-1920) of the Overholser Theatre in Oklahoma City, Oklahoma. Also in this collection are certificates of incorporation (1906-1909) of the Martin Mill and Elevator Company and posters (ca. 1925) advocating use of the new airmail service, the latter picturing the dirigible *Shenandoah*, an early touring car, and an early open-cockpit airplane.

Unpublished finding aid available.

Mason, Viola 685
Records 1902-1915
2 items

Collector. Two farm leases (1902-1915) establishing guardianship for lands owned by orphaned Seneca Indian children.

Masonic Lodge of Oklahoma Collection 686
Printed materials 1911-1936
.66 foot

Fraternal society. Copies (1911, 1925-1936) of the *Annual Proceedings* of the Grand (Masonic) Lodge of Oklahoma, and the constitution and code (1927) of the Masonic Lodge of Oklahoma.

Massad, Ernest L. (1908-1993) 687
Papers 1926-1990
9 feet

U.S. Army officer. Correspondence and supporting reports and documents (1933-1969) regarding Massad's military service in the U.S. Army, especially his command of the Ninety-fifth Training Division and his service as Deputy Assistant

Secretary of Defense for Reserve Affairs. The collection also includes correspondence and related papers (1929-1983) concerning his attendance and athletic career at the University of Oklahoma and his election to the Oklahoma Hall of Fame in 1971.

Unpublished finding aid available.

Matheney, James Curtis (b. 1880) 688
Papers 1908-1953
2 items

Physician. A letter (1953) by Matheney describing his experiences as a physician in Oklahoma between 1908 and 1953, and a news clipping (1951) regarding Matheney's retirement.

Matthews, Sam P. 689
Records 1890-1892
.10 foot

Collector. Four criminal-case docket books (1890-1892) from the court of A. D. Matthews, judge of the U.S. Circuit Court, Third Division, Indian Territory. The docket books record the names of defendants, the charges, the verdicts, and the penalties administered.

Maupin, Mary B. 690
Papers 1846-ca. 1930
.10 foot

Collector. Photocopies of Texas homestead documents (1867-1875); documents (1846-1857) concerning the estate of Lydia Loving, also from Texas; and photocopies of Guymon, Oklahoma, newspapers (ca. 1930).

Mayes, Joel Bryan (1833-1891) 691
Printed materials 1886-1905
.66 foot

Indian chief. Typescripts of newspaper articles and correspondence (1886-1905) of Mayes, a principal chief of the Cherokees, concerning tribal politics and the dissolution of tribal title to the Cherokee Strip.

Mayes, Samuel Houston (1845-1927) 692
Printed materials 1882-1928
.66 foot

Indian chief. Typescripts of newspaper articles (1882-1928) relating to Mayes's tenure as principal chief of the Cherokees and his negotiations with the Dawes Commission, the preparation of the tribal roll, and the assignment of lands.

McAlester Anniversary Incorporated Collection 693
Printed material 1949
2.33 feet

Civic organization. Programs, form letters, badges, circulars, and posters, plus nominations and voting coupons for the queen contest, all from McAlester Anniversary Incorporated, which sponsored this 1949 golden jubilee celebration in McAlester, Oklahoma.

Unpublished finding aid available.

McAlester, James Jackson (1842-1922) 694
Papers 1870-1908
58 feet

Businessman. Correspondence (1888-1908); store ledgers (1874-1903); daybooks (1870-1904); inventory books (n.d.); cash books (1889-1903); and supporting records from the J. J. McAlester Mercantile Company in McAlester, Indian Territory.

Unpublished finding aid available.

McBride, Earl D. (b. 1891) 695
Papers 1923-1954
.33 foot

Physician. Disability compensation reports (1950-1954); a copy of *Disability Evaluation* (1948) by McBride; and reprints (1923-1954) of articles by McBride, an orthopedic surgeon in Oklahoma City, Oklahoma.

McBride, Marguerite 696
Papers 1938-1943
.10 foot

Collector. Personal correspondence (1938-1943) to Marguerite McBride of Walters, Oklahoma, from Bob O'Brien, her New Zealand pen pal, plus memorabilia from New Zealand.

McCall, William (b. 1923) 697
Papers 1862-1863
2 items

Collector. Correspondence (1862-1863) from T. D. Horton, a Confederate soldier in the Civil War, to his wife and family, regarding life as a soldier and his participation in one of the Seven Days Battles at Malvern Hill (near Richmond), Virginia, a part of the 1862 Peninsular Campaign.

McCammon, J. D.   698
Papers ca. 1942
3 items

Journalist. Memoirs (n.d.) of McCammon's early career (ca. 1900) as a newspaper reporter; an article (n.d.) about Missouri judge Ernest S. Gantt; and a letter (1942) from Frank W. Taylor of the *Chicago Sun*, rejecting the article about Gantt.

McCarthy, Thomas Joseph   699
Papers 1937
6 items

Broadcaster. Newspaper clippings from McCarthy's column in *The Washington Post* regarding his travels to, and observations of life in, the former mining boomtowns of Deadwood, and Lead, South Dakota.

Eugene McCarthy Campaign Collection   700
Papers 1968
.66 foot

Political campaign organization. Correspondence, press releases and speeches, position papers, clippings, and other campaign material (all 1968), concerning Eugene McCarthy's 1968 campaign to gain the Democratic presidential nomination, and particularly concerning the organization of the Oklahoma McCarthy for President Committee and the Oklahoma State Democratic Convention.

McCarville, Mike   701
Papers 1957-1965
7 items

Author. A manuscript account (n.d.) of a 1909 lynching in Ada, Oklahoma, written by McCarville; a copy (1957) of Oklahoma City's charter; a program (1965) for a dinner at the John Fitzgerald Kennedy Library in Oklahoma City, Oklahoma; and four pieces (n.d.) of U.S. military payment script.

McClure, Tecumseh A. (b. 1830)   702
Printed material 1894
1 item

Indian chief. A typescript of a newspaper article (1894) regarding McClure's call for a special session of the Chickasaw legislature to debate the Dawes Commission proposals for the allotment of Chickasaw lands.

McClure, William L. (1896-1930) and William C. McClure (1910-1953)   703
Papers 1860-1954
3 feet

Physicians. Correspondence (1860-1954); class notes (1912-1936); case histories (1937); annuals, diplomas and certificates (1912-1953); clippings (1914-1953); and medals and medical instruments, of W. L. McClure, a surgeon at Massachusetts General Hospital, and W. C. McClure, a faculty member at the University of Oklahoma medical school.

McCornack, Ruth (b. ca. 1892) 704
Printed materials 1910-1932
.10 foot

Collector. Newspaper clippings, booklets, event programs, and broadsides (1910-1912) all regarding student life at Kingfisher College, Kingfisher, Oklahoma; an issue (1932) of the *Kingfisher College Alumni News*; and a yearbook (1913-1914) published by the Chaminade Club for the women of Oklahoma City. The collection also includes two artifacts, an official emblem of Kingfisher College, and a mortar board worn by McCornack in the college's 1912 commencement ceremony.

McCoy, James Stacy (1834-1862) 705
Papers 1859-1863
.10 foot

Soldier. Correspondence (1861-1863) to A. M. McCoy from her husband, James Stacy McCoy, captain of Company B, Twenty-sixth Alabama Infantry Regiment, and from Thomas McCoy, B. F. Thompson, and R. G. Wright; and a sales contract (1859) for slaves, stock, and farm implements sold to James Stacy McCoy by Baronett McCoy.

McCurtain, D. C. (b. 1873) 706
Printed materials. 1899-1911
7 Items.

Indian statesman. Typescripts of newspaper articles (1899-1911) regarding McCurtain's views on schools, tribal government, and related issues confronting the Choctaw Nation.

McCurtain, Edmond (1842-1890) 707
Printed materials 1875-1901
.10 foot

Indian chief. Typescripts of McCurtain's annual messages (1884-1886) to the Choctaw Nation general council; letters (1875-1877) by McCurtain to newspapers regarding various issues, including railroad right-of-way and citizenship disputes, and an obituary (1890) of McCurtain.

McCurtain, Green (1848-1910) 708
Papers 1890-1916
14.50 feet

Indian chief. Correspondence (1890-1916) to and from McCurtain regarding Choctaw Nation railroads, administrative matters, politics, Choctaw Indian claims against the United States, and the issue of separate statehood for Indian Territory, including letters from the chiefs of the other major Indian tribes in the territory; maps (1876-1908) of railroad rights-of-way and towns in the Choctaw Nation; publications (1896-1913) by political parties and citizens groups in the Choctaw Nation regarding political and judicial events and issues; publications (1892-1916) of the U.S. government regarding mineral rights of the Choctaw Nation and Indian Territory; and McCurtain's personal expense accounts (1902-1910).

Unpublished finding aid available.

McCurtain, Jackson Frazier (1830-1885) 709
Printed materials 1875-1901
.10 foot

Indian chief. Typescripts of newspaper articles (1875-1901) regarding McCurtain and his State of the Choctaw Nation speeches (1881-1883) made before the general council while he was principal chief.

McIntosh County Medical Society Collection 710
Records 1906-1948
1 foot

Professional society. Minutes of meetings (1906-1910, 1922-1923, 1939, 1943-1948); correspondence (1923-1949); resolutions and speeches from the medical society's programs; and membership records (1921-1948), all from the McIntosh County (Oklahoma) Medical Society, along with copies of the Oklahoma State Medical Association constitution and by-laws, and the American Medical Association newsletter (1948).

McIntosh, Roley Cub (b. 1858) 711
Printed materials 1835-1928
.10 foot

Indian chief. Typescripts of a speech to the Comanche and Wichita nations (1835), and the Creek Nation (1898); of McIntosh's message to the Creek Nation (1898); of newspaper articles (1871-1907) regarding McIntosh; and a biographical sketch (1928) of McIntosh.

McKenzie, (Mr. and Mrs.) W. H. 712
Printed materials ca. 1920-1938
9 items

Collectors. Clippings from the *Lawton Constitution* (1932) and the *Oklahoma News* (1938); Mother's Day cards (n.d.); a beauty-shop price list (1933); and postcard scenes (ca. 1920) of Lawton, Oklahoma.

McKeown, Roy J. (b. 1902) 713
Manuscript n.d.
1 item

Editor. A typescript (n.d.) entitled "Life History of Joannah Floyd Reed and William J. Reed, As Told by Joannah Floyd Reed," recounting their settling in Ada, Oklahoma, which was named after their eldest daughter, and where they operated several businesses.

McKinney, Raymond   714
Album ca. 1946
1 item

Collector. A Japanese picture album (ca. 1946) of World War II battle scenes in the Pacific Theater, with the text in Japanese.

McKinney, Thompson   715
Printed materials 1886-1887
2 items

Indian chief. Typescripts of two newspaper articles (1886-1887), one is McKinney's inaugural address as principal chief of the Choctaws and the other is an editorial on his handling of Choctaw Nation affairs.

McKinney, William H.   716
Manuscript 1878
1 item

Poet. A poem (1878) by McKinney written in the Choctaw language and entitled *Iti Hishi Yama Isht Chit Haya Va Lihohe* or *A Leaf That Reminds Me of Thee*. An English translation is included.

McLain, Raymond Stallings (1890-1954)   717
Papers 1920-1954
17.33 feet

U.S. Army officer. Correspondence (1929-1954) concerning McLain's personal and business affairs; orders, memoranda, reports (1920-1937), and correspondence (1939-1940) from McLain's service with the Oklahoma National Guard; speeches (1947-1954) made by McLain as Chief of Information for the U.S. Army, and as a member of the National Security Training Commission; a typescript account (n.d.) by McLain of his participation as commander of the Forty-fifth Division artillery in the Allied invasion of Sicily during World War II; and a typescript account (n.d) by McLain of the Forty-fifth Division artillery's role in the Battle of the Aisne (1918) in World War I.

McMurray, John Frank   718
Printed materials 1898-1927
.50 foot

Lawyer. Published court records (1898-1926) and correspondence (1900-1927) regarding McMurray's suit against the Choctaw and Chickasaw nations for expenses and legal fees incurred in McMurray's successful representation of Choctaw and Chickasaw Indians in a lawsuit regarding taxation of Indian lands.

McPhaul, Thomas C. 719
Records 1927-1936
2 items

Physician. Opium orders (1927) and a daybook (1935-1936) from McPhaul's Muskogee, Oklahoma, medical practice.

McReynolds, Edwin C. (1890-1967) 720
Papers ca. 1930-1967
13 feet

Professor. Correspondence (1945-1965); research notes on the southern United States, the Civil War, Missouri, and Oklahoma; manuscripts (1930-1967) of history-related books and articles; clippings and printed material (1963-1965) on President John F. Kennedy, and on McReynolds, a University of Oklahoma history professor from 1943 to 1960.

Medford Progress Club Collection 721
Records 1931-1988
2 feet

Social organization. Minutes (1931-1946); annual reports (1934-1952); yearbooks (1931-1988); correspondence (1939-1951); scrapbooks (1931-1950); and clippings (1928-1950) from the Medford (Oklahoma) Progress Club.

Medicine Shows Collection 722
Printed materials 1887-1925
.25 foot

Subject collection. Correspondence and speeches (1911-1927); recipes for patent medicines, permanent waving solutions, and cleaning solutions; and advertisements (1887-1925) for patent medicines.

Memminger, Charles B. 723
Printed materials 1913-1914
8 items

Collector. Programs and invitations (1913-1914) for University of Oklahoma social events.

Menton, John William (d. 1928) 724
Papers 1903-1915
.10 foot

Businessman. Tax receipts (1903-1908); mortgages and stock certificates (1912-

1923); and patents and deeds (1906-1915) of Menton, a Lehigh, Oklahoma, businessman.

Merrill, Maurice 725
Papers ca. 1903-1975
24.66 feet

Attorney. Correspondence (1903-1975) of Merrill; class notes (n.d.) taken by Maurice and Orpha Merrill; printed material, including copies of the *Phi Beta Kappa Key* (1911-1918), the *Supreme Court Reporter* (1964-1975), and *Proceedings* (1959-1975) of the National Conference of Commissioners of Uniform State Law.

Merriott, C. L. 726
Ledger 1937-1941
1 item

Merchant. An accounts ledger (1937-1941) from Merriott's Dry Goods Company in Walters, Oklahoma.

Mertes, John E. 727
Papers n.d.
.10 foot

A copy book (n.d.) kept by Mertes while a student at the University of Oklahoma, mostly containing biographical sketches of prominent literary figures.

Messenger, Eugene Fields (1866-1957) 728
Papers 1866-1957
2 items

Constitutional convention delegate. A typescript of Messenger's memoirs (1866-1957) detailing his role in the Oklahoma Constitutional Convention and the struggle to designate Holdenville, Oklahoma, as the county seat of Hughes County, and a newspaper obituary (1957) of Messenger.

Meyer, William (1875-1956) and Apelona Meyer (b. 1883) 729
Papers 1852-1967
5 feet

Businessman and collector. Personal correspondence (1940-1965) of Apelona Meyer; certificates and awards (1882-1931) of William Meyer; greeting cards (1930-1960); travel pamphlets and brochures (1930-1960); and other printed materials (1914-1967) relating to U.S. society, and social organization in Cuba, including invitations; programs; newspapers; and service records (1852-1893) of Spanish Army soldiers in Cuba.

Unpublished finding aid available.

Miami Lumber Company Collection 730
Records 1911-1915
3 items

Retail business. Two account ledgers (1911) and one estimate ledger (1915) from the Miami (Oklahoma) Lumber Company.

Miami, Oklahoma, Municipal Records Collection 731
Ledger 1918-1920
1 item

Municipality. A daily balance ledger (1918-1920) for the assets of the city of Miami, Oklahoma.

Micco, Hulbutta (ca. 1835-1905) 732
Printed materials 1898-1905
.10 foot

Indian chief. Typescripts of newspaper articles (1898-1905) regarding the Seminole Nation, and Hulbutta Micco, who was the last regularly elected principal chief of the Seminoles before statehood.

Midkiff, Charles F. 733
Records 1899-1917
3 items

Collector. Tax receipts, and a permit (1899-1917) issued by the Chickasaw Nation to Midkiff, a non-Indian, as permission to live in Indian Territory, and for the payment of special taxes.

Milbourn, Dolly 734
Papers 1915
2 items

Collector. Two account books (1915) from George F. Milbourn's grain business in Fairland, Oklahoma.

Milburn, George (1906-1966) 735
Papers 1912-1966
1.33 feet

Author. Correspondence (1912-1966), research notes, and manuscripts of articles (1931-1957) by Milburn; Little Blue Books (1926-1927) written by Milburn; periodicals (1929-1954) which include articles by Milburn; and clippings (1936-1966) concerning Milburn, a writer and native of Coweta, Oklahoma.

Mary Clarke Miley Foundation Collection 736
Printed materials 1900-1980
1 foot

Private foundation. Two scrapbooks (1900-1980) with clippings, programs, and photographs concerning Mary Clarke Miley, her career as a pianist, and the foundation she established.

Miller Brothers 101 Ranch Collection 737
Records 1908-1932
39.66 feet

Ranch. General correspondence (1917-1935) and financial records (1923-1924) from the Miller Brothers 101 Ranch in Marland, Oklahoma; plus general correspondence (1908-1932); legal papers and contracts (1908-1932); route schedules (1910-1929); and scrapbooks (1908-1926) from the Miller Brothers 101 Ranch Wild West Show.

Unpublished finding aid available.

Miller, Florence Graves 738
Papers 1904-1968
4 feet

Professor. Correspondence (1942-1945) from former Eastern Oklahoma A & M College students serving in the armed forces during World War II; journals (1904-1950) recounting Miller's early experiences as an educator, first in Mississippi, and, later, in Oklahoma; teaching materials (n.d.); and clippings, poems, quotations, and sermons (1935-1968).

Unpublished finding aid available.

Miller, Floyd C. (b. 1912) 739
Papers ca. 1968
.33 foot

Author. Corrected manuscripts and galley proofs of Miller's book *Bill Tilghman: Marshal of the Last Frontier*, published in 1968.

Miller, G. R. 740
Papers 1908-1936
.10 foot

Collector. Two account ledgers (1908-1920) from a Lawton, Oklahoma, business which sold goods primarily to Kiowa and Comanche Indians. The collection also contains a copy of the Comanche constitution (1936), and lists (1914-1915) of eligible Comanche voters and members of the Kiowa and Comanche tribes.

Miller, John Sinclaire (1876-1936) 741
Papers 1938
2 items

Physician. Miller's biographical data sheet (n.d.) from the Oklahoma State Medical

Society, and a clipping (1938) concerning the founding of the Choctaw (Oklahoma) Medical Society of which Miller was a founding member in 1905.

Miller, Lillie Kate (b. ca. 1882) 742
Papers 1900-1904
.33 foot

Student. Class notebooks (1900-1904) kept by Miller while attending the University of Oklahoma; Miller's diploma (1904) from the University of Oklahoma; and a cookbook (1910) entitled *Home Helps: A Pure Food Cook Book*.

Miller, Robert L. 743
Papers 1960-1975
4 feet

University employee. Correspondence (1963-1975); reports (1962-1975); and printed materials (1960-1975) relating to Indian rights and Indian education, accumulated by Miller during his tenure as director of the Indian Education Center at the University of Oklahoma's American Indian Institute.

Miller, Stephen 744
Printed material 1942-1944
.10 foot

Collector. Copies of ships' newsletters and military newspapers entitled *Patrol* (1944), the *Midway Mirror* (1944), the *Fulton Bow Plane* (1942-1944), the *Fulton Flotsam* (1944), *History of the U.S.S. Caelum* (AK-106 (ca. 1945), and a *Resume of Shanghai* (n.d.) prepared for the crew of U.S.S. *Caelum*.

Milsten, David Randolph 745
Printed material 1938
1 item

Attorney. A copy of Milsten's *Howdy Folks* (1938), the official Will Rogers poem.

Miner, Frederick William 746
Papers 1830-1947
1 foot

Attorney. Correspondence (1830-1947); legal documents concerning land (1860-1940); and school material (ca. 1880) of Miner, who moved from Virginia to Texas in 1859, and of his daughter, May Miner Dorchester.

Mitchell, (Mrs.) Alfred 747
Printed materials 1895-1910
1 foot

Collector. Typescripts of articles (1895-1910) and poems (1901-1907) written by the Creek Indian poet Alex Posey. The articles include information on Posey's actions while he was a member of the Dawes Commission, the opposition to allotment by the Snake Clan of Creek Indians, and Creek Indian opposition to Oklahoma statehood.

Mitchell, Robert Thurston 748
Papers 1937-1951
.10 foot

Collector. Memoirs (n.d.) of Robert L. Mitchell, a Vinita, Oklahoma, physician; correspondence (1938-1951) concerning the Mitchell family genealogy; newspaper clippings (1946-1951); research notes and materials relating to the Cherokee Nation, missions, education, roads, and schools in Indian Territory; and a typescript of an interview (1937) conducted by James S. Buchanan with Stanley A. Clark.

Mitchell, Sam W. 749
Papers 1899-1939
7 items

Mine worker. Contracts (1903-1939); a permit (1902); and leases (1899), all relating to the coal industry near McAlester, Oklahoma; plus a "Coal Mine Workmen's Compensation and Employers Liability Policy" (1922).

Mixon, A. M. (d. 1951) 750
Records 1914-1951
.25 foot

Physician. Account books (1914-1915, 1920); two issues of the *Oklahoma Cancer Bulletin* (n.d.); an anatomy chart (n.d.); and accounts (1951) turned over to the Interstate Reclamation Bureau for collection, all from Mixon's medical practice in Spiro, Oklahoma.

Montezuma, Carlos (1858-1923) 751
Printed materials 1921-1923
5 items

Physician. Two pamphlets by Montezuma proposing the abolition of the U.S. Indian Service and entitled *Let My People Go* (1915) and *Abolish the Indian Bureau* (n.d.); two issues of a newsletter (1921-1922) by Montezuma entitled *Wassaja: Freedom's Signal for the Indian*, and a pamphlet-length obituary (1923) of Montezuma.

Montgomery, Merle Aline (b. 1904) 752
Papers 1960-1978
2 feet

Musician. Subject files (1960-1978), including correspondence, clippings, programs, and newsletters arranged by state, from Montgomery's association with the National Federation of Music Clubs, both as president and as their representative to the United Nations.

Moore, Ercelle O'Brien Davis (b. 1903) 753
Papers 1947-1952
.33 foot

Author. Memoirs (n.d.) of Ercelle Moore; copies of journals (1947, 1975, 1982) with stories and poems by Moore; a teleplay set in Oklahoma, and entitled "Christmas at Crossroads" by Moore; and correspondence (1977) with Lawrence Kimble concerning the teleplay, along with a copy of a screenplay (1975) by James McDonald and Robert Gerlach, written for the *Mary Tyler Moore Show* and entitled "The Seminar."

Moore, Ethel and Chauncey O. Moore 754
Manuscript n.d.
1 item

Compilers. A manuscript (n.d.) entitled "Ballads and Songs of Oklahoma." An accompanying Ethel and Chauncey Moore Collection of tapes (n.d.) of American, British, and Scotch folk-songs recorded throughout Oklahoma is also in the Western History Collections.

Moore, Jessie Elizabeth Randolph (1871-1956) 755
Papers 1916-1930
6.66 feet

Court clerk. Correspondence (1927-1930) to and from Moore as clerk of the Oklahoma Criminal Court of Appeals, and clerk of the Oklahoma Supreme Court; campaign material (1926-1930); including correspondence concerning Moore's campaign for election and re-election as court clerk; personal correspondence (1926); briefs (1916-1921) filed in the state supreme court while Moore was deputy clerk; and clippings (1926-1936) concerning Oklahoma history.

Moore, John D. (b. 1886) 756
Papers 1907-1955
3 items

Physician. A biographical data sheet (1955); a reminiscence (n.d.) of his first summer of medical practice at Swink, Indian Territory, in 1907; and Moore's license (1907) to practice medicine in Indian Territory.

Moore, John H. (1939-) 757
Papers 1880-1985
16 feet

Professor. Photocopies of field notes (1933) compiled by Fred Eggan during his studies of Cheyenne and Arapaho Indian kinship, bands, societies, marriage, genealogy, ceremonies, child care, and social customs; U.S. census coding sheets (1880, 1900); Cheyenne and Arapaho Indian censuses (1888-1977); computer printouts showing Cheyenne-Arapaho allotments, census data, and kinship analyses (n.d.); printed materials and copies of records (1867-1982) relating to Northern

Cheyenne Indians; printed material and copies of records (1864-1981) relating to Sand Creek Cheyenne Indians; copies of Cheyenne Indian probate records (1920s); and grant-related records (1975-1985).

Unpublished finding aid available.

Moore, Louise Beard 758
Papers 1935-1984
7 feet

Journalist and college professor. Correspondence and subject files (1935-1984) kept by Moore while supervisor of the *Oklahoma Daily*, the University of Oklahoma student newspaper, and University of Oklahoma yearbook *The Sooner*; correspondence (1968-1971) regarding the Oklahoma Memorial Association and Oklahoma Hall of Fame; Moore's classroom teaching files (1957-1972); manuscript copies of poetry by Kenneth C. Kaufman entitled "Level Land," and volumes 1-3 of "Oklahoma Biographs."

Unpublished finding aid available.

Moore, Robb 759
Papers 1914-1949
.10 foot

Collector. Typewritten manuscripts (ca. 1949) by Ora Padgett entitled "Thirty-two Years in the U.S. Indian Service," and "The American Reservation," both regarding his experiences in the Indian Service.

Mooreland Security State Bank Collection 760
Records 1900-1920
11 feet

Bank. Financial records (1900-1920), including daily balance ledgers, account ledgers, and individual account ledgers, from the Security State Bank in Mooreland, Oklahoma.

Moorhead, Max Leon (b. 1914) 761
Papers 1600-1976
18 feet

Historian. Correspondence (1962-1976); manuscripts (1960s); microfilmed and photocopied documents (1730-1790); research notes (n.d.); lectures (n.d.); student reports (n.d.); student research papers (n.d.); and printed materials (1853-1975), including book reviews and reprints, all relating to Moorhead's teaching of Latin American history at the University of Oklahoma, and to his publications about Jacobo de Ugarte, the presidio, other Spanish colonial institutions in the southwest, and the Indians of Mexico and the southwestern United States.

Unpublished finding aid available.

Moorman, Lewis Jefferson (1875-1954) 762
Papers 1909-1953
1 foot

Physician. Typescripts of oral history interviews (1936-1937) conducted during the Indian-Pioneer Oral History Project; correspondence (1924-1953) concerning real estate transactions, Moorman's research on tuberculosis and Indian health, and other aspects of his medical career, including connections with the University of Oklahoma School of Medicine; and a stock certificate (1909) from Epworth College of Medicine in Oklahoma City, Oklahoma.

Mootz, Herman Edwin 763
Printed materials 1932-1944
6 items

Author. Two brochures (n.d.) promoting Mootz's books; two letters, one (1937) to Grace E. Ray from Grace V. Mootz, and one (1944) to Grace V. Mootz from Grace E. Ray; and two clippings (1932-1935) concerning Mootz.

Morford, Robert Boyd (b. 1876) 764
Papers 1909-1940
2 feet

Real estate agent. Business correspondence (1909-1929) concerning Morford's real estate business and the development of a cotton mill in Lawton, Oklahoma; political correspondence (1916-1929) with Senator John W. Harreld of Oklahoma, and others; Republican Party campaign literature (1936, 1940); and clippings (1913-1940).

Morgan, Clyde (b. 1886) 765
Printed materials 1899-1943
.10 foot

Collector. Newspaper clippings (1937-1938); bulletins (1936); a membership roster (n.d.); an annual reunion event program (1943) and a booklet about the U.S. Army Thirty-third Infantry Association, a veterans organization composed of members of the Thirty-third Infantry, who served in the Philippines and which had a majority of its members from Oklahoma Territory.

Morgan, (Mrs.) Lawrence Nelson 766
Papers 1837-1925
.10 foot

Collector. Photocopies of correspondence (1865-1866) from John N. Edwards, a major in the Confederate Army who emigrated to Mexico after the Civil War, to family members describing conditions in Mexico; a newspaper article (1925) about Edwards; and a copy of a treaty (1837) between the United States and the Sac and Fox Indians.

Morgan, Robert J. 767
Records 1894-1989
.33 foot

Collector. Two bound volumes (1894-1922) of handwritten minutes and reports of the trustees of Kingfisher College, Kingfisher, Oklahoma, as well as a copy of an historical newspaper article (1989) regarding Kingfisher College.

Morris, John Wesley (1907-1982) 768
Papers 1864-1982
6.66 feet

Geographer. Correspondence (1939-1982); papers (1942-1956) concerning Morris's military service in the U. S. Navy and in the U. S. Army Reserve; certificates and diplomas (1864-1982); account books (1962-1969); and manuscripts, research notes, correspondence, and contracts (ca. 1950-1982) relating to books and articles written by Morris, a University of Oklahoma geography professor.

Morrison, G. A. (1853-1925) 769
Manuscript 1912
1 item

Collector. A manuscript (1912) of an address entitled "Our Opportunity to Work Among the Negro," by Mrs. G. A. Morrison, concerning opportunities to provide education and religious training for the Afro-American population of Poteau, Oklahoma.

Morrison, W. D. and James Morrison 770
Papers 1840-1920
8 feet

Historians. Research notes and related materials (1840-1920) many concerning Choctaw and Chickasaw tribal politics, allotment of lands, and Indian participation in the Civil War, gathered by the Morrisons for the purpose of writing a history of Bryan County, Oklahoma.

Morrow, John A. (b. 1875) 771
Papers 1953-1954
2 items

Physician. Memoirs (1954) of Morrow, recounting his early medical practice (1899-1912) in Indian Territory, and biographical newspaper clippings (1953).

Mosby, George Waldo (1875-1959) 772
Ledger 1913-1941
1 item

Businessman. A ledger (1913-1941) recording mortgages issued by the Mosby and Swartz Real Estate and Insurance Company of Frederick, Oklahoma.

Moseley, John Ohleyer 773
Papers 1931-1949
.50 foot

Professor. Notes (1931-1949) on Roman law and the decline of Greco-Roman civilization, including notes (1931) for a class on Roman law taught at the University of Oklahoma by Moseley, and a scrapbook of correspondence (1935) concerning Moseley's assumption of the presidency of Central State Teachers College in Edmond, Oklahoma.

Mosely, Palmer S. (1851-1908) 774
Printed materials 1894-1904
.10 foot

Indian chief. Typescripts of newspaper articles (1894-1904) concerning negotiations with the Dawes Commission and the allotment of Chickasaw Indian lands during Mosely's two terms, 1894-1896 and 1902-1904, as governor of the Chickasaw Nation.

Mountain View Twentieth-Century Club Collection 775
Records 1904-1988
1.66 feet

Civic organization. Correspondence (1913-1946); minutes (1904-1951); account books (1903-1915); minutes of the Round Table Section (1904-1907); program calendars (1928-1950); yearbooks (1904-1988); clippings (1956-1978); and copies of *History of Mountain View* (1970), from the Mountain View (Oklahoma) Twentieth-Century Club.

Mueller, Gustav Emil (b. 1898) 776
Papers 1914-1959
3 feet

University professor. Manuscripts (1945-1968) of Mueller's published and unpublished works in English and German, including philosophical treatises, a novel, a play, and poems; notes (1938-1963) from his philosophy classes; and newspaper clippings (1914-1942) of book reviews and other articles written by Mueller and others.

Unpublished finding aid available.

Muldrow, Henry Lowndes, Jr. (b. ca. 1905) 777
Papers 1857-1898
.66 foot

Collector. Correspondence (1857-1889) between Robert Muldrow, his wife, Annie Oliver Muldrow, and their children; and a journal (1898) of Henry Lowndes Muldrow Sr.'s expedition to Alaska.

Mullen Coal Company Collection 778
Records 1900-1946
11.33 feet

Mining company. Correspondence (1902-1946); monthly account ledgers (1907-1945); payroll records (1931-1945); notebooks of production costs (1940-1943); bank statements (1909-1946); and bills and receipts (1900-1948) from the Mullen Coal Company, near McAlester, Oklahoma.

Unpublished finding aid available.

Munger, William Houston (1852-1926) 779
Records 1905-1941
.66 foot

Merchant. Account books (1906-1926); a letter book of outgoing correspondence (1917-1919); a record of funerals (1915-1921) from the W. H. Munger Hardware, Furniture & Undertaking Store in Watonga, Oklahoma; and a scrapbook (1905-1941) containing letters, clippings, programs, menus, and souvenirs collected by Munger's son, Reuben Bates Munger.

Munn, Bertha M. B. 780
Hymnal ca. 1860
1 item

Collector. A photocopy of a manuscript hymnal (ca. 1860) written in the Wyandotte (Huron) Indian language and used in mission churches before the Wyandotte removal to Oklahoma.

Murphey and Noffsinger Collection 781
Records ca. 1910-1935
.33 foot

Law firm. Legal papers (ca. 1910-1935), including court orders, appearance bonds, and arrest warrants from the law firms of Hutchings, Murphey, and German, and of Murphey and Noffsinger, in Muskogee, Oklahoma.

Murphy, William Albert Patrick (1872-1952) 782
Papers 1896-1952
.33 foot

State labor commissioner. Correspondence (1936-1947), including postcards (1907-1910) regarding family matters, Murphy's record as state commissioner of labor, and his retirement from that office; certificates (1896-1939) appointing Murphy a U.S. deputy marshal in Oklahoma Territory, incorporating the Oklahoma Association for Old Age Security, Inc., and nominating Murphy for the office of commissioner of labor; news clippings (1933-1950) regarding Murphy, and state and national labor concerns; cards (1935-1950) certifying Murphy's membership in fraternal organizations and from Murphy's re-election campaign; publications (1936-

1947), including booklets regarding national labor affairs; a campaign poster (ca. 1940) printed by the Democratic Party of Oklahoma; pocket ledgers (1907) containing names and addresses, as well as a list of delegates from Oklahoma and Indian territories attending an unidentified conference in 1907; and a funeral register (1952) signed by friends paying last respects to Murphy after his death.

Murray, Burbank (1911-1984) 783
Papers 1928-1974
1 foot

Engineer. Correspondence received by Murray from friends and relatives, including his mother, Alice (1931-1938) and father, William H. Murray (1932-1952). Also included is correspondence from Murray's brothers, Massena, Billy, and Johnston, and from his sister, Jean. The correspondence refers to Murray family affairs, the term of Oklahoma governor W. H. Murray, the family's participation in the Bolivia colony, and W. H. Murray's views regarding Oklahoma, politicians, World War II, the future of the United States and Mexico, and family members, including Burbank Murray.

Murray, Frankie Colbert (b. ca. 1900) 784
Papers 1924-1985
1.33 feet

Collector. Correspondence (1927-1980) regarding William Henry Murray, Sr., governor of Oklahoma 1931-1935, Johnston Murray, governor of Oklahoma, 1951-1955, Burbank Murray, Massena Bancroft Murray, and Frankie Colbert, Mrs. Massena B. Murray; printed material (1924-1950) regarding the Democratic Party; and clippings (1950-1985) regarding William H. Murray and Johnston Murray.

Murray, Johnston (1902-1974) 785
Papers 1950-1955
50 feet

Governor of Oklahoma. Personal papers (1950-1955), including correspondence, reports, publications, sound recordings, filmstrips, posters, and scrapbooks reflecting Murray's gubernatorial administration (1951-1955), and the affairs of state government during those years. Also included are materials from Murray's gubernatorial political campaign of 1950.

Murrow, Joseph Samuel (1835-1930) 786
Papers 1894-1928
.33 foot

Missionary. Legal documents and papers (1894-1928) relating to J. S. Murrow, his home and school for Indian orphans, and Bacone College. The collection also includes minutes and proceedings (1916-1918) of the Indian Missionary Association, and programs (1912-1921) for meetings of the Deacons and Missionaries Institute of the Cheyenne-Arapaho Baptist churches and of the Oklahoma Indian Baptist Association.

Mushulatubbee (d. ca. 1836) 787
Speech 1835
1 item

Indian chief. A typescript of a speech (1835) by Mushulatubbee regarding peace between the Choctaw Indians and neighboring tribes to the west.

Muzzy, W. J. 788
Ledger 1936-1937
1 item

Physician. A daybook (1936-1937) recording laboratory test results from the El Reno (Oklahoma) Sanitarium.

Nance, James Clark, Jr. (b. 1893) 789
Records 1911-1961
5.66 feet

Legislator. Transcripts of testimony (1922-1927); district court clerk reports (1911-1920); legislative committee reports (1956-1959); and legislative bills (1959) regarding prohibition in Oklahoma, and calls for its repeal in 1959.

Unpublished finding aid available.

National Research Council Collection 790
Records 1933-1947
.33 foot

Scientific organization. Correspondence (1933-1947); and reports (1933-1947), produced by the National Research Council's committee on the ecology of grasslands. These materials reflect the committee's work toward establishing conservation measures for the remaining virgin grasslands in the United States.

Neal, Henry 791
Records 1895-1964
.66 foot

Postmaster. A rural mail carrier's registration book (n.d.); registers of money orders issued (1906, 1910); records of registered matter (1908-1910); and related material from the Wanette, Oklahoma, post office, plus a scrapbook (1936-1964) outlining the career of Henry Neal, Wanette, Oklahoma, postmaster from 1936 to 1964.

Nelson, George (1870-1944) 792
Papers 1908-1944
1 foot

Interpreter. Personal correspondence (1912-1943); land records (1908-1929) for allotments in the Choctaw and Chickasaw nations; lists (1939-1940) of allotments available for coal leases; files (1933) on government aid given to destitute Indians; and a catechism (n.d.) written in the Choctaw Indian language.

New York Mutual Life Insurance Company Collection 793
Radio scripts ca. 1953
.10 foot

Insurance company. A series of fourteen radio scripts (ca. 1953), by Gretta Baker, on public health problems, published and distributed by the New York Mutual Life Insurance Company as an educational health service.

Newby, Errett Rains (b. 1885) 794
Printed materials 1905-1973
.66 foot

Registrar. Four University of Oklahoma catalogs (1914-1918) with Errett R. Newby's notes as university registrar (1911-1920), and which include maps of the campus (1916) and of Norman, Oklahoma (1915); a catalog (1905) for the University of Oklahoma's School of Fine Arts; a copy (1910) of the president's report to the University of Oklahoma's Board of Regents; a copy (1914) of the University of Oklahoma's biennial report; the constitution and by-laws (1914) of the University of Oklahoma's athletic association; a proposal (n.d.) for a charter for self-government by the students; the constitution and by-laws (n.d.) of the University of Oklahoma's student senate; a typescript of an editorial (n.d.) "Do the People Rule--In Oklahoma?" by Lyman Abbott; a copy (1906) of the "Voluntary Organizations Illustrations" issue of the *Bulletin* of the University of Oklahoma; and reminiscences (1973) by Newby about the university's early history.

Newkirk First National Bank Collection 795
Records 1893-1931
22 feet

Bank. Financial records (1893-1931) of the First National Bank of Newkirk, Oklahoma, prior to its merging with the Eastman National Bank of Newkirk, Oklahoma, including ledgers, draft registers, remittance registers, journals, depositors balance ledgers, discount registers, collection registers, old and new balance books, along with a ledger (1893) from the Bank of Santa Fe, also in Newkirk, Oklahoma, before it became Eastman National Bank.

Newkirk, Oklahoma, Municipal Records Collection 796
Records 1910-1947
.66 foot

Municipal government. City improvement bonds (1919-1947); bond stubs (1910-1947); paving tax receipts (1929); and a paving collection and distribution record (n.d.) from the city of Newkirk, Oklahoma.

Newland, John Lynn (1874-1941)   797
Manuscript n.d.
1 item

Newspaper editor. A manuscript (n.d.) of "The Editor's Story" by John Newland.

Newman, Coley   798
Papers 1906-1910
2 items

Collector. Two deeds (1906 and 1910) for land in Harmon County, Oklahoma.

Nice, Margaret Morse (b. 1883)   799
Papers 1905-1952
1.66 feet

Ornithologist. Correspondence (1920-1945) with other ornithologists; notebooks (1914-1929) of bird sightings in Oklahoma; note cards (1905-1929); research notes (1920-1930) of Margaret Nice; a typescript copy (n.d.) of "Wild Life of Tulsa County (Oklahoma)" by Edith R. Force; a manuscript, "Economic Value of Oklahoma Birds," by E. D. Crabb; and reprints (1930-1952) of articles about birds.

Nichols, Lea Murray (b. 1878)   800
Papers 1865-1957
1 foot

Journalist. Correspondence (1903-1951) regarding personal affairs, politicians and political events, and the National Editorial Association; speeches (n.d.) of Nichols; and publications (1917-1944) by pacifist organizations and government agencies regarding America's involvement in World War II, and Nazi Germany's relations with Poland, the Soviet Union, and other European nations.

Nieberding, Velma   801
Papers 1891-1959
.10 foot

Historian. Typescripts of interviews (1956-1959) conducted by members of the Ottawa County (Oklahoma) Semi-Centennial Committee with pioneers of Ottawa County, in which they described settlement of the area, early businesses, social activities, and interaction with the Indians of the area.

Noble First State Bank Collection   802
Records 1910-1933
6 feet

Bank. Financial records (1910-1933), including general ledgers, daily balance ledgers, daily statement ledgers, and note registers, from the First State Bank in Noble, Oklahoma.

Noble, Joseph Glass 803
Printed materials 1919-1952
.10 foot

Physician. Noble's commissions as a captain (1919) and a major (1930) in the U.S. Army Medical Corps; a paper (1931) by Noble, entitled "Examination of the Chest;" and advertisements (1940-1952) for medical products.

Norman, Oklahoma, Lions Club Collection 804
Records 1917-1955
1 foot

Civic organization. Correspondence (1917-1955); minutes (1920); and a secretary's record (1926-1930), including club rosters, dues, cash receipts and disbursements, general accounts, and attendance records of the Norman, Oklahoma, Lions Club, and printed material such as programs, brochures, and newsletters.

Norman, Oklahoma, Woden Club Collection 805
Printed materials 1953
2 items

Social organization. A history and membership list (1953) of the Woden Club of Norman, Oklahoma, plus a newspaper clipping (1953) marking the club's fortieth anniversary.

Norris, Thomas T. 806
Records 1900-1938
.10 foot

Physician. Birth records (1923-1938) and prescription slips (1936-1937) from Norris's medical practice in Krebs, Oklahoma, and a commencement announcement (1900) from the University of Nashville medical school.

Norton, Spencer Hilton (1909-1978) 807
Papers ca. 1930-1970
1 foot

Composer. Musical scores (ca. 1930-1970) of compositions by Norton, a music professor, at the University of Oklahoma, Norman, Oklahoma.

Nothstein, Charles Anderson (b. 1885) 808
Printed materials 1902-1913
.10 foot

Collector. Publications (1902-1913) reflecting social life in territorial and early statehood periods of Hennessey, Oklahoma, including programs of the town's junior and senior high school commencements, concert programs, news clippings from a local newspaper, one regarding a tornado which struck the town, and one souvenir booklet from Hennessey, Oklahoma Territory.

Nowata County Records Collection 809
Records 1909-1939
50 feet

County government. Judicial dockets (1909-1939) of the Nowata County, Oklahoma, civil and criminal courts; applications for homesteaders exemption taxes (1937); and tax assessment lists (1909-1939) for Nowata County, Oklahoma.

Unpublished finding aid available.

Nowata, Oklahoma, La Kee Kon Garden Club Collection 810
Printed material 1952
1 item

Social organization. A copy of the forty-ninth annual calendar (1952) of the La Kee Kon Garden Club of Nowata, Oklahoma, containing the club history, a membership roster, and the club's constitution and by-laws.

Office of Price Administration Collection 811
Printed materials 1942-1944
.10 foot

Federal agency. Copies of orders and regulations (1944) issued for Oklahoma by the Office of Price Adminstration (OPA) in regard to prices of commodities; publications (1942-1944) by the OPA, including a manual of procedures, bulletins, and newsletters; and posters (1943) listing grocery prices in Oklahoma.

Ogden, Florence 812
Manuscript 1868-1961
1 item

Housewife. A brief typewritten memoir (n.d.) written by Ogden recounting her childhood experiences and emphasizing her contact with local Cheyenne Indians near Thomas, Custer County, Oklahoma.

O'Hornett, Carl J. 813
Papers 1946
.10 foot

Attorney. Correspondence (1946), mostly from Carl J. O'Hornett, offering oil companies oil and gas leases on 1,250 royalty acres in the North Burbank area of Kay and Osage counties. Maps of the North Burbank area and a plat in Washita County, Oklahoma, are included in the collection.

Ohoyohoma Club Collection 814
Records 1925-1959
3.75 feet

Social organization. Scrapbooks (1925-1959) containing photographs, news clippings, programs, and mementos of the Ohoyohoma Club, a McAlester, Oklahoma, women's club that limited it membership to women of Indian descent.

Oklahoma Academy of Science Collection 815
Records 1910-1986
25.50 feet

Professional organization. Correspondence (1926-1986) regarding the academy's operation and special projects, including specialized files concerning its executive council, membership, finances, and its subsidiary organization, the Oklahoma Junior Academy of Science, and publications (1910-1985), including *The Bulletin* and *Proceedings* of the Academy, as well as the *Transactions* of the Junior Academy.

Unpublished finding aid available.

Oklahoma Association of College History Professors Collection 816
Records 1949
4 items

Professional organization. A program, sign-up sheets, and membership lists (1949) from the first annual meeting of the Oklahoma Association of College History Professors.

Oklahoma Association for Teachers Retirement Collection 817
Records 1936-1938
2 feet

Teachers organization. Correspondence (1936-1938) with professional and business organizations, school superintendents, political candidates, and others favoring legislation establishing teachers retirement provisions; and minutes (1936-1938) of the association's meetings.

Oklahoma City First National Bank Collection 818
Records 1901-1926
6 feet

Bank. Daily statement ledgers (1905-1926); general ledgers (1901-1904); personal account ledgers (1910-1911); and a Liberty Bond ledger (1918) from the American National Bank of Oklahoma City, which merged with the First National Bank of Oklahoma City in 1927. The collection also contains the general ledgers (1907-1909); draft ledgers (1907-1912); and statement books (1914-1917) from the Western National Bank of Oklahoma City, which merged with the American National Bank in 1917.

Unpublished finding aid available.

Oklahoma City Junior Symphony Orchestra Collection 819
Scrapbook 1961-1963
1 item

Youth orchestra. A scrapbook (1961-1963) of clippings, programs, promotional literature, and correspondence, relating to the Oklahoma City (Oklahoma) Junior Symphony Orchestra.

Oklahoma City Tradesmens National Bank Collection   820
Records 1919-1937
5 feet

Bank. Financial records (1919-1937) of the Tradesmens National Bank of Oklahoma City, Oklahoma, including resources and liabilities ledgers (1919-1921), and daily statements of account ledgers (1925-1937).

Oklahoma Corporation Commission Collection   821
Printed materials 1934-1948
.33 foot

State regulatory agency. Copies of monthly reports from the Oklahoma Corporation Commission, including Oklahoma allocated pools allotment reports (1945-1948), daily allocation reports (1946-1947), pipe lines run (1946-1947), notifications of intentions to drill (1946-1947), and abandoned oil and gas wells (1946-1947); and copies of monthly reports (1934-1937) on the Oklahoma labor market, from the Oklahoma Department of Labor.

Oklahoma Democratic Party Collection   822
Printed materials 1916-1955
.33 foot

Political party. Campaign brochures (1930-1958) for Democratic candidates; press releases (1949-1953) of speeches and statements given by Democratic officials; a scrapbook (1958) regarding the inaugurations of Oklahoma governors E. W. Marland, Johnston Murray, Roy J. Turner, and Raymond D. Gary; a speakers manual (1936) for the Democratic campaign in Oklahoma; official proceedings (1944) of the Democratic convention; and the Democratic campaign textbook (1916) for Oklahoma.

Oklahoma Department of Public Safety Collection   823
Printed materials 1957-1961
3 feet

State office. Scrapbooks of clippings (1957-1961) from Oklahoma newspapers on the activities of the Oklahoma Highway Patrol.

Oklahoma Farm Bureau Collection   824
Printed materials 1937-1954
.10 foot

State agricultural organization. Typescripts (1948-1954) regarding the history of the Oklahoma Farm Bureau, of proposed legislation in Oklahoma pertaining to agricultural matters, a letter sent to the county Farm Bureau offices in Oklahoma by the state office regarding the state of agriculture in Oklahoma, and of an analysis (ca. 1954) of the Oklahoma State Department of Agriculture.

Oklahoma Geological Survey Collection 825
Records 1908-1982
44 feet

State geological survey. Records of the Oklahoma Geological Survey, including correspondence (1908-1982); area geological reports (1915-1948); field notes (1908) taken during geological expeditions; reports of the governing board (1974-1979); and book manuscripts and galley proofs (n.d.) about geology in Oklahoma. Correspondence from the University of Oklahoma department of geology and geography is also present in this collection.

Unpublished finding aid available.

Oklahoma Indian Rights Association Collection 826
Records 1966-1980
11.50 feet

Indian advocacy organization. Records of the association (1966-1980), including correspondence, reports, financial records, and publications of the Oklahoma Indian Rights Association, regarding its involvement in the cause of American Indian civil rights, economic betterment, and the organization's relations with Oklahoma Indian tribes and nations.

Oklahoma Natural Mutoscene Company Collection 827
Papers 1908
6 items

Motion picture company. Correspondence (1908) to J. R. Abernathy from L. J. Simons, general manager of Oklahoma Natural Mutoscene Company, about the availability of films, financing, and advertisements for the company.

Oklahoma Ornithological Society Collection 828
Records 1949-1987
5.25 feet

Professional organization. Correspondence and reports (1949-1987) regarding the operation and status of the society, including files concerning the organization's membership, constitution, special projects, and stance regarding the official state bird of Oklahoma, and record copies of the society's publications (1951-1987), the *Oklahoma Ornithological Society Bulletin*, and *The Scissortail*.

Unpublished finding aid available.

Oklahoma Pioneer Physicians Oral History Collection 829
Papers ca. 1880-1907
.33 foot

History project. Typescripts of personal anecdotes, eyewitness accounts, and first-hand narratives (1880-1907) of physicians who were practicing medicine in Oklahoma during the late nineteenth century and early twentieth century. Also included is an interview with Oklahoma governor Johnston Murray concerning the practice of medicine.

Unpublished finding aid available.

Oklahoma Safety Council Collection 830
Printed materials 1946-1960
5 feet

Public service organization. Local reports (1948) for the National Pedestrian Protection Contest; annual inventories (1948) of local traffic safety activities; Public Safety Education Campaign material (1952-1960), including clippings, radio and television scripts; and pamphlets, along with news releases (ca. 1950) and reports (1946-1949) from the Oklahoma Safety Council.

Unpublished finding aid available.

Oklahoma School of Religion Collection 831
Records 1925-1946
10 feet

Center for religious instruction. Correspondence (1925-1946) of the director of the school regarding its functions, programs, and status; minutes (1927-1946) of meetings of the school's governing board; and publications (1927-1946), including school newsletters, catalogs, and annual reports of the First Presbyterian Church of Norman, Oklahoma, the school's sponsor.

Oklahoma Semi-Centennial Exposition Collection 832
Printed materials 1957
2.75 feet

Statehood commemorative exposition. Printed matter (1957), including leaflets, brochures, newspapers, newspaper tear sheets, and decals produced as part of the official Oklahoma Semi-Centennial Exposition in 1957.

Unpublished finding aid available.

Oklahoma Soil Conservation Service Collection 833
Printed materials 1960-1962
.66 foot

State agency. Programs and work plans (1960-1962) of the U.S. Department of Agriculture Soil Conservation Service program in Oklahoma, organized by soil conservation districts.

Oklahoma State Federation of Labor Collection 834
Records 1907-1958
43.33 feet

Labor union. Correspondence (1924-1958), transcripts (1923-1956), and published proceedings (1908-1952) of Oklahoma state labor conventions; transcripts (1907-1957) concerning administrative boards, hearings, and union meetings; publications (1915-1955) of the U.S. Department of Labor; and posters (1953-1955) encouraging the purchase of union-made products.

Unpublished finding aid available.

Oklahoma State Federation of Women's Clubs Collection 835
Printed materials 1922-1985
16 feet

Professional organization. Published material (1922-1985) from women's clubs throughout Oklahoma, including yearbooks, programs, newsletters, histories, and directories, arranged alphabetically by town and club.

Unpublished finding aid available.

Oklahoma State Grange Collection 836
Printed materials 1916-1958
.33 foot

Agricultural association. *Proceedings* (1916-1958) of the annual sessions of the Oklahoma State Grange Patrons of Husbandry.

Oklahoma State Medical Association Collection 837
Papers 1953
.66 foot

Professional organization. Biographical data sheets (1953) compiled by Oklahoma physicians regarding their lives and careers in medicine and collected by the Oklahoma State Medical Association.

Oklahoma Tax Commission Collection 838
Printed materials 1936-1959
1.33 feet

State agency. Daily report of taxes collected (1957-1959) and reports and bulletins (1936-1947) of the statistical division of the Oklahoma Tax Commission, including monthly and annual collection reports, reports of tax revenues by county and by classes of business, and reports of apportionment of taxes and state government spending, and the bulletin series (n.d.) *Know Your Government*.

Oklahoma Territorial Medical Association Collection   839
Records 1890-1904
.25 foot

Professional organization. Constitution and by-laws (1890); membership rosters (1890-1904); programs for the annual conventions (1893-1904); and minutes (1890-1904) of the meetings of the Oklahoma Territorial Medical Association.

Oklahoma Transportation Company Collection   840
Records 1902-1972
13 feet

Railroad company. Financial reports (1908-1972); executive and operating records (1902-1948), including annual reports, corporate by-laws, and minutes of the meetings of the governing board; and employee records (1931-1949) regarding the labor unions representing the Oklahoma Transportation Company work force, and wages paid.

Unpublished finding aid available.

Oklahoma Wheat Growers Association Collection   841
Records 1921-1933
.66 foot

Agricultural advocacy organization. Minutes (1921-1927) of the meetings of the Oklahoma Wheat Growers Association; audit reports (1931-1932); the association's articles of incorporation and by-laws (1921); and one copy of the *Wheat Grower's Advocate* (1933).

Oklahomans For The Right To Work, Inc., Collection   842
Printed materials 1954-1962
.25 foot

Political lobby. Organizational material (1954-1962) for county chairmen; photocopies of the articles of incorporation (1960); pamphlets (1954-1962) arguing both for and against right-to-work legislation; legislative histories (1954-1962) of state and national labor legislation; and an annotated bibliography (n.d.) from the Library of Congress Legislative Reference Service on the right-to-work controversy.

Okmulgee Abstract and Title Company Collection   843
Records 1905-1922
.10 foot

County abstract firm. Abstracts of title (1905-1922) for property in Okmulgee County, Oklahoma.

Okmulgee Civic Improvement Club Collection   844
Minutes 1906-1908
1 item

Civic club. A minute book (1906-1908) of the Okmulgee (Oklahoma) Civic Improvement Club.

Okmulgee County Medical Society Collection 845
Records 1932-1947
.33 foot

Professional organization. Correspondence (1939-1947); minutes (1940-1941); membership and dues lists (1940-1947); and membership applications (1932-1946) from the Okmulgee County (Oklahoma) Medical Society, and printed material (1940-1947) from the Oklahoma State Medical Association and the American Medical Association.

Olinger, Paul T. 846
Papers 1797-1917
.50 foot

Collector. Lecture notes (1859-1866) and theological books (1797-1866) of seminary student and, later, Indian Territory missionary, H. R. Schermerhorn; personal land records (1908-1917), including land deeds from the Choctaw and Chickasaw nations and unallotted land deeds signed by Chickasaw governor Douglas H. Johnston and Choctaw principal chief Victor M. Locke, Jr.

Oochalata Collection (d. 1891) 847
Printed materials 1875-1891
.75 foot

Indian chief. Typescripts of newspaper articles (1875-1891), including biographical items, editorials, speeches, and messages of Oochalata, also known as Charles Thompson, the principal chief of the Cherokee Nation, 1875-1878, mostly relating to education, schools, finances, Cherokee Indian lands, and tribal government in general.

Opler, Morris Edward (b. 1907) 848
Printed materials 1930-1971
1.33 feet

Anthropologist. Copies of journal articles (1930-1971) written by Opler concerning the Indian tribes of the American southwest, including the Apache and Apache subgroups, the Creek, and the Tonkawa.

Unpublished finding aid available.

Opothleyaholo Collection 849
Manuscript 1928
1 item

Indian chief. A biographical typescript (1928) commenting on Opothleyaholo's mistrust of white men.

Order of the Eastern Star Collection 850
Printed materials 1934-1935
2 items

Women's organization. *Proceedings* (1934-1935) of the twenty-sixth and twenty-seventh annual sessions of the Oklahoma chapter of the Order of the Eastern Star.

Ortenburger, Arthur Irving (b. 1898) 851
Papers 1892-1943
.25 foot

Zoologist. Consumer rationing books (1943) issued during World War II to the Ortenburger family; and journals (1892-1898) maintained by Charles C. Dean, Ortenburger's father-in-law, of visits to Florida, Mexico, and Guatemala for zoological research and vacations. Also included in this collection is a letter (1921) from Raymond L. Ditmars, whom Ortenburger considered one of the better herpetologists of his day.

Osage Indian Papers 852
Papers 1806-1957
.25 foot

Indian tribe. Photocopies of translated letters (1805-1806) from James B. Wilkinson, Pierre Chouteau, and Francisco Caso y Luenge to Osage Indian chiefs advising them of the need to comply with white authority; monthly returns (1863-1865) of ration issues to Osage Indians; an Osage tribal council statement (1953) contending that the U.S. government should supervise tribal affairs as long as there are mineral producing properties held by the tribe; and publications (1957) of the Osage Indians' semi-centennial celebration of the closing of the Osage tribal roll and allotment of Osage Indians lands in severalty.

Osborne, Lyle 853
Diary 1864
1 item

Collector. A diary (1864) of E. B. Osborne, a Union soldier, in which he relates his experiences in Tennessee near the close of the Civil War, with detailed descriptions of his company's participation in the Battle of Centerville of 1864, a trip to Georgia on the Chattahoochee, Macon, and Columbus Railroad, and a review of troops in Atlanta, Georgia, by Gen. William T. Sherman. Also included in the diary is a roster of men comprising Company I of the Thirty-first Ohio Infantry, with whom Osborne served.

Oskinson, John Milton (1874-1947) 854
Papers ca. 1917-1947
.10 foot

Author. A photo identification pass (1917) issued by the American Commission to Negotiate Peace of World War I, along with two unpublished manuscripts (n.d.), one entitled "The Singing Bird," and the other an unfinished autobiography which chronicles Oskinson's life in the Cherokee Nation and elsewhere.

Ottawa County Medical Society Collection 855
Records 1927-1949
2 items

Professional organization. Minutes and individual accounts of dues (1927-1930), and an account book (1936-1949), from the Ottawa County (Oklahoma) Medical Society.

Ourada, Patricia K. 856
Manuscript n. d.
1 item

Historian. An annotated manuscript (n.d.) of Ourada's book *The Menominee Indians: A History*.

Overton, Benjamin F. (1838-1884) 857
Printed materials 1874-1906
.33 foot

Indian chief. Typescripts of newspaper articles (1874-1906) concerning Overton as governor of the Chickasaw Nation and the Permit Law of 1876.

Owings, Donnell MacClure (1912-1966) 858
Papers 1961-1965
.66 foot

Professor. Bibliographies (1962-1965); correspondence with students (1961-1963); and syllabi, lecture outlines, and schedules for Owings's University of Oklahoma history courses entitled "The American Colonies, 1492-1789," "Historical Methods," and "Social and Cultural History of the United States 1607-1860."

Owl, Della Irene Brunsteter 859
Papers ca. 1924-1975
.33 foot

Linguist. Research notes (1924-1975) collected by Owl regarding the Cherokee Indian language and syllabary.

Paine, Mary Graham Giles 860
Printed materials 1921-1951
.10 foot

Editor. A personal account book (1935-1938); cards, programs, and directories, including the yearbook (1948-1949) for the Elliot Lee chapter (Pauls Valley, Oklahoma) of the Daughters of the American Revolution; and directories (1949-1951) for Oklahoma State Writers Inc., all belonging to Mary Giles Paine.

Palmer, Benn G. 861
Printed materials 1929-1955
.10 foot

Collector. Publications (1929-1955) by and regarding the Lions Club of Bartlesville, Oklahoma, including the weekly chapter newspaper, *The Lion's Roar* (1954-1955); a souvenir edition (1953) of a Bartlesville newspaper; and a list (n.d.) of regional secretaries of Lions clubs throughout Oklahoma.

Pantoja, Father 862
Letter ca. 1700
1 item

Priest. An unsigned, three-page draft, in Spanish, of a petition from one Father Pantoja to the king of Spain asking for the establishment of a Jesuit college in Coquimbro, Chile.

Parker, Everett C. (b. ca. 1893) 863
Manuscript n.d.
1 item

Petroleum geologist. An autobiography (n.d.) of Parker, who recounts his activities as a student at the University of Oklahoma and as a petroleum geologist for the Marland Oil Company.

Parker, Franklin (b. 1921) 864
Papers 1949-1989
.25 foot

Professor. Correspondence (1964-1966); newspaper and journal clippings (1964-1987); a press release (1966); and one newsletter (1967), all regarding the career and achievements of Parker during his years as professor of education at the University of Oklahoma and other institutions. Also included is a copy of Parker's resume (1989).

Parker, Harry (b. 1876) 865
Papers 1876-1937
.10 foot

Cattleman. The autobiography (1876-1937) of Harry Parker, an Oklahoma cattleman, in which he relates his family's migration to No Man's Land (the Oklahoma panhandle area), in 1887, describing the towns, people, and the style and standard of living in that region before it became a part of Oklahoma Territory. Included in the autobiography is an account of an immigrant family who killed several people before being caught.

Parker, Robert 866
Papers ca. 1975
11 items

Minister. Photocopies of eleven poems (ca. 1975) by Parker about God.

Parker, Thomas (1775-1890) 867
Printed materials ca. 1872, 1928
2 items

Indian chief. A biographical sketch (1928) of Parker, and, as governor, his farewell message (1872) to the Chickasaw Nation legislature.

Parks, Lucile Snider (b. ca. 1894) 868
Manuscript 1897-1903
1 item

Journalist. A photostatic copy of a typescript (n.d.) by Parks entitled "Prairie Prelude: 1897-1903" in which she describes her childhood and life in Pawnee, Indian Territory.

Parman, James Franklin (d. 1958) 869
Manuscript 1868-1904
1 item

Collector. An account (n.d.) by Will Brown of a white settlement in the Chickasaw Nation, (ca. 1868-1904), and attempts by the Chickasaw Indians to halt it.

Parnell, Charles 870
Papers 1899-1935
.10 foot

Collector. Correspondence (1899-1923); notes (n.d.) for Bible lessons; a copy of a speech (1914) by William H. Murray; two issues (1935) of the *Student's Echo* from Commercial Extension, a correspondence school in Omaha, Nebraska; and an issue (1917) of *Patton's Magazine*, all belonging to Charles Parnell.

Parrington, Vernon Louis, Sr. (1871-1929) 871
Papers 1893-1941
.10 foot

Professor. Correspondence (1908-1941); reports (ca. 1941); and a map (1931) regarding Parrington and his contributions to the University of Oklahoma, as well as efforts to name a university building for him. The collection also contains a roster of University of Oklahoma graduates from 1897-1908; a history (n.d.) of the University of Oklahoma department of English; and a report (1908) submitted by Parrington to the Board of Regents urging them to select a new campus plan and design for the University of Oklahoma. Also included is a map of the University of Washington at Seattle, Washington, showing the location of the Parrington Building there.

Patchell, O. W. (b. 1863) 872
Land patent 1850
1 item

Lawyer. A patent (1850) from the United States to Mary W. Hancock, a Choctaw Indian from Mississippi, for land granted in accordance with the 1830 Treaty of Dancing Rabbit Creek.

Pate, J. D. 873
Records 1904-1912
.25 foot

Physician. Ledgers (1904-1912) in which Pate recorded patients treated, services rendered and fees charged, and prescriptions recommended.

Patent Medicine Collection 874
Printed materials 1884-1918
.33 foot

Subject collection. Advertisements for mad stones and medicines that offer cures for snake bite, dropsy, ear ache, diseases of the eye, and rupture.

Patrick, William (1831-1909) 875
Papers 1831-1909
.10 foot

Pioneer immigrant. Photocopies of papers regarding the life of Irish immigrant William Patrick, including Patrick's diary (1857-1859) detailing his trip to California and Colorado; his Civil War service records (1864-1865); and his marriage certificate (1860).

Paul, Haskell 876
Papers 1812-1951
.10 foot

Collector. Typewritten copies of letters (1930-1951) between the Paul family of Pauls Valley, Oklahoma, and relatives in the east regarding the activities and genealogy of Smith Paul, founder of Pauls Valley, Oklahoma, before his immigration to Indian Territory.

Pauls Valley Chamber of Commerce Collection 877
Printed materials 1890-1950
.10 foot

Municipal business organization. Typescripts (n.d.) regarding the history of Pauls Valley, Oklahoma, and publications (1940-1950), including a Pauls Valley promotional pamphlet and telephone directory.

Pauls Valley First National Bank Collection 878
Records 1894-1925
11.50 feet

Bank. Financial records, including liability ledgers (1904-1910); depositor ledgers (1894-1911); discount registers (1902-1921); collection registers (1907-1924); cashier checks and drafts registers (1906-1925); stocks and securities registers (1910-1917); general journals (1916-1921); daily balance statements (1902-1921); capital stock share books (1903-1906); Liberty Loan ledgers (1917-1923); a minute book (1903-1921); and a treasurer's settlement report (1915-1920).

Unpublished finding aid available.

Pauls Valley State Training School for Boys 879
Records 1910-1939
28 feet

State reformatory. General correspondence (1924-1932); annual reports (1910-1936); storekeeper daily reports (1936-1939); commitment and parole records (1924-1929); registers of inmates (1924-1929); grade books (1924-1929); requisitions (1927-1938); remittance books (1931-1933); and related financial records (1924-1933), all reflecting the operation of Oklahoma's state reformatory for boys at Pauls Valley, Oklahoma.

Unpublished finding aid available.

Payne, David Lewis (1836-1884) 880
Printed materials 1879-1939
1.33 feet

Colonist. Typescripts of news articles (1879-1939) from Kansas, Missouri, and Indian Territory newspapers, and also from historical journals, regarding the life of David L. Payne, his leadership of the Boomer Movement, and his attempts to colonize Indian Territory before the opening of the area to white settlement.

Unpublished finding aid available.

Payne, Okemah 881
Papers 1902-1923
.10 foot

Collector. Correspondence (1908-1923) and business papers (1902-1917) of Tom Payne, a cowboy and businessman, reflecting his real estate and business interests in Indian Territory and early-day Oklahoma.

Pearson, John Cannon, Sr. (1862-1950) 882
Papers 1879-1949
5.25 feet

Merchant and mayor. Correspondence (1892-1931) regarding the administration of the cities of Pierson, Iowa, and Marshall, Oklahoma, the business ventures in which Pearson was involved, including grain elevators and trade companies, coal bins, cattle herds, real estate, and ranches, and also in regard to the Methodist Episcopal Church of Marshall, Oklahoma, the Masonic order in Oklahoma, and the 200th anniversary celebrations of George Washington's birth; minutes of meetings (1906-1912) of the Capital Grain and Elevator Company, Marshall, Oklahoma; certificates (1906-1946) of incorporation of the Capital Grain and Elevator Company, of membership in the Methodist Episcopal Church of Marshall, and others issued to Pearson by the Oklahoma State Council of Defense; legal papers (1896-1930) from the businesses with which Pearson was associated, including leases, bills of sale, insurance documents, and deeds; programs (1909-1937) from convocations, annual gatherings, and reunions of the Masonic order in Oklahoma; and publications (1879-1948), including books, periodicals, catalogs, newsletters, government documents, pamphlets, and brochures, regarding agriculture, the stock exchange system, the George Washington Monument, the coal and grain industries, and the Masonic order in the United States and Oklahoma. This collection also includes membership rosters (1895-1946) for lodges and divisions of the Masonic order in Oklahoma and Iowa, as well as the constitution, governing codes, and by-laws of the Oklahoma lodges, and the Grand Master decisions for Oklahoma and Indian territories, and the state of Oklahoma.

Unpublished finding aid available.

Pearson, Lola Clark (1871-1951) 883
Papers 1888-1950
23 feet

Editor and clubwoman. Correspondence (1888-1950) regarding the personal affairs of Pearson, the General Federation of Women's Clubs, the *Oklahoma Farmer-Stockman* magazine, and the state and national Republican parties, including letters from notables such as Eleanor Roosevelt and Patrick Hurley; speeches (n.d.) delivered by Pearson regarding communism and other matters of national concern; scrapbooks (1920-1937) containing news clippings of a general nature; certificates (1915-1948) issued to Pearson by organizations; newspaper clippings (1919-1945) regarding women's clubs, politics, and Theodore Roosevelt; propaganda posters (1929) published by the Soviet Union; pins, ribbons, and medallions (1920) worn by Pearson as a delegate to the National Republican Convention of 1920; event programs (1918-1948) published by women's clubs and other organizations, mostly relating to their annual conventions; minutes of meetings (1909-1937) of General Federation of Women's Clubs committees, along with constitutions and governing by-laws (1909-1937). Also included in this collection are newspapers, magazines, pamphlets, and booklets, including *The Clubwoman*, *General Federation Bulletin*, and *General Federation News*.

Unpublished finding aid available.

Pearson, Ralph 884
Ledger 1905-1912
1 item

Mortician. Register of funerals (1905-1912) from the Pearson Funeral Home in Walters, Oklahoma, with an inscription on the flyleaf reading "D. L. Hannifin (Emb) Randlett, OK."

Pearson, Robert Shelton, Sr. (1874-1955) 885
Papers 1923-1952
.33 foot

Artist. A scrapbook containing items reflecting Pearson's career, including correspondence (1923-1947), newspaper clippings and articles (1936-1952), ribbons (1933) awarded at a Latin American art exhibit in Florida, photographs of Pearson posing with his works, and a program (1947) of events celebrating the fortieth anniversary of Oklahoma statehood. Also included in this collection is a small landscape painting by Pearson.

Peck, Herbert Massey (b. 1890) 886
Papers 1838-1961
.66 foot

Attorney. Correspondence (1838-1961) to Peck regarding his contributions to the development of Oklahoma and Oklahoma City, and about Mrs. Peck's ancestors; certificates and diplomas (1907-1958) awarded Peck by universities and by President Woodrow Wilson, and appointing him district attorney for the western district of Oklahoma. Also in this collection are presidential invitations to Peck from Herbert Hoover and Franklin D. Roosevelt. Other correspondents include Adm. William Halsey, Frank Buttram, Edward K. Gaylord, Robert S. Kerr, Elmer Thomas, Thomas P. Gore, and Robert A. Hefner.

Peeler, Paul 887
Records 1905-1919
2 items

Collector. A financial journal (1907-1919) and a ledger (1905-1919) from the Rodger Mills Company Cooperative Association of Elk City, Oklahoma, containing a list of the association's stockholders and recording its financial transactions.

Pender, Winnfield Russell (b. 1888) 888
Manuscript 1959
1 item

Author. An unpublished novel (1959) by Pender entitled "The Treasures of Montezuma" which recounts an adventure-filled search for the fabled Aztec treasures.

Pendleton, Robert Henry (b. 1865) 889
Records 1897-1949
1.33 feet

Dentist. Ledgers in which Pendleton recorded patient accounts, dental services rendered and fees charged (1899-1907), income records (1897-1934), and appointment books (1924-1949).

Unpublished finding aid available.

Penney, Grace S. Jackson 890
Papers 1908-1958
.50 foot

University employee. Subject files (1908-1958) regarding the history and function of the Extension Division of the University of Oklahoma. The files include materials relating to the office of the director of the Extension Division (1926-1951), interscholastic meets (1929-1952), the High School Science Service (1947-1952), WNAD radio (1946-1952), the Family Life Institute (1937-1951), Interschool Speech Service (1927-1952), and other education programs (1908-1958) of the Extension Division.

Perren, Donna Lea (b. ca. 1912) 891
Records 1916-1924
.75 foot

Collector. Cash books (1920-1921) and individual account books (1916-1924) from the Perren Garage in Pond Creek, Oklahoma.

Perry, Adolphus Edward (1867-1939) 892
Papers 1907-1939
.66 foot

Politician. Correspondence (1907-1936) regarding the Republican and Progressive parties in national elections, and in Oklahoma; typed lists (1908-1920) of Republican Party officers and leaders in Oklahoma; *Proceedings* of the Republican Party Convention in the state's fourth congressional district in 1908; and newspaper articles (1908-1939) regarding the career and death of Perry.

Perry, John C. (b. 1894) 893
Printed materials 1909-1953
.10 foot

Physician. Publications (1936-1953) containing information about John C., and his father, M. L. Perry, and a typed listing of cancer patients attended by H. D. Murdock, a partner of Perry. The publications include the *Bulletin* of the Tulsa County Medical Society (1936-1944) and *The Roar* (1938-1953) of the Tulsa Lions Club.

Perryman, Joseph M. (1833-1896) 894
Papers 1883-1901
.10 foot

Indian chief. Typescripts of newspaper articles (1883-1901), including editorials, proclamations, and reports relating to Perryman, principal chief of the Creek Nation, his term of office, 1884-1888, and his service as a delegate from the Creek Nation to the Indian International Council.

Perryman, Legus Chouteau 895
Papers 1887-1907
.33 foot

Indian chief. Typescripts of newspaper articles (1887-1907) relating to Perryman as a principal chief of the Creek Nation, the Dawes Commission, Perryman's ouster from office in 1895, and his involvement with a plan for Creek Indians to emigrate to Mexico in 1905.

Peters, Kay (b. 1885) 896
Papers 1893-1935
.10 foot

Photographer. An account (n.d.) by Peters of his participation in the settlement of the Cherokee Strip during the land run of 1893; correspondence (1904) regarding settlement of the estate of a deceased relative of Peters; one warranty deed (1900) issued in Garfield County, Oklahoma Territory, and a Garfield County, Oklahoma, tax assessment list (1927) indicating the rates of taxation for farm and household items.

Peterson, Horace Cornelious (1902-1952) 897
Papers 1918-1951
9 feet

Professor. Correspondence (1918-1920) regarding his books, *Propaganda For War* and *Opponents of War*, from readers and notables, including Norman Thomas, George Creek, J. Edgar Hoover, and Roger Baldwin; manuscripts and galley proofs of the two books; scrapbooks (1918-1920) containing reviews and news items regarding his books; Peterson's research notes (n.d.) on the loyalty oath in Oklahoma, including that of the University of Oklahoma; typescripts of a journal (1918-1919) kept by Ike Hoover, a member of President Woodrow Wilson's party in Paris, France, after World War I, and a report on the negotiations for peace and an eventual peace treaty; and publications (1917-1951) regarding propaganda and World War I. Also included in this collection is a typescript account (1952) of Peterson's accidental death in a University of Oklahoma classroom building, written by Alfred B. Sears and including Sears's recommendations for removing the hazards which contributed to the death.

Unpublished finding aid available.

Pettyjohn, (Mrs.) John 898
Papers 1910-1911
4 items

Collector. An undated letter from Will Rogers to his father, Clement Vann Rogers, and three letters (1910-1911) from Betty (Mrs. Will) Rogers to Clement Vann Rogers concerning Will Rogers's horse act.

Phillips, George Wendel (d. ca. 1950) 899
Records 1901-1943
.50 foot

Physician. Patient account books (1911-1943) in which Phillips recorded fees charged; and certificates and diplomas (1901-1919) awarded Phillips by schools of medicine and by the states of Kentucky and Oklahoma, granting him the privilege of practicing medicine.

Phillips, Leon Chase (1890-1958) 900
Papers 1933-1951
10 feet

Governor. Correspondence (1934-1951) regarding Phillips's gubernatorial, legislative and political affairs; scrapbooks (1936-1941) containing loose news clippings on his political career; publications (1933-1941) about political conventions, along with event programs from numerous organizations; trial transcripts (1943-1944) from cases involving the state of Oklahoma; speeches (1936-1944) delivered by Phillips; government documents (1940); cartoons (n.d.) regarding Phillips and his political career, as well as politics and state government; and certificates (1932-1951) awarded Phillips by businesses, civic organizations, and state government. Also included in this collection is a leatherbound copy of Phillips's 1939 inaugural address.

Unpublished finding aid available.

Pi Kappa Alpha Collection 901
Records 1933-1943
6 feet

Fraternity. Records (1933-1943) of district fourteen of Pi Kappa Alpha fraternity, encompassing Oklahoma, Texas, and Arkansas, of which Ted W. Beaird and Herbert Scott were district presidents. The records consist of chapter files (1933-1943), including correspondence, reports, minutes, and financial statements from individual chapters; correspondence (1933-1938) with alumni and the Supreme Council; correspondence (1934-1940) concerning petitions, installations, and conventions; convention reports and publicity (1937-1941); and the constitution and by-laws (1933-1941).

Piburn, Anne Ross 902
Papers 1883-1958
.25 foot

Collector. Programs (1937-1958) of the yearly reunions of Cherokee seminary graduates; a report (1955) regarding the old Murrell home in Tahlequah, Indian Territory; a report (1953) regarding New Echota, Cherokee Nation; a publication (1954) of the Cherokee Foundation, Inc. entitled *Tsa La Gi' Ga Nah Se Da'*; an undated list of freedmen granted Cherokee citizenship; and memorials (1883-1899) of the Cherokee Nation and its delegation to the U.S. Congress.

Pickard, Clyde C. 903
Papers 1893-1952
8 feet

Real estate agent. Personal correspondence (1918-1952); business correspondence (1920-1947); financial records, including bank notes (1912-1946), deeds and leases (1914-1946), daily and individual account ledgers; and certificates, including a homestead certificate (1893), all from Pickard's real estate business in Norman, Oklahoma.

Unpublished finding aid available.

Pierce, Thomas Franklin, Sr. (b. 1867) 904
Papers 1867-1957
.10 foot

Professor. An autobiographical manuscript (n.d.) that includes Pierce's experiences as an educator in Indian Territory and Oklahoma; poetry (n.d.) by Pierce regarding the virtues of Oklahoma; and a manuscript account (ca. 1930) of Pierce's visit to the Grand Canyon.

Pitchlynn, Peter Perkins (1806-1881) 905
Papers 1815-1888
2.75 feet

Indian chief. Correspondence (1824-1881) of Pitchlynn with prominent citizens and family members in the Choctaw Nation regarding events and troubles within the nation; Pitchlynn's personal journals (1815); Pitchlynn's diary (1828-1832); official reports (1825-1841) of the Choctaw Academy and Missionary Station in Kentucky; and Pitchlynn family records (1806-1867). The collection also includes a signed copy of the articles of surrender and peace negotiated between the Choctaw Nation and the United States at the close of the Civil War, and extensive correspondence reflecting the state of the Choctaw Nation just prior to, and during the Civil War years, with special regard to slavery.

Unpublished finding aid available.

Pittman, F. D. 906
Letter   1930
1 item

Teacher. A letter (1930) written by F. D. Pittman, a teacher from McAlester, Oklahoma, to Louis Dakil in which Pittman describes his coming to Indian Territory in 1895 to teach, and of the growth of, and changes in the town of McAlester between 1903-1930.

Pittsburg County Medical Society Collection 907
Ledger   1917-1936
1 item

Professional organization. A ledger (1917-1936) containing the minutes and proceedings of the Pittsburg County (Oklahoma) Medical Society, including membership rosters and physician obituaries.

Planned Parenthood Association Collection 908
Papers   ca. 1935-1958
1.66 feet

Non-profit organization. Correspondence (1937-1947); reprints (1939-1955) of articles from newspapers, periodicals, and professional journals, and pamphlets relating to birth control; an unbound copy (1938) of *Season of Birth* by Ellsworth Huntington; and a bibliography (1939) of publications on birth control and related topics.

Unpublished finding aid available.

Plummer, William A. 909
Papers   1870-1895
.10 foot

Homesteader. Letters (1870-1895) from William A. Plummer to relatives in Pennsylvania concerning homesteading, agriculture, real estate, the local economy, politics, religion, Indians, and the weather in the Wichita, Kansas, area. Several letters between other Plummer family members are also included.

Pollard, Tildue H. (b. 1877) 910
Certificates   1903-1908
5 items

Physician. Certificates (1903-1904) issued to Pollard by Arkansas, Oklahoma, Indian Territory, and the Choctaw Nation granting him the privilege of practicing medicine and pharmacy within their borders.

Pomeroy, Henry Martyn (1830-1916) 911
Papers   1859-1860
.10 foot

Bookseller. A photocopy and typescript of a portion of the diary (1859-1860) of Henry M. Pomeroy in which he recorded his overland journey to California, with colorful descriptions of the gold fields, and the cities of Los Angeles and San Francisco, California. Also included are the minutes of a vigilante committee near Omaha, Nebraska, as well as an account of a massacre in Oregon Territory.

Pond, Nina Louise Phillipi (b. ca. 1905) 912
Papers 1893-1968
.33 foot

Homemaker. Typescripts (1893-1950) relating to the history of the Methodist Episcopal Church of Medford, Oklahoma Territory and Oklahoma, the history of the Grant County (Oklahoma) Historical Society, and the statement of intent of the Grant County (Oklahoma) Film Library; reports (1965-1967) of services rendered by the United Methodist Church's Oklahoma Conference Ministry to the Deaf, as well as the minutes (1966-1968) of its governing board; programs (1950-1953, 1967) of the worship services of the Methodist church of Medford, and of women's civic groups in Medford, Oklahoma, including the Mother's Club, Business and Professional Women's Club, and the Women's Society of Christian Science; and publications (1952-1968) such as *The Broadcaster*, published by the Methodist church in Medford, Oklahoma, and *The Lamplighter*, published by the Methodist Church's Oklahoma Conference Ministry to the Deaf. Also included in this collection is a cartoon history of Oklahoma, 1541-1939, published by the *Daily Oklahoman* in 1939.

Porter First National Bank Collection 913
Records 1900-1933
12 feet

Bank. Correspondence (1910-1916) and financial records (1900-1933) from the First National Bank of Porter, Oklahoma, including daybooks, tellers cash books, discount registers, distribution of expenses registers, draft registers, note registers, reconciliation of accounts books, and loan registers, along with minutes of a predecessor bank, the American Bank of Porter, Oklahoma.

Porter, Joseph L. (b. 1874) 914
Papers 1899-1938
.25 foot

Banker. The diaries (1899-1938) of Joseph L. Porter of Lawton, Oklahoma, regarding life there and his experiences as a banker and as long-time treasurer of the local board of education.

Porter, Pleasant (1840-1907) 915
Papers 1871-1902
1.66 feet

Indian chief. Typescripts of correspondence (1894-1901); speeches (1893-1907); and newspaper articles (1871-1902) relating to Porter as a principal chief of the

Creek Nation and president of the Sequoyah Convention, the allotment of lands by the Dawes Commission, the termination of tribal government, and the movement for separate statehood for Indian Territory.

Unpublished finding aid available.

Postal Records Collection 916
Records 1890-1915
7 items

Subject collection. Ledgers (1890-1915) containing equipment inventories and listings of domestic money orders issued by U.S. post offices in five towns and settlements in the territory and state of Oklahoma.

Poster Collection 917
Printed materials. 1884-1986
670 items

Series collection. Posters (1884-1986), full color and black and white, published in the United States and Europe, publicizing wild west shows, traveling medicine shows, vaudeville acts, theatrical events, political elections, and the military services of the United States. Also included are governmental propaganda posters, published in the United States, France, and Italy, during World Wars I and II, and regarding conservation of essential materials, patriotism, liberty loans, military recruitment, and other wartime themes.

Unpublished finding aid available.

Pottawatomie County Medical Society Collection 918
Records 1907-1946
2 items

Professional organization. A publication (1946) of the Pottawatomie County (Oklahoma) Medical Society entitled *The Bulletin*, along with a scrapbook belonging to the women's auxiliary of the society and containing the history of the auxiliary, which claimed to be the first women's auxiliary of a county medical society in the United States. The scrapbook also contains a copy of the first book of minutes and proceedings (1907) of the auxiliary, reflecting its preparations to host the first convention of the Oklahoma State Medical Association in 1907.

Powell, Peter J. (b. 1928) 919
Manuscript 1930-1966
1 item

Priest. An unedited version of Powell's book *Sweet Medicine* published by the University of Oklahoma Press (1969), which discusses the Cheyenne Indian sun dance and other religious ceremonies.

Prague National Bank Collection 920
Records 1902-1945
10 feet

Bank. Financial records (1906-1945) from the Prague (Oklahoma) National Bank, including balance ledgers (1906-1929); daily statement ledgers (1929-1939); daybooks (1932-1941); discount registers (1933-1945); liability registers (1929-1938); a bond register (1929-1937); certificates of deposit registers (1920-1928); and a general ledger (1928-1941). The collection also includes a liability ledger (1923-1936) from the Paden National Bank; balance ledgers (1902-1906); a tellers cash book (1902-1903); and a journal (1902-1903) from the Lincoln County Bank, predecessors of the Prague National Bank.

Unpublished finding aid available.

Pratt, Horace 921
Printed materials 1864
2 items

Indian chief. Typescripts of two conscription acts (1864) by the Chickasaw Nation legislature organizing Chickasaw Indian troops for service in the Confederate Army.

Prevost, Charles Albert 922
Papers 1918-1919
.10 foot

Investor. Correspondence, advertisements, and stock certificates (1918-1919) from the Okmulgee-Youngstown Oil Company, and the Indian Chief Oil and Gas Company, along with an advertisement (1919) regarding the productivity of the Okmulgee (Oklahoma) oil field.

Price, Charles Gary (1882-1950) 923
Papers 1903-1918
.33 foot

Physician. A notebook (1917-1918) containing transcripts of lectures given at Camp Greenleaf, Georgia, to military physicians, and poetry (1918), presumedly, by Price; a book (1903) entitled *Pocket Cyclopedia of Medicine and Surgery*, along with certificates and diplomas (1904-1914) awarded Price by medical associations and schools, including licenses to practice medicine in Oklahoma, Texas, and Georgia.

Price, Walter 924
Playbills 1935
.10 foot

Vaudevillian. Playbills (1935) advertising vaudeville and theatre productions in which Price participated.

Prisoner of War Camps Collection 925
Papers 1943-1983
.10 foot

Subject collection. Correspondence (1945-1946); publications (1945-1946); and newspaper articles (1943-1983) regarding the German prisoners of war interned in Oklahoma during World War II, and the prisoner of war camps in which they lived. Also included in this collection are the handwritten notes (1945-1946) University of Oklahoma history professor Morris L. Wardell used for his lectures to the prisoners regarding American democracy. Wardell's notes and the correspondence in this collection reflect the University of Oklahoma's efforts to educate the Germans concerning U.S. civics and government.

Proclamation Collection 926
Papers 1868-1887
1 foot

Subject collection. Proclamations issued by governors and Indian chiefs recognizing special days and events in several states and territories of the United States. Included are days of thanksgiving, fasting, prayer and humiliation, Arbor Day, and mourning for the death of President James A. Garfield.

Proctor, C. L. 927
Printed material 1918
1 item

Collector. A copy of the Saint Patrick's day issue of *The Oklahoma Daily* for 1918. Printed in green ink, this issue of the University of Oklahoma student newspaper is dedicated to the engineering students of the university and their adopted saint. It bears the banner headline "St. Pat Ran the Snakes Out of Ireland and the Engineers Will Run the Kaiser Out of Germany."

Propaganda Collection 928
Printed materials 1939-1954
.25 foot

Subject collection. Brochures, flyers, and leaflets (1939-1954) published in the United States, Great Britain, North Korea, and Australia during World War II and the Korean War. These include British publications (1943-1944) regarding World War II as well as a typescript (n.d.) on U.S. culture and customs given to British airmen enroute to America for training; leaflets (n.d.) dropped on U.S. troops in Korea by the Chinese advising them of the benefits of immediate surrender as well as the procedures for doing so; and a U.S. government list (1950) of all political and social groups in this country considered subversive.

Pruitt Gin Company Collection 929
Records 1940-1946
5 feet

Cotton gin. Daily gin reports (1940-1946); weight records (1941-1945); customer account ledgers (1940-1945); and financial records (1941-1946) of the Pruitt Gin Company of Lindsay, Oklahoma. These records reflect the trends which affected cotton gins throughout Oklahoma during this period, including the limitations and prosperity brought about by wartime conditions.

Unpublished finding aid available.

Pryor, William W. (1882-1946) 930
Printed materials ca. 1920-1938
6.66 feet

Attorney. Briefs (1920-1946) of cases reviewed before the supreme court of Oklahoma, along with related correspondence (1927-1934) and a newspaper obituary (1946) of Pryor, who served as counsel to the court.

Pugmire, Donald Ross (d. 1958) 931
Printed materials 1935-1958
.66 foot

Professor. Reports (1950-1958) issued by government and private agencies regarding education and schooling in Oklahoma, a number of which were authored by Pugmire; and Pugmire's doctoral dissertation (1936), entitled "The Administration of Personnel in Correctional Institutions in New York State."

Pumpkin, Thomas (Tah Sa Co Fah Ahwee) (1865-1899) 932
Enrollment card 1902-1909
1 item

Indian allottee. The enrollment record of Thomas Pumpkin (Tah Sa Co Fah Ahwee), a Euchee Creek Indian, as created by the Dawes Commission in 1902. Subsequent notes on the record, dated 1904-1909, establish that Pumpkin died in 1899, three years before being enrolled by the government, and ten years before the Commissioner to the Five Civilized Tribes approved his enrollment.

Purdum, Helen 933
Printed materials 1905-1907
5 items

Collector. Leather postcards (1905) sent from Ardmore, Indian Territory; and leaflets (1907) published by the Oklahoma Anti-Saloon League and addressed to the voters of Durant, Indian Territory, petitioning them to approve prohibition when Oklahoma is admitted to the Union.

Quapaw, Oklahoma, Town Records Collection 934
Records 1917-1945
1 foot

Municipality. Minutes (1931-1938) of the town board of trustees; occupational licenses (1925-1941) granted to Quapaw merchants; correspondence (1945) received by the town mayor regarding the possibility of Federal Works Agency work and planning; and municipal contracts (1919-1920) for water along with receipts of payment (1939-1941) for the same. Also included in this collection is one ledger (1917) containing town treasurer records.

Quigley, Michael 935
Papers 1857
1 item

Immigrant. Naturalization papers of Ireland native, Michael Quigley, given at Mayesville, Kentucky, in 1857.

Quong, Jennie Lou Grey 936
Papers 1923-1953
2 items

Artist. Photocopies of manuscripts (1923-1953) regarding the Korean War and the death of Quong's husband in that conflict, and the internment of Japanese-Americans in this country during World War II.

Rachlin, Carol 937
Papers 1818-1966
2.25 feet

Anthropologist. Correspondence (1954-1974); interviews (1958-1976); research notes (n.d.); manuscripts (n.d.); and publications (1818-1958) relating to Rachlin's research on the Sac and Fox and the Shawnee Indians. Also included are field notes (1954) from her archaeological research on the weaving of the mound-builders.

Unpublished finding aid available.

Rader, Jesse Lee (b. 1883) 938
Papers 1901-1952
.75 foot

University librarian. Correspondence (1906-1953) from friends and library associates regarding the Oklahoma Library Commission and Oklahoma Library Association, including a letter from University of Oklahoma president David Ross Boyd, regarding Boyd's dismissal and the dismissal of numerous faculty at the university, including Rader, by Governor C. N. Haskell; postcards (1907) of Virginia scenes; a speech (1952) delivered by Rader at a dinner in his honor; minutes (1952) of meetings of the Oklahoma Library Association; student grade reports (1905-1906) issued to Rader by the University of Oklahoma; consumer rationing books (1942-1943) used by Rader and family during World War II; publications (1901-1952), including a newspaper, the front page of which is devoted to news of the first oil well in the Oklahoma City oil field; an original book jacket for Adolph Hitler's *Mein Kampf*; a University of Oklahoma student handbook (1904-1905); a magazine *The Delta*, published by Sigma Nu; newspaper articles regarding the presidency of Theodore Roosevelt; certificates (1905-1951) issued to Rader; programs (1909-1910) of ceremonies and events conducted by University of Oklahoma fraternities and the Oklahoma Library Association; and constitutions and by-laws (1905-1907) of the Oklahoma Library Association, and of University of Oklahoma student clubs and societies, including the Websterian Literary Society and Kanuntaklage Dramatic Club. Also included in this collection is an anthropometric table (1902) used by the University of Oklahoma to measure and chart student physiques.

Rainey, George (b. 1866) 939
Papers 1880-1968
3 feet

Author. Rainey's correspondence files (1902-1954); newspaper clippings (1910-1954), including reviews of Rainey's books and other articles relating to the Rainey family and Oklahoma history; diaries and notebooks (1880-1940); pamphlets and booklets (1903-1968); and manuscripts by Rainey and others relating to Oklahoma and U.S. history; certificates (1905-1937) issued to Rainey; a copy of a patent (1904) for an adding machine; and a billfold (ca. 1890) carried by Rainey during the Oklahoma land run of 1893.

Unpublished finding aid available.

Ralls, Joseph G., Sr. (1864-1933) 940
Papers 1870-1924
9.33 feet

Attorney. Correspondence (1870-1924) and legal case files (1890-1924) from Ralls's law practice, including those concerning his representation of Choctaw Indians during the allotment of Choctaw lands and townsite payments.

Ramsay, J. J. 941
Records 1895-1934
.10 foot

Collector. Tax receipts (1895-1934) issued to Ramsay by Kay County, Oklahoma Territory and Oklahoma, listing the annual taxes levied by the county for those years.

Ramsay, James Ross (1821-ca. 1890) 942
Manuscript ca. 1890
1 item

Missionary. A typescript of Ramsay's autobiography (ca. 1890) in which he relates his education and experiences as a Presbyterian missionary among the Seminoles, hardships during the Civil War, and accounts of medical treatment.

Ramsey, Flora Belle Simmons (b. 1866) 943
Papers 1889-1897
.10 foot

Pioneer. Manuscripts (n.d.) by Ramsey recording her impressions and experiences (1889-1897) as a participant in the land run of 1889, and as a housewife in Payne County, Oklahoma Territory.

Randall, William B. (b. 1882) 944
Papers 1905-1929
.10 foot

Oil field contractor. A time book (1905-1906) kept by Randall while an oil-rig contractor; a life insurance policy (1919) issued to Randall; a certificate (1919) of his election as a trustee of Ramona, Oklahoma; and numerous novelty postcards (1907-1913). Also in this collection are a high school diploma (1914) issued by Ramona High School, a map (1904) of Oklahoma and Indian territories; and a blueprint (1934) for an oil field apparatus.

Ransom, Will Hewitt (1878-1955) 945
Papers 1847-1955
.33 foot

Collector. Correspondence (1847-1869) regarding news of a general nature, and a trip on a packet boat in 1847; a diary (1877) of an unidentified woman regarding her experiences as a teacher and her life in general; scrapbooks (1877-1882) containing calling cards, news clippings, and correspondence; and publications (1882-1955), including a premium list from the New England Agricultural Society, a teachers memorandum, and a catalog of publications by the Philip C. Duschnes Company. Also in this collection are diplomas (1876-1878) issued to Ransom's relatives by Olivet College in Michigan, and Michigan State Normal School.

Rawlinson, Sally 946
Poster 1926
1 item

Collector. A 14" x 21", black on white, poster (1926) advertising the first football game to be played at the University of Oklahoma's Owen Field, Norman, Oklahoma.

Ray, Grace Ernestine 947
Papers 1939-1982
26 feet

Journalism professor. Manuscripts (1947-1980) of articles and books by Ray; journals and newspapers (1939-1968) containing her articles; printed materials (ca. 1940-1970) and other papers used for research, along with Ray's professional correspondence. (1939-1982).

Ray, Jessie Dimple Newby (b. ca. 1888)						948
Papers 1909-1928
.10 foot

Collector. Ledgers (1919-1928) recording the daily business of the H. Warner Newby Rooming House in Oklahoma City, Oklahoma; and event programs (1909-1910) of the University of Oklahoma Class of 1910, including its graduation and senior banquet programs, along with event programs for the Senate Literary Society and the Zetaletheans. Also included is the graduation commencement program (1905) for the Logan County High School in Guthrie, Oklahoma Territory.

Reagle, James, Jr.						949
Papers 1864-1868
.10 foot

Army surgeon. Correspondence (1866-1868) to and from Reagle regarding personal matters as well as his assignment at Fort Arbuckle, Indian Territory, including some description of Indians with whom he had contact. The collection also contains Reagle's diary (1864-1867) in which he recorded his experiences as a U.S. Army surgeon in Virginia during the Civil War, and his post-war experiences with the U.S. Tenth Cavalry at Fort Arbuckle, including English translations of Chickasaw, Choctaw, and Comanche words, impressions of Indian tribes, and a sketch of a Caddo village.

Ream, Ruth K.						950
Papers 1909-1915
.33 foot

Collector. Ream's invitations to parties, weddings, and high school commencements (1910-1915), along with a report card (1909) from a Canadian County, Oklahoma, school and a souvenir (1915) from Union City Public School, Union Township, Oklahoma.

Reaves, Samuel Watson						951
Papers 1897-1914
.33 foot

Student. Lecture notes (1897-1914) taken by Reaves while a math and physics student at Cornell University and the University of Chicago.

Records, Ralph Hayden						952
Papers 1871-1968
2 feet

Professor. Magazine and journal articles (1946-1968) regarding historiography, along with a typewritten manuscript (1871-1899) by L. S. Records entitled "The Recollections of a Cowboy of the Seventies and Eighties," regarding the lives of cowboys and ranchers in frontier-era Kansas, and the Cherokee Strip of Oklahoma

Territory, including a detailed account of Records's participation in the land run of 1893.

Unpublished finding aid available.

Red Rabbit Oil Company Collection 953
Ledger 1919
1 item

Petroleum company. A ledger (1919) containing the articles of incorporation, certificate of incorporation, and minutes of the stockholders' meetings of the Red Rabbit Oil Company of Oklahoma City, Oklahoma.

Redwine Trading Company Collection 954
Records 1896-1925
21 feet

Mercantile firm. Ledgers (1896-1922) in which the daily commerce of this Spiro, Oklahoma, general store and cotton-ginning operation were recorded. Among these are day books (1898-1918); cash books and notary records (1904-1906); funeral records (1901-1911); ginners cotton books (1908-1918); and books (1903-1925) recording cotton bought and sold. Also included in this collection are a petition (n.d.) of Spiro, Indian Territory, regarding the relocation of the U.S. District Court and the treasurer's records (1907) from a Spiro-area school district. The records of this collection span thirty years and reflect the economic conditions of the Choctaw Nation, of Indian Territory, and of the state of Oklahoma, including periods of depression and prosperity.

Unpublished finding aid available.

Redwine, Wilburn Nash (b. 1862) 955
Papers 1898-1943
16 feet

Attorney. Correspondence (1898-1943) regarding Redwine's legal practice in Spiro, Oklahoma; legal case files (1898-1943) in which Redwine was involved; published legal briefs (n.d.); expense ledgers (1904-1917) in which Redwine recorded the nature of cases and the fees charged; and political posters and leaflets (1910, 1924) published during Redwine's campaigns for election to the state senate and supreme court. The expense ledgers, prior to November, 1907, reflect legal services provided for a number of Choctaw Indian families experiencing difficulty receiving or claiming allotments.

Reed, Horace 956
Papers 1901-1951
.10 foot

Physician. Typescripts (n.d.) of five articles by Reed regarding appendicitis and its treatment, as well as the treatment of ulcers, and the art of surgery, along with certificates and diplomas (1901-1951) awarded Reed by medical schools and boards.

Reed, Milo T. 957
Papers 1936-1938
2 items

Collector. A petition (n.d.) signed by approximately eighty citizens of Seminole County, Oklahoma, declaring their intent to capture the murderer of a fellow citizen and listing the rewards pledged by each for the capture of the criminal; and copies of letters (1936-1938) to Reed from Isaiah and Mary Rutherford regarding family affairs and written in Afro-American-style English.

Reeds, Clarence 958
Papers 1895-1928
.75 foot

Collector. A script for the drama production, "Our American Cousin," produced by the students of the University of Oklahoma in 1905; and publications (1905-1928) of the University of Oklahoma, including *The Sooner*, *The Umpire*, *The University Umpire*, *The University Newsletter*, *The University Oklahoman*, *The Sooner Alumnus*, and the program for the 1928 football season. Also in this collection are a number of books (ca. 1895) in German and artifacts (1905), including a beret and a football sweater marked "05."

Reeve, Lelia Hudson 959
Papers 1880-1922
.10 foot

Pioneer. Typewritten manuscripts (ca. 1922) by Reeve, entitled "Early Days in Western Kansas," "Santa Fe Trail," and "Early Days in Oklahoma."

Reidt, G. M. 960
Records 1907-1936
.33 foot

Collector. Ledgers (1907-1936) containing the minutes and proceedings of the Twentieth-Century Club of McAlester, Indian Territory and Oklahoma.

Religious Denominations of Oklahoma Collection 961
Printed materials 1895-1950
2.33 feet

Subject collection. Publications (1895-1950) of several religious denominations and individual churches in Oklahoma, including Baptists, Catholics, Congregationalists, Episcopalians, Lutherans, Mennonites, Methodists, and Presbyterians. These printed materials include church bulletins, directories, conference proceedings, and church pamphlets.

Rennie, Albert (1863-1948) 962
Papers 1900-1951
14.50 feet

Attorney. Family and business correspondence (1900-1951); legal documents (1900-1939); and printed material (1900-1951) belonging to Rennie, a Pauls Valley, Oklahoma, attorney. Much of the material relates to real estate transactions including land allotted to Choctaw and Chickasaw Indians.

Renze, Dolores C. 963
Printed materials 1892-1898
5 items

Collector. Proclamations (1892-1898) issued by the governors of Oklahoma Territory regarding the official observance of Columbus Day and Thanksgiving Day in the territory.

Reynolds, Norman E., Jr. 964
Papers 1951-1965
4 feet

Legislator and attorney. Briefs and other legal documents, correspondence, research files, maps, and printed materials relating to reapportionment in Oklahoma (1951-1965), and to the Oklahoma Turnpike Authority (1960-1961).

Unpublished finding aid available.

Rhodes, Charles B. (1862-1949) 965
Papers 1864-1950
.75 foot

U.S. marshal. Correspondence (1895-1946) regarding the Indian Territory Day celebration of 1939, and Thomas Rhodes's experiences in the military during World War I; certificates (1864-1912) appointing Rhodes a teacher in Arkansas and in the Cherokee Nation, as a U.S. deputy marshal, and exempting a relative of Rhodes from military service during the Civil War; news clippings (1905-1950) regarding lawmen, outlaws, judges, and Rhodes; postcards (1929-1949) of Colorado's Royal Gorge bridge and of the Southern Belle Railroad; a score (1894) of a patriotic hymn composed by a youth from Indian Territory; a poster (1900) advertising a reunion of the Old Settlers Band of the Cherokee Indians; poetry and short stories (1894-1942) regarding Oklahoma, Belle Starr, and the Creek National Council House at Okmulgee, Indian Territory; political ribbons (1907-1912) advertising the first Muskogee County (Oklahoma) Republican Party convention, the Muskogee County delegation to the first state Republican Party convention, and the delegation's support of William H. Taft for president in 1909; and publications (1908-1938), including programs of the reunion of former U.S. marshals in 1908, and of the forty-fifth anniversary of the First National Bank of Vinita, Oklahoma. Also in this collection is an original manuscript (1875-1907), presumably by Rhodes, regarding the U.S. District Court at Fort Smith, Arkansas, its judge, Isaac C. Parker, and the cases tried there, with commentary regarding the crimes and criminals of Indian Territory.

Richards, Aute (b. 1885) 966
Papers 1895-1950
4 feet

Zoology professor. General correspondence (1939-1947); correspondence (1934-1950) relating to the Lions Club, and to the University of Oklahoma biology department; printed material (1916-1941), including university publications and copies of Richards's published articles; scrapbooks (1931-1950) of newspaper clippings on Oklahoma history, and World War II; newspaper clippings on Norman, Oklahoma, history; books (1895-1926) on music, and prose and poetry readings; reviews (1941-1948) of scientific books; and postcards, road maps, and travel brochures (ca. 1910-1950) collected by Richards.

Richardson, David Phillip (b. 1869) 967
Papers 1890-1954
.25 foot

Banker and physician. Correspondence (1947-1948) and news clippings (1938-1939) regarding Richardson's medical career and his service as an Oklahoma banking official; publications (1906-1939), including telephone directories (1906-1907) for Union City, Oklahoma Territory, and magazines and journals such as *Harlow's Weekly* (1928) and *The Oklahoma Banker* (1928-1938) which contain articles about Richardson as a banking commissioner.

Riggs, Rollie Lynn (1899-1954) 968
Papers 1926-1966
.66 foot

Poet and playwright. Correspondence (1921-1936) with some poetry enclosed; newspaper and magazine clippings (1926-1966); and manuscripts (1924-1932) by or about Riggs and his plays and poetry, as well as his relations with the artist communities of the University of Oklahoma, Taos, and Santa Fe, New Mexico, Hollywood, California, and New York City. Correspondents include Betty Kirk Boyer and Willard Spud Johnson. The collection also includes playbills for a number of his plays.

Rinsland, Henry Daniel (b. 1889) 969
Papers 1918-1953
8.66 feet

Professor. Correspondence (1941-1953) of Rinsland with colleagues regarding his work and research in the field of education, educational testing and measurement, the study and teaching of spelling and vocabulary, and the standardization and methodology of testing, both for personnel selection and educational purposes, as well as other uses; unpublished reports (1945) of research conducted by the Works Progress Administration regarding the vocabulary and word use frequency of children; and publications (1929), including copies of *A Brief on the Rinsland Spelling Book* and guide books for *The Alice and Jerry Basic Readers* series.

Rister, Carl Coke (1889-1955) 970
Papers 1868-1951
.75 foot

Historian. Student grade books (1929-1951) from history courses taught by Rister at the University of Oklahoma; manuscripts (1889-1920) regarding the settlement of Oklahoma, written by early settlers, and relating their experiences and observations; and typescripts of the official reports (1868-1871) of generals William T. Sherman and Philip H. Sheridan regarding the actions and experiences of their units against Indians, with detailed descriptions of armed engagements, and of negotiations with chiefs and tribes. The Sherman and Sheridan reports are copies of the originals in the Library of Congress, Washington, D.C.

Rittenhouse, Frank A. 971
Records 1848-1949
.33 foot

Freemason. Financial reports (1945-1949) and by-laws (1906-1944) of the Guthrie (Oklahoma) Lodge of Freemasons; typescripts (n.d.) of speeches and presentations made by Rittenhouse to Oklahoma freemasonry groups, including one marking the seventy-fifth anniversary of Indian Territory freemasonry, the fifty-sixth anniversary of Oklahoma Territory freemasonry, as well as the fortieth anniversary of freemasonry in the state of Oklahoma, and also regarding the history of freemasonry in Indian and Oklahoma territories, along with publications (1890-1949), including *Joseph Samuel Murrow's Masonic Monitor* (1903) and a program (1949) marking the fiftieth anniversary of freemasonry in Oklahoma.

Robertson, James Brooks Ayers (1871-1938) 972
Papers 1903-1938
4 feet

Governor. Correspondence (1906-1938) regarding the Oklahoma Constitutional Convention of 1906, the condition and governance of the state after World War I, and the Okmulgee County (Oklahoma) trial incident; publications (1906-1925), including *Referendum News* and the *Oklahoma Odd Fellow* published by the International Order of Odd Fellows, of which Robertson was a member; newspaper clippings (1914-1938) regarding Robertson; scrapbooks and notebooks (ca. 1938) regarding Robertson's career and influence in politics; speeches (n.d.) by Robertson regarding his positions on prohibition, the eighteenth amendment to the federal constitution, the Oklahoma Department of Pardon and Parole, and his inauguration; along with condolence cards (1938) received by Robertson's widow and family upon his death. The collection also includes gubernatorial Special Order No. 11 (1922) regarding the membership of Oklahoma National Guard officers in the Ku Klux Klan.

Unpublished finding aid available.

Robertson, Samuel W. (b. 1860) 973
Papers 1876-1939
.33 foot

Teacher. Correspondence (1876-1931) between Robertson and his parents, mostly regarding family life and mission activities; and an autobiography of Samuel W. Robertson, with biographical information on Robertson's parents, William S. and Ann W. Robertson, the well-known Presbyterian missionaries to the Creek Indians.

Robey, Roberta (b. ca. 1891) 974
Diary 1833-1835
1 item

Missionary. A diary (1833-1835) of Cassandra Sawyer Lockwood describing her journey to the Cherokee Nation, Indian Territory, and life at Dwight Mission. The diary includes mention of efforts by the mission staff to free slaves.

Robinson, Jim Lee 975
Records 1922-1932
6 items

Collector. Chattel mortgages (1929-1932) issued in Beckham County, Oklahoma; and receipts (1922-1929) for payment of Beckham County taxes, on the reverse of which are listed tax schedules for county, city, township, and school districts for the year.

Rock Island Technical Society Collection 976
Records 1879-1987
160 feet

Historical society. Records of the Chicago, Rock Island, and Pacific Railroad Company including dismantling files (1981-1987); contract and easement listings (1981-1987); inventory records by sub-division (1980-1985); highway crossings by state and county (1973-1987); tract estimates (1972-1985); review committee reports of land sales by city (1981-1984); motor vehicle reports (1972-1987); purchasing and sales files (1971-1986); engineering files (1930-1986); law department files (1906-1984); VPO contracts (1879-1984); tax and stock reports to states (1910-1984); card files containing information on locations of gas, water, and sewer pipe lines (1914-1984); daily reports concerning the thirty-five day strike by the clerks' union (1979); inspection trip reports concerning the southern division of the railroad (1969-1976); files concerning railroad operations at El Reno, Oklahoma (1977-1979); and company general orders-southern division (1972-1977).

Unpublished finding aid available.

Rogers County Medical Society Collection 977
Records 1915-1952
1.33 feet

Professional organization. Correspondence (1915-1916, 1936-1952); minutes (1943-1951); and printed material from the records of the secretary-treasurer of the Rogers County (Oklahoma) Medical Society, which became the Rogers-Mayes County Medical Society in 1950.

Rogers-Neill Collection 978
Papers 1871-1943
1 foot

Collectors. Business correspondence and papers (1871-1935) of Fritz Sittell relating to the Choctaw Coal and Railway Company, the Choctaw Trading Company, Sittell's other business interests, and the development of the town of McAlester, Oklahoma; personal correspondence (1871-1943) including letters from Tams Bixby, Peter Pitchlynn, the Pitchlynn family, Green McCurtain, Robert L. Owen, Moritz Lippman, and others; and certificates (1890-1900) of Sittell's appointment as U.S. marshall and special deputy sheriff of Tobucksy County, Choctaw Nation, along with clippings, business cards, a sketch of house floor plans, government documents, and biographical materials relating to Sittell's family.

Rogers, Henry Collins 979
Papers 1902-ca. 1945
.10 foot

Physician. A letter (1902) to Rogers praising his services as a physician; a resolution (ca. 1945) by the Muskogee, Oklahoma, chapter of Woodmen of the World noting Rogers's death; and a diploma (1914) issued to Rogers, along with medical instruments used by Rogers in his practice.

Rogers, John Powell (b. 1892) 980
Papers 1924-1941
1.33 feet

University regent. Correspondence (1924-1941); minutes (1924-1927) of the University of Oklahoma Board of Regents; and annual reports, building reports, and financial statements (1930-1933) of the president of the university, all regarding the operation and maintenance of the University of Oklahoma. Also included in this collection are publications of the Association of Governing Boards of State Universities and Allied Institutions.

Rogers, William Charles 981
Printed materials 1893-1907
.66 foot

Indian chief. Typescripts of editorials and newspaper articles (1893-1907) concerning Rogers, the last principal chief of the Cherokees prior to statehood; a court case in 1900; the 1903 campaign for chief of the Cherokees; the closing of tribal government; and the Sequoyah Movement.

Roodhouse, Frank S. 982
Printed materials 1929-1930
2 items

Collector. Copies of "Proposed Amendments to the City Charter of Shawnee, Oklahoma" (1929), and "City Charter of Shawnee, Oklahoma: Proposed Amendments of 1930."

Rose, Noah Hamilton (d. 1952) 983
Papers 1925-1952
6.33 feet

Professional photographer. Biographies (ca. 1925) of Texans and other southwesterners; publications (1929-1933) by national councils and committees regarding cosmopolitanism, disarmament, and the League of Nations, as well as by the Nanking government of the Republic of China concerning the Sino-Japanese War; posters and placards (1931) regarding disarmament; and a newspaper (1932) published in Osaka, Japan, bearing the banner headline, "The Republic of Manchuria-Birth of a New Nation," the topic to which the entire issue is devoted.

Unpublished finding aid available.

Ross, John (1790-1866) 984
Printed materials 1829-1874
.50 foot

Indian chief. Typescripts of newspaper articles (1829-1874) regarding Ross, the history of the Cherokee Indians, and political and social conditions within the Cherokee Nation.

Ross, Leslie P., Sr. (1863-1944) 985
Papers 1892-1944
.50 foot

Territorial politician and jurist. Correspondence (1892-1916) received by Ross regarding party politics and politicians in Oklahoma Territory, and requests for appointment to political offices; a newspaper obituary (1944) of Ross; and a homestead certificate (1902) issued by President Theodore Roosevelt to a pioneer in Oklahoma Territory. A principal correspondent of Ross was William C. Renfrow, and Renfrow's letters comment on his activities before, and during, his term as governor of Oklahoma Territory.

Ross, Samuel Price (b. 1862) 986
Papers 1867-1936
.33 foot

Physician. Ledgers (1912-1922) in which Ross recorded patients attended and fees charged; certificates and diplomas (1989-1922) awarded Ross by medical schools, brotherhoods, and the medical board of the Choctaw Nation; and a typescript (1867-

1936) of an account by Mrs. Ross of her experiences as the wife of a physician in Indian Territory, describing with detail the social conditions of the area, the state and practice of medicine there, and the lives and customs of its inhabitants.

Ross, William Potter (1820-1891) 987
Printed materials 1866-1891
.75 foot

Indian chief. Typescripts of newspaper articles (1866-1891) of Ross's messages and instructions to the Cherokee Nation, the Cherokee council, and the Cherokee delegation to Washington, D.C., regarding reconstruction, tribal government, financial matters, organization of Oklahoma Territory, education, Sequoyah, and the use of lands, along with biographical information on Ross.

Rotary International of Oklahoma Collection 988
Printed materials 1914-1985
11.50 feet

Service organization. Programs (1935-1985); minutes and club records (1952-1985); club publications (1914-1985); and histories (1914-1985) of the clubs throughout Oklahoma, all accumulated in 1985-1986 by the Rotary International of Oklahoma under the direction of Doane Farr.

Unpublished finding aid available.

Ruggiers, (Mrs.) Paul Eddleman 989
Notebook 1920
1 item

Collector. A notebook (1920) in which Ruggiers's father, Morgan W. Eddleman, recorded engineering field notes and related information while an engineering student at the University of Oklahoma.

Ruggiers, Paul George (b. 1918) 990
Records 1956
.66 foot

Professor. Records (1956), including correspondence, reports, speeches, financial records, and guides produced by the Great Plains Conference on Higher Education which convened at the University of Oklahoma in 1956 to address the question, "What distinctive cultural services, both traditional and newly conceived, may our universities and colleges render to the Great Plains?"

Russell, Campbell (1863-1937) 991
Papers 1904-1937
1.33 feet

State official and politician. Correspondence (1905-1937) to and from Russell regarding the Oklahoma Corporation Commission of which he was a commissioner, and Oklahoma politics in general; political posters (ca. 1920-1930) printed by Russell to support his campaigns for election to the Oklahoma Corporation Commission and to congress, and also regarding various political issues of the day; speeches (ca. 1920-1930) delivered by Russell; by-laws and the certificate of incorporation (1933) for the Self Help Exchange, a Depression-era, unemployed persons league; and publications, including newspapers (1919-1925) printed by Russell for propaganda purposes, periodicals (1925-1936) such as *The Cactus Hornet* and *The Oklahoma Banker*, and a booklet (1919) proposing federal ownership of the railroad system, along with transcripts (n.d.) of the proceedings of the Oklahoma Supreme Court.

Unpublished finding aid available.

Russell, Earl C. 992
Records 1939-1953
4 feet

Collector. Correspondence (1949-1953); membership reports and rosters (1949-1952); financial and expense records (1952-1953); and publications (1949-1953) received or generated by the office of the district governor of the Oklahoma Regional Lions Clubs International, accumulated by Russell while serving as regional district governor of the Lions from the late 1940s through the early 1950s.

Russo, Peter E. 993
Printed materials 1946-1952
2 items

Physician. A reprint of a journal article (1952) entitled "Pioneering in the Use of X-Ray and Radium in Oklahoma" by Everett S. Lain; and a reprint of a speech (1946) by Russo entitled "Pioneer Users of X-Rays in Oklahoma."

Ruth, Kent (1916-1990) 994
Papers 1920-1990
46 feet

Writer. The original manuscript (1959), first proof, and plate proof of Ruth's book *Colorado Vacations* published by the Alfred A. Knopf Company in 1959, along with personal and professional correspondence (1920s-1980s); research files (1961-1987) for a travel series he wrote for Oklahoma newspapers; research files (1965-1988), primarily for Oklahoma and southwestern topics; research files (1956-1977) exclusively for Oklahoma places and points of interest; drafts, story lines, ideas, and manuscripts, including published items, (1928-1965) for articles and books; travel columns (1971-1985); manuscripts and published items for filler pieces (1953-1986); trip notes (1950-1985); and general research notes (1962-1990).

Unpublished finding aid available.

Rutherford, L. Morton, II 995
Papers 1940
2 items

Attorney. A report (1940) of the Oklahoma state senate Committee on Oil Investigation of which Rutherford was a member, and a letter (1940) to his son regarding the same.

Ryan, Jesse Willis 996
Papers 1888-1974
.75 foot

Collector. Correspondence (1888-1915) between family members regarding Ryan family affairs, and the move to El Reno, Oklahoma Territory, in 1902, along with newspapers (1939-1974) regarding declarations of war in 1939 and 1941, the American landings on the moon, and the resignation of President Richard M. Nixon.

Sac and Fox Indian Agency Collection 997
Records 1840-1888
.33 foot

Indian tribal agency. Ledgers (1876-1888) recording receipt of, and payment for supplies, expenditures for freight costs, the police force, employee salaries, cash payments to Indians, and names of Indians eligible for payment; along with copies of correspondence (1840-1872) from agent John Beach to the governor of Iowa and other officials regarding land distribution, employment, depredations, trade, education, and problems among the Sac and Fox; and including one letter (1872) from the governor of Kansas to Gen. John Pope regarding Indian depredations in western Kansas and the captivity of Mary Jordan by raiding Indians.

Saint John's Protestant Episcopal Church Collection 998
Records 1938-1942
.25 foot

Christian church. Six roll books (ca. 1938-1942) from the Sunday school; reports (1940) of the rector, wardens, and vestrymen; a report (1940) of the secretary of the Protestant Episcopal Cathedral Foundation of the Diocese of Oklahoma; a report (1935-1941) of property added and improvements made; a report (1942) on construction; two bulletins (April-May, 1942); and the constitution and canons (1939) of the Diocese of Oklahoma, all from Saint John's Protestant Episcopal Church in Oklahoma City, Oklahoma.

Salter, Lewis Spencer (d. ca. 1987) 999
Papers 1893-1933
.25 foot

Collector. Typescript of a diary (n.d.) by Anna K. Wood recounting her trip from Denver, Colorado, to the border of the Cherokee Outlet in preparation for the 1893 land run; minutes (1912-1921) of the Arthur Foote Music Club at the University of Oklahoma; a roster (1898) of soldiers in Company "M" of the First Volunteer Infantry Regiment, of Indian Territory; and a published history (1933) of the Men's Dinner Club in Oklahoma City, Oklahoma.

Sanders, Stella E. 1000
Manuscript 1815-1964
1 item

Professor. A dissertation (1964), bound but unpublished, written by Sanders in French for the Sorbonne University in Paris, France, and entitled "Le Theatre de Henri-Rene Lenormand." Bound-in are letters (1952-1964) from Paul Blanchart, Gabriel Marcel, and Jean-Jacques Bernard, as well as an edict (1815) authorizing Pierre-Henri-Rene Lenormand to collect taxes in his district of Paris.

Sapulpa (Oklahoma) Euchee Boarding School Collection 1001
Records 1915-1918
.25 foot

U.S. Indian Service school. Ledgers (1915-1918) recording supplies used by the school, along with the number of teachers and students in attendance.

Sapulpa (Oklahoma) Frankoma Pottery Company Collection 1002
Printed materials 1952
.10 foot

Manufacturer. A brochure (1952) and picture postcards (1952) regarding the operations and products of the Frankoma Pottery Company of Sapulpa, Oklahoma, a nationally and internationally recognized pottery manufacturer.

Savage, William Woodrow, Jr. 1003
Papers 1973-1982
2.66 foot

Professor. Original manuscripts and galley proofs (1973-1977) for Savage's books, including *The Cowboy Hero...*; *Cowboy Life*; *The Frontier*, *The Cherokee Strip Livestock Association: The Impact of Federal Regulations ...*, and *Indian Life Transforming: An American Myth*, along with correspondence and papers (1981-1982) relating to comparative frontier studies at the University of Oklahoma.

Unpublished finding aid available.

Schaefer, Hedwig 1004
Papers ca. 1914
2 items

Collector. A mimeographed Christmas letter (1914) from Hiram H. Clouse, pastor of the Rainy Mountain Baptist Mission, to supporters and friends of the mission describing the year's activities, trials, and accomplishments, along with a brochure entitled "Rainy Mountain" which gives a brief history of the mission with biographical information on the Kiowa deacons and interpreters.

Schaper, William August (1869-1955)   1005
Papers 1909-1957
1.25 feet

Professor. Correspondence (1909-1957) regarding the administration of the political science department at the University of Minnesota, Schaper's dismissal from the university faculty in 1917 due to his stance on the war with Germany, and regarding the state of the Progressive Party in the presidential election of 1912; and typescripts (ca. 1922) of a speech by university professor Frederick Hindekoper regarding military policy and history. Also in this collection are publications (1913-1917), including a booklet urging citizens of Minneapolis, Minnesota, to vote for a new charter for that city, and the proceedings of the Board of Regents of the University of Minnesota regarding Schaper's dismissal.

Unpublished finding aid available.

Schmidt, Robert W.   1006
Papers 1864-1889
5 items

Collector. Correspondence (1864-1889) received by the Schmidt family, immigrants to this country, from family members remaining in Germany. The letters are written in German.

Schmitt, Karl and Iva   1007
Papers 1947-1965
4.50 feet

Anthropologists. Field notes (1947-1951); articles (1947-1965); and other research notes (n.d.) concerning the Schmitts's work among the Wichita Indians, the Caddo, the Pawnee, and other southern plains tribes.

Unpublished finding aid available.

Schonwald, Fred P.   1008
Papers 1875-1977
.33 foot

Oil producer. Business and personal correspondence (1934-1966); catalogs (1953-1958) of art exhibits and collections; publications relating to the oil industry; a copy of a map of northwestern territories (ca. 1875); and minutes and correspondence (1962-1977) of the Indian Territory Posse of Oklahoma Westerners.

Scott, George W. (b. 1872)   1009
Papers 1904-1909
.75 foot

Indian statesman. Correspondence (1904-1909) regarding Choctaw Nation affairs and issues, including the movement for separate statehood for Indian Territory, statehood for Oklahoma, Choctaw politics, and Green McCurtain.

Scott, Howell A. 1010
Speech 1953
1 item

Physician. A typescript of a speech (ca. 1953) by Scott regarding the history of hospitals in Muskogee, Oklahoma, and the roles played by area physicians in their establishment.

Searcy, Emmett Coldwell (1865-1945) 1011
Papers 1832-1934
1 foot

Collector. Correspondence (1902) and a manuscript (ca. 1890) regarding the Red Moon Indian Boarding School for Cheyenne-Arapaho Indians; musical scores (n.d.) by Kate Searcy; publications (1892-1903) of temperance societies; items from the world fairs of 1893 and 1904; correspondence (1933-1934) from a veteran of the 1868 Battle of the Washita describing the role of George Armstrong Custer and the conflict in general; and nineteenth-century textbooks published between 1832 and 1866.

Sears, Alfred Byron (1906-1954) 1012
Papers 1917-1973
5.33 feet

Professor. Personal correspondence (1917-1973) of Sears and his wife, Helen Sears; professional correspondence (1946-1959) of Sears; research materials (1906-1954) on the history of aviation, including publications and reports of the Oklahoma Aviation Commission, magazine articles and clippings, and bibliography cards.

Seay, Abraham Jefferson (1832-1915) 1013
Papers 1832-1923
.75 foot

Territorial governor. An autobiography (1832-1893) of Governor Seay relating his childhood, his terms as an associate justice of the Oklahoma Territorial Supreme Court and later as governor of the territory; a biography (1915) of Seay, including a history of his family, written by Clark Brown; typescripts of Seay's diaries (1862-1864, 1892-1893), in which he recorded his experiences as a Union soldier in the Civil War, and his actions as governor of Oklahoma Territory. Also included in this collection are typescripts of letters (1905-1909) sent and received by Seay, regarding the events of his life after his retirement from government, and his pivotal role in early territorial politics.

Seay, Edgar W., Jr. 1014
Papers 1915-1950
2 feet

Collector. Nineteen engineering drawings, primarily by the Chicago, Rock Island, and Pacific Railroad Company, showing rights-of-way for areas in Arkansas, Louisiana, Oklahoma, and Texas.

Unpublished finding aid available.

Selby, (Mrs.) Bruce (b. ca. 1902) 1015
Papers 1917-1968
.10 foot

Collector. Correspondence (1917-1919) from American soldiers in Europe during World War I, along with World War II ration books (1942-1945).

Seminole Nation Papers 1016
Papers 1840-1979
.10 foot

Indian tribe. Typescripts of correspondence (1840-1939) and newspaper articles (1906-1933) regarding John Jumper and Seminole land disputes, along with resolutions and ordinances (1969-1979) of the Seminole General Council.

Seneca Nation Papers 1017
Papers 1892-1916
.10 foot

Indian tribe. Acts (1892) of the Seneca Nation, along with correspondence (1892-1916) regarding the allotment of tribal lands in northeastern Oklahoma and claims of the Cayuga Indians against the Seneca Nation.

Seneker, George Washington 1018
Records 1894-1913
.10 foot

Collector. Records of School District No. 11, in Kingfisher County, Oklahoma Territory, including registers of pupils (1894-1906); a receipt book (1894-1908) indicating payments for supplies purchased and wages paid; and a financial ledger (1894-1913) of the clerk of the school district in which the names of the school district officials are also recorded.

Serviss, Irma Porter 1019
Records 1894-1934
.75 foot

Collector. Territorial- and early statehood-era school records from districts in Noble and Grant counties, Oklahoma, including teachers record books (1907-1938);

school district clerks records (1915-1934); pupil rosters (1907-1917); listings of teachers and district officials (1894-1941); records of annual meetings (1915-1934); and school warrants issued (1915-1934).

Shackelford, Marshall, Jr. (b. ca. 1928) 1020
Papers 1862-1921
.10 foot

Collector. Typescripts of letters (1862-1863) written by Robert L. Shackelford, a Confederate soldier, to his parents in Georgia, describing his experiences in the Civil War. Also included is a letter (1921) from the United Daughters of the Confederacy regarding Shackelford's service record.

Shadid, Michael Abraham (1882-1966) 1021
Printed materials 1912-1984
1 foot

Physician. Newspaper and journal articles (1912-1984) and publications (1924-1947) regarding the life and career of Michael A. Shadid and his contributions to cooperative medicine, especially the Cooperative Community Hospital that he established in Elk City, Oklahoma, with information regarding its history, status, cost, and the unsuccessful attempt by the Beckham County (Oklahoma) Medical Association to close the hospital. The collection includes the *Community Hospital Bulletin* (1945-1953) and the cornerstone (1934) of the original hospital building.

Sharp, Paul F. 1022
Papers 1964-1989
8 feet

Professor and university president. Papers (1964-1989) including correspondence, speeches, book contracts, and research materials relating to Paul Sharp's presidency at Drake University, Des Moines, Iowa, and the University of Oklahoma, Norman, Oklahoma, his publications, and his attendance at conferences, commencement exercises, and inaugurations of other university presidents. Also included is information about his career in higher education and correspondence with history professor Gilbert Fite.

Unpublished finding aid available.

Sherrill, Rufus Hansen (1883-1952) 1023
Papers 1926-1930
10 items

Physician. Correspondence (1926-1930) from Indians to Sherrill, a general practitioner in Broken Bow, Oklahoma, asking for medical treatment and medicines.

Shilling, Marvin 1024
Papers 1931-1932
.33 foot

Attorney. Correspondence (1931-1932); legal documents (1931-1932); and newspaper clippings (1931-1932), all regarding the trial of two Carter County, Oklahoma, deputies charged with killing the children of two prominent Mexican families, including a relative of the Mexican president, Pascual Ortiz Rubio. The collection also contains a transcript of the preliminary hearing of the deputies, as well as telegrams and correspondence from Oklahoma governor William H. Murray concerning the delicacy of the situation and the dangers of an unjust trial.

Shippey, E. E. 1025
Records 1912-1928
.10 foot

Physician. Account books (1912-1928) in which Shippey recorded insurance policies sold to clients in the town of Wister, Oklahoma.

Shook, William Vance (b. 1871) 1026
Papers 1871-1954
.10 foot

Minister. A typewritten autobiography (1871-1953) of W. Vance Shook regarding his life as a rural circuit-riding minister in Oklahoma Territory and Oklahoma, with descriptions of the communities in which he lived, and of the churches he founded and served as pastor; newspaper clippings (1938-1957) regarding the death of Shook's wife, Lottie Lee, and the establishment of the Methodist Episcopal churches in Putnam City, Oklahoma, and at Eighth and Lee streets in Oklahoma City, Oklahoma; and publications (1918-1935), including the programs of the annual conferences of the Methodist Episcopal Church of Oklahoma, a booklet regarding the history of Methodism in Logan County, Oklahoma, and event programs issued by the Putnam City Methodist Church and the Eighth and Lee streets Methodist church in Oklahoma City, Oklahoma.

Short, George F. 1027
Letter 1962
1 item

Attorney. A letter (1962) from Lacey Mullen to Short regarding the friendship of Mullen's father with Short, and praising Short's admirable qualities.

Short, Julia A. "Julee" 1028
Papers 1832-1970
.25 foot

Author. A copy of the final issue (1968) of *The Oklahoma Advertizer*; student term papers (n.d.) and journal articles regarding the surrender of Stand Watie, the lives of Walter Campbell and Roger Williams, and Washington Irving's tour of the Oklahoma area in 1832. The collection also contains some correspondence (1967-1970) from scholars regarding the above topics.

Shumard, Evelyn H.   1029
Papers   1898-1939
2 feet

Collector. Minutes (1898-1902) of the city council of Sapulpa, Indian Territory; diaries (1915) of Evelyn Shumard; short manuscripts (n.d.) by Shumard entitled "Outlaws," "The Parade," The Spirit of Tulsa," "My Life," and "Oklahoma;" scrapbooks (n.d.) by Marion, Alice, and Gordon Shumard on various topics including "An Early History of Sapulpa," and memorabilia (n.d.) from schools attended by the Shumards.

Unpublished finding aid available.

Shumate and Sons Collection   1030
Records   1932-1935
1.33 feet

Mercantile company. Ledgers (1932-1935) recording the items sold and prices paid by customers in the Shumate Department Store in Pauls Valley, Oklahoma, during the Great Depression.

Shumate, Enola   1031
Ledger   ca. 1897
1 item

Collector. A ledger (ca. 1897) containing census cards recording members of the Seminole tribe in Indian Territory.

Sigler, Earle Marion (b. 1916)   1032
Diary   1860-1861
1 item

Collector. A photocopy of Thomas Harrison's travel diary which he kept aboard the U.S.S. *Susquehanna* while on a cruise in the Mediterranean Sea in 1860-1861. Harrison describes his impressions of ports of call, and provides a complete listing of expenses, compiled item-by-item, city-by-city.

Sigma Alpha Epsilon Collection   1033
Printed materials   1906-1954
4 feet

College social fraternity. Publications relating to the Sigma Alpha Epsilon (S.A.E.) fraternity, including a yearbook (1909-1910), a history of S.A.E. (1911), copies of *The Record* (1910-1920), *Pi Alpha* (1914-1934), and *Songs of S.A.E.*; scrapbooks (1916-1978); minute books (1906-1909, 1949-1954); and a biographical record (1909-1921) relating to the University of Oklahoma chapter of S.A.E.

Unpublished finding aid available.

Sigma Delta Chi　　　　　　　　　　　　　　　　　　　　　　　　　　　1034
Records 1948-1958
1 foot

Fraternity. Correspondence (1952-1958); reports (1948-1958); memoranda; and publications regarding the University of Oklahoma's chapter of Sigma Delta Chi, a national journalism honorary fraternity.

Sigma Nu Collection　　　　　　　　　　　　　　　　　　　　　　　　1035
Printed materials 1917-1953
1 foot

College social fraternity. Printed materials, including chapter manuals (1946-1950); a yearbook (1949); a program (1939); copies of journals (1941-1948); and reports relating to the Sigma Nu fraternity, along with autograph books (1917-1927) and receipt books (1947) from the University of Oklahoma chapter of Sigma Nu.

Simon, Earle Marvin (1895-1974)　　　　　　　　　　　　　　　　　　1036
Papers 1900-1960
7.33 feet

City clerk and civic leader. Papers (1900-1960), including pamphlets, books, newspaper clippings, and other printed materials, plus correspondence relating to the American Legion, Oklahoma City, Oklahoma, and Simon's teaching career; certificates and awards presented to Simon; and a scrapbook concerning Simon's life.

Unpublished finding aid available.

Simpson, John Andrew (1871-1934)　　　　　　　　　　　　　　　　　1037
Papers. 1889-1938
2.75 feet

Farm leader. Correspondence (1917-1934) with Simpson regarding Oklahoma Farmers Union and National Farmers Union policies, issues, stances, and activities, including financial papers and meeting minutes of the Farmers Union; Simpson's nomination for the position of U.S. Secretary of Agriculture in Franklin D. Roosevelt's first cabinet; Simpson's opposition to President Herbert Hoover and his support of Al Smith's candidacy for president; Simpson's opinions regarding bimetallism, the National Farm Board, compulsory military service, and allegiance to the state; and condolences received by Simpson's widow upon his death. Principal correspondents include Franklin D. Roosevelt, Huey P. Long, Henry Morgenthau, James A. Farley and Elmer Thomas. Also in this collection are Simpson's diaries (1924-1934); transcripts of radio and other speeches (1919-1933) delivered by Simpson; news clippings (n.d.); and newspapers (1917-1934), all relating to farm topics; and orders (1934) for Simpson's book *The Militant Voice of Agriculture.*

Unpublished finding aid available.

Simpson, (Mrs.) Morris S. 1038
Papers 1909-1925
.10 foot

Collector. Certificates of stock ownership (1909-1918) issued by the University Improvement Association in Lawton, Oklahoma, and the Crescent Mining, Milling and Oil Company, also of Lawton, Oklahoma; news clippings (n.d.) regarding Lawton, Oklahoma, citizens; a letterhead (ca. 1930) from the Lawton Mercantile Company; and a handwritten resolution (1925) composed by dinner guests of the Simpsons regarding their hosts' hospitality and kindness, and signed by all present, including Senator Elmer Thomas and several army generals stationed at Fort Sill, Oklahoma.

Skelly, William Grove (b. 1878) 1039
Speech 1954
1 item

Oil man. A typescript of a speech given by Skelley in 1954 at the University of Oklahoma Association's annual "Achievement Day."

Skinner, Esthmer H. 1040
Papers 1944-1969
.33 foot

Collector. A booklet (1969) published by Orange County, California, in tribute to President Richard Nixon; certificates (1933) issued to Skinner by the Republican Party of California, and the University of Oklahoma Foundation; and propaganda (1944-1945) printed by the Nazis and air-dropped to American troops fighting the Battle of the Bulge near Bastogne, Belgium, advising them of their certain defeat and death, and of the post-war demise of the United States. Also included are sheets of postage stamps (1948-1957) commemorating the fiftieth anniversary of Oklahoma statehood and the centennials of the petroleum industry and the Five Civilized Tribes of Oklahoma.

Slick, Thomas Baker (1883-1929) 1041
Papers 1914-1973
4 feet

Oil man. Correspondence (1920-1939); reports (1930-1939); leases and deeds (1914-1973); and tax records (1926-1933) from the estate of Tom Slick, all regarding his petroleum and real estate business interests in Oklahoma.

Unpublished finding aid available.

Slover, James Anderson, Sr. (b. 1824) 1042
Manuscript 1826-1907
1 item

Missionary. A photocopy of the autobiography (ca. 1907) of James Slover, a missionary to the Cherokee Nation during the Civil War. The typewritten manuscript contains his observations of Cherokee Indian attitudes and opinions concerning slavery, support of and participation in the Civil War, and the Confederacy, with specific reference to the Cherokee regiment organized and led by Stand Watie, and Slover's duties as regimental chaplain. Also included are accounts of post-Civil War difficulties in Arkansas due to the depressed economy, race relations, and the Reconstruction government, and Slover's subsequent decision to move to California.

Smallwood, Ben F. (1829-1891) 1043
Printed materials 1889-1891
5 items

Indian chief. Typescripts of Smallwood's messages (1889-1890) to the Choctaw Nation on the affairs of government, especially in the area of education, and articles (1891) commenting on his death and containing biographical information.

Smiser, (Mrs.) Butler Stonestreet (b. 1865) 1044
Papers 1915-1950
.10 foot

Publisher. Newspaper clippings (1935-1950) regarding the Smisers and their publishing activities and early years in Atoka, Indian Territory; a memorial (1915) to Katrina Ellett Murrow, wife of Joseph Samuel Murrow and a Baptist missionary to the Choctaw Indians; and an unpublished paper (n.d.) by John E. Dodd entitled "The Life of J. S. Murrow."

Smith, (Mrs.) E. P. 1045
Scrapbook 1832-1948
1 item

Collector. A scrapbook containing news clippings regarding the history (1832-1948) of the Hughes County, Oklahoma, region. Also included is a hand-drawn map of Hughes County, showing the route of the Texas Road and the locations of Camp Holmes, Oak Ridge Seminary, and Edwards Trading Post.

Smith, (Mrs.) Edward Needham (b. 1907) 1046
Papers 1839-1937
.33 foot

Collector. Correspondence (1852-1950) regarding the affairs and genealogy of the Needham family of Ohio and Minnesota, from whom the donor of this collection is descended, and regarding Edward Z. Needham's attempts to be awarded the Congressional Medal of Honor during the Civil War, and describing the 1863 Battle of Bristow Station, Virginia; legal documents (1853-1857), including letters of guardianship, deeds for land, a last will and testament, and a probate court record for guardianship; newspaper clippings (1870-1928) regarding the company flag of the First Minnesota Volunteer Infantry, and the Edward Smith family of Spokane, Washington, direct descendants of Needham; a proclamation (1861) by the governor of Minnesota mustering the First Minnesota Volunteer Infantry Regiment for service in the Civil War; diaries (1859-1865) of Edward Z. Needham recording his experiences immediately prior to, and during the Civil War, including entries detailing his observations of the Battle of Chickahominy, Virginia, one of the Seven Days Battles in 1862, the First Battle of Manassas, or Bull Run, in 1861, and the Battle of Sharpsburg, also known as Antietam, in 1862; pins, medals, and medallions (ca. 1899-1913) received by participants at reunions of the Civil War and Spanish-American War-era Minnesota regiments, and at encampments of the Grand Army of the Republic; and publications (1839-1935), including a two-volume history of Rome, published in 1839, a history of the United States, published in 1842, and Civil War infantry tactics and soldier sanitation guides. Also included in this collection is the official song (1861) of Company "G" of the First Minnesota Volunteer Infantry Regiment composed by Alfred L. Needham.

Smith, Franklin Campbell (b. 1874) 1047
Papers 1836-1946
.33 foot

Minister. A typescript of Smith's autobiography (1874-1946) which relates his experiences in Oklahoma Territory, and the origins of Oklahoma place names, as well as stories concerning religion, settlers, cowboys, marshals, weather, opinions about the Spanish-American War, and the Crazy Snake Rebellion in Indian Territory. The collection also includes a typescript of Smith's biography (1836-1877) of Maj. James Patrick, C.S.A., who held important commands in the southwest during the Civil War.

Smith, H. P. 1048
Diary 1901-1902
1 item

Collector. A diary (1901-1902) kept on a tour of Spain and the Middle East. The author was a Mr. Covey, who traveled with his wife. The diary includes a poem written by the Coveys regarding their travels and dedicated to their fellow passengers aboard the SS *Ramses the Great*.

Smith, Isabel Foster 1049
Papers 1887-1925
.10 foot

Collector. A diary (1887) kept by nineteen-year-old Lula Hulett until her death later in the same year; a letter (1887) regarding Miss Hulett's death; an obituary (1896) written for the Huletts' dog; and newspaper articles (1925) regarding the death of Capt. A. W. Hulett.

Smith, Joseph G. (b. 1870) 1050
Records 1888-1955
.10 foot

Physician. Records (1906-1955) kept by Smith regarding the obstetrical cases he attended in Washington County, Oklahoma; publications (1924-1946) regarding the history and future of the Methodist Episcopal Church in Bartlesville, Oklahoma; medical articles (1924-1928) published by Smith; a newsletter (1946) of the Bartlesville Rotary Club; an article (1944) regarding the Bartlesville YMCA; and certificates and diplomas (1888-1952) awarded Smith by medical schools and societies, including a license to practice (1903) in Oklahoma Territory. Also included in the collection is a letter of reference (1888) written for Smith.

Smith, Micah Pearce   1051
Papers 1930-1936
.10 foot

Historian. Manuscripts (n.d.) written by Smith and entitled "The Seminole Presbyterian Mission," "Dr. Emmet Starr," and "Daniel Collins Home;" research notes (1930-1936) on the Oklahoma towns of Fred, Ninnekah, Chickasha, and Bloomfield, along with a biographical questionnaire relating to Rhoda Gunn Colbert Potts, Daniel Collins, and the Colbert family.

Smith, Samuel Walter (b. 1877)   1052
Printed materials 1877-1949
.10 foot

Pioneer and banker. The memoirs (1877-1949) of Sam Smith, in which he recorded his and the Smith family's adventures in frontier Kansas and Colorado, and their participation in the land run of 1893 into the Cherokee Strip. Of note are his accounts of life and social conditions in a number of Kansas and Colorado towns, and also his mother's reaction to moving into the family's first sod house.

Smith, Stewart K.   1053
Papers 1896-1920
.50 foot

Mining engineer. Smith's correspondence (1902-1907), reports (1896-1920), and appraisals (1896-1920) relating to his career as a civil engineer and a mining consultant. Included in the collection are blueprints of mines (1905-1918). Most of Smith's work was with coal mines in Oklahoma, Indian Territory, Iowa, Missouri, Montana, and West Virginia.

Smithe, P. A.   1054
Records 1907-1923
.10 foot

Surgeon. Patient account records (1907-1923) of the fees charged, but not including services rendered, by Smithe; and medical artifacts used by Smithe in the Red Cross, including two hypodermic kits.

Snider, Denton Jaques (1841-1925)   1055
Manuscript ca. 1921
1 item

Author. A manuscript of Snider's book *A Biography of Ralph Waldo Emerson* published by the William Harvey Miner Company of Saint Louis, Missouri, in 1921.

Snider, Nell Achsah Smith (1873-1955) 1056
Papers 1897-1955
2 items

Collector. Typescripts (n.d.) regarding pioneer life in early Kansas and Oklahoma Territory, and the lives of Lucile Snider Parks and Nell Achsah Smith, and their experiences in Pawnee, Oklahoma Territory.

Snodgrass, Bill (b. ca. 1937) 1057
Manuscript 1959
1 item

College student. A term paper (1959) entitled "Early Development of Labor Unions in Oklahoma" in which the author details the rise of labor guilds, brotherhoods, and unions in Indian Territory and Oklahoma Territory.

Snow, Jerry Whistler 1058
Papers 1893-1915
2 feet

Collector. Correspondence (1893-1915) to and from members of the Whistler family regarding life in Oklahoma Territory, describing a first ride in an automobile, sicknesses and quarantines, floods, Sac and Fox Indian dances and customs, the Sac and Fox Indian Agency and its agent, Lee Patrick, the Chilocco Indian School, wild west shows, Christmas traditions, and Independence Day celebrations. Correspondents include Maude Mayes Whistler, Pearl Mayes Whistler, and Gertrude Nadan.

Unpublished finding aid available.

Snyder, Lawrence H. 1059
Papers 1833-1958
.10 foot

Geneticist. Sketchbooks (1833-1862) in which Snyder's mother wrote poems and drew leaves and cross-sections of flowers; and articles (1947-1958) by Snyder regarding genetics.

Society of Friends Collection 1060
Printed materials 1952-1973
.25 foot

Religious denomination. Published reports (1953-1956) of the Society of Friends (Quaker) Committee on Indian Affairs annual meetings; a report (1952) entitled "American Indian Development," by the National Congress of American Indians;

annual reports (1972-1973) of Friends Centers in Oklahoma; a checklist (n.d.) of repositories holding Society of Friends records; and related publications by the Society of Friends concerning the church's support of Indian affairs.

Sohlberg, George Gustar (b. 1863) 1061
Papers 1857-1942
7 feet

Miller. Financial papers (1883-1929) detailing Sohlberg's association with early Oklahoma City, Oklahoma, business interests, especially the milling industry; and publications (1882-1939), including books, pamphlets, brochures, and flyers on art, music, travel, and motion pictures, along with event programs from the 1914 season of the Overholser Theatre in Oklahoma City, Oklahoma, the 700th anniversary of the city of Berlin, Germany, an automobile construction and care manual published in 1919 by the Cole Motor Car Company, and numerous works regarding major cities and countries throughout the world as they were before World War I; paper money (1857) issued by a bank in Nebraska; and certificates (1909-1934) issued to Sohlberg and others, including one appointing him a member of the Oklahoma City reception committee for President Woodrow Wilson. Also in this collection are booklets detailing the status of aviation (ca. 1920) in the Kingdom of Siam.

Southeastern Oklahoma Medical Association Collection 1062
Records 1921-1942
.33 foot

Medical society. Minutes (1921-1939); correspondence (1930-1942); and the constitution (1922) of the association. The collection also includes papers (n.d.) read before the association, which consists of members from eleven southeastern Oklahoma counties.

Southern Plains Indian Agencies Collection 1063
Records 1804-1899
4.25 feet

Governmental agency. Photocopies of correspondence (1804-1899) between U.S. Indian agents throughout the southern Great Plains region and government officials, regarding the Arapaho, Cheyenne, Kiowa, Osage, Pawnee, Sac and Fox, Wichita, and other Indian tribes. Correspondents include John Beach, Lawrie Tatum, and generals E. D. Townsend, Philip H. Sheridan, and William T. Sherman.

Unpublished finding aid available.

Southwestern Association of Naturalists Collection 1064
Records 1953-1988
3 feet

Professional organization. Correspondence (1953-1981) and general files (1953-1988) regarding the operation, function, and activities of the Southwestern Association of Naturalists. Included in the collection are the minutes of the board of governors, the organization's constitution, and files regarding the history of the association.

Unpublished finding aid available.

Southwestern Oklahoma Survival Association Collection   1065
Records 1869-1959
6 feet

Citizens organization. Records (1957-1959), including correspondence, news releases, news clippings, and municipal, organizational, and legislative resolutions regarding the U.S. Army's intention in 1957 to greatly expand the land area of Fort Sill, Oklahoma, for purposes of creating a missile firing range, and the formation of a regional citizens coalition, the Southwestern Oklahoma Survival Association, which eventually thwarted those plans. Also included in this collection is information regarding prior expansions of Fort Sill, Oklahoma, 1869-1957.

Unpublished finding aid available.

Southwick, (Mrs.) Harl F.   1066
Manuscript 1898-1949
1 item

Housewife. A manuscript (ca. 1949) relating the origin and history of the Garber Christian Church in Garber, Oklahoma.

Spencer, Maude Clinkenbeard   1067
Printed materials ca. 1962
4 items

Genealogist. Genealogies (1962) of the Clinkenbeard and Willford families compiled by Maude Spencer, including an entry regarding the captivity and rescue of relatives kidnapped by Delaware Indians in 1757; and a history of the Winchester store in Winchester, Woods County, Oklahoma.

Spring, Otto F.   1068
Papers 1923-1964
.33 foot

Archaeologist. Correspondence (1923-1964) received by Spring regarding archaeological projects in Oklahoma, including excavations or explorations of mounds, earthworks, settlements, and caverns. The collection includes many items of correspondence from Joseph Thoburn of the Oklahoma Historical Society expressing that organization's interest in Spring's work.

Springstead, Clarence S., Jr. (b. ca. 1936)   1069
Papers 1882-1946
.10 foot

Collector. Correspondence (1911-1945); postcards (1934); newspaper clippings (1893); naturalization certificates (1882-1894); military records (1884-1933); and a last will and testament (1946), all regarding the immigration to the United States of Haus Kjennernd, a Norwegian, and his subsequent service in, and retirement from, the U.S. Army. Also included in this collection are maps (1881-1890) of Washington, D.C., and of Oslo, Norway.

Stafford, B. S. (b. 1853) 1070
Papers 1853-1932
.10 foot

Businessman. A manuscript (1932) of B. S. Stafford's memoirs entitled "Incidents and Recollections of My Life," in which he describes the Civil War in South Carolina, and slavery on his father's plantation. Also included are accounts of land speculation and bank failures in Oklahoma and Texas.

Stalker, Harry 1071
Papers 1892-1954
4 feet

Physician. General correspondence (1904-1950); a diploma (1896) and medical licenses (1896-1909); notebooks and correspondence relating to his education; and correspondence (1936-1948); printed material (ca. 1910-1950); ledgers (1894-1914); daybooks (1896-1951); and other financial records, all relating to his medical practice and farm in Pond Creek, Oklahoma.

Standifer, John E. (1867-1934) 1072
Records 1900-1908
3 items

Physician. Ledgers (1900-1907) in which Standifer recorded patient accounts; and certificates (1900-1908) authorizing him to practice medicine in Oklahoma. Included in the back of one ledger is a speech written by Standifer regarding an unidentified medical topic.

State Republican Party of Oklahoma Collection 1073
Records 1953-1983
128 feet

Political party. Records of the Oklahoma Republican Party, including correspondence files (1963-1981); files on the Rules Study Committee (1965-1975); minutes (1953-1980) and memoranda (1958-1983) from the State Committee; correspondence, press releases, and promotional literature (1969-1979) from the Republican National Committee; minutes and working papers (1963-1979) and budgets and reports (1963-1976) from the State Budget Committee; subject files (1964-1980) on national and state conventions; subject files (1976-1980) of the Legislative Action Committee; fund raising files (1964-1976); research files (1959-1980) by subject and by individual; county files (1968-1974); and fiscal files, including account reports (1958-1979) and payrolls (1961-1978).

Stephens, Margaret Clark (b. ca. 1920) 1074
Papers 1847-1969
.10 foot

Collector. Newspaper and magazine articles (1847-1969) regarding James Kirker (also referred to as Santiago Querque and Santiago Kirker); and a photocopy of a manuscript (1907) regarding frontier life and conditions near Arkansas City, Kansas, during the opening of the Cherokee Strip and subsequent settlement in Oklahoma Territory.

Stevens, Robert S. 1075
Papers 1870-1875
.25 foot

Railroad manager. Typescripts of letters to and from Robert S. Stevens regarding Stevens's management of the Missouri, Kansas, and Texas Railroad of which he was general manager. Included in the collection is a letter to Stevens from President U. S. Grant regarding a trip Grant made from St. Louis, Missouri, to Springfield, Missouri, and Indian Territory. The Western History Collections also holds a more complete set of the Stevens papers on microfilm. The original Stevens Family Papers are in the Division of Rare Books and Manuscripts, Cornell University Library, Ithaca, New York.

Stewart, Elijah King 1076
Papers 1950
.10 foot

Politician. Correspondence (1950) from Victor Wickersham, Oklahoma congressman, and from Elijah King Stewart regarding their contest for Wickersham's congressional seat in 1950; and one of Stewart's political posters used during the campaign. In the correspondence are allegations of wrong-doing brought by Stewart against Wickersham, as well as Wickersham's response to the charges.

Stewart, Roy Pittard (1905-1989) 1077
Papers 1980-1982
1.33 feet

Journalist. Manuscripts and galley proofs of books (1980-1982) by Stewart, including *The Turner Ranch* and *One of a Kind: The Life of C. R. Anthony*; and one unpublished manuscript, "Ambassador on Horseback," regarding the life and career of Oklahoma-born jockey, Everett Haynes. The manuscript regarding Haynes details his experiences as a jockey in Oklahoma, California, Mexico, France, and Germany, and describes with clarity the history of Germany as observed by Haynes from the mid-1920s through World War II, including accounts of his visit with President Paul von Hindenburg, the burning of the Reichstag in Berlin, in 1933, and Haynes's flight from the Nazis in 1939.

Stigler First National Bank Collection 1078
Records 1903-1940
35 feet

Bank. Financial records of the First National Bank of Stigler, Oklahoma, including general ledgers (1905-1939); tellers cash books (1903-1940); journals (1908-1940); discount registers (1918-1938); warrant registers (1914-1932); transfer ledgers (1906-1918); bank remittance ledgers (1915-1930); drafts registers (1909-1924); reconciliation of accounts books (1909-1937); individual loans registers (1920-1927); liability ledgers (1906-1927); distribution of expenses ledgers (1907-1935); bills receivable ledgers (1916-1918); certificate of deposit registers (1903-1922); and an insurance policy ledger (n.d.).

Unpublished finding aid available.

Stigler Masonic Lodge No. 121 Collection 1079
Ledger 1920-1922
1 item

Local Masonic chapter. A ledger containing the minutes (1920-1922) of the A. F. & A. M. Lodge No. 121, a Masonic order chapter in Stigler, Oklahoma.

Stith, Ruth Brewer 1080
Papers 1863-1931
.10 foot

Collector. Correspondence (1911, 1931) relating to the works of Theodore F. Brewer, and short manuscripts by Brewer concerning Methodism in Indian Territory, entitled "The Indians of Oklahoma," "Muskogee Ministerial Association," "Work Among the Indians," "A Historical Sketch of our Work in Oklahoma," "Meeting of the General Board of Education," and "Spaulding Female College." Also included is a manuscript poem (1863) entitled "Red Shiloh," attributed to Brewer, and purportedly written after his participation in the Battle of Shiloh.

Stone, DeWitt (1874-1937) 1081
Ledger 1926
1 item

Physician. A ledger (1926) in which Stone recorded patient accounts, including services rendered and fees charged.

Stone, Lucile Oliver 1082
Publications 1917-1943
.10 foot

Collector. Publications and programs (1917-1943) of P.E.O. chapter and state meetings; the Alternate Saturday Club of Pauls Valley (1917-1925); and the Music Club of Pauls Valley, Oklahoma (1917).

Stovall Museum Collection 1083
Papers 1634-1721
7 items

Natural history museum. Handprinted and painted antiphonaries, psalmody manuscripts, and a Roman missal (1634-1721), from a colonial-era church in San Lucas Camotlan, Oaxaca, Mexico.

Stovall, John Willis (1891-1953) 1084
Papers 1925-1952
3.50 feet

Paleontologist. Correspondence (1935-1952) and ledgers (1935-1938) regarding archaeological excavations in Oklahoma, sponsored by the Works Progress Administration and by the Stovall Museum of the University of Oklahoma, including site reports, findings, and operation reports and requests; and publications (1925-1950) by Stovall and others regarding zoology, evolution, and paleontology, as well as operations and procedural manuals of the Works Progress Administration. The correspondence series of this collection reflects the University of Oklahoma's involvement with the Works Progress Administration.

Unpublished finding aid available.

Stover, Samuel Murray 1085
Diary 1849
2 items

Physician. A diary kept by Stover recording his trek from Missouri to California in 1849, along with a privately printed edition of the diary published by Stover's descendants.

Stroud State Bank Collection 1086
Records 1893-1943
38.50 feet

Bank. Financial records (1893-1943) from the Stroud (Oklahoma) State Bank and its predecessors, the Sac and Fox Bank, and the Milfay State Bank, including general ledgers; cash journals; stock certificate ledgers; tellers cash books; draft registers; discount registers; insurance registers; distribution of expense ledgers; bills receivable ledgers; reconcilement ledgers; note and discount registers; and remittance registers, along with correspondence (1900-1918) from the Stroud State Bank; a bank examiner's report (1941) on the Stroud State Bank; and minutes (1919-1924) of the Milfay State Bank's board of directors.

Unpublished finding aid available.

Strough, D. F., Sr. (d. 1950) 1087
Printed material 1943
1 item

Physician. A yearbook (1945) published by the Oklahoma State Medical Association containing all state laws and regulations pertaining to the practice of medicine in Oklahoma as of 1945.

Struble, (Mrs.) Howard   1088
Papers 1885-1923
.10 foot

Collector. Profit-sharing certificates (1906) issued by Sears, Roebuck, and Company and a souvenir program (1922) from the seventieth-anniversary celebration of the Chicago, Rock Island, and Pacific Railroad Company, held in McAlester, Oklahoma. Though brief, the program contains the early railroad history of the area, as well as information regarding the settlement and subsequent growth of the towns of North McAlester, and South McAlester, Oklahoma.

Sturgis, James Wellings   1089
Papers 1931-1949
3 items

Professor. A letter (1932) from David R. Boyd congratulating Mr. and Mrs. Sturgis on receiving the "Most Useful Citizens" award from the city of Norman, Oklahoma, along with a news magazine (1949) and news clippings (n.d.) regarding the career and death of Mrs. Sturgis's brother, George Burton Parker, a nationally known journalist and former Oklahoman.

Sullivan, (Mrs.) Jim L.   1090
Records 1893-1901
2 items

Collector. A certificate (1893) appointing James Wilks as the first postmaster of Rathbone, Oklahoma Territory; and a land patent (1901) issued to the Wilkses for property in Rathbone, located in County "G," Oklahoma Territory.

Sutton, George Miksch (1898-1982)   1091
Papers ca. 1914-1967
31 feet

Ornithologist. Correspondence (1943-1982); manuscripts (ca. 1920-1967); diaries and field notes (1914-1920); artifacts relating to ornithology in Oklahoma and Mexico; and copies of dissertations (n.d.) by his students. Correspondents include George Lynn Cross, Jean and Richard Graber, John Kirkpatrick, and Olin Sewell Pettingill.

Unpublished finding aid available.

Swank, David (1931-   )   1092
Papers ca. 1965-1975
5 feet

University professor. Correspondence and legal papers (1965-1975) of Swank, along with printed materials relating to his legal research at the University of Oklahoma.

Swearingen, Martha T. (b. ca. 1873) 1093
Records 1895-1909
.10 foot

Pioneer housewife. Appraisals (1905) issued by the Townsite Commission of the Cherokee Nation for lots in Ramona, Indian Territory; a lease (1909) for land in Washington County, Oklahoma; and a work permit (1895) issued by the Cherokee Nation to one of its citizens, Whiteturkey, granting him the privilege of hiring a white non-citizen to farm his land. This collection also includes a patent (1907) for land in Ramona, Indian Territory.

Tait, J. H. 1094
Papers ca. 1920-1925
1 foot

Engineer. Correspondence (1920-1925) and reports (1920-1925) of J. H. Tait, district engineer in Muskogee, Oklahoma, for the Oklahoma Highway Commission. These materials reflect the state of highway construction in Oklahoma in the early 1920s.

Tantlinger, D. Vernon (b. 1864) 1095
Printed materials 1903-1936
.50 foot

Performer. Scrapbooks (1905-1936) and diaries (1903-1912) regarding Tantlinger's performances in wild west shows, including Buckskin Bill's Historical Wild West Show and the Miller Brothers 101 Ranch Wild West Show.

Tarpley, Bloyce 1096
Papers 1862-1863
3 items

Collector. Photocopies of correspondence (1862-1863) between Jacob Moss, a Union soldier, and his family in Missouri, who sympathized with the Confederates, regarding Moss's experiences and the issues that divided his family.

Taylor, Guy William 1097
Papers 1893-1940
5 feet

Physician. General correspondence (1893-1940); financial records (1902-1937) and personal writings of Taylor; two scrapbooks (n.d.), one of his school days, and one containing postcards; biographical materials; minutes and programs (1895-1935) of the Athenaeum Club of El Reno, Oklahoma; and personal artifacts including locks of hair, pins, beadwork, and a cloth napkin.

Taylor, John C. (d. 1935)   1098
Records 1920-1930
.10 foot

Physician. Medical case histories (1920-1924); correspondence (1920-1930) concerning cases; and notes (1920-1930) on testing and treatment procedures, all from Taylor's medical practice in Chelsea, Oklahoma.

Taylor, Joseph Richard (b. 1907)   1099
Scrapbook 1932-1969
1 item

Sculptor. A scrapbook (1932-1969) containing photographs of the Taylor family, Taylor's friends, and his works, along with news clippings and brochures regarding Taylor's career as a sculptor and professor of art at the University of Oklahoma.

Taylor, William Merritt   1100
Papers 1881-1892
3 items

Soldier. Items regarding Taylor's service in the U.S. Army's Eighth Infantry Battalion, including his copy of the *Soldier's Handbook* (1881), and certificates (1889-1892) of promotion to the ranks of corporal and sergeant, respectively.

Temple First State Bank Collection   1101
Records 1909-1925
8 feet

Bank. Correspondence (1909-1923) from the First State Bank, Temple, Oklahoma, regarding the daily commerce of the bank and general ledgers (1909-1925) in which daily financial transactions were recorded.

Territorial Oklahoma Manuscripts Collection   1102
Papers 1881-1907
.33 foot

Subject collection. Typescript and original manuscript accounts (1881-1907) by pioneers and frontiersman regarding the settlement of Oklahoma and Indian territories.

Territory of Kansas Collection   1103
Printed materials 1856-1880
.25 foot

Subject collection. Documents (1856-1880) regarding territorial and early statehood-era Kansas, including settlement leaflets and brochures; U.S. centennial celebration event programs (1876); Civil War-era government proclamations and patriotic event programs (1863-1873); a leaflet (1888) published by the Plainsville (Kansas) School Board denying the accusation that they ordered history texts sympathetic to the Confederate cause; and one leaflet (1879) regarding the influx of Afro-American settlers to Kansas from southern states.

Thompson, Alfred M., Sr. (1859-1948)   1104
Papers 1885-1948
.50 foot

Merchant. Correspondence (1902-1948) concerning the death of Thompson's son in France during World War I, and the controversy regarding a new townsite for Walters, Oklahoma Territory; publications (1913-1919) regarding the Allies' victory in World War I and Oklahoma's contributions to the cause; a program (1936) of the Wichita Mountains Easter Pageant; and certificates (1885-1920) appointing Thompson postmaster of a small city in Texas, a member of the official reception committee in Oklahoma City for President Woodrow Wilson, and chairman of the Democratic Party Precinct Committee. Also in this collection is a scrapbook and a typescript (n.d.) of a speech by Thompson regarding the origin and early years of Walters, Oklahoma Territory.

Thornton, Hurschel Vern (b. ca. 1900)   1105
Papers 1940-1951
1.66 feet

Professor. Correspondence (1940-1951) regarding the annual Boys State of Oklahoma, as well as a proposed revision of the constitution of Oklahoma. Included in this collection are budgets and procedural manuals (1940-1951) of the Boys State of Oklahoma conventions.

Three Forks Ranch Collection   1106
Papers 1835-1986
.10 foot

Ranch. Correspondence (1985-1986) with accompanying information submitted in an effort to place the ranch on the National Register of Historic Places, including maps of the ranch and environs, a history of the ranch from 1835 to 1986; and news clippings regarding the history of the town of Okay (formerly North Muskogee) in Wagoner County, Oklahoma, near where the Three Forks Ranch is located.

Tibbs, Burrell   1107
Printed materials 1898-1918
1.50 foot

Collector. Scrapbooks containing newspaper stories and clippings (1898-1918) detailing the early history of aviation in Oklahoma.

Tiger, Moty (b. 1840)   1108
Printed materials 1899-1931
.25 foot

Indian chief. Typescripts of newspaper articles (1899-1931) relating to the change in status of the Creek Nation, and the role of Tiger, its first principal chief after the amalgamation of Indian Territory into Oklahoma.

Tilghman, William Matthew (1854-1925) 1109
Papers 1843-1960
2 feet

Lawman. Correspondence (1901-1960) regarding the Tilghmans, as well as gangsters and outlaws, Communist infiltration of the Works Progress Administration in Oklahoma, and poets and writers of Oklahoma; Tilghman's personal financial records (n.d.); manuscripts and typescripts (n.d.), including the memoirs of Bill Tilghman and writings by Zoe Tilghman regarding the first Christmas in Oklahoma City, Oklahoma Territory; publications (1843-1949) by the Poetry Society of Oklahoma, the Oklahoma Authors Club, and the Women of '89 Club, including a mid-nineteenth century book on feminine etiquette; programs (1903-1934) of academic, social, charitable, and religious institutions and organizations; newspaper clippings regarding outlaws; and showbills (n.d.) for western-oriented motion pictures.

Unpublished finding aid available.

Timmons, Alice and Boyce 1110
Papers 1892-1982
.33 foot

University employees. Correspondence (1972-1976) and printed materials (1966-1982) relating to American Indian projects in which the Timmonses were interested, such as the Alaska Native Law Project, the North Slope Legal Assistance Project, the American Indian Institute, and the Alaska Legal Services Corporation.

Tittle, Leon H. (b. ca. 1895) 1111
Papers 1891-1903
.10 foot

Attorney. Legal documents (1891-1900), including tax and pay receipts; and judicial documents (1894-1899), including injunction bonds, writs of injunctions, and transcripts of court judgements, all from Greer County, Texas, and, after 1896, Greer County, Oklahoma Territory. Also included in this collection are sheriff deputization certificates (1895-1899); citizen announcements of cattle brands claimed (1894); one homestead certificate (1903); and one teacher certificate (1899), also from Greer County, Oklahoma Territory. The homestead certificate bears the signature of President Theodore Roosevelt, and a number of earlier documents bear the official stamp of Greer County, Texas. The teacher certificate is among the first issued in Greer County, Oklahoma Territory.

Tobias, Henry Jack (b. 1925) 1112
Printed materials 1913-1980
1.50 feet

Professor. A typescript (n.d.) regarding the history of Poles in Bartlesville, Oklahoma, and Martin I. Zofness; a photocopy of a thesis (1946) by Randall Falk regarding Jewry in Oklahoma; and a photocopy of a report entitled "The Story of Oklahoma Jewry," along with photocopies and original issues of Jewish newspapers (1913-1980) published in Oklahoma. The collection also includes photocopies of published biographies of prominent Oklahoma Jews and a letter (1975) by Lt. Gov. George Nigh to Zofness regarding Zofness's suggestion for promoting tourism in Oklahoma.

Unpublished finding aid available.

Tolbert, James Randolph (1862-1942) 1113
Papers 1909-1941
20 feet

Attorney. Correspondence (1909-1941) regarding Tolbert's participation in Oklahoma politics, including his election to office, terms served as a state legislator, and the Al Smith for President campaign in Oklahoma, of which he was head; reports (1923) and accompanying documentation for the impeachment proceedings and investigation of Governor Jack Walton by a special committee of the legislature, of which Tolbert was vice-chair; and posters (1942) by Norman Rockwell produced during World War II and entitled "The Four Freedoms."

Tolbert, Raymond A. 1114
Papers 1909-1951
3 feet

University regent. Correspondence (1922-1951) regarding the planning, construction, and operation of the University of Oklahoma's student union building and football stadium; the School of Law; the Alumni Association; and the university hospital, along with the articles of incorporation (1923-1928) for the Oklahoma Memorial Union board of governors.

Tolleson, William Alfred (1869-1953) 1115
Records 1893-1953
16 feet

Physician. Correspondence (1896-1953) of Tolleson in regard to personal and professional matters including Tolleson's employment as a physician for the Missouri, Kansas, and Texas Railroad; financial papers (1887-1949) of the Tolleson family; lecture notes (1894-1895) recorded by Tolleson while in medical school; newspaper clippings (1925-1942) regarding medicine; and materials from Tolleson's medical practice in Eufaula, Indian Territory, and Oklahoma, including medical equipment and supply catalogs (1928), registers of medical prescriptions given (1929-1937), and patient account and appointment registers (1875-1942). Also in this collection are posters (1895-1898) depicting seventeenth- and eighteenth-century medical practices, and certificates (1948-1949) marking Tolleson's long service to the practice of medicine in Oklahoma.

Tompkins, Stuart Ramsay (b. 1886) 1116
Papers 1917-1956
4.75 feet

Historian. Personal and professional correspondence (1932-1956); Tompkins's book manuscripts (n.d.) on the Soviet Union; lecture notes (n.d.) used by Tompkins in his classes on Russian history; student grade registers (1932-1955) from Tompkins's courses at the University of Oklahoma; and Tompkins's diary (1917) detailing his experiences with the Sixth Canadian Trench Mortar Battery in France during World War I.

Tonkawa Public Library Collection 1117
Papers 1834-1938
.10 foot

Subject collection. Typescripts (1938) of interviews with pioneers and army officers associated with the Tonkawa, Oklahoma, area regarding U.S. Army operations, Indians, the establishment of churches, schools, forts, communities, trails and roads, and the general settlement of that area occurring from 1834 forward. Also in this collection are several typescripts (1938) of news articles regarding settlement in Oklahoma and Oklahoma Territory.

Tonkawa Sunny Side Club Collection 1118
Minutes 1917-1918
1 item

Social club. A minute book (1917-1918) recording the proceedings, attendance, and activities of the Tonkawa (Oklahoma) Sunny Side Club, a literary and patriotic society formed during World War I.

Totco, Incorporated Collection 1119
Printed materials 1984
3 items

Petroleum company. Full-color posters (1984) honoring the oil field worker and oil drilling profession, 1920-1930.

Tracy, Fred 1120
Papers 1889-1911
.10 foot

Writer. Three manuscripts (n.d.) by Fred Tracy entitled "Acts of Violence in No Man's Land," "Reminiscences of No Man's Land," and "B. M. and E." all regarding the history of the Oklahoma panhandle region and the efforts to obtain railroad service in Beaver, Oklahoma.

Treat, Guy Bradford (d. 1980) 1121
Records 1903-1955
4 feet

Railroad official. Correspondence (1925-1947); reports (1906-1955); minutes (1945); financial records (1918-1946); maps (1904-1955); and publications (1909-1955) regarding the operations, financial status, and policies of railway companies in central and southeastern Oklahoma. The companies included are the Oklahoma Railway, the Oklahoma City Railway, the Metropolitan Railway, and the El Reno Interurban and the Norman Interurban railroads. The collection also contains correspondence (1947) regarding the liquidation of the Oklahoma City streetcar system, and the development of the Diamond Dishwasher Company (1925).

Unpublished finding aid available.

Truss, Sam M. 1122
Manuscript 1913
1 item

Collector. A manuscript entitled "History of the Truss Family From 1786 to 1912," by C. C. Truss.

Tucker, Fred V. (b. ca. 1895) 1123
Manuscript ca. 1890-1940
1 item

Rancher. A photocopy of an unpublished, untitled manuscript (n.d.) by Tucker, regarding life and times (1890-1940) in Kenton, Oklahoma Territory, and the surrounding region of which Tucker was an early resident.

Tucker, Hampton (b. 1870) 1124
Papers 1895-1945
15 feet

Lawyer. Legal case files (1895-1945); correspondence (1895-1945); coal mining reports (1899-1916); and related papers concerning Tucker's service as mining trustee for the Choctaw Nation, 1912-1918, national attorney for the Choctaw Nation, 1924-1929, and mining trustee for the Choctaw and Chickasaw nations, 1929-1949.

Tucker, Marshall A. (1871-1939) 1125
Papers 1896-1939
3 items

Pharmacist. A poem (1936) by Tucker regarding his deceased mother; a biographical sketch (1939) of Tucker; and a diploma (1896) awarded Tucker by the University of Oklahoma Territory. It was the second degree awarded by the university.

Tucker, R. Truman (b. ca. 1910) 1126
Papers 1930-1979
.66 foot

Rancher. A scrapbook (1930-1975) of news clippings and mementos regarding early days in Kenton, Oklahoma, and vicinity; correspondence (1975-1979) and news clippings (1975-1979) regarding the discovery of prehistoric footprints, known as the "Black Mesa footprints," on Tucker's ranch; and a blueprint of Tucker Lake.

Tuggle, C. E. 1127
Papers 1901-1921
7 items

Grocer. Letters of reference (1901) written by Texas bankers regarding Tuggle; a printed letter (n.d.) in President Woodrow Wilson's handwriting urging Americans to support the country's war effort during World War I; picture postcards (ca. 1907) of Siloam Springs, Arkansas, and the University of California at Berkeley; along with a stock certificate (1921) issued by the Grady County Park in Chickasha, Oklahoma.

Tulsa County Medical Society Collection 1128
Printed materials 1908-1945
1 item

Professional society. A booklet (1945) published by the Tulsa County (Oklahoma) Medical Society regarding its history from its establishment through World War II.

Tulsa Public Schools Collection 1129
Report 1907-1957
1 item

Public school system. A report (1957) by the Tulsa, Oklahoma, superintendent of schools entitled "Fifty Years of Progress in the Tulsa Public Schools 1907-1957." Also included in the document is the superintendent's annual report for the 1956-1957 school year.

Turbyfill, Harper Subert (b. ca. 1900) 1130
Papers 1916-1923
.50 foot

Teacher. High school yearbooks (1916-1923) from the towns of Norman, Moore, and Seminole, Oklahoma, and a scrapbook (1918-1923) containing photographs, news clippings, drama, and other event programs from Turbyfill's student days at the University of Oklahoma.

Turley, Louis Alvin 1131
Manuscript 1947
1 item

Professor. An unpublished manuscript (1947) by Turley entitled "Nephron: A Critical Study of the Data from the Structure, Pathology, and Experimentation on the Function of the Several Parts of the Kidney."

Turlington, Marcellus Martin (1868-1949)   1132
Records 1891-1937
4 feet

Physician. Ledgers (1906-1937) in which Turlington recorded medical services rendered and the fees charged. Two of these ledgers record accident and disability cases of workers from the nearby Seminole oil field, and the others document changing social and health-care conditions in Indian Territory and Oklahoma during this period. Also in this collection are certificates (1891-1906) awarded Turlington during his career.

Turnbo, S. C. (b. ca. 1844)   1133
Manuscript 1861-1865
1 item

Confederate soldier. A bound typescript (n.d.) of Turnbo's journal in which he records his personal observations regarding the actions and views of the citizens of Indian Territory and the states of Arkansas, Missouri, and Kansas during the Civil War.

Turner, Martin Luther (1863-1921)   1134
Papers 1888-1921
.50 foot

Financier. Correspondence (1888-1921); news clippings (1896-1921); scrapbooks (1896-1917); and broadsides, regarding the life of Turner, his campaign for election as U.S. senator from Oklahoma, his involvement in the world of finance, both in Oklahoma Territory and elsewhere, and his death. A number of the clippings pertain to the economic climate, politics of, and living conditions in Oklahoma Territory. Of special note are letters (1916-1920) addressed to Turner from Brig. Gen. John J. Pershing requesting Turner's assistance and influence in obtaining a promotion to major general. One letter is addressed from the headquarters of the U.S. Army Punitive Expedition in Mexico, and others are from Europe, sent by Pershing while commander-in-chief of the American Expeditionary Forces during World War I.

Turpin, Carl J. (d. 1942)   1135
Papers 1888-1941
3 feet

Railroad developer. Correspondence (1888-1941) to the Turpins regarding family and personal affairs; reports (1934-1938) of the Oklahoma State Federation of Women's Clubs; newspaper clippings (1916-1941); cancelled checks (1913-1918); and event programs (1909-1938) from organizations and clubs, including the Oklahoma Symphony Orchestra, the Oklahoma State Federation of Women's Clubs, and the New Century Club, along with the Edelweiss Club and Literary Club, both of Clinton, Oklahoma.

Turtle, Willie 1136
Papers 1901-1911, 1944
.33 foot

Collector. Land allotment documents (1901-1911) signed by William McKinley, allocating land to four Kiowa Indians. The collection also includes weekly ration coupons (ca. 1944) for the Geimansaddle family.

U. S. Army Collection: Tenth Infantry Regiment 1137
Records 1855-1903
6 feet

Military unit. Correspondence (1865-1866); reports (1855-1902); muster rolls (1865-1869); and casualty returns (1856-1868), reflecting the service of the regiment in the Minnesota, Kansas, Utah, and the Dakota territories, as well as Cuba and the Philippine Islands. Included in these registers are casualty statistics and brief action reports, several of which document engagements with Sioux and Cheyenne Indians. Those registers from the Spanish-American War forward include many enlistees from Fort Reno, Oklahoma Territory.

Unpublished finding aid available.

U. S. District Court Collection: Central District of Indian Territory 1138
Ledger 1903
1 item

Federal court. A ledger (1903) of the court entitled "Abstract of Mortgages, Liens and Deeds of Trust" in which entries regarding these documents were recorded.

U. S. District Court Collection: Northern District of Indian Territory 1139
Ledger 1897-1900
1 item

Federal court. A prisoner docket book kept by the U.S. marshal, Leo E. Bennett, of the Northern District of Indian Territory, Muskogee, Indian Territory, for the years 1897-1900. The book records prisoners' names, race, age, criminal charge, date received, arresting officer, committing judge, sentence, and dates released.

U. S. District Court Collection: Western District of Arkansas 1140
Records 1872-1903
.25 foot

Federal court. Correspondence (1872-1903) regarding U.S. District Court business and the adminstration of justice in Indian Territory. The collection includes a legal opinion by Isaac Parker regarding the case of *Ex-Parte James E. Reynolds*.

U. S. District Court Collection: Western District of Oklahoma 1141
Records 1890-1935
156 feet

Federal Court. Stenographers notebooks (1893-1910); books of statutes (1873-1912); cases and rules of procedure; U.S. marshals records (1890-1912); and court clerks records (1892-1921) concerning witness, juror, prisoner, and court staff expenses; ledgers (1898-1935); and correspondence (1894-1926) of the court clerk and the marshal with the attorney general, the U.S. attorney, and others.

Unpublished finding aid available.

U. S. Naval Bases Collection 1142
Printed materials 1941-1959
.10 foot

Military base. Newspaper articles (1941-1959) and publications (1945) regarding the U.S. Naval Air Station and the U.S. Naval Air Technical Training Center, both of which were located in Norman, Oklahoma. Included in the collection are stories regarding the establishment, operation, closing, and the condition of life at the bases, along with information on their subsequent acquisition by the University of Oklahoma.

Unger, Marion Draughon Murray 1143
Papers 1924-1936
1.25 feet

Oklahoma colonist in Bolivia. Correspondence (1924-1928) from Marion Murray, the wife of Johnston Murray, to family members in Oklahoma regarding the experiences of the Murray family in Bolivia, including accounts of their travel to Bolivia, the establishment of Murray's colony, and of its daily operation. A number of letters contain diagrams of the colony lay-out. Also included in this collection are miscellaneous items such as Bolivian travel permits, newspapers, artifacts, and newspaper articles (1932-1936) regarding William H. Murray.

Unpublished finding aid available.

United Auto Workers Collection 1144
Printed materials 1945-1957
.10 foot

Labor union. Brochures and booklets (1945-1957) published by the United Auto Workers regarding its stance on such issues as civil rights, automation, strikes, and time study, and regarding programs offered by the union, including employment plans, training programs, and guaranteed payment programs. The collection also includes copies of a journal (1956-1957) published by the union and entitled *UAW Ammunition*.

University of Oklahoma Association Collection 1145
Papers 1910-1912
.10 foot

Alumni organization. Letters (1910-1912) from each member of the university's Class of 1910, describing his or her experiences after graduation.

University of Oklahoma College of Pharmacy Collection   1146
Printed materials 1934-1948
1 foot

University college. Constitution and by-laws (1938); programs (1934-1948) of the annual conventions; programs of the annual banquets (1939-1943); and a placard (1944) of the Oklahoma University Pharmaceutical Association. The placard is for the association's War Conference and bears the inscription "Pill-Rolling for Victory." The collection also contains correspondence (1939) regarding the possible appointment of Everett E. Duncan to the Federal Trade Commission.

University of Oklahoma Press Collection   1147
Records 1928-1962
195 feet

Scholarly press. Correspondence (1928-1956) between directors of the press and University of Oklahoma officials and department heads, and with authors and prospective authors, regarding the daily operation of the press, its publishing procedures and standards, and books published. Correspondents include William Bennett Bizzell, Joseph A. Brandt, Bernard Devoto, J. Frank Dobie, and Archibald MacLeish. Also included in this collection are readers reports (1930-1956) submitted to the press critiquing authors works; book manuscripts (1934-1956) rejected by the press, and book manuscripts (n.d.) accepted, filed by author; and minutes and proceedings (1944-1961) of various working committees of the American Association of University Presses, and of the University of Oklahoma, including the Semi-Centennial Committee (1956-1957); the DeGolyer Committee (1949-1955) charged with forming what is now the University of Oklahoma's History of Science Collection; the Distinguished Service Citation Committee (1947-1955); the Committee on University and Town (1944-1945); and the Division of Manuscripts, Archives, and Rockefeller Foundation Committee (1946-1948), charged with establishing what is now the manuscript division of the Western History Collections.

Unpublished finding aid available.

Updegraff, Ruth   1148
Papers 1843-1909
3 Items

Collector. Copies of two declarations of sale (1832, 1853) of slaves in the Cherokee Nation and a declaration of land allotment (1909).

Utterback, Bert R. (1891-1926)   1149
Papers 1895-1945
.10 foot

Author. Short story manuscripts (n.d.) by Utterback written around his reminiscences (1895-1945) of territorial and early statehood-era New Mexico, with descriptions of the roles cowboys, ranches, cattle, horses, and influenza epidemics played in the social fabric and progress of the region.

Van Ausdal, Harvey G. 1150
Printed material 1898-1950
1 item

Pharmacist. A newsletter (1950) entitled *Dr. Hess Dealer News*, containing an article regarding the history of the Van Ausdal Drug Store of Centralia, Indian Territory, and, later, Welch, Oklahoma.

Van Cleave, William E. (b. 1877) 1151
Papers 1926-1940
.25 foot

Physician. Correspondence (1926-1940); manuscripts entitled "Indian Medicine" and "Important Points in the Early Diagnosis of Tuberculosis," by Van Cleave; a biographical sketch of Van Cleave; annual reports (1926-1934) of medical activity at the Choctaw-Chickasaw Sanitorium; issues of the *TB Tom Tom* newsletter (1933); and newspaper clippings about Van Cleave, the sanitorium, and his work with the Indians at the sanitorium.

Van Dyke, Gerald Mason (1895-1959) 1152
Papers 1912-1961
.10 foot

Soldier and musician. Poetry and music manuscripts (ca. 1912-1961) composed by Van Dyke about his philosophies on life and death, the Japanese attack on Pearl Harbor, and life in Cordell, Oklahoma. Also included in this collection is a biographical sketch of Van Dyke.

Vance, Leon Robert, Jr. (1916-1944) 1153
Papers 1933-1953
.50 foot

Soldier. Correspondence (1946-1953); newspaper clippings (1944-1953); and published materials, including magazines and event programs regarding Vance's death, his posthumous receipt of the Congressional Medal of Honor, the renaming of the Enid, Oklahoma, Army Air Field in his honor, and the dedication of a dormitory at the University of Oklahoma in his name, all in recognition of his wartime achievements. The collection also includes correspondence (1933-1945) regarding his father's death, as well as letters of praise he received from his parents while he was a student at the University of Oklahoma.

Vaught, Edgar Sullins, Sr. (1873-1959) 1154
Printed materials ca. 1907-1955
1 foot

Judge. Typescripts of instructions (1907-1955) to juries regarding civil and criminal cases, some rendered by Judge Vaught while presiding over the U.S. District Court, Western District of Oklahoma. Types of cases include prostitution, negligence, personal injury, mail fraud, civil rights, breach of contract, bankruptcy, conspiracy to defraud, murder, pornography, embezzlement, price fixing, and drug trafficking.

Unpublished finding aid available.

Vinita Lions Club Collection 1155
Records 1943-1955
.66 foot

Civic club. Records (1932-1955), including correspondence, reports, and membership rosters of the Vinita, Oklahoma, Lions Club.

Virden, John M. (1908-1968) 1156
Papers 1951-1968
4 feet

U.S.A.F. officer. Correspondence (1953-1968) regarding Virden's writings and other subjects; newspaper and magazine articles (1951-1968) by and about Virden; and one book-length manuscript (ca. 1965) entitled "Andrew J. Byrne," written by U.S. ambassador to France, James M. Gavin, with Virden's assistance. Principal correspondents in this collection include James M. Gavin, Carl Albert, Neill Bohlinger, Walker D. Grisso, and Arthur McAnally.

Unpublished finding aid available.

Vliet, Richard M. 1157
Papers 1934-1965
4 feet

Pharmacist. Personal correspondence (ca. 1934-1948) of Vliet and his wife, Gertrude M. Vliet; diaries (1937-1952) kept by Gertrude M. Vliet; financial records (ca. 1935-1965); and correspondence (1934-1948) relating to the Fox-Vliet Drug Store in Oklahoma City, Oklahoma.

Von Keller, Frederick Philander P. 1158
Papers 1888-1935
.10 foot

Physician. An expense book (1888-1889); student lecture notes (1895) from Von Keller's electro-therapy class; and certificates and diplomas (1888-1935) issued to him by medical schools and by the Chickasaw Nation.

Wagner, J. E. 1159
Manuscript 1874-1896
1 item

Farmer. Memoirs entitled "Memories of Oklahoma" in which Wagner relates his experiences in Texas and Oklahoma Territory.

Walker, Andrew Beattie 1160
Papers 1903-1972
.10 foot

Dentist. Manuscripts (n.d.) regarding the history of the Bank of Fairview, Oklahoma, and the arrival of the railroad in that city, along with a savings account record book (1903) from the bank; a letter (1903) regarding the Oklahoma (Territory) Dental Association and the Board of Dental Examiners; a certificate of practice (1903) issued to Walker; and news clippings (1961-1972) regarding the history of the *Fairview Republican* newspaper and of the town of Quapaw, Oklahoma.

Walker, Charles F. (b. 1875) 1161
Letter 1898-1956
1 item

Physician. A letter by Walker (1956) regarding his life and career in Grove, Indian Territory and Oklahoma.

Walker, John Riley (b. 1880) 1162
Papers 1904-1944
.33 foot

Physician. Papers (ca. 1930-1940) presented by Walker before the Oklahoma State Medical Association; and a college yearbook (1904) from Keokuk College in Keokuk, Iowa, along with a booklet (1907) also published by the college.

Walker, Tandy C. (1814-1877) 1163
Printed materials 1877-1929
5 items

Indian statesman. Typescripts of news articles (1877-1929) on the career and death of Col. Tandy C. Walker, the organizer of the first Choctaw-Chickasaw regiment for Confederate Army service.

Walker, Thelma Brown 1164
Manuscript 1889-1907
1 item

History student. A typewritten paper (ca. 1970) by Walker regarding the history of Oklahoma Territory, the Cherokee Strip, and Fairview, Oklahoma Territory.

Wallace, Cecile Boone 1165
Scrapbook 1957
1 item

Teacher. An ethnobotanical pressbook (1957) compiled by Wallace containing wild plant specimens along with descriptions of their use by Indian tribes.

Walton, John Calloway (1881-1949) 1166
Papers 1903-1948
3 feet

Governor of Oklahoma. Personal and official correspondence (1916-1948) regarding Walton's governorship, his removal from office, electioneering, and his campaign to rid Oklahoma of the Ku Klux Klan; election campaign literature and materials (1919-1938) generated during Walton's bids for public office; speeches (1922-1938) delivered by Walton as governor; newspaper clippings (1919-1943) regarding Oklahoma politics; transcripts (1923) of testimony given at trials concerning racist and Klan-sponsored incidents in Oklahoma, and Walton's impeachment; and publications (1923-1924) regarding the Klan, politics, and government.

Unpublished finding aid available.

Ward, D. C. 1167
Printed material 1889-1939
1 item

Missionary. A typescript of an article (1939) regarding the history of the Cache Creek Indian Mission, located in southwestern Oklahoma, and which ministered to Plains Indian tribes.

Wardell, Morris L. (1889-1957) 1168
Papers 1921-1956
34 feet

Historian. Correspondence (1921-1956) relating to Wardell's service as a professor of history, and an assistant to the president of the University of Oklahoma, and concerning student affairs, foreign students, curriculum, academic department administration, military training, housing, the University of Oklahoma during World War II, post-war planning, and legislative matters, as well as Wardell's involvement in civic organizations, his teaching, and his publishing activities; reports (1929-1945) from the deans, the personnel department, the registrar's office, and academic departments of the University of Oklahoma; and lecture notes, research materials, and manuscripts relating to the Cherokee Indians, and specifically Wardell's book *Political History of the Cherokee Nation*, (University of Oklahoma Press, 1938), to the Osage Indians, to historic sites in Oklahoma, and to the history of the west in general.

Unpublished finding aid available.

Watson, Archer Hunter, Sr. 1169
Papers 1910
.10 foot

State official. Correspondence (1910) from Watson to his fiancee regarding the controversial decision to move the capitol of Oklahoma from Guthrie to Oklahoma City. Watson was a member of the State Corporation Commission and these letters reflect an inside knowledge of the conflict. Also included in this collection is a news clipping regarding the hostility of citizens in Shawnee, Oklahoma, to Watson's support for the Oklahoma City site.

Watts, Charles Gordon, Sr. (1875-1964)   1170
Papers 1907-1944
113 feet

Judge. Correspondence (1907-1944) regarding Watts's personal affairs, politics and government at the state and local levels, and the progress and resolution of legal cases in which he was involved; and publications (1914-1944), also regarding politics and government at the local, state, and national levels. The correspondence series of this collection reflects Watts's interest in the welfare of the Democratic Party in all state and national elections from 1910 to 1944, with many letters and telegrams regarding the character and suitability of candidates for office.

Waynoka Commercial Bank Collection   1171
Records 1909-1940
8 feet

Bank. Financial records (1909-1940), including cash books, journals, Liberty Bond registers, treasurers warrant registers, insurance policy registers, trial balance ledgers, and general ledgers, all from the Waynoka (Oklahoma) Commercial Bank.

Wear, John B.   1172
Records 1885-1900
.10 foot

Physician. A ledger (1898-1900) in which Wear recorded services rendered to patients as well as fees charged in his Poteau, Indian Territory, medical practice, along with admission cards (1885-1887) for lectures at an Arkansas college.

Weaver, Carlton (1881-1947)   1173
Papers 1906-1924
.10 foot

Newspaper editor. Correspondence (1906-1947) to and from Weaver regarding the prospects for, and operation of, a newspaper in Ada, Indian Territory, and in the proposed state of Oklahoma, along with information regarding Ku Klux Klan activities in Oklahoma, especially the Klan's involvement in party politics and its effect upon local politicians.

Weaver, Claude Dickens, Sr. (b. 1867)   1174
Papers 1885-1934
.25 foot

Attorney. Diplomas (1885-1887) from the Gainesville (Texas) High School and from the University of Texas, along with certificates (1904-1934) authorizing Weaver to practice law in Texas and before the supreme courts of the United States and Oklahoma Territory, appointing Weaver secretary to the governor, a district judge, a delegate to the National Conference on the Interstate Liquor Question in Washington, D.C., and postmaster of Oklahoma City, Oklahoma.

Weber, S. G. (d. 1952) 1175
Records 1931-1937
.33 foot

Physician. Ledgers (1931-1937) in which Weber recorded patient accounts and fees charged at his Bartlesville, Oklahoma, medical practice, including accounts with the Indian Territory Illuminating Oil Company and Phillips Petroleum Company.

Websterian Literary Society Collection 1176
Records 1907-1931
.25 foot

Social club. Minutes (1907-1920) of meetings; membership rosters (1907-1931); event programs (1928); and the constitution and by-laws (1907) of the Websterian Literary Society of the University of Oklahoma.

Weese, Asa Orrin (1885-1955) 1177
Papers 1921-1956
3.66 feet

Professor of zoology. Correspondence (1948-1955) regarding personal matters; articles (1921-1943) published by Weese regarding zoology; reports and publications (1947-1953) of the Oklahoma Academy of Science and the Oklahoma Fish and Game Council; and minutes (1942-1956) of the meetings of the University of Oklahoma department of zoology faculty, and of the University of Oklahoma faculty senate. Also included in this collection are meteorological and climatological reports (1933-1947) compiled for the Oklahoma City, Oklahoma, area.

Welch, Oklahoma, Town Records Collection 1178
Records 1899-1926
.66 foot

Municipality. A criminal docket (1899-1909) for the municipal court of Welch, and the minutes (1911-1926) of the town council. Welch, located in the Delaware District of the Cherokee Nation, Indian Territory, is now in Craig County, Oklahoma.

Welsh, Jack D. 1179
Papers 1861-1865
2 feet

Collector. Photocopies of the service records of ninety-seven Confederate Army generals.

Weltfish, Gene 1180
Papers 1935-1954
.50 foot

Anthropologist. Analysis worksheets (1954) for Pawnee prehistoric weaving samples and microfilmed field notes (1935) relating to Weltfish's work among the Pawnee Indians.

Wenner, Fred Lincoln (1865-1950) 1181
Papers 1887-1956
3.33 foot

Journalist. Typescripts and manuscripts (1889-1939), and newspaper clippings (n.d.) regarding the settlement and history of the territory and state of Oklahoma, with information concerning schools, cities and towns, justice, government, and religion; and correspondence (1904-1950) between Wenner and the Territorial Board for the Leasing of School Lands, of which Wenner was secretary, regarding board business, and from governors and other notable personalities of Oklahoma Territory regarding politics and government, social conditions, and early territorial history. This collection also includes a warrant issued by the city of East Guthrie, Indian Territory, (later Guthrie, Oklahoma Territory) and dated June, 1889.

Unpublished finding aid available.

Westfall, Chester Harold (b. ca. 1898) 1182
Printed materials 1917-1919
.10 foot

Oil man. One copy of *Sooners in the War*, the official report of the Oklahoma State Council of Defense, of which Westfall was secretary, and seventy-five, four-color propaganda posters published by the U.S. government during World War I, including those of the U.S. School Garden Army, Red Cross, and Victory Loans series.

Wheatley, Thomas W. 1183
Papers 1905-1939
.50 foot

Coal mine operator. Correspondence (1928-1937); labor contracts (1933-1939); wage notices (1917-1936); machine contracts (1921-1939); advertising brochures (1926-1936); and orders (1937-1939) issued by the National Bituminous Coal Commission of the U.S. Department of the Interior, all in regard to the coal mining industry in southeastern Oklahoma. Included is information regarding wages, mine safety and accidents, organized labor, industry standards, coal production, mine railroads, and a 1930 mine explosion in Pittsburg County, Oklahoma, in which thirty miners were killed. This collection also contains survey reports (1905-1906) submitted to the Samples Coal Mining Company regarding the potential coal wealth of the Choctaw Nation, Indian Territory, which the Samples Company later mined.

Wheeler, J. Clyde   1184
Printed materials 1943-1955
.10 foot

Clergyman. An autographed book manuscript (1955) by Wheeler entitled "Here Lies Our Hope," about the history of the Christian faith, 1943-1955.

Whitaker, Lovie   1185
Papers 1953-1963
.10 foot

Collector. Correspondence, newspaper clippings, and printed material (1953-1963) relating to the U.S. Army's attempt to take over a part of the Wichita Mountains Wildlife Refuge for a missile firing range.

White Shrine of Jerusalem Collection   1186
Printed materials 1940
.10 foot

Charitable organization. Publications (1940) explaining the mission and purpose of the Oklahoma chapter of this women's organization devoted to helping the sick.

White, Hal H.   1187
Manuscript 1935
1 item

Physician. A paper on ureteral calculi (1935) presented at a meeting of the North Texas Medical Association.

White, (Mrs.) J. R.   1188
Warrant 1898
1 item

Collector. A warrant (1898) for fifty dollars issued by Wilson Fisher, treasurer of Red River County, Choctaw Nation, and made payable to himself.

White, Lida   1189
Papers 1891-1952
2.50 feet

Teacher. Correspondence (1891-1952) regarding White's employment, her historical research, her investments in Montana real estate, and personal matters with family and friends; leases and contracts (1936-1947); notebooks (n.d.) containing lecture notes; unorganized research notes (n.d.) entitled "Indian Lore;" and four notebooks containing typescripts of interviews (1934-1942) that White conducted with elderly Indians in Tulsa, Oklahoma, and with early settlers of the

Oklahoma City area. In addition to biographical and socio-economic information, the interviews focus on the education of Indians and the establishment of schools in Indian Territory and Oklahoma.

Unpublished finding aid available.

Whitehill, Walter Muir (b. 1905) 1190
Manuscript 1967
1 item

Author. An annotated manuscript (1967) by Whitehill entitled "Dumbarton Oaks - The History of a Georgetown House and Garden, 1800-1966."

Whitney, Charles W. 1191
Records 1864-1865
.10 foot

Army officer. Correspondence (1864-1865) of the military commissary general, Lt. C. W. Whitney, of Port Hudson, Louisiana, during the Union Army's occupation of that city.

Wichita Indian Agency Collection 1192
Papers 1871-1876
3 items

Indian agency. A letter (1872) to agent Jonathan Richards regarding the return of two Indians to the Kiowa Agency; a photostatic copy of a statement (1871) of funds remitted to the agency; and a photostatic copy of a report (1876) of the agency's employees.

Wilkins, Thurman 1193
Papers 1986
.33 foot

Author. A manuscript and galley proof of Wilkins's book *Cherokee Tragedy: The Ridge Family and the Decimation of a People* published by the University of Oklahoma Press in 1986.

Wilkinson, Otha 1194
Papers 1891-1907
.10 foot

Clergyman. A letter (1896) from Wilkinson to his family in McCloud, Oklahoma, describing his journey from Oklahoma to California; diaries (1891-1907) kept by Wilkinson detailing his evangelizing activities in Oklahoma, Kansas, and the midwest; and news clippings (1903) about church meetings and events in several Oklahoma Territory towns.

Will Rogers Scholarship Fund Collection   1195
Records ca. 1940-1955
2 feet

College scholarship fund. Scholarship applications (1941-1949) from University of Oklahoma students, along with correspondence (ca. 1940-1955) relating to the applications.

Willard, Melissa Kate   1196
Papers 1782-1852
3 items

Collector. Land registration records (1785-1786) for land located between the Tennessee and Cumberland rivers in what would become the state of Tennessee; and receipts (1851-1852) issued by the U.S. postmaster, and by a private express company, both in San Francisco, California, for a money transfer, and for the shipment of gold dust to New York City.

Williams, Arthur James (1877-1954)   1197
Papers 1905-1951
7 feet

Professor. Correspondence (1913-1930) from the Oklahoma Bureau of Geology regarding its publications and operations, and the geological and mineral characteristics and potential of Oklahoma counties; geological reports (1913-1930), with accompanying maps, regarding the geological and mineral characteristics and resources of Oklahoma counties; oil well logs (1905-1925) organized by county; and registers of students grades (1915-1951) compiled by Williams while a member of the University of Oklahoma faculty.

Unpublished finding aid available.

Williams, John Robert (1866-1931)   1198
Papers 1906-1910
.50 foot

Political campaign manager. Correspondence (1906-1910); telegrams (1909-1910); publications (1910); news clippings (1910); and broadsides (1910) regarding the Democratic and Republican parties in Oklahoma, and the campaigns of Lee Cruce and his opponent for the governorship of Oklahoma in 1910. The collection includes correspondence (1906) from Senator Gordon Russell regarding congress's plans for admitting Oklahoma to the Union.

Williams, Mary Clay   1199
Records 1871-1911
.33 foot

Collector. Receipts (1871-1911) of Henry Clay and Mary Jennings of Lancaster, Kentucky, for purchases of food, hardware, general merchandise, and carriage equipment. Also in this collection is a letter (1909) describing a collision between an early automobile and a horse-drawn buggy.

Williams, Meredith Newton (1904-1949)   1200
Papers 1919-1950
.33 foot

Journalist. Correspondence (1942-1950) from Governor Leon C. Phillips and Walter M. Harrison, a newspaper editor, praising stories Williams wrote as a reporter for the *Daily Oklahoman* newspaper, and regarding his transfer to a newspaper in Iowa; interdepartmental memos (1929-1930) of the *Daily Oklahoman* regarding the assignment of stories and potential stories; telegrams (1949-1950) and newspaper obituaries (1949) regarding Williams's death; an event program (1935) for an Oklahoma City Gridiron Club banquet; and copies of the Marshalltown, Iowa, *Times-Republican* newspaper (1945-1950) for which Williams worked after leaving Oklahoma. Also included in this collection is Williams's diploma (1919) from the Wentworth Military Academy of Lexington, Missouri.

Williams, Samuel   1201
Papers 1909-1949
.66 foot

Cotton farmer. Correspondence (1909-1949) to and from Williams regarding the Beckham County, Oklahoma, war relief and finance efforts during World War I, Williams's invention and eventual patenting of a cotton cleaning machine, and Williams's views on world and national events in the post-World War II years; blueprints (ca. 1924) for the cotton cleaning machine; a typescript (n.d.) by Williams regarding the Chisholm Trail in Beckham County; and official reports (1918-1919) regarding the progress and status of the Liberty Bond and Liberty Loan drives in Beckham County during World War I. The correspondence includes a letter (1918) from Governor Robert L. Williams regarding the war finance effort in Oklahoma.

Williams, Stephen   1202
Papers 1955
.33 foot

Professor. A photocopy of a report by Williams entitled "The Aboriginal Location of the Kadohadacho and Related Indian Tribes." Its stated purpose is to present available data concerning the location of the Caddo Indians from the period of the first recorded contact (the 1512 DeSoto Expedition) to the Treaty of 1835.

Willibrand, William Anthony   1203
Papers 1927-1955
.25 foot

Professor. Typescripts (1952) of Willibrand's speech regarding the twenty-fifth anniversary of *Books Abroad* (now *World Literature Today*), and marking the seventieth birthday of its first editor, Roy Temple House; reprints of articles, and periodicals containing articles (1940-1955) authored by Willibrand; and copies of lectures (1946) entitled "Currents in American Thought" delivered at the Fort Reno, Oklahoma, prisoner-of-war camp by a German inmate just after the close of World War II.

Willour, J. A. 1204
Scrapbook 1904-1905
1 item

Collector. A scrapbook containing letters of reference (1904-1905) from prominent citizens in the northeastern United States for F. J. Bonesteel, a lawyer from New York who settled in Indian Territory.

Wilson, Andrew R. 1205
Ledger 1907-1908
1 item

Hosteler. A guest register (1907-1908) from the Eskridge Hotel in Wynnewood, Oklahoma, listing guests, their home addresses, and prices of rooms.

Wilson, Milbourne Otto (b. 1890) 1206
Records 1926-1952
.50 foot

Professor. Student grade books (1930-1952) kept by Wilson for his psychology classes at the University of Oklahoma, along with a program (1926) from the inauguration of William B. Bizzell as president of the University of Oklahoma. The collection also includes an annual report (1935-1936) of the public schools of Glencoe, Illinois.

Wimberly, Harrington (b. 1901) 1207
Records 1924-1948
6.33 feet

Journalist and political leader. Official stenographer's reports (1945-1946) of the eight hearings of the U.S. Federal Power Commission's investigation of the natural gas industry; and reports (1947-1948) containing the findings of the commission. Also included in this collection are supporting documents (1924-1943) used during the investigation, including maps, charts, publications, and reports. Among the publications are the annual reports (1924-1940) of the Federal Power Commission, of which Wimberly was vice-chairman.

Unpublished finding aid available.

Witcher, Esther 1208
Scrapbook 1935
1 item

Librarian. A scrapbook (1935) containing newspaper clippings of Will Rogers's newspaper column and accounts of his death.

Witte, (Mrs.) Juan R.   1209
Records 1896-1921
.10 foot

Collector. Legal papers issued to Frank R. Rogers regarding the acquisition and use of lands in Georgia and Oklahoma Territory, including a mining lease (1896) for land in Georgia; a deed of conveyance (1907) for land in Gotebo, Oklahoma Territory; a homesteading certificate (1904) issued by Governor Frank Frantz and signed by President Theodore Roosevelt; and mortgage contracts (1920-1921). Also included is a grazing lease (1907), issued by Governor Frantz which specifies the conditions under which school lands could be used.

Wolf, Jonas (d. 1900)   1210
Printed materials 1884-1900
.25 foot

Indian chief. Typescripts of messages, statements, and proclamations (1884-1900) made by Wolf as governor of the Chickasaw Nation on the issues of land use, finances, allotments, and statehood, along with typescripts of newspaper articles and editorials (1894) regarding Wolf's arrest for embezzlement.

Wolfe, Oscar (1888-1963)   1211
Manuscript 1960
1 item

Pipeline consultant. A two-volume manuscript (1960) entitled "The Hydraulic Design of Oil and Gas Pipe Lines," written by Oscar Wolfe.

Wolfe, Reed E. (1885-1948)   1212
Records 1918-1948
1 foot

Physician. Account books (1918-1948) in which Wolfe recorded patient services and fees charged; and minutes (1920) of the Choctaw County (Oklahoma) Medical Society, in which a list of county physicians is included along with one letter regarding the Tri-County Medical Society of Choctaw, Pushmataha, and McCurtain counties.

Unpublished finding aid available.

Womack, John (1911-1987)   1213
Papers 1889-1984
11.33 feet

Postal employee and historian. Publications written by Womack, including manuscripts (1982-1984), newspaper clippings (1984), and pamphlets (1981-1983), along with correspondence (1980-1984) and research materials relating to these publications. The research materials include claims (1890-1920); saloon licensing papers (1896-1909); tax levies and assessments (1902-1912); bonds (1906-1912); reports (1902-1910); and related records of Cleveland County, Oklahoma, and its townships and cities.

Unpublished finding aid available.

Woman's Christian Temperance Union Collection   1214
Records 1918-1925
.25 foot

Civic organization. Minutes (1918-1925) of the Woman's Christian Temperance Union at Bismarck, North Dakota. The minutes include administrative details as well as financial statements. Also in the collection are four receipts for goods and services provided to the Methodist church where the organization met, and two announcements of meetings.

Women's History Project Collection   1215
Papers 1870-1900
.25 foot

History project. Typescripts of reports (1977) regarding the history of women and women's rights in Oklahoma, as well as biographies of historically prominent women, prepared by students participating in the University of Oklahoma Women's History Project.

Wood, Edwin K.   1216
Papers 1875-1892
.25 foot

Collector. An act (1875) of the Choctaw Nation establishing burglary as a crime; acts (1889-1892) of the Cherokee Nation appointing Elias C. Boudinot II, Thomas M. Buffington, David Rowe, and Richard M. Wolfe as Cherokee delegates to Washington, D.C., along with instructions to address land issues such as the return of Fort Gibson to the Cherokees; requests (1905-1906) for payment of salaries and expenses of the attorneys and special marshal of the Cherokee Nation; a committee report (1889) regarding payment for Cherokee lands given the Osages under the Cherokee Treaty of 1866; and a term paper (n.d.) by Wood entitled "The Indian Treaty Maker."

Woodard, Fred Barton (b. 1871)   1217
Papers 1920-1953
.33 foot

Lawyer. Personal and business correspondence (1934-1953), mostly relating to Republican Party politics, with Hamilton Fish and John H. Kane the principal correspondents. Also included are government documents and other published materials (1920s-1940s) regarding American Indians such as hearings before congressional committees on Indian affairs relating to relief of needy Indians (1940); claims of the Shawnee and Delaware tribes (1920s-1936), the Yakima tribe (1939), the Snake or Paiute tribe (1940), and the Wichita and related tribes (1939); restrictions on the lands of the Quapaw Indians (1939); a report (1946) illustrating the reduction in size of the Fort Berthold Indian Reservation; a proposed constitution for the Brotherhood of North American Indians; a tearsheet of a biographical sketch of Charles Journeycake, a chief of the Delaware, written by Woodard in 1943; and publications on Indian lands in general.

Woodrow, Thomas W. (d. 1919) 1218
Papers 1880-1918
3.75 feet

Clergyman and socialist. Manuscripts (n.d.) and sermons (1880-1891) by Woodrow regarding his views concerning God, religion, socio-economics, and socialism; ledgers (ca. 1912) containing subscription requests regarding Woodrow's publication, *Woodrow's Monthly*; and publications (1913-1918) regarding the Socialist Party in Oklahoma and in the United States, the nature of God, and German war practices during World War I.

Woods, E. K. 1219
Papers 1876-1914
.25 foot

Collector. A bibliography (1876-1914), compiled by Woods on index cards and slips of paper, regarding the Indians of North America in Indian Territory and the U.S. agencies responsible for their administration, the clothing and dress of whites and Indians of the western United States, and the cattle brands common to the Cherokee Strip and Oklahoma Territory. The information regarding cattle brands includes a drawing of the brand, the name and location of the ranch on which it appears, and the name of the proprietor of the ranch.

Woodward, Grace 1220
Manuscript 1957
1 item

Writer. A manuscript (1957) by Woodward recounting the efforts of Edward D. Hicks, a Cherokee Indian, to establish the Cherokee Telephone Company at Tahlequah, Indian Territory, in 1885.

Wooton, Esther A. Reed 1221
Papers 1860-1941
.25 foot

Collector. An unpublished, book-length manuscript (n.d.) by William E. Reed entitled "As It should Be," and letters (1941) by Reed describing the history of the town of Paris, Illinois, from the 1860s forward. The manuscript is a work of fiction set in Oklahoma at the close of the Civil War.

Worcester Academy Collection 1222
Printed materials 1885-1890
.25 foot

Indian school. Catalogs (1885-1890) of the academy listing trustees, officers, faculty, students, course offerings, and a general history and description of the school; a copy (1884) of "Pages from Cherokee Indian History" by Nevada Couch, and photocopies of documents relating to the founding and operation of the academy. Also included is a copy of the University of Oklahoma's *Extension Review* which is devoted to the life and career of Joseph W. Scroggs, the founder of Worcester Academy.

Works Progress Administration (WPA) Archaeological Survey Project Collection 1223
Records 1937-1942
1.25 feet

Federal project. Reports (1937-1942) submitted by the WPA Archaeological Survey Project of Oklahoma, regarding sites excavated in thirteen counties of Oklahoma and the findings therein. Included are reports entitled "Excavation of Prehistoric Indian Sites."

Unpublished finding aid available.

Works Progress Administration (WPA) Historic Sites and Federal Writers' Project Collection 1224
Records 1937-1941
23 feet

Federal project. Book-length manuscripts, research and project reports (1937-1941) and administrative records (1937-1941) generated by the WPA Historic Sites and Federal Writers' projects for Oklahoma during the 1930s. Arranged by county and by subject, these project files reflect the WPA research and findings regarding birthplaces and homes of prominent Oklahomans, cemeteries and burial sites, churches, missions and schools, cities, towns, and post offices, ghost towns, roads and trails, stagecoaches and stagelines, and Indians of North America in Oklahoma, including agencies and reservations, treaties, tribal government centers, councils and meetings, chiefs and leaders, judicial centers, jails and prisons, stomp grounds, ceremonial rites and dances, and settlements and villages. Also included are reports regarding geographical features and regions of Oklahoma, arranged by name, including caverns, mountains, rivers, springs and prairies, ranches, ruins and antiquities, bridges, crossings and ferries, battlefields, soil and mineral conservation, state parks, and land runs. In addition, there are reports regarding biographies of prominent Oklahomans, business enterprises and industries, judicial centers, Masonic (freemason) orders, banks and banking, trading posts and stores, military posts and camps, and transcripts of interviews conducted with oil field workers regarding the petroleum industry in Oklahoma.

Unpublished finding aid available.

Works Progress Administration (WPA) Historical
Records Survey Collection 1225
Printed materials ca. 1933-1942
24 feet

Federal project. Inventories (1937-1942) of church, county, state, and federal archives in thirty-three states, compiled by the Works Progress Administration Historical Records Survey. Included are inventories for church, state, and federal departments and agencies, and archives in eleven Oklahoma counties, as well as the vital statistics records for the state (1941) and a listing of church and religious organizations (1942) in Oklahoma. The collection also includes inventories of fifty-three Texas county archives and federal departments and agencies in that state.

Unpublished finding aid available.

Works Progress Administration (WPA) Statewide
Projects Collection 1226
Printed materials 1937-1942
.50 foot

Federal project. Publications (1937-1942) of WPA programs in Oklahoma, including the Statewide Recreation Project; the Statewide Museum Service; and the Community Service Program. The collection also includes a radio script for "The Museum of the Air" series, sponsored by the WPA on the University of Oklahoma radio station, WNAD, in Norman, Oklahoma.

World Literature Today Collection 1227
Papers 1926-1982
37.66 feet

Literary journal. Correspondence (1926-1982) between *World Literature Today* editors and University of Oklahoma administrators and faculty, and with authors and prospective authors, regarding the operation of the journal, its publishing procedures and standards, and works published. Literary correspondents include Sherwood Anderson, John Dos Passos, Upton Sinclair, Thornton Wilder, and H. L. Mencken. Also included in this collection are specialized files (1926-1951) regarding the flight of authors and playwrights from Nazi Germany and Spain, and their exile in the United States and Mexico; why women have not produced successful plays; and the special writing projects undertaken by prominent authors.

Unpublished finding aid available.

World Neighbors, Incorporated Collection 1228
Records 1951-1958
.66 foot

International relief organization. Correspondence (1954-1955); financial records (1951); and minutes of boards and committees (1951-1954); and publications (1951-

1958) of the Oklahoma-based World Neighbors, Incorporated, and its predecessor, World Assistance, Incorporated.

Woyna, Fritz Willie (1919-1965) 1229
Papers 1932-1965
11.66 feet

Television station director. Manuscripts (1941-1965) of short stories and novels by Woyna on various themes including science fiction and westerns; research material (1933-1965) used for stories and novels; subject files (1952-1961) regarding advertising statistics, methods, and budgets; subject files (1953-1959) relating to television broadcasting, including those regarding sets, cameras, procedures, and budgets, and all reflecting the philosophy and methodology of the earlier days of television programming.

Unpublished finding aid available.

Wright, Albert Daniel (b. 1863) 1230
Manuscript 1881-1947
1 item

Merchant. A typescript (1947) of an account by Wright regarding his participation in the land run of 1889, settlement in the towns of Guthrie, and Chandler, Oklahoma Territory, and his experiences and hardships in each.

Wright, Allen (1826-1885) 1231
Papers 1866-1930
2 feet

Indian chief and Presbyterian minister. Session minutes (1886-1900) of the Tali Hekia Presbyterian Church, Blue County, Indian Territory; Sunday school attendance records (1925-1926) of the Presbyterian church, Wapanucka, Oklahoma; typescripts of messages, proclamations, and statements (1866-1930) made by Wright as principal chief to the general council of the Choctaw Nation; and typescripts of Wright's letters (1866-1885) to the editor of the *Vindicator* and other newspapers, all regarding governmental issues of the Choctaw Nation. Also included are books and pamphlets (1846-1900) relating to the Presbyterian church and its missionary programs, along with a typewritten biography (1930) of Allen Wright and an inventory (n.d.) of his private library.

Unpublished finding aid available.

Wyatt, Robert Lee, III (1940-   ) 1232
Printed materials 1907-1988
5 items

Collector. Publications (1907-1988) regarding the history of the First Presbyterian Church and the First Baptist Church of Grandfield, Oklahoma, and the First Baptist

Church of Devol, Oklahoma, as well as pictorial directories of the membership of the First Baptist Church in Grandfield.

Wyatt, Rose Mary Burt (b. 1871)   1233
Papers 1886-1911
.10 foot

Collector. Printed speeches (1911) of Oklahoma senator Robert L. Owen; letters (1938-1943) from Samuel Sandheimer; and letters (1886-1889) from Mother Mary Joseph and Sister Mary Frances Bernard, Wyatt's former instructors at Sacred Heart Mission, Indian Territory. The letters were written from Saint Mary's Academy, at Sacred Heart Mission, Saint Joseph's Convent in Krebs, Indian Territory, and Saint Catharine's Convent in Lehigh, Indian Territory, and are about mission work in those respective locations and throughout Indian Territory.

Yale First National Bank Collection   1234
Records 1900-1939
28 feet

Bank. Correspondence (1917-1939), and financial records (1902-1939), including general ledgers, draft registers, tellers cash books, and daily statements, all regarding the daily business and financial status of the First National Bank of Yale, Oklahoma.

York, Bill   1235
Printed materials 1939-1949
.25 Foot

Radio station director. Song books (1939-1949) containing the music and words of songs by recording artists popular in Oklahoma in the 1940s and 1950s, including those of Roy Rogers, Ernest Tubb, and Merle Travis.

Young Mens Christian Association (YMCA) and Young
  Womens Christian Association (YWCA) Collection   1236
Records ca. 1920-1955
44 feet

Civic organizations. Activity, financial, and administrative records (1931-1948); and correspondence (1920-1950) of the University of Oklahoma branches of the YMCA and YWCA, along with bibliographies, scrapbooks, and clippings (1925-1950) relating to the organizations and their programs.

Young, Glen Olen (b. 1894)   1237
Papers 1950-1953
.10 foot

Politician. A typescript of a speech (1953) by Young to the National Conference to Abolish the United Nations entitled "U.N.-Trap Door to Stalin's Jail, Baited with the Dove of Peace"; campaign literature (1950) regarding Young's candidacy for congress; a biography (n.d.) of Young, produced for his election campaign; and publications (ca. 1953) authored by Young and produced by the Presbyterian church in Sapulpa, Oklahoma, alleging massive communist infiltration of the Presbyterian Church in the United States.

Young, Hiram 1238
Papers 1885-1921
.10 foot

Collector. Personal and family correspondence (1885-1921) between Hiram Young and other members of his family in which they describe their lives in Indian Territory and the Neosho, Missouri, area. Correspondents include L. A. Young, Ada Jones, Mollie Davidson, and W. A. Davis.

Young, James Harvey 1239
Printed materials 1953
1 item

Physician. A reprint of an article (1953) by Young entitled "Patent Medicines: The Early Post-Frontier Phase."

Yowell, Lillian J. 1240
Papers 1811-1849
2 items

Collector. A deed (1811) transferring ownership of two negro slaves, and a letter (1849) from David to Robert L. Elliott regarding his plans to settle in Texas.

Zweigel Mercantile Company Collection 1241
Records 1904-1940
51.50 feet

General store. General correspondence (1912-1930); bills of lading (1911-1921); account ledgers (1904-1928); and orders (1914-1924) of the Zweigel Mercantile Company of Atoka, Indian Territory, and Oklahoma. The collection also includes oil, gas, and mining leases (1935) to Choctaw Indian lands.

INDEX

Entry numbers in bold-face type refer to a collection of the same name as the index entry.

Abbott, Lyman: 794
Abernathy, J. R.: 827
Abrams, Abner W.: **1**
Abstracts of title (Okmulgee County, Oklahoma): 843
Achilles, Nash: 508
Ada, Indian Territory, newspapers in: 1173
Ada, Oklahoma:
  history of, 713
  lynchings, 701
Adair family, genealogy: 363
Adams, Joseph Quincy: **2**
Adams, Ramon Frederick: **3**
Aderhold, Thomas: **4**
Adkins, Art: 508
Advertisements: 226, 594, 722, 803, 874, 917, 922
Advertising cards: 532
Aeronautics (Oklahoma): 507
Africa, description and travel: 535
Afro-Americans: 273, 309, 342
  admission to University of Oklahoma, 273
  colonization (Oklahoma), 507
  dialects, example of, 957
  education (Oklahoma), 273, 769
  religious training (Oklahoma), 769
Agricultural colleges (Oklahoma): 507, 594
Agricultural colonies (Bolivia): 1143
Agriculture:
  cooperatives, 824
  legislation, 824
Agriculture (Oklahoma): 445, 507
  advocacy organizations, 841, 1037
  cooperatives, 312, 346, 441, 546, 559, 836, 887
  soil conservation, 833
Air bases (Oklahoma): 507, 1153
Airmail service, posters advocating: 684
Airports (Oklahoma): 507

Alabama Infantry Regiment, Twenty-Sixth: 650
Alaska:
  description and travel, 535, 777
  gold rush, 252
  Indians of, 285
Alaska Legal Services Corporation: 1110
Alaska Native Law Project: 1110
Albert, Carl Bert: 508, 1156
Albert Pike Hospital: **5**
Aleut Indians: 285
Alexander, Ira Olyen: **6**
Alexander family: 6
Alfalfa County, Oklahoma: 507
  Ku Klux Klan membership, 621
All Saints Hospital (McAlester, Oklahoma): **5**
Allen, Neva: **7**
Allen, Susie Keefer: **8**
Allen, Walter Bruce: **8**
Alley, Charles: **9**
Alley, John: **10**, 508
Allman, George: **11**
Alpha Epsilon Delta: **12**
Alpine, Texas, description of: 452
Alternate Saturday Club (Pauls Valley, Oklahoma): 1082
Altus, Oklahoma, attorneys: 33, 518
Alva, Oklahoma, health care: 20
Ambrose, Arthur: 200
American Association of University Presses, records of: 1147
American Association of University Women: **13**
American Bank (Porter, Oklahoma): 913
American Civil Liberties Union: 579
American Federation of Labor: 142
American Garden Service, history of: 64
American Indian File Collection: **14**

American Indian Institute (University of
    Oklahoma): **15**, 743, 1110
American Legion: 527
    posts in Oklahoma, 16, 197, 351, 1036
American Legion National American
    Commission: 197
American Legion Post 303: **16**
American Medical Association: 638
American National Bank (Oklahoma City,
    Oklahoma), records of: 818
American Party (Missouri): 605
American Red Cross: 527
    Beckham County (Oklahoma), **17**
    Cleveland County (Oklahoma), **18**, 230
Ameringer, Oscar: 508
Ames, Charles Bismark: **19**
Ames, H.B.: **20**
Amos, French Stanton Evans: **21**
Amusements (Oklahoma): 507
Anadarko, Oklahoma: 536
Anderson, R. M.: **22**
Anderson, R. R.: **23**
Anderson, Sherwood: 358, 1227
Andrus, Selden Eugene: **24**
Anglin, Tom: 508
Anthony, Charles Ross: 508
Anthony, Travis Dan: **25**
Anthony family: 25
Anthropologists:
    papers of, 757, 1180
    research of, 60, 677, 679, 848, 937, 1007
Anti-Horse Thief Association, records of: **26**
Antiphonaries: 1083
Apache Indian Mission (Fort Sill,
    Oklahoma), records of: 177
Apache Indians:
    bibliography, 562
    culture, 848
    Fort Sill band, 562
    history, 72
    land transfers, 40
    wars, 552
Apache, Oklahoma Territory, postmasters
    of: 150
Aplington, Kate Smith: 632
Apollo space missions, promotional
    literature: 458
Arapaho Indians:
    environmental studies, 483

housing surveys, 483
relations with U.S. government, 1063
wars, 552
Arapaho, Oklahoma, banks and banking: 265
Arbuckle, Matthew: 169, 302
Archaeology (Oklahoma): 507, 1126, 1223
    expeditions, 60
    projects, 1068
    sites, 1084
Architects: 415
Architecture (Oklahoma): 507
Archival administration (Latin America): 655
Archivists, writings of: 35, 655
Arkansas:
    Civil War, 1861-1865, 239
    history of, 387
    mines and mining, 589
    post-Civil War period, 1042
    railroad development, 372, 395
    state currency, 220
    western boundary of, 456
Arkansas Central Railroad: 372
Arkansas City, Kansas, opening of the
    Cherokee Outlet (Strip): 1074
Arne, Sigrid: 508
Arnold, Ben: **27**
Arnold, John D.: 229
Art (Oklahoma): 507
Art exhibits, catalogs: 1008
Arthur Foote Music Club, records of: 999
Arthur, Patti Joy: **28**
Artists: 251, 885
    Indian, 260
    Oklahoman, 557
Asahl, John: **29**
Ashbrook, William: **30**
Ashley, Charles: **31**
Asp, Henry E.: 508
Association of Governing Boards of State
    Universities: 980
Athenaeum Club (El Reno, Oklahoma),
    records of: 1097
Athletics, golf: 206
Atlanta, Georgia, cotton exposition: 399
Atlantic Oil Corporation: 575
Atoka Baptist Seminary, student
    notebooks: 366
Atoka County Medical Society, records
    of: 384

Atoka County, Oklahoma: 507
  election returns: 242
Atoka, Indian Territory: 1044
  Zweigel Mercantile Company, 1241
Atoka, Oklahoma, medical care: 384
Atoka State Bank: **32**
Attocknie, Albert: 508
Attorneys: 61, 69, 85, 290, 291, 725, 886
  Indian Territory, 96, 259
    records of, 249, 940, 955, 1124, 1204
  Oklahoma, 27, 323, 442, 518
    records of, 33, 113, 249, 351, 385, 536, 579, 633, 781, 930, 940, 955, 962, 1111, 1124
  Texas, 746
Austin, William Claude: **33**
Australia, description and travel: 210
Authors: 3, 25, 59, 82, 116, 131, 155, 214, 241, 253, 296, 340, 356, 358, 378, 381, 391, 459, 481, 499, 504, 507, 525, 538, 544, 590, 593, 611, 612, 632, 637, 656, 665, 682, 701, 735, 739, 753, 763, 776, 797, 854, 888, 897, 919, 939, 994, 1028, 1029, 1051, 1055, 1077, 1109, 1116, 1120, 1147, 1149, 1156, 1184, 1190, 1193, 1227, 1229
Autograph books: 335, 385
Automobiles: 507
  accidents, 1909, 1199
Automotive business:
  Kansas, 1
  repair, 891
Avant, James Louis: 317
Avants, Thomas Warren: 508
Aviation: 107
  history of, 1012
  Latin America, history of, 381
  Oklahoma, history of, 1107
Axton, Hoyt: 508
Aydelotte, Dora: 508
Ayer, Hugh M.: **34**
Aztec Indians, fiction: 888
Babcock, James M.: **35**
Bacon, Charles W.: **36**
Bacon Rind: 268
Bacone College (Oklahoma): 41, 582, 786
Badger, Ina: **37**
Baggett family genealogy: 578
Bailey, Hurshel: **38**

Baird College (Missouri), student life: 48
Baker, Gretta: 793
Baker, Jesse Albert: **39**
Baker, Thad J.: 508
Baldwin, Delmar H.: **40**
Baldwin, Roger, correspondence: 897
Ball, Ralph: 508
Balyeat, Frank Allen: **41**
Bandy, Mary: **42**
Bank of Augusta, Georgia, currency: 220
Bank of Santa Fe (Newkirk, Oklahoma Territory): 795
Bank of Udall (Oklahoma): **43**
Bankers, personal papers: 332, 350, 545, 569, 914, 967
Banks:
  Kansas, 77
  Oklahoma, 507, 1070, 1160
    records of, 32, 43, 160, 178, 202, 212, 233, 234, 265, 324, 327, 328, 345, 370, 379, 436, 517, 547, 592, 643, 760, 795, 802, 818, 820, 878, 913, 920, 1078, 1086, 1101, 1171, 1234
  Oklahoma Territory
    records of, 760, 795
  Texas, 1070
Baptist Church: 507, 961
  missions, 41
Baptist churches (Oklahoma), history of: 1232
Baptist Missionary Training School: 561
Barbed wire: 214
Barbour, John: **44**
Barbour, Robert: **44**
Barker, N. L.: **45**
Barking Water, copy of: 39
Barnard, Kate: 246, 508
Barnes, Arch: **46**
Barnes, Cassius McDonald: 39, 508
Barnes, D. Elijah: **47**
Barnes Medical College (Missouri), students class notes: 283
Barnes, Sudie McAlester: **48**
Barnes family: 46
Barnett, Jackson: 508
  estate of, 170
Barrett, Charles F.: 508
Barrett, Hershel: **49**
Barrett, T. H., correspondence: 474

Barthelme, Donald: 278
Bartlesville, Oklahoma:
   Lions Club of, 861
   Methodist Episcopal Church in, 1050
   physicians, 1175
   Poles in, 1112
   post office, 197
   Rotary Club, 1050
   YMCA in, 1050
Bartlett, Dewey: 508
Barton, Ray O.: 508
Bass, Altha Leah Bierbower: 50
Bass, Henry Benjamin: 51, 508
Bass, Nathan: 293
Bassett, Ann: 508
Bassett, Mabel: 508
Bataafsche Petroleum Maatshappij (Netherlands): 236
Bates, S. R.: 52
Battenburg Press (Norman, Oklahoma): 53
Battey, Thomas C.: 54
Battle, Bobby: 579
Battle vs. Park Anderson: 579
Baum, F. J.: 55
Baumgartner, Frederick M.: 56
Baumgartner, A. Marguerite: 56
Beach, John: 997, 1063
Beale, A. J.: 508
Beam, J. P.: 57
Bear, William L.: 50
Beauticians (Lawton, Oklahoma): 712
Beaver County, Oklahoma:
   description of, 528
   history of, 586
Beaver, Oklahoma, railroad service to: 1120
Beckham County, Oklahoma: 507
   American Red Cross chapters in, 17
   mortgages, 975
   taxation, 975
   teachers contracts, 274
   World War I, 1201
Beckham County (Oklahoma) Medical Association: 1021
Beecher Island, Battle of, 1868: 369
Belcher, Page Henry: 508
Bell, Earl L.: 58
Bell, Jack: 59
Bell, James Madison, papers of: 186
Bell, Robert E.: 60

Bellmon, Henry: 508
Belt, Robert V.: 61
Belvin, G. N.: 62
Belvin, Harry J. W.: 508
Bender family (Kansas): 239
Benedict, Omer K.: 508
Bennett, H. G.: 508
Bennett, Leo E.: 1139
Bennington, Oklahoma, history of: 6
Benson, Mildred June Tompkins: 63
Benson, Robert R.: 64
Benton, Joseph Horace: 65
Bentonelli, Joseph (See Joseph Horace Benton)
Bernard, Jean-Jacques: 1000
Bernard, Mary Frances (Sister): 1233
Berry, Josie Craig: 66
Berry, Roger M.: 67
Berry, Virgil: 68
Berry, William Aylor: 69
Berthrong, Donald J.: 70
Bethany College (Topeka, Kansas), student life: 331
Betts, D. C.: 71
Betzinez, Jason: 72
Bevan, Wilbur Harrison: 73
Beveridge, Albert J.: 508
Bibliographers: 456
Bienfang, Ralph David: 74
Big Bow: 508
Big Sandy Valley (Kentucky), residents of: 239
Biggers, Jesse and Helen: 75
Billings, James F.: 76
Billings family: 76
Bingham, George, estate of: 295
Birds:
   Mexico, 1091
   Oklahoma, 507, 799, 1091
Birth control: 908
Birth records:
   Kingfisher County, Oklahoma, 304
   Krebs, Oklahoma, 806
   Nowata County, Oklahoma, 336
   Payne County, Oklahoma, 509
Bismarck, North Dakota:
   Women's Christian Temperance Union, 1214
   women's clubs, 623

Bitter Creek, early settlement on: 37
Bituminous Coal Producers Board,
  reports: 227
Bixby, Tams: 508
  correspondence, 978
Bixby family, genealogy: 363
Bizzell, William Bennett: 77, 99, 1147, 1206
Bizzell family, genealogy of: 77
Blachly, Charles Dallas: **78**
Blachly, Lucile Spire: **78**
Black, Albert Hamilton: **79**
Black Beaver: 508
Black Dog: 508
Black Mesa (Oklahoma): 1126
Blackwell, A. J.: 508
Blaine County, Oklahoma Territory,
  schools: 604
Blakely, Thomas Thurston: 508
Blakemore, Jesse Lee: **80**
Blanchard, James Lyon: **81**
Blanchart, Paul, correspondence: 1000
Blanding, Donald Benson: **82**, 508
Blanton, Jr., (Mrs.) James T.: **83**
Blew, W. Bryan: **84**
Bloomfield, Oklahoma: 1051
Blue Eagle, Acee: 508
Boatman, Andrew Nimrod "Jack": **85**
Bodine, John James: **86**
Boggs, Herbert Otho: **87**
Bohlinger, Neill: 1156
Boirun, G. D.: **88**
Bolivia:
  description and travel, 1143
  Murray Colony in, 783, 1143
Bollinger, Clyde John: **89**, 508
Bond, George M.: **90**
Bond family: 90
Bonds, European: 394
Bone, Kathleen: **91**
Bonesteel, F. J.: 1204
Book collections:
  Adams and Henry Stevenson, 2
  Bizzell Memorial Library (University of
    Oklahoma), 2
Books Abroad (See also *World Literature
  Today*), 525, 1203
Boomer Literature Collection: **92**
Boomer Movement (Indian Territory): 880
Boomers: 180

Boone, Charles A.: **93**
Booth, G. R.: **94**
Boren, David: 508
Borglum, Gutzon: 361
Bosin, Blackbear, Sr.: 508
Bosworth, Caroline M.: **95**
Botanists:
  illustrations of, 624, 1059
  writings of, 624
Botany: 74, 257, 644
  societies, 1064
Boudinot, Elias Cornelius, II.: 508, 1216
Boudinot, Frank J.: **96**
Boudinot, W. P.: **97**
Boudinot family: 302
  papers of, 186
Boundaries (Oklahoma): 507
Bourland family: 6
Bowen, Myrtle Evans: **98**
Bowen family, genealogical information: 98
Bowlegs, David: 334
Bowman, Wes: 508
Boyd, David Ross: **99**, 1089
  correspondence, 938
Boyd, Mary Alice: 99
Boyd, Phleat: 508
Boyd family, geneaology of: 99, 330
Boydston, Samuel M.: **100**
Boyer, Betty Kirk: 611
  correspondence, 968
Boyer, Dave H.: **101**
Boyer, Elizabeth Mahala Kirk (See Betty
  Kirk Boyer)
Boyer, Wilfred: 101
Boyers family: 150
Boyles, Richard: 508
Boys State (Oklahoma): 1105
Braden, John: **102**
Bragg, Arthur Norris: **103**
Brandt, Joseph August: **104**, 495, 1147
Branen, Joseph L.: **105**
Braniff, Thomas Elmer: 508
Branson, Carl Colton: **106**
Brazell, J. H.: 107
Brazell, James C.: **107**
Breeding, (Mrs.) W. K.: **108**
Breen, Dick: 508
Brennan, John: **109**
Bressie, Oklahoma, history of: 110

Bressie, R. M.: **110**
Bressie family, genealogy of: 110
Brewer, Theodore F.: 1080
Brillhart, Norman W.: **111**
Briscoe, Isaac: **112**
Bristow Station, Virginia, Battle of: 1046
Broadcaster, The: 912
Broaddus, Bower: **113**
Broken Bow, Oklahoma, physicians: 1023
Bronson, Edgar S.: **114**
Brooks, Stratton Duluth: **115**, 269
Broome, Bertram C.: **116**
Brotherhood of North American Indians, constitution of: 1217
Brown, Benjamin H.: **117**
Brown Brothers Mercantile Store, records of: 120
Brown, Clark: 1013
Brown, Hugh: **118**
Brown, John: 118, 239, 467
Brown, John F.: **119**
Brown, Phillip: **120**
Brown, W. H.: **121**
Brown, Will: 869
Bruccoli, Matthew: 278
Bruner, Joe: 508
Bryan County, Oklahoma: 507
  history of, 302, 770
Bryan, Frank: **122**
Bryan, J. R.: **123**
Bryan, Joel M.: 508
Bryan, John A.: **124**
Bryan, William Jennings: 142
Bryant, William J.: **125**
Buchanan, Carl B.: 508
Buchanan, F. R.: **126**
Buchanan, James Shannon: **127**, 269
Buchanan, Joseph Rodes: 34
Buchanan family: 127
Buckskin Bill's Historical Wild West Show, performers in: 1095
Buffalo, hunting of: 488
Buffalo, Oklahoma, medical care: 148
Buffett, Richard H.: **128**
Buffington, Thomas M.: 1216
Bullock family: 149
Burch, Clarence: 397
Burchardt, August Gustave: **129**
Burchardt, George M.: **130**

Burchardt, William: **131**
Burdine, C. A.: **132**
Bureau of Government Research Collection: 133
Bureau of Indian Affairs:
  correspondence, 659
  publications, 14, 41
Buried treasure (Oklahoma): 353, 507
Burney, B. C.: **134**
Burns, David A.: **135**
Burns, Samuel Lee: **136**
Burton, Patricia: **137**
Busby, Orel: **138**
Busey, Ralph: 8
Bush, Charles C., II: **139**
Bushyhead, Dennis Wolf: **140**, 427
Business and Professional Women's Club (Medford, Oklahoma): 912
Butcher, Nahum Ellsworth: **141**
Butcher, W. H.: **142**
Buttram, Frank A.: 508
  correspondence, 886
Byington, Cyrus: 455
Byrd, William L.: **143**
Cable Temperance Union (Illinois): **144**
Cache Creek Indian Mission (Oklahoma), history of: 1167
Cactus and Succulent Society of Oklahoma City, papers of: 624
Cactus Hornet: 991
Caddo County Medical Association: **145**
Caddo County, Oklahoma: 507
  land deeds, 274
  medical care, 145
  teachers contracts, 274
Caddo Indians:
  attorneys for, 536
  Civil War, 1861-1865, 235
  claims, 536
  culture, 1007
  history of, 481, 1202
Cade, Indian Territory, general stores: 576
Calendars: 75, 385
California:
  description and travel, 112
  gold rush, 1849, 81, 112, 911
  history of, 64
  shipment of gold from, 1196
Calling cards: 945

Calloway, John R.: **146**
Calvin, Oklahoma, retail stores: 537
Camden, Arkansas, description of: 118
Camp Augur, Oklahoma: 507
Camp, Earl F.: **148**
Camp Fire Girls, costume: 199
Camp Holmes, Oklahoma: 1045
Camp Mason, Indian Territory: 169
Camp Nichols, Oklahoma: 507
Camp Radziminski, Oklahoma: 507
Camp Supply Collection: **147**
Campbell, Anson: **149**
Campbell, Charles Duncan: **150**
Campbell Funeral Home, records of: 152
Campbell, George W.: 514
Campbell Hardware Store, records of: 152
Campbell, J. E.: 540
Campbell, J. F.: **151**
Campbell, James Robert: 508
Campbell, John Sidney, Sr.: **152**
Campbell, Robert Boyers: **153**
Campbell, S. W.: **154**
Campbell, W. E.: 153
Campbell, Walter Stanley: **155**, 508, 1028
Campbell, Wilbur E.: **150**
Campbell family: 149
Canadian County, Oklahoma: 507
Canadian, Oklahoma, physicians: 640
Canton, Frank M.: **156**, 508
Canton, Oklahoma, medical care: 126
Capital Grain and Elevator Company, records of: 882
Capital punishment (Oklahoma): 507
Capitol (Oklahoma): 507
  building, 634
Capshaw, Madison T. J.: **157**
Capshaw, Walter: 157
Carlisle Barracks Collection: **158**
Carlock, Arlie Ernest: **159**
Carmen First National Bank Collection: **160**
Carpenter, Dan H., correspondence of: 161
Carpenter, Everett: **161**
Carpenter, Paul Simon: **162**
Carpenter family, genealogy of: 162
Carriker, Robert C.: **163**
Carseloway, James Manford: **164**
Carson, Christopher "Kit": 516
Carson, Frank L.: **165**
Carter, Angeline: 514

Carter, Charles D.: 508
Carter County, Oklahoma: 507
  murder of Mexican citizens, 1024
  schools, 507
Carter, Elizabeth: 514
Carter, Frank C.: **166**, 508
Carter, M. L.: **167**
Carver, George Washington: 387
Casey, Alvin Harold: **168**
Cashion, Oklahoma, retail stores: 524
Caso y Luenge, Francisco, correspondence: 852
Cass, Lewis: **169**
Catalogs:
  art exhibits, 1008
  books and publications, 945
  eyeglasses, 400
  hardware, 228
  household goods, 228
  jewelry, 228
  mail-order, 226
  medical equipment, 664
  saddlery, 228
  stoves, 228
  surgical supply, 400
Cate, Roscoe Simmons: **170**
Cates, P. M.: **171**
Catholic Church: 507, 670, 961
  programs, 11
Cattle branding: 253
Cattle brands: 1111
  Cherokee Outlet (Strip), 364, 1219
  Indian Territory, 364
  Kansas, 253, 364
  Oklahoma, 253, 350, 507
  Oklahoma Territory, 1219
  Texas, 253, 364
Cattle Brands Collection: **172**
Cattle drives: 380
  description of, 452
  Indian Territory, 501
Cattle trade: 497, 507, 882
Cattle trails: 64, 507
  Oklahoma Territory, 444
  Texas, 452
Caudron, Theophile: **173**
Cayuga Indians, claims of: 174, 1017
Cayuga Nation Papers: **174**
Celebrations:

263

centennial, 832
Christmas, 1058, 1109
89ers', 216
Independence Day, 1058
Cemeteries:
   Dyeo Mission (Lawton, Oklahoma), 268
   Indian Territory, 83, 1224
   Kiowa Indians (Duncan, Oklahoma), 268
   Oklahoma, 507, 1224
Census, 1930: 507
Centennial celebrations (Oklahoma): 832
Center for Studies in Higher Education: **175**
Central America, description and travel: 851
Central State Teachers College (Oklahoma), presidents: 773
Centralia, Indian Territory, Van Ausdal Drug Store: 1150
Certificates and Diplomas Collection: **176**
Chaat, Robert P.: **177**
Chaffin, W.A.: 508
Chambers of commerce:
   Norman, Oklahoma, 545
   Oklahoma state, 507
Chaminade Club (Oklahoma City, Oklahoma): 704
Chandler National Bank: **178**
Chandler, Oklahoma Territory:
   banks and banking, 178
   history of, 180
   settlement of, 1230
Chandler, Thomas Albert: 508
Chaney, Warren P.: **179**
Chapman, Amos: 508
Chapman, Berlin Basil: **180**
Chapman, T. Shelby: **181**
Charleston, South Carolina, cotton exposition: 399
Chattahoochee, Macon, and Columbus Railroad: 853
Chautauqua: 507
Checotah, Indian Territory, retail trade: 38
Checote, Samuel: 132, 254, 427
Chelsea (Indian Territory) Town Records Collection: **183**
Chelsea, Oklahoma:
   photography studios, 490
   physicians, 1098
Cherokee Advocate, records of: 186
Cherokee Bibliography Project: **184**

Cherokee Bilingual Education Project: **185**
Cherokee Bill (Crawford Goldsby): 508
Cherokee Commission, minutes of, 1896: 302
Cherokee County, Oklahoma: 507
Cherokee Foundation, Inc., publications of: 902
Cherokee Indians:
   allotment of land, 692
   authors, 854
   bibliography, 184
   census, 186
   chiefs, 140, 164, 186, 302, 462, 691, 692, 847, 981, 984, 987
   citizenship, 186, 477
   Civil War, 186, 1042
   claims, 186, 302
   courts, 186
   Dawes Commission, 186, 692
   delegates and agents, 164, 186
   Eastern (North Carolina) band, 186, 655
   elections, 186
   freedmen, 902
   genealogy, 302
   history of, 1193
   Keetoowah Society, 96
   land transfers, 97, 1216
   language, 185, 409, 425, 859
   laws, 186
   medicine, 484
   missionaries to, 455, 1042
   negro slavery, 1148
   Old Settlers Band, 186
   orphan asylum, 97
   per capita payments, 186
   politics, 96, 462, 691
   removal, 302
   schools, 1222
   seminary graduates, 902
   syllabaries, 41, 185, 859
   telephone companies, 1220
   tribal factionalism, 583
   tribal government, 140, 186
   tribal rolls, 692
   wars, 186
   westward migration, 606
   writings about, 1168
Cherokee Nation:
   allotment of land, 462, 492

asylum for the blind, 484
bibliography, 184
boundary surveys, 186
census, 186
Cherokee Outlet, dissolution of
 title to, 691
Cherokee Strip Livestock Association, 140
Civil War, 186
courts, 186, 498
crime, 186
description of, 363, 854
description of life in, 1861-1865, 368
disputes with the federal government, 186
economy, 363
education, 186, 748, 847, 987
elections, 186
financial affairs, 186, 847, 987
geographical studies of, 492
history of, 363, 616, 984, 1168
insane asylum, 186
intruders, 186
land transfers, 462, 498, 847
law enforcement, 186
laws, 186
leases, 186
legal affairs, 186
licenses, 186
memorials and resolutions, 902
missionaries, 338, 368, 974, 1042
missions, 748
New Echota Church, 338
officials, 186
oil wells in, 164
pensions, 484
permits & fees, 186
politics, 363, 484, 984
Presbyterian Church, 338
prisons, 186
railroads, 97, 186
reconstruction in, 987
records of, 186
roads, 748
schools, 748, 847
slavery in, 974, 1148
smallpox, 186
social conditions in, 984
statehood, 987
town lots, 186
township maps, 492

tribal government, 462, 847, 987
 closing of, 981
 Vann murder case, 186
Cherokee Nation Papers: **186**
Cherokee National Party: 484
Cherokee Outlet (Strip): 186
 cattle brands used in, 1219
 cowboy life in, 952
 dissolution of Indian title to, 691
 history of, 1164
 land run of 1893, 39, 319, 410, 474,
  896, 952, 1052, 1074
 maps, 303, 474
 social history, 533
Cherokee Strip Livestock Association: 140
 history of, 1003
Cherokee Telephone Company: 1220
Cherokee Treaty Fund, claims: 186
Cheyenne and Arapaho Indian Baptist
 Mission: 561
Cheyenne Indians:
 environmental studies, 483
 housing surveys, 483
 probate records, 757
 relations with U.S. government, 1063
 relations with whites, 812
 religion and mythology, 919
 rites and ceremonies, 919
 Sand Creek band, 757
 sun dance, 302, 919
 wars, 369, 552, 1137
Cheyenne-Arapaho Indian Agency: 252, 614
Cheyenne-Arapaho Indians:
 allotments, 757
 bands, 757
 census, 757
 ceremonies, 757
 child care, 757
 farming, 614
 genealogy, 757
 history, 91
 kinship, 757
 missions to, 561
 religion and mythology, 79
 schools, 1011
 social customs, 757
 societies, 757
 wars, 147
Chi Delta Phi Collection: **187**

Chi Upsilon Collection: **188**
Chiang Kai-Shek, (Madame): 668
  correspondence of, 543
Chicago, Rock Island, and Pacific
  Railroad: **189**
  health & pension plans, 389
  history of, 1088
  physicians, 360
  records of, 503, 976, 1014
Chicago, Texas, and Mexican Central
  Railway Company: 456
Chickahominy, Virginia, Battle of: 1046
Chickasaw Indians:
  allotment of land, 91, 259, 702, 770, 774,
    846, 962
  attorneys, 718
  banks and banking, 569
  business interests, 569
  cemeteries, 83
  chiefs, 134, 463, 435, 463, 573, 655,
    702, 774, 857, 867, 1210
  citizenship claims, 249, 259
  Civil War, 1861-1865, 770, 921
  conscription, 921
  Dawes Commission, 702
  health care, 1151
  land transfers, 91, 315, 846, 962
  language, 949
  litigation, 249, 718
  mineral resources of, 1124
  relations with U.S. government, 1124
  relations with whites, 869
  slaves, ownership of, 573
  taxation, 718
  tribal factionalism, 463
  tribal government, 134, 143
  tribal politics, 770
Chickasaw Nation:
  allotment of land, 463, 792, 1210
  chiefs, 466
  claims, 573
  description and travel, 179
  education, 573
  elections, 435, 463
  finances, 573, 1210
  history of, 655
  land transfer, 179, 190
  land use, 1210
  laws, 190

  legislation, 466
  mineral resources, 573
  mining trustee for, 1124
  Oklahoma statehood, 1210
  Permit Law of 1876, 857
  schools, 463
  tribal factionalism, 463
  tribal government, 190, 573
  tribal legislation, 435
  white settlement in, 869
Chickasaw Nation Collection: **190**
Chickasha Milling Company Collection: **191**
Chickasha, Oklahoma: 1051
  clubs and societies, 37
  Grady County Park, 1127
  milling companies, 191
Child labor (Oklahoma): 276
Children, research on vocabulary of: 969
Children's literature: 538, 637, 682
Childs, (Mrs.) William Oscar: **192**
Chile, Jesuits in: 862
Chilocco Indian School:
  Indian Territory, 287
  Oklahoma, 1058
China, foreign relations, 1939-1946: 543
Chisholm, Jesse: 508
Chisholm Trail: 507
  in Oklahoma, 444, 1201
Chisum family: 6
Choate, Mary Treadwell: **193**
Choctaw Academy and Missionary Station
  (Kentucky): 905
Choctaw-Chickasaw Sanitorium: 1151
Choctaw Coal and Railway Company: 978
Choctaw County, Oklahoma: 507
  medical care, 167
  Medical Society, records of, 1212
Choctaw Indians:
  allotment of land, 194, 469, 580, 770,
    846, 940, 955, 962
  attorneys, 718
  chiefs, 10, 125, 224, 316, 469, 523, 555,
    580, 636, 646, 657, 707, 708, 709, 715,
    787, 905, 1043, 1231
  citizenship, 249, 302
  Civil War, 609, 770
  culture, 533
  education, 231, 1043
  general stores, 576

health care, 1151
history, 237, 302, 350
land transfer, 179, 315, 846, 872, 962
language, 62, 792, 949
  correspondence, 366
  example of, 576, 716
  hymnal, 366
  religious texts, 383
  textbooks, 383
libraries, private, 1231
litigation, 249, 718, 955
minerals
  resources of, 1124, 1183, 1241
  rights, 580
missionaries to, 455, 609
Mississippi band, 543
poets, 716
relations with other Indians, 787
relations with U.S. government, 1124
relations with white settlers, 560
religious texts, 366
removal of, 87, 609
slavery, 392, 609
social history, 533
taxation, 718
townsite payments, 940
tribal council proceedings, 224
tribal government, 10, 194, 224, 1043
tribal politics, 87, 580, 770
Choctaw Nation:
  allotment of land, 194, 315, 392, 543, 657, 792
  attorneys of, 543, 668, 1124
  businesses in, 954
  citizenship, 707
  Civil War, 1861-1865, treaty of peace, 905
  claims, 543
  coal lands royalties, 224
  coal mining, 396, 1183
  courts, 224, 249, 396
  crime and criminals, 1216
  description and travel, 179
  elections, 194
  financial affairs, 392
  general council records, 194, 366
  general council, speeches to, 576
  history of, 655
  intruders, 224
  land transfers, 194, 543
  laws, 194, 366
  legislation, 396
  mineral rights, 708
  mining trustee, papers of, 1124
  politics, 194, 316, 708, 1009
  railroads, 707, 708
  schools, 316, 396, 706
  slavery, 392, 609, 905
  statehood, 708, 1009
  stock raising, 316
  timber lands, 396
  townsites, 708
  treasurers of, 1188
  tribal citizenship, 224
  tribal factionalism, 392
  tribal government, 194, 316, 657, 706, 707, 708, 709, 715, 905
Choctaw Nation Papers: **194**
Choctaw, Oklahoma, Medical Society: 741
Choctaw Trading Company: 978
Choska Trading Company Collection: **195**
Chouteau, Auguste: 196
Chouteau, Edward L.: 268
Chouteau, Indian Territory, medical care: 68
Chouteau, Jean Pierre: 169, 196, 508
Chouteau, Myra Yvonne: **196**, 508
Chouteau, Pierre, correspondence: 852
Chouteau, Rosalie Capitaine: 268
Christian Church, history of in Oklahoma: 1066
Christianity, history of: 1184
Christie, Ned: 508
Christmas traditions: 1058, 1109
Christopher, Ernest Randell: **197**
Chupco, John: **198**
Church of Jesus Christ of Latter-Day Saints, currency issued by: 220
Churches:
  Baptist, 507
  Catholic, 507
  Christian, history of, 1066
  Disciples of Christ, 507
  Episcopal, records of, 998
  Mennonite, 507
  Methodist, 507
  Presbyterian, 507
Churchill, Winston: 358
  correspondence, 543

Ciereszko, Leon: 199
Cigar bands: 385
Cimarron County, Oklahoma: 507
Cimarron Rose (Rose Dunn): 508
Cities Service Oil and Gas Corporation
    Collection: 200
Civil Rights Commission (Oklahoma): 201
Civil War, 1861-1865:
    Arkansas, 1133
    border states, 387
    Bristow Station, Battle of, 1046
    Centerville, Battle of, 1864, 853
    Chickahominy, Battle of, 1046
    CSA Indian policy, 235
    correspondence about, 231, 339, 650
    damage claims, 291
    historical fiction, 593
    history of, 51, 720
    Indian Territory, 402, 609, 1042, 1133
    Indian troops, 921, 1042, 1162
    infantry tactics, 1046
    Kansas, 239, 344, 1133
    Manassas, First Battle of, 1046
    maps of battlefield maneuvers, 432
    military sanitation guides, 1046
    military service records, 875
    Missouri, 1133
    naval engagements, 270
    oath of allegiance to the U.S., 602
    personal narratives, 9, 107, 109, 255,
        270, 291, 339, 404, 429, 432, 605, 697,
        705, 853, 949, 1013, 1020, 1046, 1096,
        1133
    poetry about, 1080
    regimental songs, 1046
    Seven Days Battle, 1046
    Sharpsburg, Battle of, 1046
    Shiloh, Battle of, 1080
    South Carolina, 1070
    Tennessee Theatre, 853
    trans-Mississippi west, 339, 387
    U.S. occupation of Louisiana, 1191
    veterans reunion memorabilia, 1046
Civil War Centennial Commission: 468
    records of (Oklahoma), 51
Claremore, Oklahoma:
    index to records of, 31
    mayors of, 31
    utility rates, 515

Clarita Farmers State Bank Collection: 202
Clark, B. C.: 508
Clark, Ben: 203
Clark, Carter Blue: 204
Clark, Joseph J.: 205, 508
Clark, Stanley A.: 748
Clarke, Georgia Lee: 206
Clarke, (Mrs.) Hulbert S.: 206
Clarke, John R.: 207
Clarkson, Addie W.: 208
Classen, Anton H.: 209
Clay Center, Kansas: 76
Clay, Henry: 1199
Cleckler, Frank Stuart: 210
Clements, Frank B.: 211
Cleo Springs, Oklahoma, banks and
    banking: 212
Cleo State Bank: 212
Clergymen: 430, 866, 1026, 1042, 1047,
    1080, 1184, 1194
    papers of, 1218, 1231
Cleveland County, Oklahoma: 507
    American Red Cross chapters in, 18
    history of, 1213
    medical care, 213
    records of, 1213
Cleveland County (Oklahoma) Children's
    Clinic: 213
Clifton, Robert T.: 214
Climatology: 507
Cline, (Mrs.) B. F.: 215
Clinkenbeard family, genealogy of: 1067
Clinton, Oklahoma:
    Edelweiss Club, 1135
    Literary Club, 1135
    physicians, 626
Clouse, Hiram H.: 1004
Clubb, Laura: 508
Clubs:
    civic, 775, 805, 1082, 1118, 1155
    garden, 810
    Lions International, 84, 105, 129, 168,
        211, 272, 584, 652, 804, 861
    mens, 684, 988, 999
    music, 506, 511, 752, 999
    Oklahoma, 507, 844, 883, 960, 988
    political, 498
    professional, 1109
    Rotary International, 988

social, 1176
women's, 37, 230, 277, 386, 617, 704, 721, 814, 835, 850, 860, 883, 912, 1135
Coaches, football: 666
Coachman, Ward: **217**, 254
Coal mining:
 Arkansas, 589
 Indian Territory, 589, 1053
 Iowa, 1053
 Missouri, 1053
 Montana, 1053,
 Oklahoma, 227, 507, 589, 749, 778, 1053, 1183
 West Virginia, 1053
Cobb, Isabel: **218**
Cobb, William, murder case of: 186
Cobblers: 306
Cocke family, records of: 38
Cody, William F. (Buffalo Bill): 356, 508
Coffey, John L.: **219**
Coins, Tokens and Money Collection: **220**
Colbert, Winchester: **221**
Colbert family: 1051
Colcord, Charles Francis: **222**, 508
 memoirs of, 459
Colcord, Harriet Scoresby: 222, 508
Colcord, Ray: 222
Colcord, Sidney: 222
Colcord, Will C.: 222
Colcord family, genealogy: 222
Coldiron, Daisy Lemon: **223**, 508
Cole, Coleman: **224**
Cole Motor Car Company: 1061
Cole, Redmond S.: **225**
Coleman, Emma Alberta White: **226**
Colleges and universities:
 course outlines, 440, 858
 deans, 513
 diplomas, 945
 faculty attitude toward WWI, 1005
 faculty lecture notes, 77, 139, 165, 341, 375, 606, 655, 681, 761, 773, 858, 925, 1116, 1168
 fraternities, records of, 901, 1033, 1034, 1035
 libraries, 240
 loyalty oaths, 180
 medical students, 12, 159, 377, 509, 520, 539, 654, 680, 703, 1158
 Oklahoma, 507
 presidents, 773, 980, 1022
  Oklahoma, 77, 338, 938
  Texas, 77
 professors, 155, 162, 246, 269, 278, 286, 309, 310, 325, 341, 347, 375, 412, 440, 480, 489, 502, 513, 525, 606, 631, 655, 656,.659, 670, 673, 681, 720, 761, 762, 768, 773, 776, 807, 858, 864, 871, 904, 938, 947, 966, 969, 1000, 1003, 1005, 1012, 1022, 1092, 1099, 1116, 1168, 1177, 1197, 1203, 1206
 publications, 1162
 school songs, 406
 student
  class notes, 77, 283, 365, 366, 377, 450, 455, 509, 520, 539, 654, 703, 725, 727, 742, 846, 951, 989
  grade reports, 938, 1116, 1197, 1206
  life, 25, 28, 48, 50, 162, 331, 412, 704
  writings, 269, 681, 761, 1057
Collins, Arza Bailey: **229**
Collins Coal Company: **227**
Collins, Daniel: 1051
Collins Hardware Store: **228**
Collums, (Mrs.) Garner G.: **230**
Colonial Dames Collection: **231**
Colony Mercantile Company (Oklahoma): 607
Colony, Oklahoma, medical care: 275
Colorado, mines and mining: 589
Columbus Day, proclamation of (Oklahoma Territory): 963
Comanche County, Oklahoma: 507
 history of, 491
 school boards, 491
Comanche Indian Mission (Fort Sill, Oklahoma): 177
Comanche Indians:
 Civil War, 1861-1865, 235
 census, 740
 constitution, 740
 customs, 294
 dictionaries, 294
 encounters with whites, 663
 land transfers, 40
 language, 294, 949
 wars, 552, 578

Comanche, Oklahoma, buried treasure: 353
Combest, George Marion: 232
Commerce First State Bank: 233
Commerce, Oklahoma, municipal
 records: 233
Commercial National Bank: 234
Committee on Oil Investigation: 995
Commonplace books, Elizabethan: 2
Communism, attitudes toward: 883, 1237
Community Hospital Bulletin: 1021
Composers: 612, 807
Confederate States of America:
 army
  26th Alabama Infantry, 650
  Dublin Provost Guard, 602
  general officers, 1179
  Indian troops, 1162
 conscription of Indian troops, 921
 currency, 220, 684
 Indian policy, 235, 302, 1042
 soldiers, personal narratives, 109, 650,
  697, 705, 1020, 1133
 veterans, 454
Confederate States of America Indian Affairs
 Collection: 235
Congregationalist Church: 961
Conkling, Richard A.: 236
Conlan, Madeline Czarina Colbert: 237
Conn, J. L.: 238
Connelley, William Elsey: 239
Conner, Bart: 508
Connors State Agricultural College: 240
Conservation:
 advocacy organization, 1065
 grasslands, 790
Conservationists: 425, 1185
Conservatoire National (France): 162
Constant, Alberta Anne Wilson: 241
Constant, Edwin, correspondence: 241
Constitutional Convention (Oklahoma): 39,
 473, 556, 972
 history of, 544, 728
 records of, 133
Consumer cooperatives: 361
Continental Asphalt and Petroleum
 Company: 128
Continental Investment Corporation, records
 of: 575
Coocoochee: 645

Cook, Benjamin R.: 242
Cook, F. L.: 243
Cookbooks: 75, 385, 742 (See recipes also)
Cooksey, Harold S.: 244
Cooper, Ann Mayer: 245
Cooper, Leroy (Gordon): 508
Cooperative Community Hospital (Elk City,
 Oklahoma): 1021
Co-operative Publishing Company: 216
Copeland, Edith: 246, 508, 571
Copeland, Fayette, Jr.: 246, 508
Coppadge, Ethel: 247
Coquimbro, Chile, Jesuit college of: 862
Cordell, Oklahoma:
 description, 1152
 physicians, 599
Cornell, Kearns Bryon: 248
Cornish, Cecil: 508
Cornish, Melven: 249
Correspondence schools: 870
Costumes: 507
Cotton:
 cleaning machines, invention of, 1201
 gins and ginning, 439, 929, 954
 trade expositions, 399
Cotton County, Oklahoma: 507
Cotton trade:
 Indian Territory, 954
 Oklahoma, 120, 929, 954
Couch, Nevada: 1222
County government (Oklahoma):
 court records, 809
 financial records, 370, 809
Court, Nathan Altschiller: 250
Courts:
 Arkansas, 317, 965
 district court clerk reports, 789
 Indian Territory, records of, 1138, 1139,
  1140
 Oklahoma, 507, 755
  records of, 113, 809, 1141, 1154
 Oklahoma Territory, records of, 1141
Covey, Arthur: 251
Covington, J.A.: 252
Cowboys: 155, 253, 446, 452, 478, 507,
 528, 586, 881, 952, 1003, 1047, 1149
Cowles, Fred G.: 672
Coyle, Oklahoma, retail stores: 524
Crabb, E. D.: 799

Crawford, L. E.: **253**
Crazy Snake Rebellion: 10, 1047
Creek County, Oklahoma: 507
Creek, George, correspondence: 897
Creek Indians:
  allotment of land, 427, 747
  census, 302
  chiefs, 182, 217, 427, 457, 554, 711, 849, 894, 895, 915, 1108
  constitution of 1867, 217
  culture, 848
  history, 302, 427
  immigration to Mexico, 895
  lands in Alabama, 427
  language of, 62
  missionaries to, 973
  Oklahoma statehood, opposition to, 747
  poets, 747
  relations with whites, 849
  removal, 427
  Snake Clan, 747
  speeches, 711
  towns
    Alabama, 170
    Oklahoma, 170
  tribal factionalism, 217, 427, 554, 645
  tribal government, 182
  tribal politics, 427
Creek Nation:
  allotment of land, 427, 915
  boundaries of, 663
  courts, 254
  Dawes Commission, 895
  finances, 554
  general stores, 195
  Green Peach War, 427
  land titles, 254, 554
  land transfers, 427
  politics, 427, 895
  records of, 254
  statehood for Indian Territory, 915
  tribal government, 254, 457, 554, 711, 894, 915
Creek Nation Collection: **254**
Crescent Mining, Milling, and Oil Company (Lawton, Oklahoma): 1038
Cress, Sherry Marie: **255**
Crime and criminals:
  Carter County, Oklahoma, 1024
  Cobb, William, murder case of, 186
  criminals conferences on, 51
  Fountain, Albert Jennings, murder case, 43
  Indian Territory, 689, 965, 1139, 1140, 1178
  Kelly, George "Machine Gun", 633
  No Man's Land (Oklahoma Panhandle), 865
  Nowata County, Oklahoma, 809
  Oklahoma, 507, 610, 1141, 1154, 1178
  Oklahoma Territory, 1141
  Seminole County, Oklahoma, 957
  Urschel kidnapping case, 222
Crittendon, William Dial: **256**
Cross, George Lynn: **257**, 1091
Cross, John M.: 508
Crouch, Aziel Henry: **258**
Cruce, Cruce, and Bleakmore Collection: **259**
Cruce, Lee: 259, 508, 684
  campaign for governor of Oklahoma, 1198
Crumbo, Woody: **260**
Cuadra, José de la: 525
Cuba: 729
Cuddeback, Frank J.: **261**
Curry, Arthur R.: **262**
Cushing Refining and Gasoline Company: **263**
Custer County Medical Society: **264**
Custer County, Oklahoma: 507
  banks and banking, 265
  medical care, 264
Custer County, Oklahoma Territory, frontier and pioneer life: 812
Custer County State Bank: **265**
Custer, George Armstrong: 111, 1011
Cutler, Violona: **266**
Cutlip, C. Guy: **267**
Czechoslovakians in Oklahoma: 486
Dahlberg, Sophie Little Bear: **268**
Dairy farmers league, creation of (Oklahoma): 559
Dakota Territory:
  Sisseton Indian reservation, 474
  Wahpeton Indian reservation, 474
Dale, Edward Everett: 99, **269**, 495
Dalton brothers: 356, 508
Dalton family: 10

271

Dams and reservoirs (Oklahoma): 164, 507
Danforth, Thatcher O.: **270**
Dangerfield, Royden James: **271**
Daniel, Harley A.: **272**
Daniels, Opherita Eugenia: **273**
Danner, Clyde: **274**
Darlington, Brinton: 331
Darnell, E. E.: **275**
Darrow, Clarence: 358
Daugherty, Charles L.: **276**
Daughters of the American Revolution: **277**
  Elliot Lee chapter, 860
Davidson, Frank (See Elmer McCurdy)
Davidson, Mollie: 1238
Davis, Jefferson, correspondence: 530
Davis, Robert Murray: **278**
Davis, W. A.: 1238
Davison, Oscar William: **279**
Dawes Commission: 48, 119, 132, 140, 179, 186, 194, 392, 462, 747, 774, 932
Dawson, Herron Victor: **280**
Dawson, Winnie M.: **281**
Day County, Oklahoma Territory: 507
Day, John Lewis: **282**
Deacons and Missionaries Institute: 786
Deadwood, South Dakota, description of: 699
Deal [Photography] Studio (Chelsea, Oklahoma), records of: 490
Dean, Charles C.: 851
Dean, Samuel C.: **283**
DeBarr, Edwin S.: **284**
DeBarr family: 284
Debo, Angie Elbertha: **285**, 508
  publication of *And Still the Waters Run*, 495
Decker, Charles Elijah: **286**
DeGolyer, Everette Lee: 508
  correspondence, 450
DeKnight, Emma H.: **287**
Delaware Indian Agency: **288**
Delaware Indians:
  captives of, 1067
  chiefs, 1217
  claims against U.S. government, 1217
  land transfers, 288
  removal, 288
Delta Kappa Gamma, publications of: 127
Delta Tau Delta Collection: **289**

Deming, Samuel A.: 632
Democratic Club (Vinita, Indian Territory), records of: 498
Democratic Party (Oklahoma): 595
  campaigns, 69, 138, 595, 700, 822, 1170, 1198
  elections, 1170
  labor legislation, 276
  publications of, 784
Democratic Party Convention, 1900: admission ticket to, 498
  Oklahoma, 1944, proceedings, 822
Dennis, Frank Landt, Sr.: **290**
Dentists (Oklahoma), records of: 889
Denton, B. E. "Cyclone": 508
Denver, James William: **291**
Denver family: 291
Department stores (Oklahoma), records of: 215, 1030
DeRosier, Arthur H.: **292**
DeStwolinski, Louis C.: **293**
Detrick, C. H.: **294**
DeVilliers, Myrtle: **295**
Devol, Oklahoma, First Baptist Church: 1232
Devoto, Bernard: 1147
Dewey County, Oklahoma: 507
Dewey, Frederick Stanley: 680
Dewey, George H.: 680
Dewey, Oklahoma, hotels: 7
Dewlen, Al: **296**
D'Hanis, Texas, history of: 390
Diamond Dishwasher Co., history of: 1121
Diamond Jubilee Commission: **297**
Diaries (See journals also): 9, 48, 51, 54, 154, 155, 170, 210, 229, 232, 239, 252, 255, 267, 287, 302, 307, 331, 338, 351, 361, 363, 390, 404, 413, 429, 431, 432, 440, 450, 455, 491, 582, 645, 646, 738, 853, 875, 905, 911, 914, 939, 945, 949, 974, 999, 1013, 1029, 1032, 1046, 1048, 1049, 1085, 1091, 1116, 1157, 1194
Dill, C.A.: **298**
Dinkler, Frank A.: **299**
Diplomas (See Certificates and Diplomas Collection)
Diplomats (United States), personal papers: 401, 543

Dirkson, Everett: 59
Disarmament: 78
  posters about, 983
  publications about, 983
Disciples of Christ Church: 507
Disney, Dorothy Cameron: 508
Disney, Richard Lester: 300
Ditmars, Raymond L., correspondence: 851
Ditzler, Walter Linginfelter: 301
Division of Manuscripts Collection: 302
Division of Manuscripts Map Collection: 303
Dixon, A.: 304
Doan's Crossing (Oklahoma): 507
Dobie, J. Frank: 1147
Dodd, John E.: 1044
Dodge City, Kansas, description of: 452, 528
Doggett, E. J.: 2
Doherty, Henry: 200
Donnelley, Herndon Ford: 305
Donnelley family: 305
Doody, Maurice: 306
Doran, Lowry A.: 307
Dorchester, May Miner: 746
Dorrance, Lemuel: 308
Dos Passos, John: 1227
Dowd, Jerome H.: 309
Drake, Noah Fields: 310
Drake University (Des Moines, Iowa), presidents: 1022
Drug stores (See pharmacies also):
  Indian Territory, 1150
  Oklahoma, 44, 1150
    records of, 233, 581, 613, 646, 1157
  Oklahoma Territory, 299, 646
    records of, 613
Drury College (Missouri): 77
Dry goods stores, records of: 726
DuBois family: 311
Duffy, Homer: 312
Dugan, Eva Ellsworth: 313
Duke Indian Oral History Collection: 314
Duke, James Monroe: 315
Dukes, Gilbert W.: 316
Dumbarton Oaks, history of: 1190
Dunbar, Diana: 292
Dunbar, William: 292
Duncan, Everett E.: 1146
Duncum, Floy: 317

Dunn, Jesse J.: 508
Dunn, Rose "Cimarron Rose": 508
Durant, William A.: 318
Dust storms (Oklahoma): 475
Dutch Reformed Church (Indian Territory): 177
Duvall, Preston Van Buren: 319
Dwight Mission: 320, 418
  description of, 974
Eagle-Picher Mining and Smelting Company: 321
Earlsboro, Oklahoma Territory: 49
Eason Oil Company: 575
East Guthrie, Indian Territory: 1181
Eastern Oklahoma A&M College (Wilburton): 738
Eddleman, Morgan W.: 989
Edelweiss Club (Clinton, Oklahoma): 1135
Editors: 97, 797
Education:
  higher, 990, 1022
  Oklahoma, 507, 931
  research, 969, 990
  trends (United States), 306
  testing and measurement, 969
  text books, 40
Educators:
  correspondence of, 76
  writings of, 864, 969
Edwards, Archibald Cason: 322
Edwards, John N., correspondence: 766
Edwards, R. J. Inc., records of: 322
Edwards, Thomas Allison: 323
Edwards family, correspondence of: 322
Edwards Trading Post (Hughes County, Oklahoma): 1045
Eggan, Fred, field notes of: 757
Eisenhower, Dwight David: 59
El Meta Bond College (Oklahoma): 41
El Reno Citizens National Bank: 324
El Reno Interurban Railway Co., (Oklahoma), records of: 1121
El Reno, Oklahoma:
  banks and banking, 324
  clubs, 1097
  railroad operations at, 976
El Reno (Oklahoma) Sanitarium: 4, 788
Ela, George: 239
Elder, Frederick Stanton: 325

Election returns Atoka County, Oklahoma: 242
Elections:
 Oklahoma, 207, 276, 507, 892
 United States, 892
Elk City Community Hospital: 326
Elk City Farmers National Bank: 327
Elk City First National Bank: 328
Elk City, Oklahoma:
 agricultural cooperatives, 887
 banks and banking, 327, 328
 hospitals, 1021
 medical care, 326
Elkins, Harrison H.: 329
Elliott, J. Ross: 330
Elliott, Robert L.: 1240
Ellison, (Mrs.) C. D.: 331
Ellison, Ralph: 66
Emblems, state (Oklahoma): 507
Emerson, Caro: 331
Emerson, Ralph Waldo: 1055
English, Frank Miller: 332
English, William M.: 333
Enid, Oklahoma:
 physicians, 603
 training school for nurses, 603
Enid (Oklahoma) Army Air Field, naming of: 1153
Enid, Oklahoma Territory, settlement of: 410
Epidemics, influenza: 157
Episcopal Church: 961
Epton, Hicks Byers: 334
Epworth College of Medicine (Oklahoma City, Oklahoma): 762
Epworth Spotlight, The: 625
Equal Rights Amendment (Oklahoma): 496
Erdmann, E. M.: 335
Erwin, A. M.: 336
Eskridge Hotel (Wynnewood, Oklahoma), records of: 1205
Eta Kappa Nu Collection: 337
Ethnobotany: 1165
Ethnology (Oklahoma): 507
Ethopian/Amharic language, manuscripts in: 158
Etiquette, book of: 1109
Euchee Boarding School (Sapulpa, Oklahoma), records of: 1001

Euchee Indians, schools: 1001
Eufaula, Indian Territory, physicians: 1115
Eufaula, Oklahoma:
 general stores, 120
 physicians, 1115
Eureka Springs, Arkansas, development of railroads: 395
Europe, description and travel, 535, 1032
Evans, Arthur Grant: 338
Evans, Arthur W.: 338
Evans, Charles: 339
Evans, Luther H.: 35
Evans, Oren F.: 340
Ewing, Amos, correspondence: 238
Ewing, Cortez Arthur Milton: 63, 341
Exchange National Bank (Tulsa, Oklahoma), correspondence: 350
Expeditions, southwestern United States: 390
Ezell, John Samuel: 342
Fairland, Indian Territory, retail trade: 152
Fairland, Oklahoma:
 grain businesses, records of, 734
 municipal government, records of, 343
 retail trade, 152
Fairland, Oklahoma, Municipal Records Collection: 343
Fairview, Oklahoma:
 banks, 1160
 newspapers, 1160
 physicians, 565
 railroads, 1160
Fairview, Oklahoma Territory, history of: 1164
Family Life Institute (University of Oklahoma): 890
Fanciers organizations (Oklahoma): 594
Farley, Alan W.: 344
Farley, James A.: 1037
Farm Credit Administration, publications of: 441
Farm relief programs: 361
Farmers: 88
Farmers Cotton Gin Company, records of: 439
Farmers National Bank (Hydro, Oklahoma), records of: 547
Farmers National Grain Corporation, records of: 441
Farmers State Bank: 345

Farmers Union Cooperative Gin
  Company: 346
Farms and farming: 501
  Indian Territory, 88
  Kansas, 239, 909
  mortgages, 166
  Oklahoma, 546, 559
  Oklahoma Territory, 1159
  Texas, 88, 1159
Farr, Doane: 988
Faulk, Odie B.: 508
Fauna (Tulsa County, Oklahoma): 799
Feaver, John Clayton: 347
Federal district courts, records of: 113
Federal Home Loan Bank (Topeka, Kansas),
  records of: 77
Federal Power Commission:
  annual reports of, 1207
  investigation of natural gas industry, 1207
Feed stores (Oklahoma), records of: 407
Ferguson, Lucia Loomis,
  correspondence: 350
Ferguson, Milton James: 348
Ferguson, Thompson Benton: 349, 350
Ferguson, Walter Scott: 350, 508
Feuquay, Courtland Matson: 351
Feuquay, J. W.: 351
Field, J. Walker: 352
Fields, John: 419
Fillman, Irvin: 353
Financial firms (Oklahoma), records of: 322
Findlay, James Franklin: 354
Fink, John Berlin: 355
Finley, Ira M.: 204
Finney, Frank Florer: 356
Finney, Thomas McKean: 356
Finney family: 356
First, Francis Ray, Sr.: 357
First National Bank (Carmen,
  Oklahoma): 160
First National Bank (Oklahoma City,
  Oklahoma), records of: 818
First State Bank (Noble, Oklahoma): 802
Fish, Hamilton: 1217
Fisher, Clyde, publications of: 359
Fisher, Daniel G.: 358
Fisher, Te Ata: 359
Fisk, Charles W.: 360
Fite, Gilbert C.: 361

Fitzpatrick, H. L.: 362
Five Civilized Tribes: (See also individual
  tribes)
  Civil War, participation in, 235, 302
  principal chiefs of, 10, 302
Flags:
  state (Oklahoma), 507
  United States, poems about, 422
Flenner, John W.: 494
Fletcher, Margaret Catherine: 363
Fletcher family genealogy: 363
Flint District, Cherokee Nation, description
  of: 363
Flint, Indian Territory, retail stores: 530
Flipper, Henry O.: 508
Flitch, Sylvester: 364
Floods and flood control (Oklahoma): 507
Flora (southwestern United States): 624
Flora, Snowden Dwight: 365
Florida, description and travel: 851
Floyd, Charles "Pretty Boy": 508
Floyd, Gilbert: 122
Fluke, Louise: 508
Folk songs: 754
Folsom, David: 455
Folsom, Israel: 455
Folsom, Lee W.: 366
Folsom, Nathaniel: 455
Folsom family, correspondence: 366
Folsom Reunion Association, records of: 367
Folsom Training School: 367
Football, play diagrams: 666
Force, Edith R.: 799
Ford, Oklahoma, history of: 110
Foreign policy, United States: 307
Foreman, Carolyn Thomas: 508
Foreman, Grant: 508
Foreman, James, death of: 583
Foreman, Stephen: 368
Foreman family: 302, 368
Forests and forestry (Oklahoma): 507
Forsyth, George Alexander: 369
Fort Arbuckle, Indian Territory: 507, 949
Fort Berthold Indian Reservation: 1217
Fort Cobb, Oklahoma: 507
Fort Coffee, Indian Territory: 507
Fort Davis, Indian Territory: 507
Fort Gibson First National Bank: 370
Fort Gibson, Indian Territory: 1216

275

cemetery, 606
　establishment of, 606
Fort Gibson, Oklahoma: 507
　banks and banking, 370
　financial records, 370
Fort Gibson Quartermaster Collection: 371
Fort Griffin, Texas, description of: 452
Fort McCulloch, Indian Territory: 507
Fort Marion, Florida: 507
Fort Reno, Oklahoma Territory: 507, 1137
　description of, 452, 488
Fort Sill, Oklahoma, missile firing
　　range at: 1065
Fort Sill, Oklahoma Territory: 507
　description of, 488
Fort Smith, Arkansas: 507
　description of, 363
　history of, 402
　U.S. district court at, 965
Fort Smith, Subiaco, and Eastern Railway
　Company: 372
Fort Supply, Indian Territory: 507
　description of, 452
　history of, 163
Fort Towson, Indian Territory: 507
Fort Union, New Mexico, records from: 390
Fort Washita, Indian Territory: 507
Fort Washita, Oklahoma: 111
Fort Wayne, Indian Territory: 507
Forts (See also camps and military posts)
Foster, Del Oneita: 373
Fountain, Albert Jennings, murder case: 43
Four Mothers Society: 62
Fourche family, estate of: 219
Fowler, David: 374
Fowler, Richard Gildart: 375
Fox-Vliet Drug Store, (Oklahoma City,
　Oklahoma) records of: 1157
France:
　theatrical history, 1000
　transfer of real property, 256
Frankhoma pottery: 1002
Franklin, William Monroe: 376
Fraternal Order of Eagles, correspondence
　relating to: 500
Fraternal organizations:
　proceedings of, 615
　publications, 686
　ribbons and buttons, 438

Fraternities, records of: 901, 1033, 1034,
　1035
Frayser, E. B.: 377
Fred, Oklahoma: 1051
Frederick, Oklahoma:
　mortgages, 772
　realtors, 772
　telephone directory, 1926, 130
Frederickson, Mary Brownlee: 378
Freedom State Bank: 379
Freeman, Margaret: 380
Freeman family: 380
Freemasonry (See Masonry)
Freudenthal, Elsbeth Estelle: 381
Frick, Charles D.: 283
Friends Hillside Mission (Indian Territory),
　records of: 430
Fritts, Mary: 382
Frontier and pioneer life:
　Colorado, 1052
　Indian Territory, 1102, 1238
　Kansas, 76, 528, 1052, 1056, 1074, 1103
　New Mexico, 1149
　Oklahoma, 49, 98, 410, 528, 808, 1047,
　　1058
　Oklahoma Territory, 1056, 1074, 1102,
　　1117, 1123, 1134, 1159, 1181, 1230
　Texas, 380, 1159
Frontiers, comparative studies of: 1003
Fuller, Agnes: 383
Fulton Bow Plane: 744
Fulton Flotsam: 744
Fulton, J. S.: 384
Funeral homes:
　Indian Territory, 152, 954
　Oklahoma, 152, 884, 954
　records of, 530, 779, 884
Funk, John: 385
Funk, Rose: 385
Funk family: 385
Furniture stores, records of: 779
Gaillardia Garden Club: 386
Gainer, Ina: 476
Gaither, Edna: 387
Galen Society: 388
Gallaher, William M.: 389
Gamble, Richard Dalzell: 390
Gambling (Kansas): 342
Gantt, Ernest S.: 698

276

Garber, Oklahoma, Christian Church at: 1066
Gardner, Florence Guild Bruce: **391**
Gardner, Jefferson: **392**
Gardner, Oscar: **393**
Garfield County, Oklahoma: 507
 taxes, 896
Garfield, James A.: 427
 death of, 926
Garland, Hamlin: 358
Garner, James: 508
Garretson, Henry David: **394**
Garrett, Buck: 508
Garrett, Lyle, correspondence: 339
Garrett, Patrick: 508
Garrity, Richard M.: **395**
Garvin County, Oklahoma: 507
Garvin, Isaac L.: **396**
Gary, Raymond Dancel: **397**, 508
 inauguration of, 822
Gassaway, Percy Lee: **398**
Gatchell, Theodore Dodge: **399**
Gavin, James M.: 1156
Gaylord, Edward King: 508
 correspondence, 886
Gee, Robert L.: **400**
Geissler, Arthur H.: **401**
General Federation of Women's Clubs (Oklahoma): 883
General stores:
 Indian Territory, 195, 242, 530, 576, 694, 954
 Oklahoma, 120, 524, 537, 954
Genetics: 1059
Geographers:
 research of, 89, 492
 writings of, 768
Geologists, 122, 236, 286, 310, 340, 421, 423, 450, 863
Geology (Oklahoma): 507, 825, 1197
George, David Lloyd: 358
Georgia:
 land records, 1209
 state currency, 220
Gerlach, Robert: 753
German State Bank (Elk City, Oklahoma), records of: 327
Germany:
 bonds of, 394

 description of, 1933-1939, 1077
 foreign relations with Europe, 800
 German prisoners of war in Oklahoma, 1203
 immigration of authors from, 1227
Geronimo: 285, 508
Ghost towns:
 Indian Territory, 1224
 Oklahoma, 1224
Gibson, Arrell Morgan: **402**, 508
Gibson, Iva Thomas: **403**
Gibson, Rosemary: 508
Giessmann, Gary: **404**
Gilcrease, Thomas: 508
Gildart, J. B.: **405**
Gildart, W. B.: **405**
Gildart family: 405
Giles, Albert S.: 204
Gilkey, Jessie Lone Clarkson: **406**
Gilkey, John E.: **407**
Gillespie, F. E.: **408**
Gillespie, John D.: **409**
Gilliland, J. W.: **410**
Girl Scouts of America: 230
Gist, Chris: **411**
Gittinger, Roy: **412**
Gladney, Essa: **413**
Glasstone, Samuel: **414**
Glencoe, Illionis, public school system of: 1206
Glickman, Mendel: **415**
Goddard, Eunice May Stewart: **416**
Gold miners, personal narratives: 81, 112
Goldsby, Crawford "Cherokee Bill": 508
Goldwater, Barry: 59
Golf: 206
Golobie, John: **417**, 568
Gomes, Pat: **418**
Good, Nancye: **419**
Gooding, Henry Leavenworth: 508
Goodland Indian Mission (Oklahoma): 588
Goodland Indian Orphanage and School (Oklahoma): 393
Goodland Indian School: **420**
Goodnight, Charles: 64
Goodnight, Oklahoma, retail stores: 524
Goodrich, Harold Beach: **421**
Gordon, Charles Ulysses: **422**
Gore, Thomas Pryor: 508

correspondence, 886
Gould, Charles Newton: 423
Governors:
  Oklahoma,
    impeachment of, 1166
    personal papers, 445, 473, 574, 783, 785, 900, 972, 1166
  Oklahoma Territory, 985
    personal papers, 1013
Governor's Interstate Indian Council: 424
Graber, Jean: 1091
Graber, Richard: 1091
Grady County, Oklahoma: 507
Grady County Park (Chickasha, Oklahoma): 1127
Graham, Gideon Wesley: 425
Grain trade (Oklahoma): 191, 734, 882
Grand Army of the Republic, encampment programs: 429
Grand Canyon (Arizona), description of: 904
Grand River Dam (Oklahoma), history of: 164
Grandfield, Oklahoma:
  First Baptist Church, 1232
  First Presbyterian Church, 1232
Granite, Oklahoma, physicians: 628
Grant County (Oklahoma) Film Library: 912
Grant County (Oklahoma) Historical Society, history of: 912
Grant County, Oklahoma, school district records: 1019
Grant, Ulysses S.: 1075
Grass, Frank: 426
Grass, Patty: 426
Grasslands (United States), conservation of: 790
Gray Horse, Oklahoma Territory: 356
Gray Horse Trading Post: 356
Grayson, Ambrose T.: 428
Grayson, George W.: 182, 427
Grayson, Washington: 427
Grayson Family Papers: 427
Great Britian, foreign relations, 1939-1946: 543
Great Plains Conference on Higher Education, records of: 990
Great Plains, Indian tribes of: 70
Green Peach War: 427
Greer County:
  Oklahoma, 507
    description, 560
  Oklahoma Territory, 1111
  Texas, 1111
Greeting cards: 75, 385, 646, 712, 729
Gregory, A. R.: 520
Grey, Lucy: 1
Griffith, Alfred: 429
Griffitts, James Addison: 430
Grimes, Mary E.: 431
Grisso, D. Horton: 432
Grisso, Walker D.: 433, 1156
Grocery stores (Oklahoma) records of: 407
Grove, Indian Territory, physicians: 1161
Guaranty Bank (Oklahoma City, Oklahoma): 643
Guatemala:
  description and travel, 86, 851
  U.S. ambassador to, 401
Guess, George (See Sequoyah)
Guthrie District Medical Association Collection: 434
Guthrie Lodge of Freemasons (Guthrie, Oklahoma), records of: 971
Guthrie, Oklahoma:
  89er celebration, 216
  drugstores, 646
  history of, 216, 646
  Lions Club, 168
  retail stores, 524
  state capitol, movement of, 1169
Guthrie, Oklahoma Territory, settlement of: 1230
Guthrie, Woody: 508
Guthrie family genealogy: 363
Guy, William M.: 435
Guymon First National Bank: 436
Guymon, Oklahoma:
  banks and banking, 436
  newspapers, 690
Haas, Mary R.: 437
Hackett, Helen: 438
Haddix, J. F.: 439
Hadsell, Sardis Roy: 440
Hague, Lyle L.: 441
Hainer, Bayard Taylor: 442
Haines, Sarah Deborah: 443
Hair, Fannie M. Townsend: 444
Hall, David: 445, 508

Hall, Horace Mark: 446
Hall, Joseph S.: 446
Hallinen, Andrew, estate of: 447
Hallinen, John A., Jr.: 447
Hallinen, Joseph E.: 447
Halsell, Harold Hallet: 448
Halsell, Oscar D.: 448
Halsey, William, correspondence: 886
Hamilton, (Mrs.) C. P.: 449
Hamilton, Charles W.: 450
Hamilton Hardware Store (Hollis, Oklahoma), records of: 449
Hamilton, Robert: 561
Hamon, Earl: 451
Hancock, Mary W.: 872
Hancock, William Box: 452
Handbook of Oklahoma Writers: 673
Handy family, correspondence of: 322
Hannifin, D. L.: 884
Harbison, Robert B.: 33, 453
Hardin, Joe: 454
Hardman, P. V.: 298
Hardware stores:
 Indian Territory, 29, 152
 Oklahoma, 152, 228, 449
 records of, 449, 779
Hardy, Summers: 39
Hargett, Jay L.: 455
Hargrett, Lester: 456
Harjo, Lochar: 457
Harkins, George: 87
Harlow, James Gindling: 458
Harlow, Victor E.: 459
Harmon County, Oklahoma, land deeds: 798
Harper, Robert Henry: 460
Harrall, Stewart: 461
Harreld, John W., correspondence: 764
Harriman, Averell, correspondence: 543
Harris, C. Johnston: 462
Harris, Cyrus H.: 463, 508
Harris, Fred: 508
Harris, Giles Edward: 464
Harris, Harvey: 465
Harris, James A.: 465
Harris, Robert M.: 466
Harris family, genealogy: 465
Harrison, Jacob: 467
Harrison, Walter M.: 468, 1200
Harrison, William H.: 469

Harrod, Neva Belle: 470
Hart, (Mrs.) Hugh: 471
Hartshorne, Oklahoma, hospitals: 159
Harvard University (Massachusetts), faculty: 269
Haskell and LeFlore Counties Medical Society: 472
Haskell, Charles Nathaniel: 473, 508, 938
Haskell County, Oklahoma, medical societies: 472
Hastings, William Wirt: 315, 508
Hatfield, Edna Greer Porter: 474
Hathaway, A. H.: 475
Havemeyers-Seamans Oil Company: 128
Hayes, James H.: 476
Haynes, Everett: 1077
Haynes, Micajah P.: 477
Healdton Petroleum Company: 128
Healy, Frank Dale, Jr.: 478
Healy, George Henry: 478
Healy, William D.: 302
Healy family, history of: 478
Heffner, Edna Swenson: 479
Heffner, Roy E.: 480
Heflin, Cleo Eugene: 481
Hefner, Robert Alexander: 482, 508
 correspondence, 886
Hefner family, genealogy: 482
Helpenstein family, correspondence: 426
Henderson, Arnold G.: 483
Hendricks, James R.: 484
Hendrickson, Gwen: 485
Hendrickson, Samuel Harvey: 485
Hennessey High School: 486
Hennessey, Oklahoma:
 history of, 486, 808
 medical care, 304
 tornados, 808
Hennessey, Oklahoma Territory:
 drug stores, 299
 settlement of, 410
Hennings, A. E.: 487
Henryetta, Oklahoma: 173
Hensley, Claude: 488
Herbert, Harold Harvey: 489
Herpetologists: 851
Herring, Alvin J.: 490
Hertzog, Anna Laura Brisky: 491
Hester Mercantile Store (Boggy Depot,

Indian Territory): 242
Heston, J. Edgar: 200
Hewes, Leslie: 492
Hewitt, Robert C.: 493
Hewitt family: 493
Heydrick, L. C.: 494
Hickok, James Butler "Wild Bill": 239
Hicks, Edward D.: 1220
Hicks, Jimmie: 495
High School Science Service: 890
Higher education: 461
Hilbert-Price, Shirley: 496
Hill, Francis M.: 497
Hill, George Washington: 498
Hill, Weldon: 499
Hindekoper, Frederick: 1005
Hine, L. T.: 500
Hines, M. D.: 501
Hinkel John W.: 502
Hinkhouse, Steven: 503
Hinsdale, Harriet: 504
Hipes, Jessie James: 505
Hirsch, Leon: 204
Hisel, (Mrs.) O. R.: 506
Historians: 1051
  papers of, 1116, 1168
  research notes, 155, 390, 402, 720, 770, 1012
  writings of, 34, 64, 70, 139, 155, 163, 164, 180, 237, 269, 285, 342, 361, 506, 533, 544, 606, 720, 761, 856, 970, 994, 1003, 1022
Historic buildings (Oklahoma): 507
Historic Oklahoma Biographies Collection: 508
Historic Oklahoma Collection: 507
Historic sites:
  Oklahoma, 507, 1224
  Indian Territory, 1224
Hobart, Oklahoma, crime and criminals: 610
Hoffman, Roy V.: 10, 508
Holbrook, Mabel Jackson, correspondence: 510
Holbrook, Ralph Winfrey: 509
Holbrook, Richard Burkey: 510
Holdenville, Oklahoma: 728
  clubs, 511
Holdenville Schubert Music Club: 511
Holidays:

Indian Territory, proclamations of, 926
Oklahoma Territory, proclamations of, 963
United States, proclamations of, 926
Holland, W. B.: 351
Hollem, Anna Iverson: 512
Hollem, Charles L.: 512
Hollis, Oklahoma, hardware stores: 449
Holloway, William Judson: 508
Holmberg, Gustaf Fredrik: 513
Holt, James Doepel: 514
Holt, Smith Lewis: 514
Holtzendorff, Chrichton Brooks: 515
Homestead certificates: 985
Homesteading (Texas): 380, 690
Honey Creek Ranch (Grove, Oklahoma): 497
Hoops, Mary Griffith: 516
Hoover, Herbert: 356, 668
  correspondence, 543, 886
Hoover, Ike: 897
Hoover, J. Edgar: 51, 59
  correspondence, 897
Hopeton State Bank: 517
Hopkins, Harry, correspondence: 543
Horses (Oklahoma): 507
Horton, Guy K.: 518
Horton, T. D., correspondence: 697
Horton family: 518
Hoskinson, Thomas Bowman: 519
Hoskinson, William Earl: 519
Hoskinson family, history: 519
Hospitals:
  cooperative, 326, 1021
  mental, 570
  Muskogee, Oklahoma, 1010
  Oklahoma, 4, 117, 159, 326, 507
  records of, 5, 213
Hoss, Henry Sessler: 520
Hosterman, Jacob: 521
Hotchkiss and Cronkhite Loan & Investment Company: 522
Hotels (Oklahoma): 7, 507, 948, 1205
Hotema, Solomon E.: 523
Houghton, Fred Ernest: 524
House, Roy Temple: 525, 1203
Houses, floor plans of (Indian Territory): 978
Houston, Temple: 526
Howard, Walter Alonzo: 527
Howdy Folks: 745

Howe, A. N.: **528**
Howell, O. E.: **529**
Hoxie, Jack: 508
Hudson, Wadie: **530**
Hudson family: 530
Huff, Thomas J.: **531**
Huffman, Jacob C.: 532
Huffman, John: **532**
← Huggard, Christopher James: **533**
Hughes County, Oklahoma: 507
  county seat, 728
  history of, 1045
Hughes, Jim: **534**
Hughes, John Elmer: **535**
Hughes, Oklahoma, medical care: 94
Hugo, Oklahoma:
  medical care, 400
  physicians, 567
Hulett, A. W.: 1049
Hulett, Lula: 1049
Hull, Cordell, correspondence: 543
Hume, Carlton Ross: **536**
Humphrey, Hubert H., interview with: 59
Hundley, John: **537**
Hungary, bonds of: 394
Hunt, Blanche Seale: **538**
Hunt, J. O.: **539**
Hunter, H. A.: **540**
Hunter, Thomas W.: **541**
Hunting Horse: 508
Huntley, A. A.: **542**
Hurley, Alice: 668
Hurley, Patrick Jay: **543**
  correspondence, 668, 883
Hurst, Irvin: **544**
Hutchings, Murphey, and German law firm, records of: 781
Hutto, Robert W.: **545**
Hyde, Clayton H.: **546**
Hydro First National Bank Collection: **547**
Hydro, Oklahoma:
  banks and banking, 547
  hardware stores, 228
Hymnals: 519
  Protestant, 281
Illustrators: 637, 1059
Immigrants:
  German, family correspondence, 1006
  in the U.S., 1069

naturalization records, 935
personal narratives, 417
Impson, Hiram: **548**
Independent Oil and Gas Company: 575
Independent Order of Odd Fellows: **549**
Indian agencies, records of: 1063, 1192
Indian Chief Oil and Gas Company: 922
Indian International Council, Creek Indian delegates to: 894
Indian Missionary Association, records of: 786
Indian-Pioneer Papers: **550**
Indian Territory:
  attitude toward Oklahoma Territory, 987
  attorneys, 1204
  banks and banking, 878
  business permits, 644
  businessmen, 881
  cemeteries, 1224
  Civil War, 1861-1865, 402, 683
  clubs, 960
  coal mining, 396, 1183
  courts, 689
    records of, 249, 1138, 1139, 1140
  crime and criminals, 689, 1139, 1140, 1178
  description of, 132, 179, 363, 404, 548, 636, 645, 663, 683
  education, 630
  elections, 498
  fiction about, 1221
  First Volunteer Infantry Regiment, 999
  forts, 371, 1224
  fraternal organizations in, 549
  frontier and pioneer life, 98, 132, 550, 560, 636, 645, 801, 868, 683, 986, 1102, 1238
  funeral homes, records of, 954
  general stores, 694, 954
  ghost towns, 1224
  history of, 269
  holiday proclamations, 926
  Indian Meridian, 284
  intruders, 733
  judges, 689
  labor unions in, 1057
  land surveys, 292
  legality of marriages performed in, 598
  letterheads, 639

libraries, private, 1231
maps of, 303
masonry (Scottish Rite) in, 971
medical care, 68, 181
medical societies, records of, 551
Methodism in, 1080
military posts, 371, 1224
mineral resources, 396
mines and mining, 589
missionaries, 974
missions, 748, 1233
municipal government, 183
newspapers in, 1173
oil wells in, 164
patriotic hymns, 965
physicians, 771, 986, 1161
  personal narratives, 756
  records of, 1172
place names, 1224
political organizations, 498
publishers, 1044
realtors, 881
retail stores, 1241
roads, 748
schools, 231, 287, 295, 316, 338, 396,
  588, 630, 706, 748, 1080, 1189, 1222
Seminole Nation, description of, 548
settlement of, 550
statehood, 316, 338, 683, 708, 747, 904,
  915, 981, 1009, 1108, 1210
telephone service in, 488, 1220
timber resources, 396
townsites, 292
trading posts, 1224
white settlement in, 880
women in, 363, 986
work permits, 1093
Indian Territory Illuminating Oil
  Company *News*: 356
Indian Territory Medical Association: 551
history of, 181
proceedings, 360
Indian Union: 224
Indian University (Oklahoma): 92
Indian War Veterans: 552
Indiana, Eleventh Volunteer Infantry: 255
Indians of Mexico: 761
  fiction, 888
Indians of North America:

advocacy organizations, 15, 826, 1110
alcohol use, 572
allotment of land, 469, 580, 683, 770,
  846, 657, 692, 702, 774, 852, 915
antiquities, 937
archaeological sites (Oklahoma), 1223
art, 155, 260, 507
authors, 854
banks, 1086
bibliography, 1219
cemeteries, 83
censuses, 1031
chiefs, 10, 119, 125, 134, 140, 155, 164,
  182, 198, 217, 224, 302, 316, 318, 392,
  396, 427, 435, 457, 463, 466, 467, 469,
  522, 523, 554, 555, 573, 576, 580, 585,
  587, 636, 655, 657, 691, 692, 702, 707,
  708, 709, 711, 715, 732, 774, 787, 849,
  857, 867, 894, 895, 905, 915, 926, 981,
  984, 987, 1033, 1108, 1210, 1217, 1231
civil rights, 15, 743, 826
Civil War, 1861-1865, 235, 609, 770
claims, 259, 302, 536, 573, 1217
colleges, 582
conversion to Christianity, 177
costume and dress, 1219
courts, 396
culture, 314, 677, 679, 848, 1007
dances, 919
depredations, 997
descriptions of, 949
diseases of the skin, 625
education, 15, 41, 54, 302, 573, 743, 997,
  1043
employment, 997
environmental studies, 483
ethnobotany, 1165
farming, 614
fiction, 116
folklore, 359, 677, 937, 1189
government relations, 70, 198, 302, 659
health care, 302, 1151
historic sites (Oklahoma), 1224
history, 155, 237, 314, 320
housing, 483
hymnals, 780
intertribal relations, 787
land titles, 554
land transfers, 40, 91, 311, 392, 427, 462,

846, 847, 997, 1217
languages, 239, 437
leases of agricultural lands, 295
libraries, private, 1231
medical research, 762
medical treatment, 1023
mineral resources, 396, 573, 792, 1183, 1241
mineral rights, 580
missionaries to, 41, 302, 455, 587, 609, 645
missions to, 1167
oral history, 314, 1189
organizations, 424
orphanages, 393, 420
Peace Council of 1874, 587
per capita payments, 997
performers, 359
peyotism, 356, 507, 679
physicians, 751
poets, 747
police forces, 997
poverty among, 1217
relations with
  Spain, 553
  U.S. government, 852, 1063
  whites, 239, 812, 849, 852
religion and mythology, 79, 239, 679, 919
removal, 302, 609
reservations, 474, 759, 1217
rites and ceremonies, 314, 919
schools, 295, 316, 317, 367, 393, 396, 420, 463, 609, 706, 847, 1058, 1189, 1222
slaves, ownership of: 573
social conditions, 826
social life and customs, 1180
social welfare, 792
speeches, 711
storytellers, 359
taxation of lands, 718
timber resources, 396
traders with, 356, 607
trading posts (Oklahoma), 1224
treaties, 70, 198
tribal council proceedings, 15
tribal factionalism, 463, 645
tribal government, 143, 224, 254, 295, 316, 392, 462, 554, 573, 657, 706, 708,
   847, 915
tribal politics, 427, 580, 691, 770
wars, 10, 427, 552, 662, 970, 1137
weaving, 937, 1180
white captives, 311, 997, 1067
women, 937
youth programs, 15
Individual Opportunity Achievement Ranch (Perkins, Oklahoma): 305
Indochina, description and travel: 535
Industry (Oklahoma): 507
Infantry:
  Eleventh Indiana Volunteer, 255
  First Minnesota Volunteer, 1046
  Twenty-third Iowa, 339
Inskip, Diana: 305
Internal Provinces of New Spain: 553
International relations: 271
Interschool Speech Service (University of Oklahoma): 890
Investment firms (Oklahoma), records of: 322
Invitations: 729
  commencement, 607
  social events, 723, 950
  weddings, 607, 950
Iowa:
  Fifth Volunteer Cavalry, 9
  Keokuk College, 1162
  newspapers, 1200
  shoemakers, 521
  Twenty-third Infantry, 339
Iowa Indians:
  agriculture, 229
  land leases, 229
  lands, 245
Irelan, Singer B.: 200
Irving, Washington, in Oklahoma, 1832: 1028
Isparhecher: 254, 554
Ivask, Ivar: 508
Jackson County, Oklahoma: 507
  state senators, 453
Jackson, Jacob Battiest: 555
Jackson, Robert Edward, Jr.: 556
Jackson, Samuel D.: 514
Jacobson, Oscar Brousse: 508, 557
James, Jesse: 508
James, Marquis: 508

James, Will: 358
Jameson, John: **558**
Jameson family: 558
Jamestown, Virginia, cotton exposition: 399
Jamieson, W. C.: **559**
Japan, World War, 1939-1945, battle scenes: 714
Jarboe, (Mrs.) W. C.: **560**
Jayne, Mary Prosser: **561**
Jazhe, Benedict: **562**
Jennings, Al J.: 508
Jennings, Mary: 1199
Jessup, Thomas S.: 170
Jesuits (Chile): 862
Jet, Oklahoma: 507
Jewel Drug Store (Hennessey, Oklahoma Territory): 299
Jews (Oklahoma): 1112
Joblin, Walter Ridgway: **563**
Jockeys: 1077
John, Walter N.: **564**
Johnson, B. F.: **565**
Johnson, Bob: **566**
Johnson County, Oklahoma: 507
Johnson, Edgar Allen: **567**
Johnson, Edith Cherry: **568**
Johnson, Edward Bryant: **569**
Johnson, Henry Lee: **570**
Johnson, Lyndon B., interview with: 59
Johnson, Martha Sherwood Finch: **571**
Johnson, Willard Spud, correspondence: 968
Johnson, William E.: **572**
Johnston, Douglas H.: 508, **573**, 655
Johnston, Henry Simpson: **574**
Johnston, Paul Imrie: **575**
Jones, Ada: 1238
Jones, Dovie: 576
Jones, John Paul: **577**
Jones, Lydia Caroline Baggett: **578**
Jones, Stephen: **579**
Jones, Wilson N.: 576, **580**
Jones family, genealogy: 578
Jordan Drug Store: **581**
Jordan, Glenn: **582**
Jordan, John D.: **583**
Jordan, Mary: 997
Jordan, Omar L.: **584**
Journalism, history of: 246
Journalists: 59, 114, 223, 246, 290, 350, 358, 468, 489, 510, 568, 590, 611, 698, 797, 800, 947, 994, 1077, 1173
papers of, 758, 994, 1181, 1200
Journals (See diaries also): 73, 88, 118, 291, 298, 302, 368, 484, 663, 680, 777, 851, 897, 905
Journeycake, Charles: **585**, 1217
Judges:
Indian Territory, 267, 484, 689
Oklahoma, 27, 90, 113, 138, 225, 267, 300, 398
Oklahoma Territory, 39, 225, 442
papers of, 1154, 1170
Judy, Thomas J.: **586**
Jumper, John: **587**, 1016
Juvenile delinquency (Oklahoma): 309
Kagey, Joseph Newton: **588**
Kali-Inla Coal Company: **589**
Kane, John H.: 1217
Kansa (Kaw) Indians:
allotments, 591
agriculture, 591
financial affairs, 591
history, 474
land transfers, 591
Kansas:
agriculture, 909
Civil War, 1861-1865, 239
crime and criminals, Bender family, 239
description and travel, 1908, 566
farm life, 239
frontier and pioneer life, 516, 909, 959, 1074
gambling, 342
history of, 239, 344, 387
homesteading, 909
Indian wars, 344, 997
Indians in, 909
mines and mining, 261
politics, 909
preachers, 1194
ranches and ranching, 952
real estate, 909
religion, 909
settlement of, 344
Kansas Territory: **1103**
frontier and pioneer life, 1103
Kanuntaklage Dramatic Club (University of Oklahoma): 938

Kaufman, Kenneth Carlyle: **590**
  poetry of, 758
Kaw Indian Agency: **591** (See also Kansa Indians)
  history of, 356
Kay County, Oklahoma:
  banks and banking, 592
  oil and gas leases, 813
  taxation, 941
Kay County, Oklahoma Territory, taxation: 941
Kay County State Bank: **592**
Keefer, Ann: 8
Keefer, Lewis: 8
Keeler, William A.: 508
Keetoowah Society: 96
Keezer, William Stillman: 682
Keith, Harold: **593**
Keller, Helen: 358
  correspondence, 543
Keller-Clarke Seed Store: **594**
Kelley, Francis Clement: 508
Kelly, George "Machine Gun": 633
Kendall, George Wilkins: 246
Kennedy, John C.: **595**
Kennedy, John Fitzgerald: **596**, 720
  assassination of, 596
  interview with, 59
Kennedy, Kay Don: **597**
Kennedy, L. P.: **598**
Kennedy, Robert F., interview with: 59
Kennerly, Caleb Burwell Rowan: 390
Kenton, Oklahoma, description of: 1126
Kenton, Oklahoma Territory, description of: 1123
Keokuk College (Iowa), publications of: 1162
Kerley, J. W.: **599**
Kerr, Robert Samuel: 508, **600**
  correspondence, 886
Kerr-McGee Corportion: **600**
Kibbey, W. Beckford: **601**
Kibler, Nell: **602**
Kickapoo Indians, lands: 245
Kidd, Robert L.: 200
Kiebler, W. G.: **603**
Kiel, Oklahoma, medical care: 304
Kimble, Lawrence: 753
Kinder, George: **604**

King, (Mrs.) A. J.: 605
King, Charles Francis Xavier: **606**
King, Donald: **607**
Kingfisher College (Oklahoma): 10, **608**, 704
  history of, 767
  publications of, 608
  records of, 608, 767
Kingfisher County, Oklahoma: 507
  land deeds, 42
  school district records, 1018
Kingsbury, Cyrus: 455, 508, **609**
Kiowa County Historical Society: **610**
Kiowa County, Oklahoma: 507
  history of, 408
  schools, 41
Kiowa Indians:
  allotment of land, 1136
  cemeteries, 268
  census, 740
  land transfers, 40
  missions, 1004
  relations with
    U.S. government, 1063
    white settlers, 560
  schools, 317
  wars, 552
Kirk, Betty: **611** (See also Betty Kirk Boyer)
Kirker, James (Santiago): 1074
Kirkpatrick, Albert J.: **612**
Kirkpatrick, Jeanne: 508
Kirkpatrick, John: 1091
Kjennernd, Haus: 1069
Klapps Drug Store: **613**
Kliewer, Heinrich: **614**
Knights of Labor: 142
Knights Templar of Oklahoma: **615**, 675
Knott, Charles: 255
Know Your Government: 838
Kobel, Raleigh: **616**
Korean War, 1950-1953: 936
  propaganda, 928
Korn, Anna Lee Brosius: **617**
Kowetah Manual Labor Boarding School: 507
Kraettli, Emil Rudolph: **618**
Krebs, Indian Territory, missions at: 1233
Krebs, Oklahoma:
  coal mining, 227

physicians, 806
Krugers, Albert: **619**
Kruis, Roland: **620**
Ku Klux Klan:
  Oklahoma, 204, 507, 621, 1166, 1173
  publications, 204
Ku Klux Klan Women: **621**
Kuyrkendall, Louis C.: **622**
La Kee Kon Garden Club, records of: 810
L'Amour, Louis: 508
Labor legislation (Oklahoma): 276, 534, 842
Labor litigation: 589
Labor market (Oklahoma): 821
Labor relations:
  railroads, 976
  strikes, 976
Labor unions: 142, 374, 589, 1144, 1183
  Oklahoma, 100, 173, 279, 534, 834, 840, 1057
Lacey, Oklahoma, medical care: 304
Lacy, A. J.: 302
Ladies' Aid Society: **623**
Lafferty, John F.: 432
Lahman, Marion Sherwood: **624**
Lain, Everett S.: **625**
Lake Thunderbird (Oklahoma): 244
Lakes (Oklahoma): 507
Lamar, L. Q. C., correspondence: 530
Lamb, Ellis: **626**
Lamplighter, The: 912
Land deeds:
  Georgia, 498
  Indian Territory, 498, 651
  Missouri, 30
  Oklahoma, 42, 619, 798, 903
  Oklahoma Territory, 651, 798, 896
  Vermont, 619
  Wisconsin, 293
Land grants, Maxwell: 433
Land speculation:
  Oklahoma, 1070
  Texas, 1070
Landon, Alfred M.: 559
Langsford, William: **627**
Lansden, J. B.: **628**
Lardner, Ring: 358
Las Dos Americas: **629**
Latimer County, Oklahoma: 507
Latin America:

  archival administration, 655
  history of, 761
  librarianship, 655
Latty, James Monroe: **630**
Law enforcement (Oklahoma): 507, 823, 1109
Law enforcement officers:
  Alaska, 156
  Indian Territory, 965, 978
  Oklahoma, 156, 739, 1109
  reminiscences, 317
  Texas, 156
  Wyoming, 156
Lawson, E. B.: 540
Lawton, Oklahoma: 712
  banks and banking, 332, 914
  cotton mills, 764
  description of life in, 914
  fiftieth anniversary celebration, 674
  history of, 1038
  lumberyards, 512
  real estate businesses, 764
  retail stores, records of, 740
Lawton Pioneer Club (Lawton, Oklahoma), yearbook: 674
Lawton, Sherman Paxton: **631**
Layton, Helen Elizabeth Blackert: **632**
Lead, South Dakota, description of: 699
League of Nations: 983
League of Women Voters, publications of: 63
Leatherwork: 306
Ledbetter, Eugene P.: **633**
Ledbetter, Walter A.: **634**
Lee, Ottie: **635**
Lee, R. C. "Crockett": 635
Lee Vining Creek, California, history of: 64
LeFlore, Basil L.: 508, **636**
LeFlore, Carrie: **636**
LeFlore County, Oklahoma: 507
  medical societies, 472
LeFlore, Greenwood: 508
Legends (Oklahoma): 507
Legislature (Oklahoma): 507, 789, 900
Lehigh, Indian Territory, missions at: 1233
Lenormand, Henri-Rene: 1000
Lenski, Lois: **637**
Leslie, Samuel B.: **638**

Letterheads: **639**
Lewallen, Wesley P.: **640**
Lewis, Powell K.: **641**
Lewis, Walter E.: **642**
Lewis, W. M.: 514
Liberty National Bank: **643**
Librarians: 262, 348, 413, 670, 673, 938
Librarianship (Latin America): 655
Libraries:
  Oklahoma, 507
  private, 447, 1231
Ligon, Mary Louise: **644**
Lilley, (Mrs.) John B.: **645**
Lillie, Foress B.: **646**
Lillie, Gordon William: **647**
Lillie's Drug Store (Guthrie, Oklahoma): 646
Lincoln, Abraham: 51, 670
Lincoln County Bank (Prague, Oklahoma), records of: 920
Lincoln County Medical Society: **648**
Lincoln County, Oklahoma: 507
  history of, 245
  medical care, 648
Lincoln County, Oklahoma Territory, history of: 180
Lindbergh, Charles A.: 358, 470
Lindsay, Oklahoma:
  cotton gins, 929
  history of, 149
Lindsey, Newton Harvey: **649**
Lindsey, Ray H.: **650**
Lindsey, Thomas G., correspondence: 650
Lininger, Herbert K.: **651**
Linzee, E. H.: 488
Lions Club: **652**
Lions International: **653**
Lions International, Oklahoma:
  club reports, 272
  conventions, 211
  correspondence about, 966
  directories, 653
  history of district 3-A, 584
  publications, 129, 211, 272, 584, 804, 861, 893
  records of, 84, 105, 129, 168, 211, 584, 652, 804, 992, 1155
Lisbon, Portugal, description of: 429
Literary Club (Clinton, Oklahoma): 1135
Literary criticism: 278

Literary societies: 187, 1176
Little Bear, Haynes: 268
Little Bear family, genealogy: 268
Little Bighorn River, Battle of, 1876: 669
Little, Jesse Samuel: **654**
Little Jim: 508
Little River Reservoir (Oklahoma): 244
Litton, Gaston: **655**
Livezey, William Edmund: **656**
Locke, Newt: 410
Locke, Victor M., Jr.: 10, **657**
Lockwood, Cassandra Sawyer: 974
Logan County High School, commencement program, 1905: 948
Logan County, Oklahoma: 507
  history of, 216
  records of, 658
  roads, 658
Logan County Road Record Collection: **658**
Logan, Leonard M.: **659**
Long, Charles Alexander: **660**
Long, Huey P.: 1037
Longstreet, James: **661**
Los Angeles, California, description of: 911
Lottinville, Savoie: **662**
Love County, Oklahoma: 507
Lovelace, Bryan W.: **663**
Loving, Lydia: 690
Loy-McDonald Clinic: **664**
Loyalty oaths (Oklahoma): 897
Luce, Henry: 668
Lucka, Emil: 525, **665**
Ludlow, Edwin, correspondence: 455
Lumber companies: 730
  records of, 233
Lumberyards (Oklahoma): 512
Luster, Dewey William "Snorter": **666**
Lutheran Church: 961
Lyles, Harold L.: **667**
Lynchings (Ada, Oklahoma): 701
MacArthur, Douglas: 59, 391
  correspondence, 543
Mackey, (Mrs.) Clifton Marion: **668**
MacLeish, Archibald: 1147
McAlester Anniversary Incorporated Collection: **693**
McAlester, Indian Territory:
  clubs, 960
  description, 906

McAlester, James Jackson: 48, 508, 694
McAlester Mercantile Company, records
   of: 694
McAlester News-Capital, history of: 672
McAlester, Oklahoma:
   clubs, 960
   development of, 978
   fiftieth anniversary celebration, 693
   medical care, 181
   Ohoyohoma Club, 814
   physicians, 622
McAlester (Oklahoma) General Hospital: 5
McAnally, Arthur: 1156
   correspondence, 433
McBride, Earl D.: 695
McBride, Marguerite: 696
McCall, William: 697
McCammon, J. D.: 698
McCarthy (Eugene) Campaign
   Collection: 700
McCarthy, Thomas Joseph: 699
McCarville, Mike: 701
McClain County, Oklahoma: 507
McClure, Tecumseh A.: 702
McClure, William C.: 703
McClure, William L.: 703
McCormick, Ada P., correspondence: 525
McCornack, Ruth: 704
McCoy, James Stacy: 705
McCoy, Thomas: 705
McCurdy, Dave: 508
McCurdy, Elmer (Frank Davidson): 508
McCurtain County, Oklahoma: 507
McCurtain, D. C.: 706
McCurtain, Edmond: 707
McCurtain, Green: 708, 1998
   correspondence, 978
McCurtain, Jackson E.: 508
McCurtain, Jackson Frazier: 709
McCurtain, James Austin: 508
McDonald, James: 753
McGee, Dean A.: 600
McIntosh County Medical Society: 710
McIntosh County, Oklahoma: 507
   medical societies, 710
McIntosh, Roley Cub: 711
McIntosh family: 508
McKennon, Paul: 548
McKenzie, W. H.: 712

McKeown, Roy J.: 713
McKinley, William, assassination of: 470
McKinney, Raymond: 714
McKinney, Thompson: 715
McKinney, William H.: 716
McLain, Raymond Stallings: 508, 717
McMurray, John Frank: 718
McPhaul, Thomas C.: 719
McReynolds, Edwin C.: 444, 720
McReynolds, S. A.: 612
McSpadden, Sallie Rogers: 508
Madsen, Christian C.: 40, 508, 669
Maguire, Grace Adeline King: 670
Maguire, James D.: 670
Majestic Cookbook: 385
Major County, Oklahoma: 507
Malone, E. L.: 671
Manassas, Virginia, First Battle of: 1046
Mangum, Oklahoma, medical care: 151
Manos, Grace C.: 672
Mantle, Mickey: 508
Mao Tse-tung, correspondence: 543
Maps: 303
   Indian Territory, 1904, 944
   military posts, 355
   northwestern territories (United States),
      1008
   Oklahoma, 507
   Oklahoma Territory, 1904, 944
   road maps, 966
Marable, Mary Hays: 673
Marcel, Gabriel, correspondence: 1000
March, (Mrs.) Abe: 674
Marcy, Randolph B.: 508
Marion, Kansas, description of: 516
Marland, Ernest Whitworth: 135, 508, 676
   inauguration of, 822
Marland Oil Company: 863
Marlow, Oklahoma, telephone service: 684
Marquart, Vida: 675
Marriott, Alice: 508, 677, 679
Marriott, Sydney C.: 678
Marriott-Rachlin Collection: 679
Marrs, Frederica S. Dewey: 680
Marrs, James Wyatt: 681
Mars (planet): 414
Marshall, Oklahoma:
   Christian Church, 105
   government of, 882

granaries, 882
Methodist Episcopal Church, 882
Marshals, United States: 507
Martin, Cy: **682**
Martin Mill and Elevator Company, articles of incorporation: 684
Martin, Richard L.: **683**
Martin, Thomas Pugh, Jr.: **684**
Mary Joseph (Mother): 1233
Mason, Viola: **685**
Masonic Lodge of Oklahoma: **686**
Masonry (Scottish Rite): 142, 192, 882, 971
  publications of, 686, 971
  records of, 267, 1079
Massad, Ernest L.: **687**
Mathematicians, publications of: 250
Matheney, James Curtis: **688**
Mathews, John Joseph: 508
Matthews, A. D.: 689
Matthews, Sam P.: **689**
Maupin, Mary B.: **690**
Maxwell land grant: 433
Mayes County, Oklahoma: 507
Mayes, Joel Bryan: 302, **691**
Mayes, Samuel Houston: **692**
Maysville, Oklahoma:
  cotton gins, 439
  general stores, 171
Medford, Oklahoma:
  churches, 912
  clubs, 721
  department stores, 215
  women's clubs, 912
Medford, Oklahoma Territory, churches: 912
Medford Progress Club: **721**
Medical associations and societies: 1160
  history of, 1128
  Oklahoma, 1021
    publications of, 893, 918
    records of, 434, 472, 845, 855, 907, 918, 977, 1062, 1212
  Oklahoma Territory, records of, 839
  records of, 384, 527, 551, 638, 648, 710
Medical care:
  Oklahoma, 4, 5, 20, 52, 55, 57, 80, 145, 243, 264
  Texas, 45, 47
Medical clinic, records of: 664
Medical education: 4, 12, 22, 123, 283, 1158
Medical equipment: 1115
Medical instruments: 703, 979
Medical literature: 55, 389, 527, 695
Medical research: 1131, 1162, 1187
Medicine (Oklahoma): 507, 1087
Medicine, patented: 722, 874, 1239
Medicine Shows: **722**
  posters, 917
Mediterranean area, description and travel, 1860-61: 1032
Meigs, Return J.: 427
Mein Kampf, original book jacket of: 938
Memminger, Charles B.: **723**
Mencken, H. L.: 1227
Mennonite Church: 507, 961
Menominee Indians, history of: 856
Men's Dinner Club (Oklahoma City, Oklahoma), history of: 999
  program from, 684
Mental hospitals: 570
Menton, John William: **724**
Menus: 428
Meridian, Oklahoma, retail stores: 524
Merrill, Maurice: **725**
Merrill, Orpha: 725
Merriott, C. L.: **726**
Merriott's Dry Goods Company (Walters, Oklahoma), records of: 726
Mertes, John E.: **727**
Messenger, Eugene Fields: **728**
Mesta, Perle Skirvin: 508
Meteorology: 365
Methodism:
  Logan County, Oklahoma, 1026
  Oklahoma, 1026
Methodist Church: 507, 961
  Indian Territory, 1080
  mission schools, 367
Methodist Episcopal Church:
  Bartlesville, Oklahoma, 1050
  Marshall, Oklahoma, 882
  Medford, Oklahoma, 912
  Norman, Oklahoma, 286
Methodist Episcopal Church of Oklahoma: 1026
Metropolitan Railway Co., (Oklahoma), records of: 1121
Mexican Coal and Coke Company

(Mexico): 455
Mexican Gulf Oil Company,
   correspondence: 450
Mexican Revolution, 1910-1921, description
   of: 450, 601
Mexico:
   Confederate Army emigrés, 766
   currency, examples of, 684
   description and travel, 86, 766, 851
   history of, 611, 761
   international relations, 611
   revolutionary activities in Sonora, 1929,
      601
   Spanish colonial institutions, 761
Meyer, Apelona: 729
Meyer, William: 729
Miami Lumber Company Collection: 730
Miami, Oklahoma:
   lumber companies, 730
   municipal government, records of, 731
   retail stores, 233
Micco, Hulbutta: 732
Michigan Territory, frontier and pioneer
   life: 602
Mid-Continent Farmers Cooperative,
   records of: 312
Mid-Continent Petroleum Corporation: 575
Middle East:
   description and travel, 1901-1902, 1048
   foreign relations, 1939-1946, 543
Midkiff, Charles F.: 733
Midway Mirror: 744
Milbourn, Dolly: 734
Milbourn, George F.: 734
Milburn, George: 662, 735
Miles, Nelson A.: 203
Miley (Mary Clarke) Foundation: 736
Milfay State Bank (Stroud, Oklahoma),
   records of: 1086
Military posts (See also forts and camps):
   Indian Territory, 147, 371, 1224
   New Mexico, 390
   Oklahoma Territory, 355, 1224
Miller Brothers 101 Ranch: 737
Miller Brothers 101 Ranch Wild West Show,
   performers in: 1095
Miller County, Oklahoma: 507
Miller, Florence Graves: 738
Miller, Floyd C.: 739

Miller, Freeman E., correspondence: 502
Miller, G. R.: 740
Miller, Joe: 508
Miller, John Sinclaire: 741
Miller, Lillie Kate: 742
Miller, Robert L.: 743
Miller, Stephen: 744
Miller, Zack T.: 508
Milling companies: 191, 1061
Millington, Oklahoma, medical care: 208
Milsten, David Randolph: 745
Minco, Oklahoma, physicians: 654
Miner, Frederick William: 746
Mineral Point, Wisconsin, land deeds: 293
Mines and mining:
   Chickasaw Nation, 1124
   Choctaw Nation, 1124, 1241
   coal, 396
   Indian Territory, coal, 1053
   Iowa, coal, 1053
   labor unions, 374, 1183
   mine safety, 1183
   Kansas, lead and zinc, 261
   Missouri
      coal, 1053
      lead and zinc, 261
   Montana, coal, 1053
   Oklahoma, 321, 507, 1197
      coal, 227, 749, 778, 1053, 1183
      equipment sales, 71
      lead and zinc, 1, 261
      private investment, 24
      Wichita Mountain area, 491
   West Virginia, 1053
Mining companies, records of: 321
Mining engineers, personal papers of: 1053
Mining equipment suppliers, records of: 71
Minion, John A., correspondence: 669
Ministers:
   circuit riding, 1026
   Oklahoma, 1026
   Oklahoma Territory, 1026, 1047
Minneapolis, Minnesota, city charter
   of: 1005
Missals: 1083
Missionaries: 368, 480, 582, 846, 1042
   Baptist, 41, 561
   Brazil, 660
   Indian Territory, 786, 974

290

Methodist, 660, 1080
Muskogee, Oklahoma, 506
Nigeria, 479
Peru, 479
Presbyterian, 338, 506, 609, 645, 942, 973, 1051, 1231
Society of Friends (Quaker), 54, 331, 430, 1060
Missionary Federation of Muskogee, Oklahoma, history of: 506
Missions:
  Indian Territory, 1233
  Nebraska, 231
  Oklahoma, 507, 1167
Missouri:
  history of, 387, 617, 720
  mines and mining, 261
  political parties, 605
Missouri, Kansas, and Texas Railroad Company: 622, 1075, 1115
  officials of, 635
Missouri Medical College (Missouri): 159
Missouri River, description and travel, 1803: 302
Mitchell, (Mrs.) Alfred: 747
Mitchell, Robert Thurston: 748
Mitchell, Sam W.: 749
Mitchell family, genealogy: 748
Mix, Tom: 508
Mixon, A. M.: 750
Model Railroad Interest Group, newsletters of: 395
Molesworth, Charles: 278
Momaday, N. Scott: 508
Monroney, Mike (Almer Stillwell): 508
Montague County, Texas, frontier and pioneer life: 578
Montezuma, Carlos: 751
Montgomery, Merle Aline: 752
Monuments (Oklahoma): 507
Moore, Chauncey O.: 754
Moore, Ercelle O'Brien Davis: 753
Moore, Ethel: 754
Moore, Jessie Elizabeth Randolph: 755
Moore, John D.: 756
Moore, John H.: 757
Moore, Louise Beard: 758
Moore (Oklahoma) High School, yearbooks: 1130

Moore, Robb: 759
Mooreland, Oklahoma, banks and banking: 760
Mooreland Security State Bank: 760
Moorhead, Max Leon: 761
Moorman, Lewis Jefferson: 508, 762
Mootz, Grace V.: 763
Mootz, Herman Edwin: 763
Morford, Robert Boyd: 764
Morgan, Clyde: 765
Morgan, (Mrs.) Lawrence Nelson: 766
Morgan, Robert J.: 767
Morgenthau, Henry: 1037
Morris, John Wesley: 768
Morrison, G. A.: 769
Morrison, James: 770
Morrison, W. D.: 770
Morrow, John A.: 771
Mortgages (Oklahoma): 772
Mosby, George Waldo: 772
Moseley, John Ohleyer: 773
Mosely, Palmer S.: 774
Moss, Jacob: 1096
Mother's Club (Medford, Oklahoma): 912
Motion pictures, advertising: 529, 827, 1109
Mount Holyoke Female Seminary (Massachusetts), student essays: 50
Mount Pleasant School (Blaine County, Oklahoma Territory): 604
Mount Rushmore national monument: 361
Mountain View, Oklahoma:
  clubs, 775
  history of, 775
Mountain View, Oklahoma Territory, history of: 180
Mountain View Twentieth-Century Club: 775
Mountbatten, Louis, correspondence: 543
Mower, George: 566
Mueller, Gustave Emil: 776
Muldrow, Annie Oliver, correspondence: 777
Muldrow, Henry Lowndes, Jr.: 777
Muldrow, Henry Lowndes, Sr.: 777
Muldrow, Robert, correspondence: 777
Mullen Coal Company Collection: 778
Mullen, Lacey: 1027
Munger Hardware, Furniture and Undertaking Store, records of: 779
Munger, Reuben Bates: 779

Munger, William Houston: **779**
Municipal government (Oklahoma): 63, 343
  financial records, 370, 796, 934
  records of, 934
Munn, Bertha M. B.: **780**
Murdock, H. D.: 893
Murphey and Noffsinger Collection: **781**
Murphy, William Albert Patrick: **782**
Murray, Alice Hearrell: 508
  correspondence, 783
Murray, Billy, correspondence: 783
Murray, Burbank: **783**, **784**
Murray County, Oklahoma: 507
Murray, Frankie Colbert: **784**
Murray, Johnston: 508, 784, **785**, 829, 1143
  correspondence, 783
  inauguration of, 822
  political campaign, 1950, 461
Murray, Massena Bancroft: **784**
  correspondence, 783
Murray, William Henry (Alfalfa Bill): 39, 508, 618, 783, 784, 870, 1024, 1143
Murray family: 1143
Murrell, George Michael: 508
Murrell home (Tahlequah, Indian Territory): 902
Murrow, Joseph Samuel: 41, 508, 582, **786**, 1044
Murrow, Katrina Ellett: 1044
Museum of the Air, radio program script: 1226
Museums (Oklahoma): 507
Mushulatubbee: **787**
Music:
  classical, 612
  country and western, 1235
  folk songs, 754
  Japanese, 65
  manuscripts, 612, 1083, 1152
  Oklahoma, 507
  performance, 612
  professional organizations, 752
  published, 431
  sacred, 1083,
  teachers, 431
Music Club (Pauls Valley, Oklahoma): 1082
Musical compositions: 373, 678
Musical productions and performances:
  programs of, 65, 162, 313, 322, 531
  reviews of, 65
Musical scores, 65, 108, 162, 280, 391, 406, 807, 1011
Musicians: 752
Muskogean languages: 437
Muskogee County, Oklahoma: 507
  financial records, 370
Muskogee Ministerial Association (Oklahoma): 1080
Muskogee, Oklahoma:
  attorneys, 113
  banks and banking, 234
  hospitals, 117
  law firms, 781
  medical care, 80, 520
  physicians, 719
Muzzy, W. J.: **788**
Nadan, Gertrude: 1058
Nagle, Patrick Sarsfield: 508
Nance, James Clark, Jr.: **789**
Napoleonic wars: 292
Nash, Frank: 610
Nashville, Tennessee, cotton exposition: 399
National Aid Life Association: 678
National Bituminous Coal Commission: 1183
National Board of Farm Organizations: 559
National Conference of Commissioners of Uniform State Law: 725
National Conference on Higher Education, Sixth Annual: 461
National Cowboy Hall of Fame: 468
National Editorial Association: 800
National Farmers Union: 312, 1037
National Federation of Music Clubs: 752
National Research Council: **790**
National Security Training Commission: 717
Natural gas industry: (See also petroleum industry)
  corporate records, 575
  investigation of, 1207
  leases, 633
Naturalists: 447
  societies, 1064
Neal, Henry: **791**
Nebraska Territory, description and travel, 1849: 566
Needham, Edward Z.: 1046
Needham family, genealogy of: 1046
Nelson, George: **792**

Nelson, Indian Territory, postal service: 124
Neosho, Missouri, description of: 1238
New Century Club (Oklahoma): 1135
New Echota, Cherokee Nation: 902
New Echota Church (Cherokee Nation),
 records of: 338
New Hope Seminary (Indian Territory): 429
New Mexico:
 frontier and pioneer life, 1149
 Spanish colonial records of, 553
New Orleans, Louisiana:
 cotton exposition, 399
 description, 292
New Spain, Spanish colonial records of: 553
New York Mutual Life Insurance
 Company: 793
New Zealand, description of: 696
Newby, Errett Rains: 794
Newby Rooming House (Oklahoma City,
 Oklahoma), records of: 948
Newkirk First National Bank: 795
Newkirk, Oklahoma:
 banks and banking, 795
 high school, 451
 municipal records, 796
Newland, John Lynn: 797
Newman, Coley: 798
Newspapers:
 Japanese, 983
 military, 1939-1945, 744
Nice, Margaret Morse: 799
 correspondence, 642
Nichols, Lea Murray: 800
Nieberding, Velma: 801
Nigeria, missionaries in: 479
Nigh, George: 508
Ninety-six ("96") Ballard Oil and Gas
 Company, records of: 202
Ninnekah, Oklahoma: 1051
Nixon, Richard M.: 59, 1040
 resignation as president, 996
No Man's Land (Oklahoma Territory): 507
 crime and criminals, 865
 history of, 586, 865
 ranching in, 865
Noble County, Oklahoma, school district
 records: 1019
Noble, Ed: 508
Noble First State Bank: 802

Noble, Joseph Glass: 803
Noble, Oklahoma, banks and banking: 802
Norbeck, Peter: 361
Norman Interurban Railway Co.,
 (Oklahoma), records of: 1121
Norman, Oklahoma:
 banks and banking, 569
 chamber of commerce, 545
 city government, 63
 clubs and societies, 230
 DAR, Black Beaver Chapter, records of,
  277
 drug stores, 44
 First Presbyterian Church, 831
 Gaillardia Garden Club, records of, 386
 grocery stores, 407
 high school, yearbook, 1130
 history of, 966
 Lions Club, records of, 804
 mayors, 63
 Methodist Episcopal Church, 286
 Oklahoma School of Religion, 831
 printers, 53
 radio station WNAD, 655, 890
 realtors, 903
 records of, 63, 67
 retail stores, 670
 schools, 141
 U.S. Naval Air Station, history of, 416,
  1142
 U.S. Naval Air Technical Training
  Center, 416, 1142
 utility companies in, 127
 Woden Club, 805
Norman, Oklahoma Territory, medical
 care: 157
Norris, Thomas T.: 806
North America, description and travel, 18th
 century: 302
North Burbank (Oklahoma) area, map
 of: 813
North Carolina, state currency: 220
North Dakota, women's societies and
 clubs: 623, 1214
North McAlester, Oklahoma, settlement
 of: 1088
North Muskogee, Oklahoma, history
 of: 1106
North Slope Legal Assistant Project: 1110

Northern Pacific Railroad Company, land
 sales: 58
Northwestern State Teachers College (Alva,
 Oklahoma): 526
Norton, Spencer Hilton: **807**
Notary records (Tahlequah, Indian
 Territory): 530
Nothstein, Charles Anderson: **808**
Nowata County, Oklahoma:
 courts, 809
 medical care, 336
 records of, **809**
 taxation, 809
Nowata, Oklahoma:
 La Kee Kon Garden Club, **810**
Nuclear weapons (United States): 78
Numismatics: 220
Nurseries (plants): 501
Oak Ridge Seminary (Hughes County,
 Oklahoma): 1045
O'Brien, Bob: 696
Ocean travel:
 descriptions of, 1860-1861, 1032
 descriptions of, 1901-1902, 1048
Office of Price Administration: **811**
Ogden, Florence: **812**
Oge ranch (San Antonio, Texas): 452
Ohio, Thirty-first Infantry: 853
O'Hornett, Carl J.: 302, **813**
Ohoyohoma Club: **814**
Oil production (See petroleum industry):
Okay, Oklahoma, history of: 1106
Okfuskee County, Oklahoma: 507
Oklahoma:
 agricultural advocacy organizations, 841
 agricultural legislation, 824
 agriculture, 445, 507, 546, 824
 agriculture cooperatives, 312, 346, 441,
  559, 824, 836, 887
 archaeological sites, 1223
 art and artists, history of, 557
 automobile travel, 1930, 559
 aviation, 1107
 banks and banking, 32, 43, 265, 324, 327,
  328, 345, 436, 507, 517, 545, 547, 592,
  643, 760, 795, 802, 818, 820, 878, 913,
  967
 bibliography, 507
 birds of, 642, 799, 828

 budget, 397
 buildings
  historic, 507
  public, 507
  state capitol, 634
   location of, 1169
 cartoon history of, 912
 cemeteries, 1224
 chamber of commerce (state), 507
 child labor, 276
 churches, 961
 commisssioner of labor, personal papers,
  782
 congressmen, 1076
 conservation
  soil, 833
  wildlife, 244, 425, 507
 constitution, 507, 556, 1105
 Constitutional Convention, 39, 127, 133,
  544, 556, 728, 972
 courts, 225, 507, 755, 789, 809
  records of, 1141, 1154
 crime and criminals, 40, 222, 507, 610,
  633, 809, 1141, 1154, 1178
 Democratic Party in, 822
 description of, 559, 566, 994
 disaster relief, 445
 dust storms, 475
 economic conditions, 507
 education, 279, 931
 elections, 276, 419, 892
 emblems, 507
 farm markets, 559
 flags, state, 507
 floods and flood control, 507
 folk songs, 754
 forests and forestry, 507
 fraternal organizations in, 549, 615
 frontier and pioneer life, 49, 98, 410, 808,
  1047, 1058
 general stores, 954
 geology of, 106, 423, 507, 825, 1197
 ghost towns, 1224
 government, 271, 397, 900
 governors
  inaugurals, 684, 822, 972
  personal papers, 397, 445, 473, 574,
   783, 785, 900, 972, 1166
 health care, 36, 659 (See also medical

care)
highway construction in, 1094
historic sites, 994, 1168, 1224
historical fiction, 241
history of, 64, 155, 269, 302, 331, 387, 423, 507, 720, 755, 939, 966, 994
hospitals, 326, 507
hotels, 507
immigration, Czechoslovakian, 486
industry, 507
Jews in, 1112
juvenile delinquency, 309
Ku Klux Klan, 507, 1166, 1173
labor legislation, 312, 534
labor market in, 821
lakes, 507
land run of 1889, 216, 271, 507, 943, 1230
land run of 1893, 39, 49, 319, 410, 474, 507, 896, 952, 999, 1074
land runs, 92, 245, 507
  opening of the Cheyenne and Arapaho lands, 485
law enforcement, 507, 823
legends, 507
legislation, 397, 496, 507, 789, 824, 900
legislators, 518
  papers of, 351, 376, 453, 789, 1113
letterheads, 639
libraries, 507
loyalty oaths, 897
maps of, 303
Masonry (Scottish Rite) in, 971
medical care, 4, 5, 20, 23, 68, 326, 434, 464 (See also health care)
medical laws, 389
military posts, 507
mines and mining, 261, 491, 507, 589, 749, 778
monuments, 507
motion picture industry, 827
music, 754
newspapers, 1200
oil investigations, 995
organized labor, 6, 100, 276, 279, 507, 534, 589, 782, 834, 840
panhandle area, history of, 586, 865, 1120
  description of, 478
parks, 507

petroleum industry, 421, 433
pharmacists, 36
pharmacy laws, 646
place names, 423, 507, 994, 1047, 1224
poetry about, 965
political appointments, 276
politics, 19, 85, 101, 138, 166, 207, 248, 259, 271, 419, 507, 518, 574, 595, 635, 755, 785, 892, 900, 972, 991, 1037, 1073, 1113, 1134, 1166, 1170, 1198, 1217
post offices, 41, 916
practice of medicine in, 1087
preachers, 1194
prison reform, 309
prisons, 445, 507, 879, 972
prohibition, 507, 572, 789, 933, 972
public health, 464
racism, 507
railroad development, 395
railroads, records of, 840
reapportionment, 964
reformatories, 879
Republican Party, 892
retirement systems, 817
right-to-work issue, 842
roads, 658
rural life, 25, 518
schools, 412, 507, 931, 1181, 1189
  sale of lands, 325
Selective Service registration, 464
settlement of, 970, 1181
sites, historic, 507
social welfare, 266
Socialist Party in, 133
state records inventories, 1225
statehood, 19, 316, 683, 708, 747, 1009, 1198
statehood celebrations, 297, 832
supreme court, clerks of, 755
supreme court justices, salaries of, 633
taxes and taxation, 507, 809, 838, 896
teachers retirement, 397
tourism, 507, 994
trading posts, 1224
traffic safety, 830
transportation, 507
unemployment, 991
utilities, public, 507

utility rates, 515
water resources, 507
weather conditions, 475
workers compensation cases, 622
World War II, 1939-1945, price controls, 811
zoology of, 103
Oklahoma Academy of Science: **815**, 1177
records of, 286
Oklahoma Advertizer, The: 1028
Oklahoma Agricultural & Mechnical College (Stillwater, OK.): 502
bond issues, 1903, 597
Oklahoma Almanac, publication of: 362
Oklahoma Anti-Saloon League: 933
Oklahoma Association for Old Age Security: 782
Oklahoma Association for Teachers Retirement: **817**
Oklahoma Association of College History Professors: **816**
Oklahoma Authors Club, publications of: 1109
Oklahoma Aviation Commission: 1012
Oklahoma Bankers' Association: 545
Oklahoma Bar Association, board of governors records: 267
Oklahoma Boys State convention: 1105
Oklahoma Children's Sooner Orchestra: 313
Oklahoma City First National Bank: **818**
Oklahoma City Junior Symphony Orchestra: 819
Oklahoma City, Oklahoma:
attorneys, 633
banks and banking, 643, 818, 820
businesses, 1061
city charter, 701
city clerks of, 1036
city councilmen, papers of, 468
civic leaders, 1036
clubs, 684, 704, 999
development of, 886
drug stores, 581
Episcopal churches, records of, 998
First National Bank Building, 482
Fox-Vliet Drug Store, 1157
history of, 448
housing, 78
mayors, 482

medical care, 78
Methodist Episcopal church in, 1026
orchestras, 819
Overholser Theatre programs, 1061
physicians, 627, 695
politics, 19
public library, 701
rooming houses, 948
streetcar system, 1121
weather reports for, 1177
Oklahoma City Railway Co., records of: 1121
Oklahoma City Symphony: 313
Oklahoma City *Times* Company, report of earnings: 19
Oklahoma City Tradesmens National Bank: **820**
Oklahoma Civil Liberties Union: 579
Oklahoma Club, program from: 684
Oklahoma Commissioners of Charities and Corrections, report: 275
Oklahoma Corporation Commission: **821**, 991
Oklahoma County Consumers Council, records & publications of: 78
Oklahoma County, Oklahoma: 507
Oklahoma Daily, The, special St. Patrick's day issue: 927
Oklahoma Democratic Party: **822**
Oklahoma Department of Pardons and Parole: 972
Oklahoma Department of Public Safety: **823**
Oklahoma Department of Public Welfare, physicians for: 622
Oklahoma Diamond Jubilee Commission, records of: 297
Oklahoma Education Association, legislation supported by: 279
Oklahoma Equal Rights Amendment: 496
Oklahoma Farm Bureau: **824**
Oklahoma Farmers Union: 1037
publications, 376
records of, 312
Oklahoma Federation of Music Clubs, history of: 506
Oklahoma Fish and Game Council: 1177
Oklahoma Geological Survey: 106, **825**
expedition of 1900, 440
Oklahoma Goodwill Industries, Inc.: 568

296

Oklahoma Grain Growers Association, records of: 441
Oklahoma Hall of Fame: 687, 758
Oklahoma Highway Commission: 1094
Oklahoma Highway Patrol: 823
Oklahoma Imprints: 456
Oklahoma Indian Baptist Association: 786
Oklahoma Indian Rights Association: 826
Oklahoma Jim (See James Shears)
Oklahoma Junior Academy of Science, records of: 815
Oklahoma-Kansas Natural Gas Company, records of: 575
Oklahoma Library Association: 938
Oklahoma Library Commission: 938
Oklahoma McCarthy for President Committee: 700
Oklahoma Medical Research Foundation: 487
Oklahoma Memorial Association: 758
Oklahoma Memorial Union: 1114
  records of, 656
Oklahoma National Guard: 717, 972
Oklahoma Natural Gas Company: 515
Oklahoma Natural Mutoscene Company: 827
Oklahoma Normal School, bond issues, 1903: 597
Oklahoma Odd Fellow: 972
Oklahoma Ornithological Society: 828
Oklahoma Pharmaceutical Association, constitution of: 646
Oklahoma Pioneer Physicians Oral History: 829
Oklahoma Public Services Corporation, records of: 575
Oklahoma Railway Co., records of: 1121
Oklahoma Safety Council: 830
Oklahoma School of Religion: 831
Oklahoma Semi-Centennial Exposition: 832
Oklahoma Soil Conservation Service: 833
Oklahoma State Archaeological Society, records of: 60
Oklahoma State Board of Medical Examiners: 638
Oklahoma State Council of Defense, report of: 1182
Oklahoma State Democratic Convention, 1968: 700
Oklahoma State Department of Agriculture: 824
Oklahoma State Federation of Labor: 834
Oklahoma State Federation of Women's Clubs: 835
  reports of, 1135
Oklahoma State Grange: 836
Oklahoma State Highway Department: 595
Oklahoma State Legislative Council, reports of: 133
Oklahoma State Medical Association: 638, 837
  constitution and by-laws, 710
  membership lists, 124
  proceedings, 360
  publications of, 360, 845
Oklahoma State Planning Board, reports of: 133
Oklahoma State Public Health Department, report of 1910-1912: 464
Oklahoma State University, loyalty oaths: 180
Oklahoma State Writers, Inc., directories of: 860
Oklahoma Supreme Court, proceedings of: 991
Oklahoma Symphony Orchestra: 1135
Oklahoma Tax Commission: 838
  reports of, 133
Oklahoma Territorial Board of Pharmacy, records of: 646
Oklahoma Territorial Medical Association: 839
Oklahoma Territorial Supreme Court, justices of: 1013
Oklahoma Territory:
  annual reports, 350
  banks and banking, 760, 795
  cattle brands used in, 1219
  college bond issues, 1903, 597
  courts, 442
    records of, 1141
  crime and criminals, 40, 1141
  description of, 671
  economy of, 1134
  forts, 1224
  fraternal organizations in, 549
  frontier and pioneer life, 410, 426, 474, 491, 550, 560, 586, 808, 943, 959, 970, 999, 1047, 1074, 1102, 1117, 1123,

1134, 1159, 1181, 1230
governors, 39, 40, 307, 349, 350, 605, 985
personal papers, 1013
history of, 180, 488, 507
holidays, proclamation of, 963
judges, 39, 442
labor unions in, 1057
land claim litigation, 680
land records, 1209
letterheads, 639
maps of, 303
Masonry (Scottish Rite) in, 971
medical societies, records of, 839
military posts, 355
No Man's Land, 507, 586
opening of Indian lands, 40
place names, 507
politics, 238, 985, 1013, 1134
post offices, 916
preachers, 1194
schools, 1181
settlement of, 550, 943, 1181
statehood, 338, 708, 747
Indian opposition to, 683
supreme court justices, 1013
territorial records, inventories, 1225
vigilante groups, 26
women, 943
Oklahoma Territory Dental Association: 1160
Oklahoma Transportation Company: 840
Oklahoma Tuberculosis Association: 223
Oklahoma Turnpike Authority: 964
Oklahoma University Pharmaceutical Association, publications of: 1146
Oklahoma Wheat Growers Association: 841
Oklahoma Wildlife Conservation Commission, records of: 244
Oklahomans, biographical information: 508
Oklahomans For The Right To Work, Incorporated: 842
Okmulgee Abstract and Title Company: 843
Okmulgee Civic Improvement Club: 844
Okmulgee County Medical Society: 845
Okmulgee County, Oklahoma: 507
abstracts of title, 843
martial law in, 180
Okmulgee, Oklahoma:
clubs, 844
medical care, 68
Okmulgee-Youngstown Oil Company: 922
Oktaha, Oklahoma, physicians: 529
Olds, Frederick: 508
Olinger, Paul T.: 846
Omaha Indian Mission (Nebraska): 231
Omaha, Nebraska, vigilante committee at: 911
Oochalata: 847
Opler, Morris Edward: 848
Opothleyaholo: 170, 508, 849
Oral histories:
Indian Territory, 550
Indians, 314
Oklahoma Territory, 550
physicians, 829
Orchestras (Oklahoma): 819
Order of the Eastern Star: 850
Oregon Territory, massacres: 911
Oregon Trail, travel accounts (See also overland journeys): 154
Organized labor: 142, 374, 589, 1144, 1183
Oklahoma, 6, 100, 173, 276, 507, 534, 782, 834, 840, 1057
Ornithologists: 642, 799
papers of, 1091
Ornithology:
Mexico, 1091
Oklahoma, 1091
research, 56, 799
societies, 828
Orphanages for Indians: 393
Orr, Kenneth: 60
Ortenburger, Arthur Irving: 851
Osage County, Oklahoma: 507
oil and gas leases, 813
Osage Indian Agency, history of: 356
Osage Indian Papers: 852
Osage Indians:
allotment of land, 852
Civil War, 1861-1865, 235
encounters with whites, 663
history, 356
oil and gas leases, 356
relations with U.S. government, 852, 1063
relations with whites, 852
songs, 268
traditions, 268

tribal council, 852
tribal roll, 852
writings about, 1168
Osborne, Kansas, founding of: 50
Osborne, Lyle: **853**
Osceola: 508
Oskinson, John Milton: **854**
Oto Indians, schools: 287
Ottawa County (Oklahoma) Semi-Centennial Committee: 801
Ottawa County Medical Society: **855**
Ottawa County, Oklahoma: 507
  history of, 801
  treasurer's records, 233
Ourada, Patricia K.: **856**
Overholser Theatre (Oklahoma City, Oklahoma), showbills: 684
Overland journeys to the Pacific: 81, 154, 291, 390, 875, 911, 1085, 1194
Overton, Benjamin F.: **857**
Owen, Robert Latham: 358, 508
  correspondence, 978
  speeches of, 1233
Owings, Donnell MacClure: **858**
Owl, Della Irene Brunsteter: **859**
Packet boats, account of travel on: 945
Paden National Bank (Paden, Oklahoma), records of: 920
Padgett, Ora: 759
Pah Se To Pah, Dora: 268
Paine, Mary Graham Giles: **860**
Paiute Indians:
  claims against U.S. government, 1217
  wars, 552
Paleontologists, papers of: 1084
Palmer, Benn G.: **861**
Palo Pinto County, Texas, history of: 426
Pan American Airways: 381
Pantoja, (Father): **862**
Paris, Illinois, history of: 1221
Paris, Texas:
  history of, 6
  medical care, 45
Park Hill, Oklahoma, banks and banking: 345
Parker, Cynthia Ann: 508
Parker, Everett C.: **863**
Parker, Franklin: **864**

Parker, George Burton: 99, 1089
Parker, Harry: **865**
Parker, Isaac C.: 598, 965, 1140
Parker, Quanah: 488, 508
Parker, Robert: **866**
Parker, Thomas: **867**
Parking meter: 507
  invention of, 121
Parks (Oklahoma): 507
Parks, Lucile Snider: **868**, 1056
Parman, James Franklin: **869**
Parnell, Charles: **870**
Parrington, Vernon Louis: 67, 440, **871**
Patchell, O. W.: **872**
Pate, J. D.: **873**
Patent medicines: 226, **874**, 917, 1239
Patrick, James, biography of: 1047
Patrick, Lee: 1058
Patrick, William: **875**
Patrol: 744
Patterson, L. E.: 426
Paul, Haskell: **876**
Paul, Smith: 83
  genealogy of, 876
Pauls Valley Chamber of Commerce: **877**
Pauls Valley First National Bank: **878**
Pauls Valley, Indian Territory:
  banks and banking, 878
  cemeteries, 83
Pauls Valley, Oklahoma:
  attorneys, 962
  banks and banking, 878
  history of, 877
  medical care, 146
  physicians, 649
  Presbyterian church in, 471
  reformatory for boys, 879
  social clubs, 1082
  telephone directory, 877
  women's clubs, 860
Pauls Valley State Training School for Boys: **879**
Pawhuska, Oklahoma:
  history of, 356
  medical facilities, 664
Pawnee County, Oklahoma: 507
Pawnee Indians:
  culture, 1007
  relations with U.S. government, 1063

social life and customs, 1180
weaving, 1180
Pawnee, Oklahoma, description of: 510
Pawnee, Oklahoma Territory, description of life in: 1056
Payne County, Oklahoma: 507
medical care, 509
Payne County, Oklahoma Territory, homesteading in: 943
Payne, David Lewis: 180, 508, **880**
Payne, Okemah: **881**
Payne, Tom: 881
Pea Ridge, Battle of: 507
Pearl Harbor, Hawaii, attack by Japanese: 1152
Pearson Funeral Home (Walters, Oklahoma): 884
Pearson, John Cannon, Sr.: **882**
Pearson, Lola Clark: **883**
Pearson, Ralph: 884
Pearson, Robert Shelton, Sr.: **885**
Peck, Herbert Massey: **886**
Peek, George: 361
Peeler, Paul: **887**
Pender, Winnfield Russell: **888**
Pendleton, Robert Henry: **889**
Penney, Grace S. Jackson: **890**
P.E.O., publications of: 1082
Peoples, William T., murder trial of: 667
Performers:
dancers, 196
musicians, 736
storytellers, 359
wild west show, 737, 898
Perren, Donna Lea: **891**
Perren Garage (Pond Creek, Oklahoma), records of: 891
Perry, Adolphus Edward: **892**
Perry, John C.: **893**
Perryman, Joseph M.: 254, **894**
Perryman, Legus Chouteau: **895**
Perryman family: 508
Pershing, John J.: 684
correspondence, 1134
Peru, missionaries in: 479
Peters, Kay: **896**
Peterson, Horace Cornelious: **897**
Petroleum companies (Oklahoma): 236
Petroleum geologists:
papers of, 161
personal narratives, 863
Petroleum industry:
corporate history, 200, 600
corporate records, 575, 600, 953
development of (Oklahoma), 507, 821, 1041
equipment, 944
geology reports, 310, 450
history of, 356
Oklahoma, 433, 494, 938
investigative reports (Oklahoma), 995
literature about, 378, 421
natural gas industry, investigation of, 1207
oil and gas leases (Choctaw Nation), 1241
oil discovery (Oklahoma), 494, 938
oil field contractors, 944
oil field workers, 11, 671, 1224
injuries to, 1132
oil leases, 500, 633
oil production in,
Middle East, 450
Oklahoma, 421, 450, 821
South America, 450
oil reserves in California, 421
oil well logs, 1197
pipelines, development of, 1211
poster art, 1119
price controls, 263
private investment, 24, 192, 150, 153, 222, 569, 922
publications, 1008
refineries, records of, 263
storage tanks, 263
World War II and rationing, 263
Pettingill, Olin Sewell: 1091
Pettyjohn, (Mrs.) John: **898**
Pharmacies, records of: 44, 93, 299, 581, 613 (See also drug stores)
Pharmacists: 1125, 1157
Oklahoma, 36, 44, 74, 93, 308, 646
professional societies, 388
Phi Beta Kappa Key: 725
Philatelists: 74, 102, 1040
Phillips, Frank: 508
Phillips, George Wendel: **899**
Phillips, Leon Chase: 508, **900**, 1200
Photographers: 226, 480, 983

Photography studios (Chelsea, Oklahoma),
    records of: 490
Physicians: 377
    Indian Territory, 136, 159, 232, 429, 829,
        910, 986, 1161
        personal narratives, 68, 756, 771
        records of, 539, 563, 1115, 1132, 1158,
            1172
    military, 232, 680, 803, 923, 949
    Oklahoma, 78, 117, 123, 159, 258, 360,
        428, 464, 507, 520, 638, 741, 748,
        829, 893, 967, 979, 1010, 1151
        biographical information, 837
        cooperative medicine, 1021
        correspondence, 1023
        lecture notes, 165, 283
        obstetricians, 567, 1050
        personal narratives, 68, 157, 529, 535,
            688
        publications of, 146, 165, 282, 542,
            622, 625, 695, 803, 956, 993
        records of, 20, 23, 52, 55, 57, 80, 94,
            126, 146, 148, 151, 167, 181, 205,
            208, 218, 275, 282, 283, 304, 336,
            357, 384, 389, 400, 475, 476, 487,
            505, 509, 527, 563, 564, 565, 577,
            599, 603, 622, 625, 626, 627, 628,
            635, 640, 641, 695, 703, 719, 750,
            788, 806, 873, 899, 986, 1050,
            1054, 1071, 1072, 1081, 1097,
            1098, 1115, 1132, 1175, 1212
        reference books, 570
        research, 542, 625, 762
        wives of, 649
        women, 218
        World War I service, 165
        writings, 243, 389
        x-ray use, 993
    Oklahoma Territory, 829
        records of, 627, 654
    Texas, records of, 45, 47
Physics, research: 375
Pi Kappa Alpha: 901
Piburn, Anne Ross: 902
Pickard, Clyde C.: 903
Pickens County, Indian Territory: 507
Pickett, Bill: 508
Pierce, Thomas Franklin, Sr.: 904
Pierson, Iowa, government of: 882

Pike, Albert: 170, 302
Pilgrims of the Plains: 632
Pioneer Club (Chickasha, Oklahoma): 37
Pioneers, personal narratives: 319
    (See also frontier and pioneer life)
Pitchlynn, E. P.: 541
Pitchlynn, Ernest: 508
Pitchlynn, Peter Perkins: 87, 198, 455, **905**
    correspondence, 978
Pitchlynn family: 978
    records of, 905
Pitman shorthand, 19th-century examples
    of: 432
Pittman, F. D.: **906**
Pittsburg County Medical Society: **907**
Pittsburg County, Oklahoma: 507
    land titles, 394
    mine explosion, 1930, 1183
Place names:
    Indian Territory, 1224
    Oklahoma, 507, 1047, 1224
Planned Parenthood Association: **908**
Playwrights: 968
Plummer, William A.: **909**
Plummer family, correspondence: 909
Poetry Society of Oklahoma, publications
    of: 1109
Poets and poetry: 82, 223, 301, 302, 329,
    378, 403, 422, 423, 454, 455, 476, 571,
    590, 716, 745, 747, 753, 776, 866, 904,
    923, 968, 1059, 1080, 1125, 1152
Political appointments (Oklahoma): 276
Political campaigns: 69, 138, 166, 207, 248,
    259, 271, 376, 419, 461, 574, 676, 755,
    785, 1166
    Democratic Party of Oklahoma, 822
    pamphlets and brochures, 700, 764, 822
    posters, 917, 955, 991
    presidential, 700
    ribbons and buttons, 438, 883, 965
    U.S. Senate, 1134
Political conventions:
    Democratic (Oklahoma), 822
    publications, 900
Political memorabilia: 498
Political organizations (Indian Territory): 498
Political pamphlets and brochures, 142, 248,
    376, 461, 468, 496, 531, 1073
Political parties (Oklahoma): 822, 1073

Political posters: 1076
Political theory: 341
Politics:
 agricultural, 546, 1037
 cartoons, 900
 Equal Rights Amendment, 496
 Ku Klux Klan, 1173
 Missouri, 605
 municipal, 63, 225
 national, 192, 238, 611, 635, 892, 1073
 Oklahoma, 445
 publications, 225, 271, 382
 state, 69, 101, 166, 207, 223, 225, 248, 259, 376, 453, 465, 496, 574, 800, 892, 900, 972, 991, 1073, 1076, 1113, 1134, 1166, 1170, 1198, 1217
 territorial, 238, 985, 1013
Pollard, Tildue H.: 910
Pomeroy, Henry Martyn: 911
Ponca Indians, history: 474
Pond Creek, Oklahoma:
 garages, 891
 physicians, 1071
Pond, Nina Louise Phillipi: 912
Pontotoc County, Oklahoma: 507
 political campaigns, 138
Pony Express: 507
Porter First National Bank: 913
Porter, Indian Territory:
 general stores, 195
 physicians, 563
Porter, Joseph L.: 914
Porter, Oklahoma:
 banks and banking, 913
 physicians, 563
Porter, Pleasant: 427, **915**
Portillo, Jack: 268
Posey, Alexander Lawrence: 508, 747
Post cards: 75, 385, 966, 1002, 1097, 1127
 leather, 933
 Virginia scenes, 938
Post offices:
 Indian Territory, records of, 124
 Oklahoma, 41
 records of, 197, 791, 916
 Oklahoma Territory, records of: 916
Post, Wiley: 508
Postage stamps: 74, 102, 1040
Postal Records Collection: 916

Postal service, airmail: 684
Poster Collection: 917
Posters:
 disarmament, 983
 football games, 946
 Norman Rockwell, 1113
 petroleum industry, 1119
 political campaign, 991
 World War I, 1914-1918, 1182
Postmasters:
 Oklahoma, 150, 197
 Oklahoma Territory, 1090
Potawatomi Indians, art: 260
Potaway: 508
Poteau, Indian Territory, physicians: 1172
Poteau, Oklahoma, Afro-Americans: 769
Pottawatomie County Medical Society: 918
Pottawatomie County, Oklahoma: 507
Pottery, manufacture of, (Oklahoma): 1002
Potts, Rhoda Gunn Colbert: 1051
Powell, Peter J.: **919**
Power resources (Oklahoma): 507
Prague National Bank: **920**
Prairie Oil Company: 150
Pratt, Horace: **921**
Presbyterian Church: 507, 961
 communist infiltration of, 1237
 Indian Territory,
  ministers, 1231
  records of, 1231
 Norman, Oklahoma, 831
 Oklahoma
  history of, 506, 1232
  ministers, 523
 Pauls Valley, Oklahoma, history of, 471
Presidios, history of: 761
Prevost, Charles Albert: **922**
Price, Charles Gary: **923**
Price controls (Oklahoma), World War II, 1939-1945: 811
Price, Walter: **924**
Printers (Oklahoma): 53
Printing, examples of: 53
Prison reform (Oklahoma): 309, 579
Prisoner of war camps: **925**
 American, 69
 Fort Reno, Oklahoma, 1203
 German, 1203
Prisons:

302

New York, 931
Oklahoma, 8, 445, 507, 879, 1224
Proclamation Collection: 926
Proctor, C. L.: 927
Proctor family: 508
Professional societies: (See also medical associations and societies)
  pre-medical, 12
  sciences, 815
  women's, 13
Progressive Party: 892, 1005
Prohibition: 248
  Oklahoma, 507, 933
Propaganda Collection: 928
Propaganda, Nazis: 1040
Protestant Episcopal Cathedral Foundation (Diocese of Oklahoma): 998
Proxmire, William: 59
Pruitt Gin Company: 929
Pryor, William W.: 930
Public buildings (Oklahoma): 507
Publishers and publishing:
  academic, 104, 1147
  Indian Territory, 1044
  Oklahoma, history, 216
Pugmire, Donald Ross: 931
Pulitzer Prize Board: 468
Pumpkin, Thomas: 932
Purcell, Oklahoma, realtors: 500
Purdum, Helen: 933
Pushmataha: 508
Pushmataha County, Oklahoma: 507
Putnam City, Oklahoma, Methodist Episcopal church in: 1026
Quakers (See Society of Friends)
Quantrill, William: 239
Quapaw Indians:
  claims against U.S. government, 1217
  farm leases, 295
  schools, 295
  tribal government, 295
Quapaw, Oklahoma:
  mining equipment stores, 71
  municipal records of, 934
Quigley, Michael: 935
Quinton, Indian Territory, land titles: 394
Quong, Jennie Lou Gray: 936
Rachlin, Carol: 679, 937
Racism (Oklahoma): 507

Rader, Jesse Lee: 938
Radio:
  advertisements, 594
  operators, amateur, 293
  scripts, 631, 655, 793, 830
    "Labor's Side of the News", 631
    "Museum of the Air,", 1226
    "Wake Up to Yesterday", 631
    "Great Men and Books", 655
  shows, educational, 793
  stations, WNAD (Norman, Oklahoma), 890
Railroads:
  books, 355
  Chicago, Rock Island, and Pacific, 189, 976
  depots and stations, 189
  equipment, 189
  federal owenership of, 991
  Fort Smith, Subiaco, and Eastern, 372
  health and pension plans, 389
  history of, 355
  Indian Territory, 97, 707
  interurban, 1121
  labor relations of, 976
  land, sales and transfers, 58, 189
  leases, 633
  litigation, 351
  mines and mining, 1183
  Missouri, Kansas, and Texas Railroad Company, 622, 635, 1075
  modeling groups, 395
  Oklahoma, 507, 1121
  Oklahoma Transportation Company, 840
  operations, 976
  physicians, 360, 622
  records of, 189, 372, 503, 840, 976, 978, 1014, 1121
  rights-of-way, 456
  rolling-stock, 189
  street, 1121
  strikes, 976
  timetables, 355
Rainey, George: 939
Rainey family: 939
Rainy Mountain Baptist Mission (Oklahoma): 1004
Ralls, Joseph G., Sr.: 940
Ramona, Indian Territory: 1093

retail trade, 29
Ramsay, J. J.: **941**
Ramsay, James Ross: **942**
Ramsey, Flora Belle Simmons: **943**
Ranches and ranching: 253, 501, 569, 1123, 1149
  Cherokee Outlet, 952
  Dakota Territory, 452
  Indian Territory, 558
  Kansas, 952
  Oklahoma, 478, 497, 507, 647, 737, 882, 1106
  Oklahoma Territory, 586, 865
  Sonora, Mexico, 601
  Texas, 380, 446, 452, 478
Randall, William B.: **944**
Ransom, Will Hewitt: **945**
Ransom family: 945
Rascoe, Burton: 358, 508
Rasmus, William F.: 530
Rathbone, Oklahoma Territory: 1090
Rawlinson, Sally: **946**
Ray, Grace Ernestine: 763, **947**
Ray, Jessie Dimple Newby: **948**
Reagle, James, Jr.: **949**
Real estate (Oklahoma): 1, 120, 150, 882, 1041
Realtors:
  personal papers, 465, 500, 764, 881, 903
  records of, 772
Ream, Ruth K.: **950**
Reapportionment (Oklahoma): 964
Reaves, Samuel Watson: **951**
Recipes (See also cookbooks): 37
  ink, 521
  medicines, 193, 484, 539, 558, 613, 641, 722
Records, L. S.: 952
Records, Ralph Hayden: **952**
Red Bird: 508
Red Buck: 508
Red Cross chapters (Oklahoma), records of: 17, 18
Red Fork, Oklahoma, discovery of oil at: 494
Red Moon Indian Boarding School: 1011
Red Rabbit Oil Company Collection: **953**
Red Rock Indian Agency (Indian Territory), schools: 287

Red Store Trading Post (Fort Sill, Oklahoma Territory): 294
Redwine Trading Company Collection: **954**
Redwine, Wilburn Nash: **955**
Reed, Horace: **956**
Reed, Joannah Floyd: 713
Reed, Milo T.: **957**
Reed, Nathaniel "Texas Jack": 508
Reed, William J.: 713
Reeds, Clarence: **958**
Reeve, Lelia Hudson: **959**
Reeves, Bass: 508
Referendum News: 972
Reformatories (Oklahoma): 879
Reidt, G. M.: **960**
Relief organizations, (Oklahoma), records of: 1228
Religion: 507
Religious Denominations of Oklahoma Collection: **961**
Religious viewpoints: 460
Religious writings: 459
Renfro, Isaac: 644
Renfrow, William C., correspondence: 985
Rennie, Albert: **962**
Renze, Dolores C.: **963**
Repplier, Agnes: 358
Republican Party:
  national convention, 1920, 883
  Oklahoma, 465, 764, 892, 1217
  campaigns, 1198
  convention proceedings, 1908, 892
  United States, 892
Republican Party of Oklahoma: **1073**
Retail stores:
  Indian reservations, 607
  Indian Territory, 29, 38, 152, 195, 242, 267, 294, 530, 576, 694, 954, 978
  records of, 1241
  Missouri, records of, 404
  Oklahoma, 71, 120, 152, 171, 215, 228, 233, 449, 524, 537, 594, 607, 646, 670, 726, 730, 740, 779, 954, 978, 1030
  history of, 1067
  records of, 407, 1241
  Oklahoma Territory, 299, 646
  trade tokens, 220, 524
Retirement systems, Oklahoma teachers: 817

304

Revolutions, American: 311
  description of, 292
Rewards, payment of: 633
Reynolds, James E.: 1140
Reynolds, Norman E., Jr.: 964
Rhodes, Charles B.: 965
Rhodes Legal History Collection: 662
Richards, Aute: 966
Richardson, David Phillip: 967
Ridge, John R., correspondence: 583
Ridge family: 302, 1193
  papers of, 186
Riggs, Rollie Lynn: 65, 508, 968
Right-to-work issue (Oklahoma): 842
Rinsland, Henry Daniel: 969
Ripley, Oklahoma, development of
  railroads: 395
Rister, Carl Coke: 970
Rittenhouse, Frank A.: 971
Rivers (Oklahoma): 507
Roads (Oklahoma), construction of: 658, 1094
Roberts, E. N.: 662
Roberts, John: 662
Roberts, Oral: 508
Robertson, Alice: 50
Robertson, Ann Eliza Worcester: 508, 973
Robertson, James Brooks Ayers: 39, 972
Robertson, Samuel W.: 973
Robertson, William S.: 973
Robey, Roberta: 974
Robinson, Jim Lee: 975
Rock Island Technical Society: 976
Rockefeller, Nelson A.: 59
Rockport, Texas, description of: 452
Rockwell, Norman, posters of: 1113
Rodeos (Oklahoma): 507
Rodger Mills Company Cooperative
  Association, records of: 887
Roger Mills County, Oklahoma: 507
Rogers, Betty (Mrs. Will): 898
Rogers, Charles S.: 231
Rogers County Medical Society: 527, 977
Rogers County, Oklahoma: 507
Rogers, Henry Collins: 979
Rogers, John Powell: 980
Rogers-Neill Collection: 978
Rogers, Roy, songs recorded by: 1235
Rogers, Will (William Penn Adair Rogers):
  102, 508, 620, 745, 898, 1208
Rogers, William Charles: 981
Romback family, genealogy: 291
Roodhouse, Frank S.: 982
Roosevelt, Eleanor, correspondence, 78, 883
Roosevelt, Franklin D.: 668, 1037
  correspondence of, 173, 207, 543, 886
Roosevelt, Theodore: 883, 938
  correspondence of, 209
Rose, Noah Hamilton: 983
Ross, John: 302, 508, 984
Ross, Leslie P., Sr.: 985
Ross, Samuel Price: 986
Ross, William Potter: 987
Ross family, genealogy of: 99
Rotary International of Oklahoma: 988
Rough Riders, reunions (Oklahoma): 40, 209
Rowe, David: 1216
Roxana Petroleum Corporation (Ardmore, Oklahoma): 236
Ruggiers, (Mrs.) Paul Eddleman: 989
Ruggiers, Paul George: 990
Russell, Campbell: 991
Russell, Earl C.: 992
Russell, Gordon: 1198
Russia (See also Soviet Union):
  description and travel, 572
  propaganda posters from, 883
Russo, Peter E.: 993
Ruth, Kent: 994
Rutherford, David Ross: 33
Rutherford, Isaiah: 957
Rutherford, L. Morton, II: 995
Rutherford, Mary: 957
Ryan, Jesse Willis: 996
Ryan family: 996
Sac and Fox Bank (Stroud, Oklahoma),
  records of: 1086
Sac and Fox Indian Agency (Oklahoma):
  229, 997, 1058
Sac and Fox Indians:
  agriculture, 229
  banks, 1086
  biography, 937
  customs, 1058
  dances, 1058
  depredations, 997
  education, 997
  employment, 997

land leases, 229
land transfers, 997
lands, 245
per capita payments, 997
police force, 997
relations with U.S. government, 1063
trade, 997
treaties, 766
women, 937, 1058
Sacajawea: 662
Sacred Heart Abbey (Oklahoma): 87
Sacred Heart Mission, Indian Territory: 1233
St. Catharine's Convent (Lehigh, Indian Territory): 1233
St. John's Protestant Episcopal Church Collection: **998**
St. Joseph's Convent (Krebs, Indian Territory): 1233
St. Louis and San Francisco Railway Company: 456
St. Mary's Academy: 1233
St. Michael's Catholic Church (Henryetta, Oklahoma): 173
Sallisaw, Oklahoma, history of: 616
Saloons: 433, 644
   Indian Territory, records of, 88
Salter, Lewis Spencer: **999**
Samples Coal Mining Company: 1183
San Antonio, Texas, description of: 452
San Carlos, Arizona, description of, 1880s: 552
San Francisco, California, description of: 911
Sanborn Fire Insurance Company maps: 303
Sand Creek Massacre: 662
Sanders, Stella E.: **1000**
Sanders family: 404
   genealogy, 363
Sandheimer, Samuel: 1233
Santa Fe Trail: 959
Santos-Dumont, Alberto: 381
Sapulpa, Indian Territory:
   Euchee Boarding School, **1001**
   history of, 1029
   records of, 1029
Sapulpa, Oklahoma:
   Frankoma Pottery Company, **1002**
   physicians, 641
   Presbyterian church, 1237

Sarokin, Pitirim, correspondence: 78
Sassoon, Sigfried: 358
Satank: 508
Satanta: 508
Saudia Arabia, training of educators: 175
Savage, William Woodrow, Jr.: **1003**
Schackelford, Robert L., correspondence: 1020
Schaefer, Hedwig: **1004**
Schaper, William August: **1005**
Schermerhorn, H. R.: 846
Schmidt, Robert W.: **1006**
Schmidt family, correspondence: 1006
Schmitt, Karl and Iva: **1007**
Schonwald, Fred P., Sr.: 508, **1008**
Schools:
   Carter County, Oklahoma, 507
   commencement programs, 479, 948, 950
   diplomas, 944
   Germany, grade books, 335
   Grant County, Oklahoma, 1019
   Hennessey, Oklahoma, 486
   Illinois, 1206
   Indian, 393, 420, 1080
      boarding, 1001, 1011
      mission, 367
   Indian Territory, 231, 287, 295, 338, 396, 588, 706, 748, 1189, 1222
   Kingfisher County, Oklahoma, 1018
   Kiowa County, Oklahoma, 41
   leasing of school lands (Oklahoma Territory), 1209
   Noble County, Oklahoma, 1019
   Norman, Oklahoma, 141
   Oklahoma, 412, 507, 931, 1181, 1189
      construction of, 451
      immunization programs, 434
      sale of lands in, 325
   Oklahoma Territory, 1181
   Poland, 250
   religious, 831
   report cards, 950
   Spiro, Indian Territory, records of, 954
   student term papers, 1028
   student writing assignments, 486
   superintendents of, 76
   text books, 40, 602
   Tulsa, Oklahoma, public schools, history of, 1129

Wanette, Oklahoma, 281
women's, 1080
Scott, Angelo C.: 508
Scott, George W.: **1009**
Scott, Howell A.: **1010**
Scott, William R.: 499
Scrapbooks: 431
Scroggs, Joseph W.: 1222
Sculptors: 1099
Seal, notary public: 438
Sealey Chapel Methodist Church, history of: 367
Seamans Oil Company: 128
Searcy, Emmett Coldwell: **1011**
Searcy, Kate: 1011
Sears, Alfred Byron: 897, **1012**
Sears, Helen: 1012
Sears, Roebuck and Co., profit sharing certificates: 1088
Seay, Abraham Jefferson: 307, **1013**
   correspondence, 605
Seay, Edgar W., Jr.: **1014**
Seay family: 1013
   history of, 605
Seed stores (Oklahoma), records of: 594
Selby, (Mrs.) Bruce: **1015**
Self Help Exchange, by-laws of: 991
Sellers family: 6
Seminole County, Oklahoma: 507
   crime and criminals, 957
   history of, 267
Seminole (Oklahoma) High School, yearbooks: 1130
Seminole Indians:
   allotment of land, 267
   censuses, 1031
   chiefs, 119, 467, 587, 732
   crime and criminals, 548
   freedmen, 334
   land disputes, 1016
   medical care, 68, 942
   military service, 334
   mining and grazing leases, 119
   missionaries to, 645, 942, 1051
   slavery, 645
   tribal factionalism, 645
   tribal government, 119
Seminole Nation:
   Civil War, 1861-1865, 942

   crime and criminals, 548
   description of, 548, 645
   general council records, 1016
   missions, 587
   tribal government, 732, 1016
   tribal politics, 1016
Seminole Nation Papers: **1016**
Senate Literary Society (University of Oklahoma): 948
Seneca Indian School: 588
Seneca Indians:
   farm leases, 685
   green corn festival of, 50
   schools, 588
Seneca Nation:
   allocation of land, 1017
   tribal government, 1017
   tribal politics, 1017
Seneca Nation Papers: **1017**
Seneker, George Washington: **1018**
Sentinel, Oklahoma, drug stores: 93
Sequoyah (George Guess): 41, 508, 987
   death of, 409
Sequoyah Convention: 915
Sequoyah Movement: 981
Servant indentures: 651
Serviss, Irma Porter: **1019**
Seven Days Battle, 1862 (Virginia): 697, 1046
Shackelford, Marshall, Jr.: **1020**
Shadid, Michael Abraham: **1021**
Shaffer County, Oklahoma: 507
Sharp, Paul F.: **1022**
Sharpsburg, Virginia, Battle of: 1046
Shattuck, Oklahoma, land sales and rentals: 333
Shawnee (Oklahoma) Fanciers Association, records of: 594
Shawnee Indians:
   biography, 937
   claims against U.S. government, 1217
   women, 937
Shawnee, Oklahoma:
   city charter of, 982
   missionaries, 561
   physicians, 535
   retail stores, 594
Shears, James "Oklahoma Jim": 508
Sheridan, Philip H.: 970, 1063

Sheriffs: 156
Sherman, William T.: 970, 1063
Sherrill, Rufus Hanson: 1023
Shetland ponies: 137
Shilling, Marvin: 1024
Shippey, E. E.: 1025
Shirk, George H.: 508
Shirley, Glenn: 508
Shirley Trading Post: 536
Shoemakers (Iowa), records of: 521
Shoemaking: 306
Shook, Lottie Lee: 1026
Shook, William Vance: 1026
Short, George F.: 1027
Short, Julia A. "Julee": 1028
Shorthand, examples of: 432
Shumard, Evelyn H.: 1029
Shumate and Sons: 1030
Shumate Department Store (Pauls Valley, Oklahoma), records of: 1030
Shumate, Enola: 1031
Shunatona, Baptiste: 508
Sigler, Earle Marion: 1032
Sigma Alpha Epsilon: 1033
Sigma Delta Chi: 1034
Sigma Gamma Epsilon: 286
Sigma Nu: 1035
  publications of, 938
Silkwood, Karen: 508, 600
Siloam Springs, Arkansas, postcard views of: 1127
Simon, Earle Marvin: 1036
Simons, L. J., correspondence: 827
Simpson, John Andrew: 1037
Simpson, (Mrs.) Morris S.: 1038
Sinclair, Upton: 358, 1227
Sino-Japanese Conflict, 1937-1945: 543, 983
Sioux Indians, wars: 155, 1137
Sisseton Indian reservation, survey of: 474
Sittell, Fritz: 978
Sittell family: 978
Sitting Bull: 155, 508
Skeleton, The: 603
Skelly, William Grove: 1039
Skinner, Esthmer H.: 1040
Slavens, T. H.: 552
Slaves and slavery: 302
  bills of sale for, 1240
  Cherokee Nation, 1148
  contract for sale of, 705
  description of (South Carolina), 1070
  receipt of sale, 477
Slick, Thomas Baker: 1041
Slover, James Anderson, Sr.: 1042
Smallwood, Ben F.: 1043
Smiser, (Mrs.) Butler Stonestreet: 1044
Smith, Al, presidential campaign in Oklahoma: 1113
Smith, (Mrs.) E. P.: 1045
Smith, Edward, family of: 1046
Smith, (Mrs.) Edward Needham: 1046
Smith, Franklin Campbell: 1047
Smith, H. P.: 1048
Smith, Isabel Foster: 1049
Smith, Jedidiah Strong: 508
Smith, Joseph G.: 1050
Smith, Joseph R.: 663
Smith, Micah Pearce: 1051
Smith, Nell Achsah: 1056
Smith, Orville, correspondence: 474
Smith, Samuel Walter: 1052
Smith, Stewart K.: 1053
Smithe, P. A.: 1054
Smithville, Oklahoma, Indian school at: 367
Snake Indians, claims against U.S. government: 1217
Snider, Denton Jaques: 1055
Snider, Nell Achsah Smith: 1056
Snodgrass, Bill: 1057
Snow, Jerry Whistler: 1058
Snyder, Lawrence H.: 1059
Social work (Oklahoma): 266
Socialist Party:
  Oklahoma, 133
  publications of, 1218
Socialists, papers of: 1218
Socialized medicine: 78
Society of Friends (Quakers): 1060
  locations of records of, 1060
  missionaries, 54, 430
  relations with Indians, 1060
Sociologists, writings of: 309, 681
Sod houses: 528, 1052
  description of, 474
Sohlberg, George Gustar: 1061
Soil conservation programs (Oklahoma): 833
Song books, religious: 281
Song writers: 108, 280, 373, 406

Songs:
    country and western, 1235
    Oklahoma Territory, 528
South America, description and travel: 535
South Dakota:
    description and travel, 699
    governors, 361
South McAlester, Oklahoma, settlement of: 1088
Southeastern Oklahoma Medical Association: **1062**
Southern Plains Indian Agencies: **1063**
Southwest Merchandise Company (Missouri), records of: 404
Southwestern Association of Naturalists: **1064**
Southwestern Oklahoma Survival Association: **1065**
Southwick, (Mrs.) Harl F.: **1066**
Soviet Union (See also Russia):
    foreign relations, 1939-1946, 543
    history of, 1116
Space flight: 458
    manned, 290
    moon landings, 996
Spain:
    colonial institutions in America, 761
    colonial records of, 553
    description and travel, 1901-1902, 1048
    immigration of authors from, 1227
    soldiers' service records, 729
Spanish-American War: 1047
    personal narratives, 232
    U.S. Army in, 1137
Spaulding Female College (Indian Territory): 1080
Spelling, research on teaching of: 969
Spencer Academy (Indian Territory): 231
Spencer, Maude Clinkenbeard: **1067**
Spiro, Indian Territory:
    cotton gins and ginning, records of, 954
    funeral homes, records of, 954
    general stores, records of, 954
    school district records, 954
Spiro, Oklahoma:
    attorneys, records of, 955
    cotton gins and ginning, records of, 954
    funeral homes, records of, 954
    general stores, records of, 954

    physicians, 750
Sports (Oklahoma): 507
Spring, Otto F.: **1068**
Springstead, Clarence S., Jr.: **1069**
Springston family: 302
Stafford, B. S.: **1070**
Stalker, Harry: **1071**
Standifer, John E.: **1072**
Standing Bear: 50
Stansberry, Robert: 404
Stapler and Son funeral home: 530
Starr, Belle: 387, 508
Starr, Emmett: 508, 1051
Starr, Henry: 508
State Capitol Printing Company, history of: 216
Steed, Tom: 508
Stephens County, Oklahoma: 507
Stephens, Margaret Clark: **1074**
Stephenson, Thomas J.: 58
Stevens, Robert S.: **1075**
Stevens family: 1075
Stevenson, Adams: 2
Stevenson, Adlai E.: 59
Stevenson, Henry: 2
Stevenson, Robert Louis: 504
Stewart, Elijah King: **1076**
Stewart, Roy Pittard: **1077**
Stigler First National Bank (Oklahoma): **1078**
Stigler Masonic Lodge No. 121 (Oklahoma): **1079**
Stillwater, Oklahoma Territory, history of: 180
Stillwater, Oklahoma Woman's Relief Corps: 247
Stilwell, Giles "Jack": 508
Stilwell, Joseph, correspondence: 543
Stith, Ruth Brewer: **1080**
Stock certificates: 128
Stockyards National Bank (Oklahoma City, Oklahoma): 643
Stokes, Montfort: 169
Stone, DeWitt: **1081**
Stone, Lucile Oliver: **1082**
Storms: 365
Stovall, John Willis: **1084**
Stovall Museum: **1083**, 1084
Stover, Samuel Murray: **1085**

Stroud State Bank (Oklahoma): **1086**
Strough, D. F., Sr.: **1087**
Strubble, (Mrs.) Howard: **1088**
Student's Echo: 870
Stumbling Bear: 508
Sturgis, James Wellings: **1089**
Sullivan, (Mrs.) Jim L.: **1090**
Sunday schools (Indian Territory): 1231
Sutton, George Miksch: **1091**
Swain, John: 508
Swank, David: **1092**
Swanson County, Oklahoma: 507
Swearingen, Martha T.: **1093**
Sweezy Carl William: 508
    art of, 155
Swink, Indian Territory, physicians: 756
Tah Sa Co Fah Ahwee (see Pumpkin, Thomas)
Tahlequah, Indian Territory:
    description of, 363
    notaries public, records of, 530
    telephones in, 1220
Tait, J. H.: **1094**
Tali Hekia Presbyterian Church, records of: 1231
Tallchief, Maria: 356, 508
Tamagno, Francesco: 65
Tanning of leather: 306
Tantlinger, D. Vernon: **1095**
Tarpley, Bloyce: **1096**
Tatum, Lawrie: 1063
Taxation (Oklahoma): 507
Taxes, state and county (Oklahoma): 838, 896, 941, 975
Taylor, Frank W.: 698
Taylor, Guy William: **1097**
Taylor, John C.: **1098**
Taylor, Joseph Richard: **1099**
Taylor, William Merritt: **1100**
Teachers:
    Arkansas, 274
    Indian Territory
    personal narratives, 54, 287, 904, 906
    Oklahoma
      Afro-American, 273
      contracts for employment, 274, 383
      lecture notes, 1189
      personal narratives, 141, 323, 904, 945
      personal papers of, 431, 470, 1036, 1189
    retirement systems, 817
    Oklahoma Territory, personal papers, 512
Tecumseh: 139
Tecumseh, Oklahoma, drug stores: 613
Telegraph code books: 385
Telephone directories:
    Oklahoma, 11
    Texas, 11
    Union, City, Oklahoma Territory, 967
Telephone service:
    Indian Territory, 488
    Oklahoma, 684
Television shows:
    "The Open Window," 631
    scripts and publicity, 631, 753, 830
Television stations:
    operating records of, 1229
    programming, 1229
Temperance societies:
    publications of, 1011
    records of, 144, 1214
    songs of, 144
Temple First State Bank (Oklahoma): **1101**
Tennessee, land records: 1196
Terrill, A. W.: 302
Territorial Board for the Leasing of School Lands (Oklahoma):1181
Territorial Oklahoma Manuscripts Collection: **1102**
Texas:
    attorneys, 746
    biographies of Texans, 983
    cattle brands, 172
    frontier and pioneer life, 578, 1159
    homesteading in, 690
    Indian wars, 661
    state records inventories, 1225
Texas A&M College: 77
Texas County, Oklahoma: 507
Texas Jack (See Nathaniel Reed)
Texas Road, the: 1045
Text books:
    Choctaw Indian language, 383
    nineteenth-century, 1011
    spelling, 40
    theological, 846
    used in missions, 430
Thames, Battle of the, 1813: 139

Thanksgiving, proclamations of: 926, 963
Theatrical productions and performances:
    playbills, 684, 968
    posters, 917, 924
    programs of, 322, 531
Thoburn, Joseph: 1068
Thomas, Elmer: 508, 1037
    correspondence, 886
Thomas, Henry Andrew (Heck): 508
Thomas, Norman, correspondence: 897
Thomas, Oklahoma Territory, frontier and pioneer life: 812
Thompson, Alfred M., Sr.: **1104**
Thompson, B. F.: 705
Thompson, Charles: 847
Thornton, Hurschel Vern: **1105**
Thorpe, Jim: 508
Three Forks Ranch: **1106**
Tibbs, Burrell: **1107**
Tiger, Moty: **1108**
Tilghman, William Matthew: 508, 739, **1109**
Tilghman, Zoe: 1109
Tillman County, Oklahoma, state senators: 453
Timmons, Alice: 508, **1110**
Timmons, Boyce: **1110**
Tinker, Clarence L.: 508
Tishomingo, Indian Territory, description of: 132
Tittle, Leon H.: **1111**
Tobias, Henry Jack: **1112**
Tolbert, James Randolph: **1113**
Tolbert, Raymond A.: **1114**
Tolleson, William Alfred: **1115**
Tolleson family: 1115
Tomer, John, correspondence: 642
Tompkins, Charles Harland: 508
Tompkins, Stuart Ramsay: **1116**
Tonkawa Indians:
    culture, 848
    history, 474
Tonkawa, Oklahoma:
    history of, 1117
    public library, **1117**
    Sunny Side Club, **1118**
Tornadoes: 365, 507, 808
Torrey, Charles C.: 320
Totco, Incorporated: **1119**
Tourism (Oklahoma): 507

Townsend, E. D.: 1063
Tracy, Fred: **1120**
Trade tokens: 220, 524
Tradesmens National Bank (Oklahoma City, Oklahoma), records of: 820
Trading posts (Oklahoma): 356, 1224
Traffic safety (Oklahoma): 830
Trails (Oklahoma): 507
Trails, Santa Fe: 959
Transcontinental Oil Company: 575
Transportation (Oklahoma): 507
Travel:
    accounts of, 210, 945, 994
    brochures, 75, 385, 729, 966
    publications regarding, 210, 994
Travis, Merle, songs recorded by: 1235
Treat, Guy Bradford: **1121**
Tri-County Medical Society (Oklahoma): 1212
Truman, Harry S.: 59
Truss, Sam M.: **1122**
Truss family, history: 1122
Tubb, Ernest, songs recorded by: 1235
Tucker, Fred V.: **1123**
Tucker, Hampton: **1124**
Tucker Lake (Oklahoma): 1126
Tucker, Marshall A.: **1125**
Tucker, R. Truman: **1126**
Tuggle, C. E.: **1127**
Tulsa County Medical Society (Oklahoma): **1128**
    publications of, 893
Tulsa County, Oklahoma, fauna: 799
Tulsa, Oklahoma:
    Lions Club, 211
    public school system, history of, 1129
Tulsa Public Schools: **1129**
Tunica Indians, language: 437
Turbyfill, Harper Subert: **1130**
Turbyfill, Mark: 508
Turley, Louis Alvin: **1131**
Turlington, Marcellus Martin: **1132**
Turnbo, S. C.: **1133**
Turner, Martin Luther: **1134**
Turner, Roy Joseph: 508
    inauguration of, 822
Turpin, Carl J.: **1135**
Turpin family: 1135
Turtle, Willie: **1136**

Twentieth-Century Club (McAlester, Oklahoma): 960
Two Feathers, Abraham Isaac: 508
U.S.:
　Afro-Americans, 309
　ambassador, 668
　civil rights, 382
　conservation of grasslands, 790
　description and travel, 994
　ecology, 382
　education, trends, 306
　foreign policy, 307, 611
　foreign relations, 668
　foreign service officers, 401
　frontiers, comparative studies, 1003
　government
　　foreign policy, 1939-1946, 543
　　Indian policy of, 14, 61, 70, 97, 169, 302, 371, 759
　　subversive organizations, 928
　history of, 939
　international relations, 611
　maps of, 303
　marshals, 156, 507, 782, 965, 978, 1109, 1139, 1141
　medical care, 78
　southwest, history of, 433
　exploration of, 390
　Spanish borderlands, history of, 761
　tourism, 994
　trade expositions, cotton, 399
U.S. Army:
　1st Volunteer Infantry Regiment (Indian Territory), 999
　5th Iowa Cavalry, 9
　10th Cavalry, 949
　10th Infantry Regiment, 1137
　11th Indiana Volunteer Infantry, 255
　23rd Iowa Infantry, 339
　31st Ohio Infantry, Company I, 853
　33rd Infantry Association, 765
　45th Infantry Division, 507, 717
　95th Training Division, 687
　Air Force, personal narratives, 493
　Indian Territory, correspondence, 371
　Indian troops, 334
　Indian wars, 369, 552, 661, 662, 1137
　land acquisition, Wichita Mountains (Oklahoma), 1185
　military payment script, 701
　officers
　　correspondence, 291, 1191
　　personal narratives, 298, 1117
　　personal papers of, 687, 717
　　Oklahoma, enlistments, 1137
　　physicians, 680, 949
　　records and correspondence, 147, 371, 390, 1137
　　recruitment posters, 917
　　reserve affairs, 687
　　scouts, 203, 344
　　soldiers,
　　　papers of, 1100
　　　letters, 669
　　Spanish American War, 1137
U.S. Board of Indian Commissioners, annual reports: 366
U.S. Board of Tax Appeals, opinions of: 300
U.S. Circuit Court (Indian Territory), records of: 689
U.S. Civil Aeronautics Administration, medical reports: 622
U.S. Commission on Civil Rights: 201
U.S. Department of Agriculture, publications of: 441
U.S. Department of Interior, Bureau of Indian Affairs: 14, 659
U.S. District Court:
　Central District of Indian Territory: **1138**
　Northern District of Indian Territory: **1139**
　Western District of Arkansas: 317, **1140**
　Western District of Oklahoma: **1141**, 1154
U.S. Indian Service: 751, 759
U.S. Naval Air Station (Norman, Oklahoma), history of: 416, 1142
U.S. Naval Air Technical Training Center (Norman, Oklahoma), history of: 416, 1142
U.S. Naval bases: **1142**
U.S. Navy:
　expedition to Darien, Panama, 429
　physicians, 429
U.S. Secretary of War, correspondence: 543
U.S. Selective Service, directives of: 351
U.S. Veterans Bureau, physicians: 527
U.S.S. *Caelum* (AK-106): 744
Unger, Marion Draughon Murray: **1143**

Union City, Oklahoma Territory, telephone directories: 967
Union Mutual Insurance Company, records of: 312
United Auto Workers: 1144
United Daughters of 1812 (Oklahoma), publications of: 617
United Methodist Church (Oklahoma), ministry to the deaf: 912
United Mine Workers Local #1864 (Oklahoma), records of: 100
United Nations: 1237
  delegates to, 595
University Improvement Association (Lawton, Oklahoma): 1038
University of Arkansas, faculty: 310
University of California (Berkeley, Calif.), postcard views of: 1127
University of Minnesota:
  faculty attitude toward WWI, 1005
  political science department, 1005
University of Oklahoma:
  accreditation reviews, 175
  Achievement Day at, 1039
  administrators, 1168
  Afro-Americans, admission of, 273
  alumni, 308, 536, 593, 1145
  Alumni Association, 85, 1114
  American Indian Institute, 743
  athletes, 687
  athletic association, by-laws of, 794
  athletic event programs, 593
  Athletics Council, 175
  athletics, football, 604, 618, 666, 946
  biology department, 966
  bond issues, 1903, 597
  Books Abroad (See also *World Literature Today*), 525, 1203
  Budget Council, 175
  buildings, 1114, 1153
    Carpenter Hall, 162
    chemistry, 284
    dormitories, 322
    Memorial Union, 302, 322
    Vance Hall, 1153
  campus master plan, 871
  carillons, 192
  civil defense preparations, 557
  class of 1910, 948, 1145
  class of 1913, 443
  clubs and societies, 230, 354, 629, 938, 948, 999, 1176
  College of Arts & Sciences, 342, 347, 489
  College of Business Administration, 133
  College of Fine Arts, 162
  College of Pharmacy, 1146
  commencement exercises, 675
  commencement programs, 479
  Commission on Curriculum, 347
  course catalogs, 794
  curriculum, 440, 1168
  deans, 342, 513, 1168
  DeGolyer Committee, 1147
  Department of
    Communication, 631
    English, 440, 871
    Geography, 825
    Geology, 825
    History, 269, 1116
    Sociology, 77
    Zoology, 1177
  diplomas, 742
  Distinguished Service Citation Committee, 1147
  Extension Division, 890
  faculty, 10, 21, 65, 77, 89, 99, 127, 155, 162, 246, 269, 271, 284, 286, 309, 341, 342, 347, 375, 412, 440, 483, 489, 513, 525, 557, 618, 631, 655, 656, 673, 681, 703, 720, 758, 761, 762, 768, 773, 776, 807, 858, 864, 871, 897, 925, 938, 947, 966, 970, 1003, 1012, 1022, 1092, 1099, 1116, 1168, 1177, 1197, 1203, 1206
  faculty club, 230
  Family Life Institute, 890
  finances, 440
  fine arts events, 99, 419
  fraternities, 289, 337, 901, 938, 1033, 1034, 1035
  Galen Society, records of, 388
  grade books, 21, 348, 970, 1116
  graduates, 1897-1908, 871
  history of, 99, 127, 412, 440, 794
  hospital, 1114
  Independent Men's Association, 354
  Indian Education Center, 743

integration, 273
Interschool Speech Service, 890
lecture notes, 341
librarians, 262, 348, 938
library, 2
literary societies, 187, 352
maps of campus, 302, 794
medals and pins, 443
memorabilia, 958
musical performances, programs, 322
newspaper, 758
Owens Field, 946, 1114
presidents, 77, 99, 104, 115, 127, 269,
 338, 361, 794, 938, 980, 1022, 1206
President's Class, 656
Press, 104, **1147**
professional societies, 12, 13, 188, 286,
 337, 388
publications of, 75, 99, 480, 938, 958
radio station WNAD, 890
regents, 138, 284, 433, 618, 980, 1114
registrars, 794, 1168
research centers, 175
Rockefeller Foundation Committee, 1147
School of Fine Arts, 513, 794
School of Journalism, 246, 489
School of Law, 1114
School of Medicine, 762
School of Social Work, 273
seal of, 175, 662
Semi-Centennial Committee, 1147
Sigma Gamma Epsilon, 286
social events, 723
songs and music, 99, 406
special collections, library, 35
sports, 99
student life, 67, 141, 290, 536, 863
student senate, constitution and
 by-laws, 794
student union, 1114
students, 25, 28, 208, 342, 660, 687, 269,
 412, 489, 593, 727, 742, 794, 938, 989,
 1125, 1130, 1153, 1168, 1197, 1206
students, medical, 12
theatrical performances and programs,
 322, 958
University and Town Committee, 1147
university constitution, 347
veterans organizations, 16

Websterian Literary Society, 1176
Will Rogers Scholarship Fund, 1195
Women's Club, 230
Women's History Project, 1215
World Literature Today (See also
 Books Abroad), 1227
World War I, 115
World War II, 1168
YMCA branch,
 event programs, 99
 records of, 1236
YWCA branch,
 event programs, 99
 records of, 1236
 yearbook, 758
University of Oklahoma Association: **1145**
University of Washington, map of: 871
Updegraff, Ruth: **1148**
Urschel, Charles F., kidnapping case: 222
Utterback, Bert R.: **1149**
Valentines: 531
Valliant, Oklahoma, medical care: 208
Van Ausdal, Harvey G.: **1150**
Van Cleave, William E.: **1151**
Van Dyke, Gerald Mason: **1152**
Vance, Leon C.: 508
Vance, Leon Robert, Jr.: **1153**
Vann, Joseph: 508
Vaudeville, posters: 917, 924
Vaught, Edgar Sullins, Sr.: 331, **1154**
Venereal diseases: 55, 243
Vera, Indian Territory, missions: 430
Verdi, Giuseppe: 65
Vestal, Stanley (See Walter Stanley
 Campbell)
Veterans (Oklahoma): 507
Veterans organizations:
 33rd Infantry Association, 765
 records of, 16
Vian, Oklahoma, census of, 1910: 302
Vietnam War: 382
Vigilante committee (Omaha, Nebraska),
 records of: 911
Vigilantes (Oklahoma Territory): 26
Vinita, Indian Territory, political
 organizations: 498
Vinita, Oklahoma:
 Lions Club, **1155**
 physicians, 748

Virden, John M.: **1156**
  correspondence, 433
Vliet, Gertrude M.: **1157**
Vliet, Richard M.: **1157**
Von Keller, Frederick Philander P.: **1158**
Wagner, J. E.: **1159**
Wagoner County, Oklahoma: 507
Wagoner, Indian Territory, medical care: 68
Wagoner, Oklahoma:
  health care, 52
  real estate, 465
Wahepton Indian Reservation, survey of: 474
Walker, Andrew Beattie: **1160**
Walker, Charles F.: **1161**
Walker, John Riley: **1162**
Walker, Tandy C.: **1163**
Walker, Thelma Brown: **1164**
Wallace Cecile Boone: **1165**
Wallace, Henry, correspondence: 543
Wallis, Indian Territory, physicians: 539
Wallock, Anthony Mark: 391
Walters, Oklahoma:
  funeral homes, 884
  high school teachers, 431
  retail stores, 726
Walters, Oklahoma Territory:
  history of, 1104
  townsite controversy, 1104
Walton, John Calloway "Jack": 204, 419, 508, 684, 1113, **1166**
Wanette, Oklahoma:
  history of, 281
  post office, 791
  schools, 281
Wapanucka, Oklahoma, Presbyterian church: 1231
Ward, D. C.: **1167**
Wardell, Morris L.: 925, **1168**
Warm Springs Apache Indians, missions: 177
Warner, Oklahoma, Jacob Johnson Library: 240
Washington County, Oklahoma: 507
Washita, Battle of the, 1868: 298, 606, 1011
Washita County, Oklahoma: 507
  map of, 813
Washita County, Oklahoma Territory, pioneer life: 323
Wassaja: Freedom's Signal for the

Indian: 751
Water resources (Oklahoma): 507
Watie, Sarah C., correspondence and papers of: 186
Watie, Stand: 221, 455, 508, 583, 593, 1028, 1042
  correspondence and papers of, 186
Watie family: 302
Watonga, Oklahoma:
  financial institutions, 522
  funeral homes, 779
  retail stores, 779
Watson, Archer Hunter, Sr.: **1169**
Watts, Charles Gordon, Sr.: **1170**
Waugh, Evelyn: 278
Waynoka Commercial Bank (Waynoka, Oklahoma): **1171**
Wear, John B.: **1172**
Weather (Oklahoma): 507
Weaver, Carlton: **1173**
Weaver, Claude Dickens, Sr.: 508, 667, **1174**
Weber, S. G.: **1175**
Websterian Literary Society (University of Oklahoma): 938, **1176**
Weese, Asa Orrin: **1177**
Welch, Oklahoma:
  crime and criminals, 1178
  municipal records, **1178**
  Van Ausdal Drug Store, 1150
Welsh, Jack D.: **1179**
Weltfish, Gene: **1180**
Wenner, Fred Lincoln: 508, **1181**
  map collection of, 303
Wentz, Lewis Haines: 135, 508
West Virginia, mines and mining: 589
Western History Collections: 1147
  history of, 35
Western National Bank (Oklahoma City, Oklahoma), records of: 818
Western Writers of America: 131
Westerners International, Indian Territory Posse: 1008
Westfall, Chester Harold: **1182**
Wetumka, Oklahoma, medical care: 68
Wewoka, Indian Territory:
  history of, 267
  Masonry (Scottish Rite), 267
  retail stores, 267

Wewoka Masonic Lodge, records of: 267
Wewoka Trading Company: 267
Wheat Grower's Advocate: 841
Wheatley, Thomas W.: **1183**
Wheeler, Homer W.: 344
Wheeler, J. Clyde: **1184**
Wheeler, John F.: 616
Wheeler family: 616
Whistler, Maude Mayes: 1058
Whistler, Pearl Mayes: 1058
Whistler family: 1058
Whitaker, Lovie: **1185**
White, Greenup: 411
White, Hal H.: **1187**
White, (Mrs.) J. R.: **1188**
White, Lida: **1189**
White Shrine of Jerusalem (Oklahoma): **1186**
Whitebead, Indian Territory, cemeteries: 83
Whitehill, Walter Muir: **1190**
Whitney, Charles W.: **1191**
Wichita Indian Agency: **1192**
Wichita Indians:
　claims against U.S. government, 1217
　culture, 1007
　land transfers, 40
　relations with U.S. government, 1063
Wichita, Kansas, description: 909
Wichita Mountains Easter Pageant: 1104
　history of, 391
Wichita Mountains (Oklahoma), mines and mining: 491
Wichita Mountains Wildlife Refuge: 1185
Wickersham, Victor: 1076
Wild Cat: 645
Wild west shows: 1058
　performers, 1095
　posters, 917
　publications of, 40
　records of, 647, 737
Wilder, Thornton: 1227
Wildlife conservation (Oklahoma): 507
Wilkins, Thurman: **1193**
Wilkinson, James B., correspondence: 852
Wilkinson, Otha: **1194**
Wilks, James: 1090
Will Rogers Memorial Commission, records of: 468
Will Rogers Scholarship Fund: **1195**
Willard, Melissa Kate: **1196**

Willey family: 418
Willford family, genealogy of: 1067
Williams, Arthur James: **1197**
Williams, John Robert: **1198**
Williams, Mary Clay: **1199**
Williams, Meredith Newton: **1200**
Williams, Robert L.: **1201**
Williams, Roger: 1028
Williams, Samuel: **1201**
Williams, Stephen: **1202**
Williamson, Halsell, Frasier Grocer Company: 448
Willibrand, William Anthony: **1203**
Willour, J. A.: **1204**
Wills: 302
Wilson, Andrew R.: **1205**
Wilson, Charles Banks: 508
Wilson, Milbourne Otto: **1206**
Wilson's Creek, Battle of, 1861: 507
Wimberly, Harrington: **1207**
Winchester Store (Winchester, Oklahoma), history of: 1067
Wingate, Beni: 566
Wister, Oklahoma, insurance agents: 1025
Witcher, Esther: **1208**
Witte, (Mrs.) Juan R.: **1209**
Woden Club (Norman, Oklahoma), history of: 805
Wolf, Jonas: **1210**
Wolfe, Oscar: **1211**
Wolfe, Reed E.: **1212**
Wolfe, Richard M.: 1216
Womack, John: 508, **1213**
Woman's Christian Temperance Union: **1214**
Woman's Relief Corps, Stillwater, Oklahoma, chapter: 247
Women:
　anthropologists, 677, 679
　athletes, 206
　charitable organizations, 1186
　clothing, 226
　college professors, 670, 673, 738, 758
　college students, 48, 50, 331, 704
　editors, 883
　equal rights (Oklahoma), 496
　historians, 285
　illustrators, 1059
　Indian Territory, 636, 645, 986
　journalists, 223, 350, 568, 611, 758

Ku Klux Klan membership, 621
librarians, 413, 670, 673
Oklahoma, 507
ornithologists, 799
photographers, 226
physicians, 78, 218
physicians' wives, 649, 986
pioneer narratives, 516, 560, 578, 645, 812, 868, 943, 959, 974, 986, 999
playwrights, 1227
poets, 223, 571, 1059
societies and clubs, 37, 188, 277, 386, 617, 621, 623, 835, 850, 860, 883, 912, 918, 1109, 1135
suffrage, 223
teachers, 127, 273, 383, 431, 470, 945, 1189
temperance societies, 1214
writers, 50, 241, 246, 350, 378, 381, 391, 403, 538, 611, 632, 637, 677, 679, 753, 860, 1029, 1109, 1220
Women of '89 Club, publications of: 1109
Women's History Project: **1215**
Women's Society of Christian Science: 912
Wood, Anna K.: 999
Wood, Charles L.: 292
Wood, Edwin K.: **1216**
Woodard, Fred Barton: **1217**
Woodard Ranch (San Antonio, Texas): 452
Woodrow, Thomas W.: **1218**
Woods County, Oklahoma: 507
Woods, E. K.: **1219**
Woodward County, Oklahoma: 507
Woodward, Grace: **1220**
Wooton, Esther A. Reed: **1221**
Worcester Academy: **1222**
Worcester, Samuel A.: 508
Worcester, Sarah: 50
Workers compensation cases (Oklahoma): 622
Works Progress Administration: 507
   Archaeological Survey Project, **1223**
   Federal Writers Project, **1224**
   Historic Sites Project, **1224**
   Historical Records Survey, **1225**
   Indian-Pioneer Papers Project, 269
   Oklahoma, 1109
    records of, 1084
   project records, 1223, 1224, 1225, 1226

Statewide Projects, **1226**
World Assistance, records of: 1228
World fairs, memorabilia: 1011
World Literature Today (See also *Books Abroad*): **1227**
World Neighbors, Inc.: **1228**
World War I, 1914-1918:
   American participation in, 19
   artillery, role of, 717
   attitude toward, 1005, 1104, 1127
   civil defense, 557
   correspondence with U.S. soldiers, 470
   Germany, 1218
   Liberty Bond sales (Oklahoma), 818, 1201
   Liberty Loan records, 878, 1201
   newspaper clippings regarding, 557
   Oklahoma participation in, 1182, 1201
   patriotic society, records of, 1118
   peace treaty, 897
   personal narratives, 115, 1116
   posters, 917, 1182
   propaganda, 338, 897
   relief of sick and wounded, 18
   selective service registration, 464
   soldiers' correspondence, 1015
World War II, 1939-1945:
   battle scenes, 714
   blockade of Germany, 271
   civil defense, 557
   Far Eastern Theatre, 543
   German prisoners of war, 925, 1203
   Japanese-Americans, internment of, 936
   Medal of Honor recipients, 1153
   military newspapers, 744
   musical compositions about, 391
   news clippings regarding, 274, 313, 470, 966, 996
   origins of, 307
   Pacific Theater, 714
   pacifist publications, 800
   personal narratives, 493, 738
   posters, 917
   price controls, 811
   propaganda, 928, 1040
   ration books, 11, 95, 851, 938, 1015, 1136
   rationing, gasoline, 263
   soldiers' correspondence, 593
   U.S. involvement in, 800

Woyna, Fritz Willie: **1229**
Wright, Albert Daniel: **1230**
Wright, Allen: 508, **1231**
Wright, Frank Lloyd, correspondence: 415
Wright, Harriet Bunce: 50
Wright, Muriel Hazel: 508
Wright, R. G.: 705
Writers (See also authors and women writers):
 free lance, papers of, 994
 travel, 994
Wyandotte Indians:
 hymnals, 780
 language, example of, 780
Wyatt, Robert Lee, III: **1232**
Wyatt, Rose Mary Burt: **1233**
Wyncoop, Frank M.: 662
Wynnewood, Oklahoma, Eskridge Hotel: 1205
Yakima Indians, claims against U.S. government: 1217

Yale First National Bank (Yale, Oklahoma): **1234**
Yazoo land frauds: 21
York, Bill: **1235**
Young, Glen Olen: **1237**
Young, Hiram: **1238**
Young, James Harvey: **1239**
Young, L. A.: 1238
Young Men's Christian Association: 99, **1236**
Young Women's Christian Association: 99, 230, **1236**
Yowell, Lillian J.: **1240**
Yugoslavia, description of life in: 417
Zetaletheans (University of Oklahoma): 948
Zofness, Martin I.: 1112
Zoologists:
 personal papers of, 1177
 research of, 103, 851, 966
Zweigel Mercantile Company: **1241**

www.ingramcontent.com/pod-product-compliance
Lightning Source LLC
Chambersburg PA
CBHW050335230426
43663CB00010B/1861